# dynamics
# of the cuban
# revolution

# dynamics of the cuban revolution

## the trotskyist view
## by joseph hansen

**PATHFINDER PRESS**
New York and Toronto

Copyright © 1978 by Pathfinder Press
All rights reserved
Library of Congress Catalog Card Number 78-59357
ISBN 0-87348-558-0 cloth / 087348-559-9 paper
Manufactured in the United States of America

First edition 1978

Published in the United States by Pathfinder
Press, 410 West Street, New York, N.Y. 10014, and
simultaneously in Canada by Pathfinder Press, Ltd.,
25 Bulwer Street, Toronto, Ontario.

# Contents

# Introduction

Because of its rising prominence in African political affairs, Cuba is again very much in the news. Not since the downfall of Batista and the overturn of capitalist property relations in Cuba has there been such controversy over the actions of the Castro regime.

The most ominous reaction to Cuba's role in providing material aid to Angola, and later to Ethiopia, has come from the White House. Before he lost office, President Ford branded the Castro government as an "international outlaw." Carter promised to take a different course, and for a time he intimated that a dialogue might be opened with the Cubans. This proved to be little more than a demagogic interlude in the general policy followed by Eisenhower, Kennedy, Johnson, Nixon, and Ford. Carter now insists that Castro withdraw Cuban forces from Angola and Ethiopia or suffer the consequences. The State Department has increased pressures on the diplomatic level, and threats have been made to resort to military measures.

Washington's reaction emanates from fear that the Cuban presence in Africa means further weakening of the imperialist grip in that area, strengthening of Soviet influence, and fresh encouragement to revolutionary forces capable of moving in the direction of socialism.

The resumption of the imperialist campaign against the Cuban revolution is of top concern to everyone opposed to war and in favor of the right of self-determination. It means rallying in a vigorous way on an international scale in defense of the Cuban revolution against the renewed threat of American imperialism to crush it.

One of the byproducts of Cuba's fresh leap into world prominence has been a renewal of interest in the nature of the Cuban revolution, in the political character of its leadership, and in the relationship between Moscow and Havana. Questions such as the following are being discussed: Does the presence of Cuban advisers and troops in Angola, Ethiopia, and elsewhere in Africa prove—as Washington's propaganda machine alleges—that Castro is serving as a puppet of Moscow? Or is the Cuban government seeking to advance a policy of its own that happens, for the time being, to be congruent with Moscow's aims? What does Havana's rising influence in African affairs show about the present status of the Cuban revolution? Has a parasitic caste become entrenched in Cuba? Has the revolution degenerated to such a point that it must now be said that a Stalinist regime has usurped power? With the wisdom of hindsight must it now be acknowledged that the Cuban revolution was Stalinist-led from the beginning? Or do the new developments speak otherwise, indicating continuation of a policy to extend the revolution internationally, thus cutting across the Stalinist policy of "peaceful coexistence" with the imperialist powers and their capitalist system?

Questions running along these lines are not new. They were raised and debated during the first years of the Cuban revolution. The initiatives taken by the Cubans on the African continent place them on the agenda for rediscussion.

It takes something more than careful study of the current developments to find correct answers to these questions, particularly in view of the absence of information on some essential points such as the calculations of Havana on the one hand and Moscow on the other. At present these can only be surmised or deduced.

An obvious requisite is accurate knowledge of the background. Articles featuring "in depth" analysis of Cuba's rising role in Africa are strikingly inadequate if they fail to refer to the patterns followed by the Cuban leaders in carrying through the revolutionary struggle in Cuba.

For dialectical materialists it is imperative to go back to the origin of the Cuban revolution. There is no other way to establish the continuity (or discontinuity) of the processes that have, among other results, now received spectacular expression in Africa. Moreover, there is no other way to determine the meaning of the Cuban revolution as it has evolved. Here it is not necessary to begin from zero—the problem presented to Marxist theory by the uniqueness of the events was solved at the time. The conclusions reached then have proved of immense service in analyzing subsequent developments.

One of the purposes of this compilation is to present those theoretical conclusions. They are included in documents that were part of a free internal discussion held in the Socialist Workers Party in 1960-61 while the party at the same time carried out energetic defense work in support of the Cuban revolution and against the American imperialist effort to smash it.

Other documents in the book include polemics against protagonists of State Department positions, exposures of Cuban Stalinist hacks who sought to besmirch the record of the Trotskyists, and articles representative of hundreds by many different writers that were published in the *Militant* and other Trotskyist journals in defense of the Cuban revolution when it was the target of the heaviest blows. These documents indicate where the Trotskyists stood on other fronts as they sought, through use of the dialectical method, to ascertain the place of the Cuban revolution in the chain of socialist revolutions that began in Russia in 1917.

\*           \*           \*

At present Washington is pushing the line that Cuba has become completely dependent on the Soviet Union, abjectly obeys orders from the Kremlin, and has sent its troops to Africa to serve as surrogates for Soviet troops. These allegations conform to the pattern of the State Department's well-aged propaganda picturing the Soviet Union as an aggressive power intent on conquering the world. The truth is that the main objective of foreign policy as pursued by the Soviet ruling caste is maintenance of the status quo; that is, "peaceful coexistence" with the imperialist powers and the capitalist system.

If it were true that Brezhnev had shifted from this policy to one of extending Soviet power and influence through the use of armed force, the turn would represent a new element of transcendent importance in world affairs. A reassessment of the nature of the Soviet government would be called for, along with a possible redetermination of the revolutionary Marxist attitude toward the ruling caste. The analysis might place the Cubans in a favorable light as the spearhead chosen to open the offensive decided on by Brezhnev.

However, the State Department is not acting on the assumption that Brezhnev has adopted a class-struggle policy. The State

Department distinguishes Castro from Brezhnev. Friendly relations are maintained with the Russian leader even while new weapons of the most fiendish kind are developed by the Pentagon for use in a projected war against the Soviet Union. Castro, on the other hand, is kept at the top of the State Department's list of enemies, and the CIA has attempted on a number of occasions to apply the order issued against him, "Terminate with extreme prejudice."

Washington's attitude is hardly surprising—it is simply an imperialistic reaction to the efforts made by the Cuban leadership to defend their revolution by extending it.

The course of the Cubans can be conveniently divided into three phases:

1. In the great wave of enthusiasm over the Cuban revolution following its victory, many attempts were made in Latin America to emulate the July 26 Movement. These attempts were supported by Havana both politically and materially. Extension of the Cuban revolution appeared to hinge on extension of the methods used by the July 26 Movement—mainly the initiation and pursuit of guerrilla warfare. This period reached its high point at the OLAS conference held in Havana in August 1967. There Castro subjected the reformist Latin American Communist parties to scorching criticism for their sabotage of guerrilla war. At that moment, Che Guevara was in Bolivia conducting the experiment that was to end in his death.

Ill-conceived though it was, Guevara's attempt to set off a revolution in Bolivia testified to the international outlook of the Castro team. One of Guevara's aims was to create a new front that would help the Vietnamese in their struggle against the American invasion in Indochina.

It is worth recalling that on March 10, 1965, Castro publicly offered to send arms and men to aid the Vietnamese. On March 16, in a widely publicized speech appealing to Peking and Moscow to close ranks against the common foe, Castro said: ". . . we think Vietnam should be given all the necessary aid . . . we are in favor of aid in arms and men . . . we are for the socialist camp risking everything required for Vietnam."

Cuba's offer to send "arms and men" was turned down by the National Liberation Front. As it was, Cuba was the first workers' state to make this kind of public offer. The initiative may have been decisive in compelling Moscow and Peking to follow with similar statements.

2. The crushing of Guevara's ambitious project capped a series of defeats for the groups that took the road of guerrilla war. Castro now made a turn. Since this occurred only months after the OLAS conference in 1967, and since no critical appraisal of the previous course was presented publicly, a good deal of confusion was created among supporters of the Cuban revolution. While still giving some aid—principally training— to the protagonists of guerrilla war in Latin America, the Cubans ceased fostering it as the royal road to success.

The economic situation in Cuba also worried them; the American blockade was inducing strains. The Cuban leaders stepped up the goals on the economic front, hoping by extraordinary exertion to overcome the effects of the American stranglehold. Unrealistic goals, notably in the 1970 campaign to produce ten million tons of sugar, resulted in dislocations of economic planning and exhaustion among the workers.

In view of such consequences, the Cuban leaders had to reassess priorities and set more modest goals. The pause for reflection over the meaning of the failures of guerrilla war and consideration of possible alternatives lasted until 1975.

Washington evidently interpreted the downturn in guerrilla war in Latin America as evidence of the domestication of the Cuban revolution; and the State Department—whose blockade had failed to isolate Cuba—began probing ways to bring Castro under the general framework of "peaceful coexistence."

3. The breakup of the Portuguese empire, with climactic liberation struggles in the colonies and the toppling of the Salazar-Caetano dictatorship in Lisbon, presented new openings for the Cubans. They had already established ties with various guerrilla forces in Africa, Guevara himself having participated in this work. In Angola, the Cubans granted aid—most noticeably in the form of combat troops—to counter the imperialist efforts of Washington and Pretoria to block the liberation struggle. Cuban belief in the preeminent role of armed force in and of itself—a belief that discounts the power of a correct political program—is being tested in an even clearer way than in Latin America.

A new aspect of this involvement is its legality. The Cubans were invited by the People's Movement for the Liberation of Angola (MPLA), which received international recognition as the legitimate government of Angola, to send material aid, including troops, to boost the country's defense against the efforts of South Africa and the United States to reimpose imperialist rule. In responding to the appeal, the Cubans acted in accordance with international law. The pattern was repeated in the case of Ethiopia. Today Cuban consultants and advisers are to be found in a number of countries in Africa.

\*       \*       \*

Moscow has supplied material aid, armaments in the first place, to both Angola and Ethiopia. This represents nothing new. Similar aid has been extended by the Kremlin in the past to other African countries and to countries elsewhere in the world—Cuba itself is an outstanding example. The Soviet ruling caste is compelled to do this, in part to meet Peking's challenge, in part to give some substance to its pretense of standing for socialism, and mostly to gain leadership of forces heading in an anticapitalist direction, the better to use them in bartering with the American imperialists. Moscow's objectives fall within the general context of the détente. All that is sought is more elbowroom for maneuver.

\*       \*       \*

The American Trotskyists have criticized Havana's foreign policy on several counts:

1. The extrapolation on a continental scale of the efficacy of guerrilla war seemed to us to be based on a misjudgment of both the Cuban experience and the possibilities for its repetition. The key to the toppling of Batista was the rise in the class struggle in Cuba. The rise was not "sparked" by the guerrilla actions; on the contrary, the rise made it possible *in this instance* to win even through guerrilla actions.

American imperialism and its satellite forces in Latin America, learning from what happened in Cuba, resorted to more repressive regimes to suffocate the class struggle; hence the installation of military dictatorships that in their first actions sought to stamp out all organizations of the working class. As the masses fell back in face of the murderous onslaught, it became increasingly difficult for guerrilla movements to gain headway. The problem of linking up with the masses could not be solved by them.

The general conclusion to be drawn from this turn of events is that more effective means than a guerrilla band is required to lead the struggle for socialism. What is required is a mass working-class party of the Leninist type.

2. Guided by their desire to construct a common front against American imperialism, the Cubans failed to distinguish the components of this front according to program. Thus supporters of the capitalist system were hailed, provided that they were "progressive," i.e., denounced imperialism or spoke well of the Cuban revolution. Confusion was thus sown among supporters of the Cuban revolution, with the consequence that many of them were diverted down false trails.

A case in point was the support given the Chilean regime headed by Salvador Allende. Although Castro may have sensed a coming showdown in Chile when he was there on tour—his parting gift to Allende was a submachine gun—the support he offered the regime appeared to be support for its adherence to capitalism. Allende's failure to act against the plotters in the military forces cost him his life. More important, the seizure of power by Pinochet dealt a cruel blow to the cause of socialism in Latin America, and a deadly enemy was added to the roster of regimes hostile to the Cuban revolution.

3. Similar criticisms can be made of Cuban policy in Africa today. The programs of the Neto regime in Angola and the Mengistu regime in Ethiopia have not been presented for what they are—commitments to maintain capitalist relations in those countries.

The Cubans seem to be primarily interested in bolstering the *anti-imperialist* aspects of the upheavals in these areas. But to overlook the struggle for *socialist* goals can only prove counterproductive. And it is dangerous to believe that an anti-imperialist struggle automatically reinforces the struggle for socialism. Such a view can lead to defeats for socialism, as was shown in Chile. In both Angola and Ethiopia we have already seen repressive measures taken against revolutionary socialists.

In the case of Eritrea, the Cuban government at first supported the national liberation struggle there. As the Dergue organized expeditionary forces with the objective of smashing the rebellion by military means, the Cubans appeared to be having difficulty deciding what to do—participate, stand aside, or withdraw? Havana's hesitancy demonstrated how dangerous an inconsistent anti-imperialist line can be.

What does Cuba's new role in African affairs tell us about the nature of the Cuban revolution and its leadership? Let us recall that when Havana responded to the MPLA's plea for aid, the shipment of troops received wide acclaim in the left. It was argued that the support granted by Havana not only proved how internationally minded the Castro regime was, it proved the progressiveness of the Neto government.

However, this argumentation was shelved when the Mengistu regime appealed for similar aid and the Cubans responded favorably. Castro plummeted in leftist opinion. According to this view, Castro's granting aid to Ethiopia was a sure sign of the degeneration of the Cuban revolution.

It is unfortunate that these analysts lacked the capacity to maintain both arguments simultaneously. Had they insisted that their deductions held with equal force in both cases, they would have provided us with an educational demonstration of the traps awaiting those who believe Havana's relations with the Angolan and Ethiopian regimes offer fresh evidence concerning the nature of the Castro regime and the status of the Cuban revolution.

The same goes for the contention that the Cuban role in Africa amounts to providing surrogate troops for the Kremlin. It might be argued that the State Department's propaganda on this point does not necessarily mean that it is untrue. We can agree with that. However, this does not alter the questions that arise if we take a close look at the propaganda rather than simply brushing it aside.

Why did the Kremlin select the Cubans for this role and not the Latvians, the Poles, or the Czechs? Was it because Cuba is the farthest from the scene and the transport problems from there are the greatest? Did the Cuban record in guerrilla war tip the scales? Did Moscow calculate that the White House would react most angrily to the choice of Cuba, thereby assuring a rise in tensions between Havana and Washington? Or did the Kremlin have more devious reasons for wanting to incite the Americans?

The answers to such questions and to others of similar nature point to the conclusion that the Castro regime exercised a certain initiative in bringing Cuban influence to bear in the struggle against imperialism on the African continent.

As for the argument that Havana's rising prominence in Africa indicates the crystallization of a hardened bureaucratic caste in Cuba, the available evidence would seem to indicate the contrary. Hardened bureaucratic castes, such as the ones in the Soviet Union and China, characteristically display conservatism, even a counterrevolutionary outlook, particularly in foreign policy; hence their pursuit of "peaceful coexistence," of "détente," of deals with the imperialist powers at the expense of the masses. But in Africa, Cuban activities have greatly increased instability at the expense of the imperialist powers. Castro has followed a course that closed off rather than invited a deal with American imperialism. This fact alone speaks decisively against the contention that the events in Africa offer proof that a hardened bureaucratic caste has taken over in Cuba.

The Cuban course in Africa requires no essential alterations in the Marxist analysis of the lines of action adopted by the Castro team after they had consolidated the victory of the revolution.

\*       \*       \*

Cuba's influence in African affairs appears completely out of proportion to the size of this small Caribbean country. How is this anomaly to be explained? The answer is obvious—it lies in the power of the Cuban revolution.

The record is there for all to see: First, in the contrast between the Cuba that *was,* under the American puppet Batista, and the Cuba that *is,* under a revolutionary regime. Second, in the contrast between today's Cuba and the rest of Latin America. Cuba demonstrates what can be done under a planned economy to improve the standard of living of the poor. Countries like Chile are hangmen's showcases.

The achievements made possible by toppling capitalism are impressive. The list includes the elimination of unemployment, once the scourge of the Cuban working class; the banning of racism; the promulgation of equal rights for women; the setting up of child-care centers on a national scale; the construction of a free educational system that provides not only books but food and clothing to students; the establishment of a model social-security system, including health care; the slashing of rents and initiation of an ambitious program to end the acute shortage of housing, inherited from the past; and an agrarian reform that was decisive in establishing the firm worker-peasant alliance on which the first workers' state in the Western Hemisphere depends.

The government's concern for the needs of youth should be added to the list. In the first period following the victory, when one of the most pressing needs was reliable personnel, teen-agers were given responsible posts throughout the island. The perspectives for young people in Cuba today include broad educational and job opportunities on a scale that cannot be matched in any capitalist country.

It is the *example* of Cuba, the example of achievements made possible by the revolution, that accounts for Havana's standing among the peoples of the colonial and semicolonial countries and thereby its political weight internationally.

An accounting of developments within Cuba, particularly in the last decade, is of course required in any balance sheet of the revolution as a whole. Such a balance sheet is not included in the documents in this book, which center on defense of the revolution in the early years and on analysis of the particular pattern that made possible a socialist victory without the presence of a Leninist party. Nonetheless, a few points should be taken up.

The Cuban revolution faced extreme difficulties from the beginning. Inadequacies of leadership counted among them, the prime one being, as I have indicated, reliance on guerrilla war to extend the revolution. Another was the failure to proceed immediately to establishment of forms of proletarian democracy.

However, the main source of the difficulties was American imperialism. The mightiest military power on earth, located only ninety miles away, decided to strangle the Cuban revolution. Castro was marked for assassination. Farm animals were inoculated with contagious diseases. Saboteurs set bombs. The blowing up of a merchant ship in Havana harbor and arson that succeeded in burning down one of Havana's biggest department stores were two of the more spectacular incidents. Forays of this kind were topped by the armed invasion at the Bay of Pigs. Worst of all was the blockade, which completely disrupted Cuba's traditional pattern of trade with the United States and greatly reduced the possibilities of free trade with other countries. Tiny Cuba, dependent on imported oil as its source of energy, was truly an isolated fortress under heavy siege. In defense of the revolution, the Castro team placed Cuba under wartime regulations.

Wall Street and its political agents in Washington bear full responsibility for blocking the Cuban revolution from developing freely. This should never be forgotten in criticizing the weaknesses and mistakes of the Castro regime.

The Kremlin must be held responsible for another source of difficulties. Without help from the Soviet Union, the Cuban revolution would certainly have been smashed by either Eisenhower or Kennedy. The Cubans were completely correct in seeking that aid. It was due them in accordance with the program of world revolution supported by the Soviet government when it was headed by Lenin and Trotsky.

Stalin's heirs felt obliged to respond to the Cuban plea, but instead of providing aid free of charge, as was their duty, they demanded that a price be paid—principally on the political level. In short, to get the required aid the Cubans had to let the red glow of the Cuban revolution shine on Khrushchev and Brezhnev.

From many things that have appeared in the record—a good example is Castro's criticisms of the Soviet invasion of Czechoslovakia, which he reluctantly supported—it is clear that the price demanded by the Kremlin for Soviet aid rankled with the Cubans. They had to forego speaking out freely. While they were able to get the required material aid in time to save the revolution, the cost was heavy in terms of their political independence.

Both the American campaign to crush the revolution and the strings attached to Soviet aid must be taken into consideration in dealing with the problem of bureaucratism in Cuba. By isolating and further impoverishing the country, the blockade helped increase the social importance of the layers charged with the defense. In the distribution of scarce supplies top priority had to be given the armed forces. One of the consequences was an army now recognized as the best in Latin America. Another consequence, however, was the introduction of ranks, a sign of bureaucratization. The Kremlin's influence was shown in the growth of bureaucratic tendencies under the auspices of figures who were prominent in the Stalinist apparatus in Batista's time. These case-hardened bureaucrats were met head-on by Castro. A more difficult problem is the example set by the Soviet ruling caste, which liquidated the proletarian democracy fostered under Lenin and Trotsky. No model of proletarian democracy exists in the world today to counter the totalitarian forms of rule upheld by the Kremlin.

It would be untrue to say that the battle against bureaucratism has been won in Cuba. The indications are that this insidious social disease has gained, as the introduction of ranks in the armed forces would indicate. Similar signs include the continuation of the ban on formation of tendencies and factions in the Communist Party and the jailing of the independent-minded poet Heberto Padilla on March 20, 1971; the brush-off given to protests against the jailing by leftist intellectuals like Carlos Fuentes, Gabriel García Márquez, Octavio Paz, Jean-Paul Sartre, and Mario Vargas Llosa; the show trial of Padilla, which included a Moscow style "confession" by the poet; and the accompanying clampdown in the cultural field, where the Cubans had previously shown their intent to make the revolution a "school of unfettered thought" in opposition to bureaucratic practices. Another bad indication has been the pillorying of homosexuals.

However, the headway made by bureaucratism has not reached such a degree that one must conclude that a hardened bureaucratic caste has been formed, exercises dictatorial power, and cannot be dislodged save through a political revolution. No qualitative point of change has yet been adduced to substantiate this hypothesis.

\*        \*        \*

The stand taken by the Socialist Workers Party towards the Cuban revolution flows from its initial analysis of that event. It can be summarized in three points:

1. For defense of the Cuban revolution against all its enemies. As a party within the United States, the SWP considers it to be its special duty to foster the strongest possible political opposition to the main enemy of the revolution, American imperialism. This defense is unconditional—it does not hinge on the attitudes or policies of the Cuban government.

2. For the development of proletarian forms of democracy in Cuba. The purpose of this is to bring the masses into the decision-making process in the most effective way, thereby strengthening the struggle against bureaucratism. The initiation of workers' councils would add fresh power to the Cuban revolution as living proof that socialism does not entail totalitarianism but on the contrary signifies the extension of democracy to the oppressed in a way that will lead eventually to the withering away of the state.

3. For the formation of a Leninist-type party that guarantees internal democracy, that is, the right of critical opinion to be heard. The power of a party that safeguards the right to form tendencies or factions was demonstrated by the Bolsheviks. A replica shaped in accordance with Cuban particularities could do much to induce the formation of similar parties in the rest of the

world. This would greatly facilitate resolving the crisis in leadership faced by the proletariat internationally, thereby assuring a new series of revolutionary victories.

May 1, 1978

# THE TRUTH ABOUT CUBA

*"The Truth About Cuba" appeared as a series of articles in the Militant from May 9 to August 15, 1960, and later was published as a pamphlet by Pioneer Publishers. This was part of the Socialist Workers Party's effort to educate workers in the United States about the Cuban revolution and help build a movement to defend that revolution against Washington's efforts to crush it. Also at that time, SWP presidential candidate Farrell Dobbs made defense of the Cuban revolution the focus of his campaign, and the party worked with other political tendencies and prominent individuals in the Fair Play for Cuba Committee, an organization that sought to disseminate accurate information about Cuba.*

*Reprinted here with minor editorial changes, these articles provide an overview of the background of the revolution—the growth of American economic domination and the repression under puppet dictators from the Spanish-American War to the fall of Batista. They outline the program and evolution of the July 26 Movement, drawing parallels between the aspirations of the Cuban leaders and those of the leaders of the American Revolution, showing why the Cuban struggle for independence and the socialist measures undertaken by the new government deserve the full support of American workers. They also trace the counterrevolutionary record of the pre-1959 Cuban Communist Party and discuss the differences between Stalinism and the Castro leadership during the early battles of the revolution.*

# The Truth About Cuba
## (1960)

One of the things that rankle with the Cubans is a long-standing tendency in Washington to look at their country as a prize to be taken like Texas, California, and the other parts of the West which we seized from Mexico. They can quote declarations going back as far as Thomas Jefferson and John Quincy Adams on the advisability of eventually grabbing Cuba. They cite proposals of statesmen of the Southern slavocracy to wrest Cuba from Spain and make it another slave state.

Cuba's struggle for independence from Spain began in 1868. It is the conviction of the Cubans that this struggle could have been won rather rapidly had aid been forthcoming from America. Instead, Washington's policy was to prevent Cuba from gaining her independence, the reasoning being that it was better to let the declining Spanish empire retain rule until the "fruit" became "ripe," whereupon it could be expected to drop into waiting American hands.

Cuba's freedom fighters continued to battle against the Spanish tyranny. By 1898 victory was in their hands. However, in January of that year President McKinley began open preparations for war on Spain. At the end of the month, the U.S. battleship *Maine* was sent to Havana harbor. On February 15 it blew up, with a loss of 266 lives. The true cause of the explosion was never determined, but the suspicion remains that it was a cloak-and-dagger operation plotted in Washington.

In any case, utilizing the explosion as a pretext, Congress voted $50 million "for the national defense" and on March 25 declared that a state of war had existed with Spain for four days.

American troops were landed in Cuba under the proclaimed aim of aiding the Cuban struggle for independence. The Spanish-American War was short. Spain signed a peace treaty on December 10 ceding the Philippines, Guam, and Puerto Rico outright to the United States and relinquishing Cuba. But American troops did not leave the island. They stayed four years as an army of occupation.

Among the things this army did was to prevent the Cubans from forming a government of their own free choice. The Wall Street interests sought to annex Cuba. However, public clamor rose in the United States against such a brazen move. The Democratic Party, in striking contrast to its present-day, bipartisan, "me too" attitude, made an issue in the 1900 elections of "Republican imperialism." Imperialism, whether Republican or Democratic, was an accurate label for America's new role in world affairs.

Today, to expose the hypocrisy of State Department propaganda, the Cubans remind Americans of that army of occupation. "You demand that the Castro government hold immediate elections," they say. "But when your army occupied our country, you prevented elections from being held for four years."

President McKinley sent American troops to intervene in the civil war in Cuba in 1898 ostensibly to aid the independence movement. His real reason was to make Cuba safe for American investments. That was why the troops were kept there for four years. By the time they were ready to leave, Cuba was safe for the Almighty Dollar.

By 1959 private American capital investments were listed at around $850 million. This does not sound like very much compared, say, to the some $2 billion which the Pentagon and State Department are reputed to take out of the public till each year for nothing but worldwide spying. But America's financial sharks are noted for their exceptionally strong parental instincts. They suffer agonies if the smallest investment is endangered; they will fight ferociously to protect it from harm; and they are fabled for their solicitude in providing it with human flesh, bones, and nerves so that it will prosper and grow.

Thus, a half century after the American troops were withdrawn, at least 40 percent of the sugar production in Cuba was held by U.S. corporations. About 90 percent of the island's mineral wealth was in the hands of Americans, and 80 percent of public utilities. Cuba's oil resources were completely owned by American and British corporations. The biggest cattle ranches were likewise listed in the investment portfolios of American coupon clippers.

How much wealth was funneled from Cuba into American

bank accounts after Cuba fell into Wall Street's orbit is not known. At present the Cuban government has been opening the books of the big corporations to try to get an idea. When the facts are made public, they should make interesting reading.

Even worse than the exhausting drain of profits wrung from the toil of the Cuban workers and *campesinos* were the pernicious effects on the structure of the economy. Cuba became a one-crop country.

This does not mean much to American workers when they first hear about it. "So what?" they ask.

If we had a worldwide, integrated economy run according to scientific plan, a small country would very likely find it advantageous to concentrate on what its resources, climate, and skills best enable it to produce. Bolivia's tin, Venezuela's oil, and Cuba's sugar might then be regarded as the most important contributions to the satisfaction of humanity's material needs that could be produced in these countries for some time to come. Under capitalism, however, a one-crop economy compounds and intensifies the ordinary evils of this antiquated way of producing our basic necessities. The life of an entire nation becomes subject, sometimes to a disastrous degree, to the vagaries of the market and to the whims and calculations of a handful of ruthless, profit-minded monopolists.

In Cuba, sugar customarily accounted for two-thirds of the national income and 80 percent of exports. Property holdings became so concentrated that until the agrarian reform of a year ago, 75 percent of all the cultivated land was held by some 8 percent of the country's property owners. About 700,000 peasants held no land at all.

In the *Nation* of January 23, 1960, Robert Taber summarizes figures indicating the situation facing the working class as follows:

Of the total Cuban labor force of 2,204,000, some 361,000 persons were wholly unemployed throughout 1957; 150,000 were employed only part of the time; 154,000 were engaged in unremunerated labor—e.g., as domestic servants, working for their meals and lodgings. Of 1,539,000 Cubans gainfully employed, 954,000 earned less than $75 a month in a nation where the peso was on a par with the dollar and had even less purchasing power in Havana than in New York.

These are graphic figures; but they fail to indicate the plight of the 500,000 sugar workers in Cuba's main industry. Employment for them existed each year only during the four months of the harvest. The other eight months were known as the "dead time."

For American workers to grasp the meaning of that, they would have to recall in all its vividness the Great Depression of the thirties. That was a "dead time" in the richest country in the world, when it seemed hopeless to find work and millions found themselves reduced to beggary.

In poverty-stricken Cuba, eight months out of each year counted as a major depression for the bulk of the working people. The misery, suffering, and hopelessness they experienced make for bleak reading. It is must reading, however, if you want to understand the reasons for the sensitivity of the Cubans to what happens in Washington and the countinghouses of Manhattan.

They ate malanga, which is something like a straight potato diet. Sugar cane was a second staple. Thus they grew up stunted and subject to vitamin deficiency diseases.

They lived in huts called *bohios*. No floor, just the bare earth. A roof made of thatch from the royal palm, much appreciated by all kinds of insects.

Their clothes, more often than not, were patched rags.

They went barefoot, although this is hazardous in tropical countries.

They went without dental care, losing their teeth when they were still young. And they went without medical care.

As for education, some two million Cubans could neither read nor write.

Tens of thousands of fertile acres, growing to weeds, were available for cultivation, but feudal-minded landlords barred this. Cuba's long-suffering victims of chronic hunger, malnutrition, and abysmal poverty had to avoid trespassing on land that really belonged to the people as a whole. To heighten their bitterness, Wall Street's propagandists made sure that they heard all about the "free world" and its wonders, particularly the prosperous "American Way of Life."

The American propagandists need not have rubbed it in. The Cuban masses were well prepared to desire a change in their way of life.

*          *          *

American domination of Cuba can be divided into five stages. First came the period of direct military rule over the island under General John R. Brooke and later Major General Leonard Wood. The aim of U.S. military occupation was to make the country safe for American investments. This included such progressive things as stamping out yellow fever and introducing modern sanitation, but these measures were linked with a major political objective: to block the Cuban independence fighters from government office and to set up a structure of rule best suited to guarantee high profits.

By May 20, 1902, when the army of occupation was withdrawn, Cuba was well prepared for penetration of the dollar. Elections had been supervised by the American military forces, the candidates thoroughly screened. The constitution had been processed under General Wood's vigilant eye. As a final guarantee, an amendment to the constitution, fathered by Senator Orville H. Platt of Connecticut, had been forced down the throat of the new Cuban government.

This notorious appendix obliged the Cubans to ratify everything done by the military occupation, forbade any government loans that could not be paid off through an excess above current revenues, forbade any foreign treaties not approved by Washington, gave the U.S. the right to intervene in Cuba's internal affairs whenever necessary to maintain "a government adequate for the protection of life, property and individual liberty," and, finally, to make everything doubly sure, gave the U.S. the right to buy or lease lands necessary for military bases.

Under the latter clause, American troops have been stationed in Cuba ever since. These have been supplemented from time to time by the landing of marines to maintain the kind of government favored by Wall Street.

In the second stage of American domination the Wall Street locusts settled on highly profitable economic concessions and contracts.

Under the administration (1909-13) of José Miguel Gómez, a typical Latin American *caudillo,* or military chief, the third stage of American economic domination opened. This was the period of the sugar barons, who converted Cuba to a one-crop economy. They consolidated their position under President Mario G. Menocal, an employee of the Cuban-American Sugar Company, who stole a second term and remained in office under the protection of U.S. marines until 1922.

During Menocal's second term a new stage of American domination opened. The Morgan gang, National City Bank, the

Royal Bank of Canada, and Chase National Bank became the real rulers of Cuba, and they rapidly brought the sugar industry under their control. They entrenched themselves under Alfredo Zayas, who stole the 1921 elections, and Gerardo Machado (elected 1925, overthrown 1933).

Finally we come to the Batista period, which lasted with interruptions from 1933 to 1959. We will consider this stage later.

Carleton Beals, in his book *The Crime of Cuba,* describes the first four stages in considerable detail. He summarizes the economic side as follows:

1900 to 1917 marks the gradual infiltration of American capital, the pace ever quickening toward the end of the span. 1917 to 1922 marks a virtual tidal wave of American capital investment. Those years also mark the beginning of bankers' control over sugar and other resources. By the 1922 crisis J. P. Morgan and Company, Chase National Bank, National City Bank, and allied Canadian institutions moved into dominance, ever expanding their equities in the industrial and agricultural enterprises. 1922 to 1933 marks the definite consolidation of bankers' control. Through the Electric Bond and Share Company and the International Telephone and Telegraph Company, close to the house of Morgan, public utilities were gathered into the fold. Most railroads, not in English hands, are controlled by the Tarafa-Woodin-Rubens-Lakin-Rockefeller combination, closely harmonized with the American Car and Foundry Company and the National City Bank. Cubans own far less of the wealth of their country than in 1895.

Beals indicates the extent of American domination of Cuba by 1933 as follows:

One-third of Cuba's territory, nearly 90 percent of the cultivated lands of the island, is owned or controlled by long-time leases by Americans or American corporations. The remainder is largely mortgaged to American banks and creditors. Eighty percent of the sugar industry belongs to citizens of the United States; the rest is controlled chiefly by American creditors. Cuba's second industry—tobacco—is also mostly American. Nearly all the banks, railroads, street-car lines, electric plants, telephone systems and other public utilities are owned by capital from the United States.

Subservient to Washington to begin with, Cuba's governments came increasingly into the service of American imperialism. Shocking poverty and lack of economic opportunity helped foster the growing corruption of public office. Once behind a government desk, the average Cuban official immediately went to work to sweeten up his own bank account at the expense of the public treasury. In this he was abetted by the American ambassadors, for they were there, among other things, to facilitate plunder of the Cuban treasury, in the form of loans, by Manhattan's financial pirates.

As public dissatisfaction and unrest mounted over this state of affairs, Cuba's military forces grew in size, venality, and ferocity. This tendency, deliberately fostered by Wall Street and the State Department, reached its culmination in the government of Gerardo Machado. His became known as the regime of the "Sawed-Off Shotgun." He smashed the trade unions, murdering their leaders. He butchered politically minded students, finally closing down the University of Havana and many lesser schools. He suppressed all opposition, jailing, torturing, and killing any who dared to hint lack of enthusiasm about the way he ran things. Professional criminals, preferably murderers, became candidates for his gangs of killers, both official and unofficial, and he put his armed henchmen in control of the most ordinary civic institutions to prevent them from becoming centers of resistance.

Resistance mounted, nevertheless. The dictator, relying on the backing of the U.S. government, refused to give an inch. He swore that no power would dislodge him from office. On May 20, 1930, reviewing his troops, he declared, "Before resigning the Presidency of the Republic, I will drown the island in blood."

Among those who joined conspicuously in the applause was Ambassador Harry F. Guggenheim, of Anaconda Copper, the American Smelting and Refining Company, and the New York banks interested in Cuban sugar.

Ruling as a political servant of America's top financial interests, dictator Gerardo Machado brought Cuba's army to peak strength. Since the country has no land frontiers to dispute over, the desire to have a big military machine appeared irrational to many Cubans. However, from the viewpoint of the cold-eyed men who survey this world from the countinghouses of Manhattan, nothing is more reasonable than a disciplined body of killers, armed with modern weapons, to protect the source of your profits.

The Cuban people did not yet grasp the full meaning of this murderous force, bristling with arms, which had been put together under the political guidance of the State Department and trained under American officers. They saw Machado, not the military institution, as the prime source of the terror inflicted upon them. And it must be recognized that Machado did all he could in a personal way to deserve the nationwide fear, bitterness, and hatred turned in his direction.

The people acted as people will under tyranny. Some tried shortcuts, venting their feelings in individual heroic—if ineffective—acts, such as exploding bombs and killing the worst public officials, in suicidal gestures of despair. The students began organizing more effective political protest demonstrations. Spontaneous strikes broke out. The Communist Party, although it had been outlawed since 1925, gained recruits from all sides. A Havana bus strike spread like a chain reaction throughout the island. "This general strike is a marvelous thing," the wife of the *New York Times* correspondent wrote in her diary August 6, 1933. "An entire nation folds its arms and quits work."

Sumner Welles had arrived as American ambassador in May. He began his work by urging Machado to resign. But the dictator took a stubborn attitude. The culmination of Welles's intervention was action by the military staff. For the first time in Cuba, the army displayed the power it had gained. The top brass informed Machado, who had built the military institution into a main instrument of rule, that his usefulness as president had ended. They advised him to resign within twenty-four hours.

Machado decided that the advice was good. On August 12 he took a "leave of absence" and left for the U.S., bullets whistling past his plane as it rose from the field.

On August 14 Carlos Manuel de Céspedes was sworn in. The conservative son of an illustrious leader in Cuba's struggle for independence from Spain, he had proved his docility by serving in Machado's cabinet. He was the choice of Sumner Welles.

But the concession of putting the name Céspedes in office did not halt the developing revolutionary movement. The people were in the streets by this time, hunting down the worst government gunmen and executioners. The strikes continued. Workers took possession of plantations, mills, and factories. In places they elected shop committees.

As the news came over the ticker tapes, the Wall Street operators deduced what might come next. They could lose their Cuban holdings. In those circles, that is a fate worse than death. Where could a new strong man be found in a hurry?

On September 5 a "Revolutionary Junta" under the leadership of one Fulgencio Batista y Zaldívar seized power. The junta represented principally the lower officer caste in the army; but Batista shrewdly involved the leaders of the radical student forces. The junta appointed five commissioners to form a new government, and Batista went to see Sumner Welles.

The students pressed hard for Dr. Ramón Grau San Martín, a member of the commission of five, to be named president. Welles didn't like the university professor, whom Machado had imprisoned on the Isle of Pines. Obviously a leftist egghead.

But the pressure was so great that Batista kicked out Céspedes and named Grau to the job September 10. Washington refused to recognize the new government and recalled Welles. On December 18 Jefferson Caffrey arrived in Havana as "special representative" of President Roosevelt. Apparently some of FDR's famous "charm" had rubbed off on Caffrey. Things began to happen. On January 15, 1934, on Batista's order, Grau resigned.

Batista made Carlos Hevia president. That was only a tactical step aimed at confusing political opposition groups. Hevia lasted exactly two days. On January 18 Batista put in Carlos Mendieta. This was the candidate Washington wanted. In face of protests from the Cuban students at having to swallow this reactionary, Roosevelt recognized the new government January 23. Batista then moved swiftly to smash the protest demonstrations and to arrest the leaders.

Some observers have concluded that this opening stage of Batista's rise to power was nothing but pure chaos. They are wrong. The revolutionary pressure had risen high. Batista gave the appearance of bending with it. He did this until its strength was down and his own base was firm; then he moved against it.

During that period he had demonstrated his ability to control the army in the interests of American capitalism. At the same time, he had shown that he was genuinely popular among the majority of the professional officer caste and even the ranks of the army—he was a talented demagogue. His replacement of one president after another demonstrated his tactical suppleness and his ability to confuse and break up the civilian political opposition. In Wall Street's balance sheet he was evidently not only willing to play ball but was well qualified. No one else in Cuba came near him as a military politician.

Something else had been proved. The military machine was now so powerful in Cuba, and in such skilled and understanding hands, that it was obviously no longer necessary for American imperialism to use direct intervention. The crude use of marines had become outmoded.

This provided a promising opportunity to prove the sincerity of Roosevelt's "Good Neighbor Policy." The Democratic chief now gave Batista a powerful assist. He granted a concession. To show that American capitalism had reformed and could now be counted on to behave as a big brother who would never again use a club on small children, Roosevelt agreed to a new treaty annulling the hated Platt Amendment. This was signed on May 29, 1934.

The rejoicing at this concession was great in Cuba, but somewhat premature. Batista, the enigmatic maker and unmaker of presidents, was busy polishing up the army, oiling its special privileges, adjusting the placement of henchmen, tuning up his military-political machine.

In 1935 a great strike wave hit Cuba. To push back the workers, Mendieta suspended constitutional law and declared a state of siege in Havana. These acts conferred still more dictatorial power upon Batista.

Cuba's new strong man felt so well entrenched that he decided he could afford to stage a normal election. A genuine democratic facade, ending the "provisional" government, would have a lot of advantages. Just before the election Mendieta suddenly resigned. But Batista simply appointed José A. Barnet as the fifth provisional president since the fall of Machado.

On January 10, 1936, in what appeared to be a fairly honest election (women voted in Cuba for the first time), Dr. Miguel Mariano Gómez y Arias won a majority. He was sworn in May 20.

But he didn't last long. Gómez tried to trim Batista's power. He dismissed 3,000 government employees who owed their posts to the dictator. That was a move Batista had not written in his book. Maybe this democracy stuff was going a bit too far after all. He had Gómez impeached. On December 22 the trial began. Within two days the president had been found guilty and removed from office.

A Senate committee told Vice-President Federico Laredo Brú that he was now it. Laredo proved to be a more satisfactory occupant of the president's swivel chair.

Batista's main base of power was the army. So long as that base remained seemingly impregnable, however, and the class struggle was not acute, he sought to clothe his rule in at least the forms of democracy.

In preparation for assuming the presidency himself, he had a constitution drawn up that even recognized the right of the people to revolt against a despotic government. He had already managed to give his brass a "New Deal" shine, achieving this partly by cultivating Roosevelt's friendly patronage, and partly by legislation that could be read as quite prolabor.

An expensive campaign helped give Batista the majority of the votes in the 1940 election. Under his presidency the war boom that ended the depression in the United States also gave Cuba a measure of prosperity, and the class struggle became relatively quiescent.

In the 1944 elections, Batista decided to run a puppet, Carlos Saladrigas. The opposition ran Grau San Martín. The Cubans took the election seriously, and Grau won by a landslide. He took office October 10 amid celebrations from one end of the island to the other. The hope was that Grau would now convert the forms of democracy into genuine substance. Batista's departure to live in Florida seemed to make this hope even more realistic.

Grau did do a few startling things, such as seizing the American-owned Havana Electric Railway; but his regime quickly settled down to the main preoccupation of bourgeois politicians in Cuba—self-enrichment. Fraud and corruption flourished as before.

The sinister army, too, remained as before. Grau dismissed some of the most notorious Batista supporters among the officer caste, but he altered nothing essential. As the decisive means of rule, the military machine remained intact.

Upon the outbreak of the cold war in 1946 and the launching of the witch-hunt shortly thereafter in the United States, Grau veered from New Dealism to anticommunism. In 1947, the same year that Truman decreed the infamous Loyalty Oath, the Cuban president appointed Carlos Prío Socarrás as minister of labor. Prío initiated repressive measures against the Communist Party and then in 1948 campaigned for the presidency on an anticommunist platform. His victory on such a platform was ominous for the future of Cuban politics. Even more ominous was the victory of Batista as a senator, although he still lived in Florida.

Truman's anticommunism paved the way in the United States for the rise to prominence of the fascist-minded Senator McCarthy and the worst wave of witch-hunting in the history of the country. In Cuba the anticommunism of Prío Socarrás paved the way for Batista's return to power and a regime worse than anything yet seen.

Batista was running as a poor third in the presidential elections in 1952. When polls indicated that Ignacio Agramonte of the Ortodoxo Party was quite certain to win, Batista moved. He got together the key officers in the army. With their support he announced March 10 that he had taken power in order to forestall a coup d'etat by Prío Socarrás.

The incumbent president took refuge in the Mexican Embassy as Batista declared over the radio, "I have been forced to carry out this coup because of my love for the people." Besides this love, he said he also had in mind "to save the country from chaotic conditions which endangered lives and property." He suspended all constitutional guarantees and canceled the June elections, thus making himself absolute dictator. At the same time he announced that if the United States was attacked by or involved in a war with the Soviet Union, Washington could count on his support. He also promised, naturally, to protect American investments. In a couple of weeks—on March 27, to be exact—he received U.S. recognition, and on April 3 he broke off diplomatic relations with the USSR.

Thus began the bloodiest chapter in Cuba's unhappy history. The total number of victims in the next seven years is estimated at around 20,000.

But business, especially American business, never had it so good in Cuba. Batista, in addition, initiated the most ambitious construction program in all Latin America, including highways, tunnels, office buildings, apartment houses, hospitals, and orphanages. Dickey Chapelle writes in the April 1959 *Reader's Digest:*

Havana was the chief beneficiary of this face lifting. But two out of three Cubans live in small towns or as squatters beside sugar and coffee plantations. The outpouring of capital and cement did not reach their earth-floored huts. They still ate less than their stomachs craved, their roads remained potholed and flooded, their school buildings jerry-built or in disrepair, their hospitals only paper promises.

Soon it became commonly accepted that at least one dollar out of every five spent in the country's building boom was lining the personal pocket of a Batista henchman. The dictator himself piled up a fortune estimated at 300 million dollars. A minister of the treasury, debt-ridden when he took office, became a multimillionaire in a matter of weeks. Hundreds of other fortunes—large and small—were made as the government steadily robbed the poeple. (One senator, Rolando Masferrer, maintained a private army of more than 1000 men.)

Robert Taber cites an authoritative estimate that out of a public-works budget of $800 million, the graft came close to $500 million.

How the Wall Street financiers made out in this rain of dollars is indicated by Carleton Beals in *Liberation* magazine:

In 1957, immediately after the brutal murder of one of the finest men in Cuban public life, Pelayo Cuervo (on orders of Detective Chief Orlando Piedra after personal consultation with Batista), Ambassador Arthur Gardner, accompanied by American Embassy economic advisers and officials of the Cuban Telephone Company (subsidiary of I.T. & T.) entered the National Palace, which was still stained with the blood of unsuccessful revolt, to sign a new contract raising telephone rates. According to documents found in the office of Edmund Chester, Batista's public relations adviser, this arrangement was achieved by the persuasive outlay of three million dollars. Our latest ambassador, Philip W. Bonsal, was for years a top official of this same telephone company.

Little was overlooked that might serve to line a pocket with pesos. According to an authoritative Cuban estimate in 1958, nearly 27,000 persons lived on the take from gambling, and 11,500 on prostitution. Havana swarmed with American tourists attracted by the daiquiris, gambling casinos, and lurid burlesque shows. Ten thousand slot machines were under the personal control of Batista's brother-in-law. In similar fashion Havana's parking meters were operated by the family of the mayor.

Batista could maintain himself in power only by the most brutal force. To supplement the army and the police, he shaped his secret service along the lines of Hitler's Gestapo. As under Machado, sadistic murderers were recruited from the underworld to serve as professional butchers in uniform. Political opposition was met with the submachine gun. Virtually every police station had its torture room. Dickey Chapelle writes:

On my desk before me are two signed statements documenting the terrorism. One is from a 50-year-old schoolteacher, mother of three children. The Havana police thought she knew where rebel arms were hidden. They arrested her in the middle of the night, and she tells how she was violated with a soldering iron in Havana's XII District police station on February 24, 1958. A physician's certificate confirms her assertion.

This instance was not exceptional. The police often gouged out eyes and castrated their victims before bashing in their heads. The bodies were commonly thrown in the streets or dumped in wells. Chapelle reports a typical experience:

One rebel told me he had searched for the remains of his father among 92 bodies piled at a Havana street intersection one morning. "He was one of the last I looked at," he finished.

Ruby Hart Phillips, Havana correspondent of the *New York Times,* reports a case in her book *Cuba, Island of Paradox,* which vividly indicates what Batista's henchmen were like. Nine Cuban youths had taken political asylum in the Haitian Embassy, where, according to international law, they could not be touched. While the Haitian ambassador was out to lunch, General Salas Canizares, chief of the national police, raided the embassy and shot down all the young political exiles. One of them, dying, managed to draw a pistol and shoot the police chief in the lower abdomen. Cuba's head cop was taken to the hospital.

"Ernestina Otero rushed out to Camp Columbia Hospital where she knew the General would be taken," continues Mrs. Phillips. Ernestina was ordered out.

But instead of leaving, she slipped into a small room adjacent to another operating room. Then she heard the siren of an ambulance. There was a window in the little room which permitted her to look into the operating room. It was the type of glass through which one can see without being seen from the other side. She watched as two boys were brought in, still alive, although riddled with bullets. They were dumped onto the operating tables like bags of flour. One lifted his head, stared around, then dropped back. The other was moving his lips. He lifted his hand and let it fall back. An officer came in. He consulted with one of the orderlies. "Get a doctor for them," he said. Just then Captain Moryon, an aide of Colonel Salas Canizares [the general's brother] burst in. He looked at the two wounded men, then shouted, "Never mind the doctor." He grabbed a knife from a table covered with instruments and cut the throats of both boys. Ernestina said she would never forget the scene.

\*           \*           \*

Americans acquainted to the least degree with the history of their own country should have no difficulty understanding why the Cuban people revolted against the Batista dictatorship. The rebel spirit that animated the Boston Tea Party, the encampment at Valley Forge, the type of fighting seen at Concord and Lexington, inspired comparable actions in Cuba of the 1950s.

The Cuban revolutionaries felt kinship to the rebels of 1775-83, but their immediate models were their own countrymen who opened the struggle for independence from Spain in 1868 and carried it on for thirty years. Today's revolutionaries felt themselves to be the direct heirs of this cause, among other reasons because Batista was not just a Cuban dictator but the representative of a new foreign oppressor—the United States. This may sound strange to Americans who have not studied the role of our country in Cuba; but it happens to be the fact.

In the early Cuban independence fighters, the revolutionaries of the 1950s found worthy models. Men like José Martí were not just nationalists in the narrow sense of the word, but partisans of the great ideas of freedom and equality that inspired the American and French revolutions.

The young men and women who finally succeeded in toppling Batista provided new examples of self-sacrifice, singleness of purpose, energy, and heroism which the youth of the world might well study as they consider taking up the great causes that move humanity forward, such as socialism.

The first important action following Batista's seizure of power was a raid organized by Fidel Castro on the Moncada fortress at Santiago on July 26, 1953. It was something like John Brown's raid on Harper's Ferry in 1859. The American abolitionist hoped that his action would serve as a spark to set off a slave rebellion. The Cuban rebel counted on a comparable response. The immediate consequences for the revolutionaries were similarly tragic. The young Fidel (he was not yet 27) escaped death only by sheer accident. Those in his small band of fewer than 200 who did not lose their lives in the attack were hunted down and implacably slaughtered, some after revolting torture. A few managed to escape, but Castro and other main leaders were sentenced to long terms in the penitentiary on the Isle of Pines, Castro being condemned to fifteen years.

In a certain sense John Brown succeeded in his raid even though he was hanged. He became an inspiration to the Northern haters of slavery and, as the battle hymn declares, his soul went marching on. The Moncada raid had a similar fate in Cuba; it served to inspire the rebel youth. When Fidel Castro and his comrades were released under an amnesty granted to political prisoners in 1955, Havana's radical-minded students already hailed them as national heroes.

Under the title of its closing words, "History will absolve me!" Castro's five-hour address to the court in his own self-defense, October 6, 1953, became one of the most important documents in the movement that finally overthrew Batista. To this day it is well worth studying as an indictment of Batista's tyranny and as a passionate defense of the right of a people to revolt against oppression.

On the legal side, the youthful lawyer based his case on the constitution of 1940, which recognizes the right of revolt. Under the same constitution, and the penal Code of Social Defense, Batista's seizure of power was clearly illegal and subject to heavy punishment.

Proceeding along these lines to accuse Batista and thus turn the defense of the Moncada action into a prosecution of the criminal regime, Castro appealed to the revolutionary will of the people as the final authority in questions of government. This was true, he pointed out, even in ancient times and in the Middle Ages. Most of his examples, of course, were taken from modern history. "It is well known that in England during the eighteenth century two kings, Charles I and James II, were dethroned for despotism. These acts coincided with the birth of liberal political philosophy and provided the ideological foundation for a new social class, which was then struggling to break the bonds of feudalism."

John Milton, John Locke, Jean Jacques Rousseau, Thomas Paine, the Declaration of Independence, the French Declaration of the Rights of Man were among the authorities cited by Castro to prove that "the right to rebellion is at the very roots of Cuba's existence as a nation."

As can be seen, Castro's legal defense did not interfere with his use of the trial to present his political views. He and his comrades were performing their duty as citizens, he said. "We are Cubans, and to be Cuban implies a duty. Not to fulfill that duty is a crime, is treason." He continued:

We are proud of the history of our country. We learned history in school and we have grown up hearing of liberty, justice and human rights.

We were taught to venerate the glorious example of our heroes and our martyrs. Céspedes, Agramonte, Maceo, Gómez and Martí were the first names engraved in our minds. We were taught that the titan Maceo had said that liberty is not begged but is won with the blade of a machete.

We were taught that for the guidance of Cuba's free citizens the Apostle [José Martí] wrote in his "Book of Gold":

"The man who conforms by obeying unjust laws and permits anybody to trample the country in which he was born, the man who so mistreats his country, is not an honorable man.

"In the world there must be a certain degree of decorum just as there must be a certain amount of light. When there are many men without decorum, there are always others who bear in themselves the dignity of many men. These are the men who rebel with great force against those who steal the people's freedom—that is to say, against those who steal human dignity itself."

Perhaps the most eloquent section of Castro's speech before the court was his defense of the martyrs who fell in the Moncada assault. Castro is not the flowery type of orator; his eloquence resides in the marshaling of facts and explanations. In front of the judges assigned to condemn him, he described the financial sacrifices these young people had made to buy guns, the risks they had accepted to carry out the assault, and the heroism with which they laid down their lives in the cause of freedom and justice. In stark contrast to this he described the corruption, foulness, and barbarous acts of Batista and his butchers. It was an account that could not but stir the youth of Cuba—and youth everywhere.

Castro explained exactly what the attack on the fortress sought to accomplish, exactly how it was organized, who the leaders were, and how they intended to proclaim their aims over the radio station that was listed for capture. Today greatest interest attaches to the program he outlined. It included much more than "restoration of public liberties and political democracy."

It advocated granting land to the smallholders, making the property "not mortgageable and not transferable." For the workers Castro proposed "the right to share 30% of the profits of all the large industrial, mercantile and mining enterprises, including the sugar mills." A new revolutionary government would order "the confiscation of all holdings and ill-gotten gains of those who had committed frauds during previous regimes, as well as the holdings and ill-gotten gains of all their legatees and heirs." To implement this, special courts would be given full powers to look into the records of all corporations.

In addition another series of laws would be promulgated such as "the Agrarian Reform, Integral Reform of Education, nationalization of the Utilities Trust and the Telephone Trust, refund to the people of the illegal excessive rates this company has charged, and payment to the Treasury of all taxes brazenly evaded in the past."

The rebel leader outlined in some detail from the prisoner's docket what he considered to be Cuba's six main problems: land, industrialization, housing, unemployment, education, and health. Here is a section of his speech that indicates how he proposed to solve these:

It is not by statesmen such as Carlos Saladrigas [Batista's nominee for the presidency in 1944], whose statesmanship consists of preserving the status quo and mouthing phrases like the "absolute freedom of enterprise," "guarantees to investment capital" and "the law of supply and demand," that we will solve these problems. . . . In this present-day world, social problems are not solved by spontaneous generation.

A revolutionary government with the backing of the people and the respect of the nation, after cleaning the various institutions of all venal and corrupt officials, would proceed immediately to industrialize the country, mobilizing all inactive capital, currently estimated at about 150 million dollars, through the National Bank and the Agricultural, Industrial and Development Bank, and submitting this mammoth task to experts and men of absolute competence, completely removed from all political machinations, for study, direction, planning and realization.

After settling the one hundred thousand small farmers as owners on land which they previously rented, a revolutionary government would proceed immediately to settle the land problem. First, as the Constitution ordains we would establish the maximum amount of land to be held by each type of agricultural enterprise and would acquire the excess acres by: expropriation, recovery of the lands stolen from the State, improvement of swampland, planting of large nurseries and reserving zones for reforestation. Secondly, we would distribute the remaining land among peasant families with priority given to the larger ones, and would promote agricultural cooperatives for common use of expensive equipment, freezing plants and a single technical, professional directing board in farming and cattle raising. Finally, we would provide resources, equipment, protection and useful guidance to the peasants.

A revolutionary government would solve the housing problem by cutting all rents in half, by providing tax exemptions on homes inhabited by the owners; by tripling taxes on rented homes; by tearing down hovels and replacing them with modern multiple-dwelling buildings; and by financing housing all over the island on a scale heretofore unheard of; with the criterion that, just as each rural family should possess its own tract of land, each city family should own its home or apartment. There is plenty of building material and more than enough manpower to make a decent home for every Cuban. . . . On the other hand, today there are greater than ever possibilities of bringing electricity to the remotest corner of the island. The use of nuclear energy in this field is now a reality and will greatly reduce the cost of producing electricity.

With these three projects and reforms, the problem of unemployment would automatically disappear and the work to improve public health and to fight against disease would be made much less difficult.

Finally, a revolutionary government would undertake the integral reform of the educational system, bringing it in line with the foregoing projects with the idea of educating those generations who will have the privilege of living in a happy land. . . .

Where will the money be found for all this? When there is an end to embezzlement of government funds, when public officials stop taking graft from the large companies who owe taxes to the State, when the enormous resources of the country are brought into full use, when we no longer buy tanks, bombers and guns for this country (which has no frontiers to defend and where these instruments of war, now being purchased, are used against the people), when there is more interest in educating the people than in killing them—then there will be more than enough money.

Cuba could easily provide for a population three times as great as it now has, so there is no excuse for the abject poverty of a single one of its present inhabitants. The markets should be overflowing with produce, pantries should be full, all hands should be working. This is not an inconceivable thought. What is inconceivable is that anyone should go to bed hungry, that children should die for lack of medical attention; what is inconceivable is that 30% of our farm people cannot write their names and that 99% of them know nothing of Cuba's history. What is inconceivable is that the majority of our rural people are now living in worse circumstances than were the Indians Columbus discovered living in the fairest land that human eyes had ever seen.

To those who would call me a dreamer, I quote the words of Martí: "A true man does not seek the path where advantage lies, but rather, the path where duty lies, and this is the only practical man, whose dream of today will be the law of tomorrow, because he who has looked back on the upheavals of history and has seen civilizations going up in flames, crying out in bloody struggle, throughout the centuries, knows that the future well-being of man, without exception, lies on the side of duty."

By 1954 Batista appeared impregnable. His army, equipped with the latest American weapons and advised by an American military mission, held the island's political life in a tight net. Police terror kept the meshes of the net in good repair. Business was booming and the dictator enjoyed the full support of Wall Street and the State Department. It appeared a propitious time to add some democratic camouflage. A presidential election, held November 1, was won handily by Batista after the sole token oppositional candidate, Dr. Ramón Grau San Martín, withdrew in despair and disgust.

In another step calculated to reduce dissatisfaction with his rule, Batista granted a concession after being sworn in as president. On May 13, 1955, he signed a bill providing a general amnesty of political prisoners.

Castro had been approached in prison with an offer of freedom in return for modifying his opposition to the dictatorship. He refused such a deal, however; and, upon arriving in Havana on May 17, resumed his political attacks on the regime.

But Castro found the avenues for democratic expression so meager as to be of little consequence. He decided to go into exile in Mexico in order better to organize an underground struggle.

How serious Castro was in this aim can be gathered from the fact that one of his first efforts was directed at overcoming a weakness which he and his followers felt keenly—their lack of military training. Castro succeeded in persuading Colonel Alberto Bayo to give a select group of cadres theoretical and practical training in guerrilla warfare. Bayo was well known in Latin America as an expert in this field, having served in the Spanish forces that fought Abd El Krim in Morocco. The colonel became an admirer of the Moroccan guerrilla fighters and made a study of their tactics, which he sought, unsuccessfully, to place at the disposal of the republican government of Spain in the civil war against Franco.

Castro himself participated only to a limited degree in this training. As the main political organizer, he spent the greater part of his time among refugee circles in Miami, Key West, Tampa, and New York in search of funds and recruits.

Cuban refugee circles were divided at the time into many groups and tendencies. Castro was a member of the bourgeois-democratic Ortodoxo Party, but soon found himself embroiled with the leadership over what to him was the key question—the necessity for serious preparation and active organization of the armed overthrow of the Batista dictatorship. Finally on March 19, 1956, disillusioned with the vacillations and compromises of the Ortodoxo chieftains on this issue, he announced the formation of the July 26 Movement as an independent revolutionary organization.

The most noteworthy feature of this political formation in the following years was its consistent refusal to compromise on the basic platform on which it stood—active organization of a popular uprising against Batista. Several attempts were made by leaders of the Auténtico and Ortodoxo parties to get Castro to subordinate his aims to a common front in which they would have decisive voice. In each case he refused, although he at the same time sought united action, particularly if it would facilitate getting material aid for the rebel forces in Cuba.

The year 1956 marked a significant turning point in Cuban politics. On April 4 a conspiracy was discovered between the "Monte Cristi" group and some lower officers in the army headed by Colonel Ramón Barquín. The officers were court-martialed and sentenced to the Isle of Pines. The conspiracy was of symptomatic importance, revealing that a section of the officer caste were uneasy over the unpopularity of Batista and thinking of finding a more acceptable figure.

On April 29 a small group attempted, in emulation of Castro's Moncada raid, to seize the Goicuria army fortress at Matanzas. The attempt was smashed.

Apparently Castro judged that such actions indicated a rise in revolutionary sentiment in Cuba. On November 15 he announced his intention to invade the island as the first step in leading a popular insurrection.

The story of his landing is now well known. On a small yacht, the *Granma,* capable of holding a couple of dozen men, Castro set out from Mexico with a force of eighty-two and all the arms and ammunition that could be put on board. An uprising in Santiago was timed for November 30 to divert attention from the landing. The uprising went through on schedule and was put down. But due to bad weather and engine trouble, the *Granma* was delayed until December 2, and the landing was made at an unfavorable, swampy spot where the arms could not easily be unloaded.

Batista learned of the landing the same day that it was made, and by December 5 the small "invasion" force was surrounded. They suffered a heavy defeat, only twelve men managing to evade the attackers and eventually assemble in a safe place in the Sierra Maestra. Batista claimed, and apparently believed, that Castro had been killed. For a time it was difficult to obtain evidence to the contrary. Nevertheless, this small band of twelve was to swell in less than two years to an army powerful enough to defeat Batista's well-trained and well-equipped forces and topple the dictatorship.

The leaders of the July 26 Movement ascribe their final success principally to their tactics. It must be noted, however, that the best of tactics are of little avail in the absence of favorable social and political conditions. These were quite ripe for revolution, as can be judged from the fact that on July 31, 1957, a spontaneous general strike occurred in Santiago and spread swiftly throughout the country.

It should be noted, too, that in the political atmosphere generated under Batista another leadership, much like the July 26 Movement in composition and political coloration, had formed in Havana. This was the Directorio Revolucionario, a group centered among the university students. Under José Antonio Echevarria, the Directorio staged a raid on the Presidential Palace on March 13, 1957, in an attempt to assassinate Batista. This terroristic action, heroic as it was, proved crippling; some of the best leaders of the group, including Echevarria, were killed, and Batista received only a bad scare.

As a major tactic, the July 26 Movement sought a base in the Cuban peasantry. Its main appeals were directed to the countryside, where it hoped to recruit its fighting forces. The leading slogan was "Land to the *Campesinos!*"

Setting up what was in effect a dual government in the Sierra Maestra, Castro sought to give an example to the farmers, sharecroppers, and field workers of what they could expect from the July 26 Movement in contrast to Batista's regime in Havana. The example was quite convincing, for the July 26 Movement was a spartan organization that sought to live according to what it taught. The *campesinos* began to support it actively and then to join its guerrilla forces in increasing numbers. By the summer of 1958 the point of qualitative change was reached—the guerrilla bands became large enough to operate as an army in the field.

Batista, like Chiang Kai-shek in China in the 1940s, sought to crush the guerrillas by an ambitious military drive. Like Chiang's troops, however, the ranks of Batista's army proved receptive to revolutionary appeals and began to join the rebels. Finally, like the Chinese revolutionary leaders, the Cubans launched a counterattack that brought them to power.

On the political side, Castro sought from the beginning to speak for Cuba as a whole. His principal appeal was to end Batista's bloody, dictatorial rule and put a government in power that was responsible to the people. He received some support from individuals in bourgeois circles, but it is worth observing that the class as a whole did not rally to his banner. The most powerful ones stuck with Batista. When the dictatorship was collapsing, a junta of generals was set up that evidently enjoyed the backing of these interests. They sought to negotiate with Castro, but he refused to deal with them. Having learned from the experience of the Guatemalan revolution that failure to break up the old army is a fatal error, Castro did not intend to walk into that trap. Out of tactical considerations he took the far-reaching measure, upon reaching Havana, of breaking up both Batista's army and Batista's police.

Not even the middle class in the cities appears to have been enthusiastic over Castro's July 26 Movement. The upper petty-bourgeois layers that opposed Batista, including businessmen and manufacturers, tended to support the Auténtico or Ortodoxo parties and a clandestine organization, the Civic Resistance Movement, which included professors, teachers, and white-collar workers in its ranks. This underground action group, centered principally in Havana, had three sections: propaganda, fundraising, and supplies. The sections were divided into cells of ten persons, each of whom sought to enlist another ten persons to form a new cell. By the beginning of 1958, as the July 26 Movement grew in weight, the Civic Resistance Movement began to note a sharp rise in financial contributions. In January these were $7,000; in March, $20,000.

As for the working class, it was caught without an effective political leadership of its own. The trade unions were dominated by venal officials holding their posts through Batista's favor. The Communist Party was discredited because of its support to Batista in the past. Moreover, it had no independent policy. Like the Communist Party in the United States, its main concern was to advance the Kremlin's foreign policy of maintaining the status quo. Consequently, the Cuban workers tended to favor the July 26 Movement and to support it actively insofar as they could without a dynamic leadership and fighting organizations of their own.

\*          \*          \*

If words could destroy, a single day's production of "hate Cuba" language in the American capitalist press would suffice to make Havana look like Hiroshima on the evening of August 6, 1945.

Even the staid newspapers, those that believe a public image of dignity pays off best, are in the firing line, bucket in one hand, filth in the other. Here, for instance, is a sampling of loaded words from a single article by Tad Szulc, special correspondent of the *New York Times,* datelined from Camaguey, June 20, 1960:

Doubt about the eventual outcome of Cuba's social revolution is becoming manifest in the island's rich provinces. . . .

. . . shrinking ranks of those still unquestioningly supporting the Castro regime. . . .

. . . the revolutionary program is at best in very serious difficulties and at worst in danger of possible disintegration. . . .

. . . the picture is one of mismanagement, economic deterioration and declining social standards. . . .

. . . the situation now developing in the provinces appears to be breeding palpable discontent and fear for the future, although it has not yet taken the shape of open opposition. . . .

What are the facts?

The Castro regime is without the slightest doubt the most popular government Cuba has ever enjoyed.

To anyone with an open mind who cares to take the ten-dollar flight from Florida to Havana to see firsthand, the contrast between the propaganda in the American capitalist press and the real attitude of the Cuban people could not be more startling.

But we needn't rely on personal impressions, which may be colored or one-sided. Facts are available that speak so emphatically about the popular attitude that even the most ardent backers of the Batista dictatorship find them difficult to deny.

On June 26, 1960, the Cuban magazine *Bohemia* published a nationwide poll. The rating of the government can be judged from the following: 81.17 percent of the population considered everything the government was doing "perfect"; 12.14 percent thought it was doing well, with qualifications ranging from "few exceptions" to "both good and bad"; 0.48 percent thought it was bad with "few exceptions"; 0.17 percent considered it "extremely bad"; 0.96 percent answered "don't know"; and 5.08 percent said they didn't care to answer.

Those were the figures for the country as a whole. In the rural areas the response was even more impressive: 89.67 percent answered "perfect"; 6.61 percent had some qualifications; 0.14 percent considered it "extremely bad"; 1.65 percent didn't know; and 1.93 percent didn't care to answer.

The poll included dozens of questions designed to explore attitudes toward all the many fields of activity in which the government is engaged, from the agrarian reform to international relations. These made it possible to get an accurate picture of shifts in sentiment since the previous poll a year earlier. Here are the conclusions drawn by *Bohemia:*

(1) The Revolutionary Government continues to enjoy the support of public opinion to a degree unequaled by any other government in our memory.

(2) This support has suffered in the year since our last survey only a slight decline of 2%. This decline has been compensated by a slight increase in the intensity of support.

(3) The source of the decline is in the upper and middle class. And this is compensated by an increase in the working class.

(4) The highly favorable opinion of the Revolutionary Government is due principally to the measures and actions undertaken by the Revolutionary Government in defense of the popular economy.

(5) Economic motives continue to constitute for our people the fundamental forces that shape their opinions.

*Bohemia*'s survey was confirmed by another one, under American auspices, published August 1. This survey, based on a thousand interviews in Havana and other cities and therefore reflecting urban sentiment, was made in May under the direction of the Institute for International and Social Research, of Princeton, N.J., headed by Lloyd A. Free.

"If this report is at all accurate," Peter Edson was forced to, admit in the rabidly anti-Castro *New York World-Telegram,* "it should dispel any hopes that the Castro regime is about to be overthrown."

Eighty-six percent of the Cuban people support Fidel Castro's revolutionary government, finding conditions now better than they were under the Batista regime overthrown in 1959. Eight percent rate the Castro regime worse than Batista's. Three percent believe the two about equal. And 3 percent refuse to express an opinion.

Like the *Bohemia* survey, the Princeton sampling indicated the class division over the new government. Edson noted:

The eight to 11 percent of the Cubans who oppose the Castro regime . . . are made up largely of the older, better educated, middle and upper-income-bracket groups. Eighty percent of Castro's opposition is concentrated in the Havana area. In rural Cuba, Castro is supreme. . . .

Half of the 86 percent believing conditions in Cuba today are better than they were under Batista are classified as "fervent" Castro supporters. The other half are "moderate" supporters. . . .

Only three out of ten expressed any disapproval of the Castro government. Of this minority, 25 percent mentioned "lack of freedom"; 18 percent "intervention with private property and private enterprise"; 9 percent "bad foreign policy"; 9 percent "lack of democracy and failure to hold elections."

Reasons listed for satisfaction with the Castro government included the following:

Approval of its agrarian reform program, 26 percent. Educational reform and campaign against illiteracy, 18 percent. Social justice and concern for workers, farmers and the poor, 17 percent. Economic progress and concern over unemployment, 8 percent. Inculcation of nationalism and patriotism among the people, 6 percent. Safety of the individual with an end to killing and physical abuses by the police, 6 percent.

The statistics speak for themselves. They register overwhelming approval of the sweeping measures taken since the revolution toppled the Batista dictatorship.

If these measures are borne in mind it is not difficult to understand why enthusiasm is so high. Under Batista, Cuba was like a concentration camp. Today the fortresses that housed the dictator's murderous armed forces have been torn down or converted into schools. To most Cubans, this change alone symbolizes what the revolution has accomplished.

But that was only the beginning. For the ordinary person, economic conditions in Cuba in Batista's time were like those of the Great Depression of the thirties in the U.S.A. As the first installment on their promises, the revolutionary leaders slashed rents, lowered essential food costs, raised wages, and began tackling the unemployment problem.

Then came the agrarian reform. This recovered the fertile land that had been fenced in by giant American corporations and feudal-minded Cuban landholders. Land is now being parceled out to family farmers. The government at the same time initiated a cooperative movement that holds great promise. Cuba's basic labor force, the sugar workers, saw a new future opening up—an indescribably bright future, if it is recalled that under Batista normal unemployment lasted eight to nine months a year.

As America's corporate interests sought to counter such progressive measures by savage economic and political attacks, the Cuban government responded by taking control of many of their holdings. "Intervention," the establishment of control, was followed quite frequently by nationalization. Each time this occurred on a dramatic scale, as in the case of the oil refineries, the island resounded with shouts of approval.

Intervention and nationalization have gone so far that all of Cuba's major industries, including the key plantations and sugar mills, are now in government hands. Wall Street investments, rated as high as $1 billion among the stock gamblers and their Democratic and Republican spokesmen in government, have reverted to the Cuban people. At this writing, the only major property still held by Wall Street is in Cuba's rich mineral resources. These, however, appear marked for early nationalization.

The beginnings of planned economy were established in the fall of 1959 during a series of great public demonstrations of approval. The beginnings proved successful. Planned economy—the first in the Western Hemisphere!—is now destined for rapid growth in Cuba.

Even if the Cubans find themselves compelled to make quite a few sacrifices because of the terrible pressures that the American monopolists can exert, they have already demonstrated that they will respond with the greatest determination and heroism.

They have begun to win their way out of the prison of capitalism and, as the polls show, they see no reason for returning.

\*          \*          \*

It is difficult to find an article about the Cuban revolution or even a dispatch from Havana nowadays in the capitalist press that does not include wringing of the hands or frothing at the mouth over the "advance of communism" under the Castro government. In Cuba, on the other hand, most of the people you talk with indignantly dismiss the charge as slander.

Is all that smoke in the press about "communism" just a Wall Street smudge or is there, perhaps, some fire behind it? To answer this question, we had best begin by attempting to discover what is meant by "communism."

To some capitalists, and they happen to be among the most powerful, any public measure that puts limits to "free enterprise" signifies "communism." They consider it "communism," for instance, to prevent them from plundering our natural resources, or from raiding the public treasury. A lot of Wall Street's clamor about what is going on in Cuba refers to restrictions of this type.

Among many radicals and even socialists, the term *communism* refers to something quite different—it means the antidemocratic practices, including one-party slates, blood purges, frame-up trials, and similar manifestations of dictatorial rule that have occurred in the Soviet Union under Stalin and his heirs.

This is also pretty much the popular view. When ordinary people today express fear of "communism," what they think of is the lack of democracy and civil liberties in the Soviet bloc countries. They say quite rightly, "We don't want concentration camps in America, or the cult of an individual like Stalin." Thus they find it depressing to hear about Cuba going "communist." Why would the Cubans want a regime like Stalin's?

Among Marxists, *communism* has still other meanings. First of all, it is the name of the society toward which all countries are clearly evolving, a society of complete freedom based on a cooperative, planned world economy that has achieved unlimited abundance and thereby brought the painful class differences, the wars and depressions and hatreds of our time to an end. Secondly, it is the name of the international political movement organized under the leadership of Lenin and Trotsky in 1919 to fight for and hasten the inauguration of this abundant communist society of the future.

In the early twenties and even into the thirties this was the splendid meaning of the word *communism*, and that was the way most people thought of it—even opponents—when they considered it honestly.

Clearly enough, the Stalinist displacement of Leninism brought communism into evil repute, converting the word in the popular mind into the opposite of its real meaning and offering reactionaries an invaluable propaganda advantage. But all this is another story. For our present purpose we need consider only two possibilities that people think of when they ask about Cuba going "communist": (1) inroads on capitalist property relations; (2) a shift in government that would give power to Stalinism. The two possibilities are not at all synonymous or dependent on each other.

Most workers and farmers tend to favor inroads on capitalism. So let us consider the second possibility as the one of real concern. Is there anything in the record of the Cuban Communist Party (it has called itself the Popular Socialist Party since 1944) to indicate that it might seek power in opposition to the July 26 Movement, which led the revolution against Batista?

The communist movement, as Lenin and Trotsky conceived it, began in Cuba in the early twenties in Oriente, the traditional revolutionary center. Outlawed by dictator Machado in 1925, the party fought in the underground. But with the rise of Stalinism, the Cuban Communist Party, like its sister parties throughout the world, was converted from an expression of Cuban revolutionary protest into an agency of Soviet foreign policy. With the fall of Machado, it engaged in wild ultraleftist adventures typical of the "third period" of Stalinism. (In the United States, by way of parallel, Franklin D. Roosevelt was labeled a fascist.)

After Hitler walked into power in Germany without a fight from either the Communist Party or the Social Democracy, Stalin shifted to a tactic of the most cynical class collaboration with what he called the "peace-loving" powers. Class collaboration, scored since the time of Marx and Engels as betrayal of the interests of the working class, was given new packaging and labeled the "popular front."

Stalin began to make this turn about the time Roosevelt recognized the Soviet Union in 1933. One of the services which Stalin offered Roosevelt in the negotiations leading up to recognition was help in stemming revolutionary unrest in Cuba. That was how the *Militant* analyzed it, as can be seen from an editorial printed December 16, 1933:

Cuba may very well turn out to be the Achilles' heel of the Wall Street monster. The contradictions between its domination by U.S. imperialism and the life interests of the masses are at the explosive point there. For many weeks now the struggle has been blazing into a conflagration which the whole world could see. The workers on their own initiative have been taking possession of American properties and have even, in some instances, proceeded to the formation of local Soviets. The island is small, but the uprising of its people has an enormous strategical importance and moral power. The Wall Street bandits justly regard it with apprehension as the peoples of Latin America and the conscious workers in the U.S. look to it with sympathy and hope. The U.S. bandits stand ready to crush the revolt with the brutal force of armed intervention. The workers and the peoples ought to be shown the way to unify all their efforts with those of the Cuban workers for the frustration of these designs. . . .

In the present instance, filled with such great potentialities, the Comintern of Stalin remains as silent as the grave. And as for Stalin himself, the "best disciple of Lenin," his mouth, as the saying goes, might be filled with water—he cannot utter a word of advice, encouragement or hope on the grandiose events in Cuba.

Is this "nonintervention" in the Cuban revolution a deliberate policy? Was an *express promise* to keep "Hands off Cuba" a part of the Washington agreement for recognition? If not, please explain the precise meaning of the following clause in Litvinoff's letter:

"(4) Not to permit the formation or residence on its territory of any organization or group—and to prevent the activity on its territory of any organization or group, or of representatives or officials of any organization or group, which has as its aim the overthrow of, or bringing about by force of a change in, the political or social order of the whole or any part of the United States, *its territories or possessions.*"

This treacherous pledge, which brings the blush of shame to every revolutionist, does not refer to some territory on the moon. It refers, directly and concretely, *and at the present moment,* to Cuba.

In our opinion, and we say it with blunt and brutal frankness, it was explicitly so discussed and understood in the negotiations. . . .

Batista's rule was so bloody, as the Cuban dictator aped some of the practices of Mussolini and Hitler, that it was not easy for the leaders of the Communist Party to overcome the revolutionary sentiments of the rank and file and get them to support the dictatorship. But by 1938, the party was following Stalin's "popular front" line as assiduously as its American counterpart, which was now under Browder's guidance, helping to spread the cult of "FDR." In August of 1938 the Plenum of the Central Committee of the Cuban Communist Party openly resolved "to take a more positive stand towards Colonel Batista since he has ceased to be the center of reaction and now professes democracy."

Batista reciprocated by immediately legalizing the Communist Party. Blas Roca, general secretary of the party, explained the Cuban popular front on a visit to New York: "It must be remembered that Colonel Batista himself comes of the people. He was a worker, the leader of the greatest democratic movement we've had."

In 1940 the Communist Party was conspicuous in the coalition that Batista put together around the slogan "Batista for President!" On March 6, 1943, the dictator appointed a Communist Party leader, Juan Marinello, to his cabinet, and on March 14 of the following year, he added another, Carlos Rodríguez.

In the 1944 elections the Communist Party supported Saladrigas, a Batista puppet, for the presidency, against the opposition candidate, Dr. Grau San Martín. When Grau won, the Communist leaders saw that they had made an error in sticking so faithfully to Batista. However, they speedily rectified the error. They ran after the bandwagon of the new president after it was unhitched in the presidential palace. Grau let them climb on the tailboard.

With the beginning of the cold war and the opening of the witch-hunt in the United States, the Grau government altered its policies to conform with those of Washington. Batista had utilized the services of the Communist Party principally to keep the trade unions under government control. Grau's minister of labor, Carlos Prío Socarrás, began a government witch-hunt of "communists" in 1947, the same year that Truman issued his infamous decree requiring a "loyalty" oath of government employees. Prío sought to oust trade union leaders under Communist Party influence and replace them with officials selected from his own Auténtico Party. In 1948 he ran for the presidency and won on an anticommunist plank. In office he continued the witch-hunt, in imitation of Truman.

When Batista seized power again in 1952, he kept up the Cuban emulation of McCarthyism, breaking off diplomatic relations with the Soviet Union on April 3, 1952, and outlawing the Communist Party on October 31, 1953. However, the Communist Party never suffered, even in the worst, final years of Batista's murderous rule, as did the July 26 Movement and similar revolutionary-minded groups. In fact, it appeared that Batista had a working arrangement under which the Communist Party, in return for a lenient attitude, utilized its positions in the trade unions to block the working class from militant action. The Communist leaders, of course, never supported the July 26 Movement during Batista's terror; in fact, they attacked it.

Today the Cuban Communist Party press is sweet as molasses toward the July 26 Movement. Whether the leaders of the "barbudos" find this thick praise very palatable may well be doubted. Certainly it has not served to rehabilitate the Communist Party in the eyes of the Cuban people.

We are fairly safe in concluding that a party that could toady up to Stalin and Batista for a quarter of a century is not exactly the kind that will seriously contend for power. That the leaders will seek government posts and special privileges is, of course, to be expected. In that they remain true to their past record.

*          *          *

At a public meeting sponsored by the Fair Play for Cuba Committee in New York on April 24, 1960, Waldo Frank, the well known liberal who heads the committee, warned that Cuba could meet with a tragic fate like that of the Spanish Republic. A counterrevolutionary movement such as the one headed by Franco might gain headway under foreign inspiration and succeed in toppling the new government. Analyzing the downfall of the elected Spanish government at the hands of the fascists, Frank recalled that the help received by the republican government from the Soviet Union was delayed and grudging. Arms were shipped only in return for gold, and onerous political strings were attached.

Waldo Frank's main point was to defend Cuba's right as a sovereign nation to deal with other powers as it sees fit, despite any dangers, real or alleged. He scored the economic and political pressure placed on Cuba by the State Department and American monopoly interests, and demonstrated how hypocritical it was of these forces to denounce the Cuban government for turning in the Soviet direction for help.

Every fair-minded person must certainly agree that the Castro government not only had the right but the duty to seek aid from other countries in face of Wall Street's evident aim of strangling the Cuban revolution. Everyone who really believes in democracy, in equality among nations, and in the efforts of oppressed colonial peoples to achieve independence will support the new government in the courageous way it has asserted Cuba's sovereignty.

However, Waldo Frank is quite right in indicating that dangers are involved. The parallel with Spanish experience is pertinent. But if the causes of the tragedy in Spain are fully understood there is no reason whatever for Cuba to suffer a similar fate. The leaders of the Cuban revolution have already demonstrated their capacity to avoid the errors that proved fatal in Guatemala; we can expect that they will demonstrate similar capacity to learn from the costly experience of the Spanish revolution.

What assured defeat at the hands of Franco was acceptance of the political strings that Stalin put on aid sent from the Soviet Union. The Spanish revolutionaries were under no obligation whatever to agree with these. In the first place, they had to pay cash on the barrelhead for the arms they received. In the second place, to submit to political guidance from the Kremlin meant to betray the political independence of their own movement. Independent political action was of decisive importance to the success of the Spanish revolution; arms from the USSR were not.

Stalin's policy in Spain was to retain capitalist property relations, including Spanish possession of the Moroccan colony. Thus the Spanish republican forces had no effective appeal that could have disintegrated Franco's forces; and they had no program of basic social change to inspire the Spanish workers and peasants. The final consequence was to assure Franco's victory. This in turn paved the way for World War II and Hitler's invasion of the Soviet Union. Stalin's policy proved disastrous to the interests of the USSR, not to speak of the interests of socialism on a world scale.

On the surface, the danger of repeating this bleak course appears considerable. Khrushchev's foreign policy is essentially the same as Stalin's; he seeks to maintain the status quo by selling out the interests of revolutionary movements and of small countries in big-power deals. All that Khrushchev has granted Cuba is a trade pact, one that is advantageous to the Soviet Union. He is not giving any handouts. Instead he is obviously seeking political profit in Cuba, Latin America, and the rest of the colonial world. Can Khrushchev succeed in Cuba in the unfortunate way Stalin did in Spain?

On close consideration, the possibility of repeating in Cuba what happened in Spain appears remote. The Cuban leaders are different from the Spanish revolutionaries in their tendency to carry things through to the end. Although they began by seeking only an end to Batista's dictatorship, they have proved far bolder in upsetting property relations, under the demands of political necessity, than the Spaniards with all their lip service to socialist and communist ideology. This difference alone can turn out to be decisive.

In addition, they passed a stern test which the Spaniards failed—they won a civil war. This has placed them in an extremely strong domestic position, for they came to power *after* the civil war with the Cuban Franco, not before. Their resulting strength and confidence are displayed by a dramatic fact—in the face of the threat from Wall Street to smash the revolution, they gave guns to the people, arming the entire population.

Finally, they appear to have realized the importance of widening the base of their defense to all of Latin America, instead of confining it to the small island of Cuba. They honestly and frankly recognize their military weakness, their small size, the great difficulties that confront the Cuban revolution; but they seek to make up for this by utilizing the revolution as an *example* to inspire all of Central and South America.

The international situation is also much more favorable for the Cuban revolution than the Spanish. In 1936 Mussolini, Hitler, and the Mikado were riding high, fascism was on the march, and the prestige and power of the Soviet Union had reached the ebb marked by Stalin's infamous purges and frame-up trials.

Today the colonial independence movement is sweeping with enormous force, bringing even the most underdeveloped nations of Africa into the stream of world politics. Cuba stands in a fraternity of small powers whose voices resound out of all proportion to their economic and military strength.

World imperialism is far weaker; the British, French, Dutch, and Belgian empires are disintegrating. In contrast, Eastern Europe and China now stand in the Soviet camp, and the Soviet Union itself has outstripped the Western European powers and stands second only to the United States.

Besides this, the monolithism of Stalinism has been broken. Moscow can no longer speak without taking into account rejoinders or amendments from Belgrade and Peking, which are no doubt carefully studied in Cuba for independent evaluation. And the revolutionary socialist voice of Trotskyism begins to be heard more frequently, as in the student demonstrations in Japan.

With such a relationship of forces, the fear that Cuba may fall like a ripe fruit into the hands of Khrushchev does not seem well founded. It is more likely that the Cuban example will prove to be a fresh source of inspiration to the Russian workers in their own struggle to win back the democracy they knew under Lenin and Trotsky.

*         *         *

In observance of France's national holiday commemorating the fall of the Bastille, July 14, 1789, *Revolución,* the newspaper of Cuba's July 26 Movement, paid high tribute to the great social upheaval that sounded the death knell of European feudalism. A columnist, "El Jacobino," recalled the role of the Jacobins in leading the French revolution and praised the thorough way in which Desmoulins, Danton, and "above all Robespierre, Saint-Just, Hébert and Marat" carried out the historic mission of their epoch.

El Jacobino describes the major stages of the revolution—the popular one in which the feudal rubbish was swept away; and then the stage of reaction:

> With the fall of Robespierre on the ninth of Thermidor (July 27, 1794), the glorious, Jacobin, popular stage of the great French Revolution closes. Power passed into the hands of the industrial and commercial bourgeoisie, who hastened to elevate to the level of eternal categories the new relations of economic production, forgetting that the feudal regime which had just been overthrown was also convinced of the eternalness of its supremacy and of its despotism over the people.

The Cuban revolution, in El Jacobino's opinion, is not only analogous to the French revolution; it is in its tradition:

> If the French revolution did not resolve all the problems, other revolutions followed in the heritage, such as the victorious revolution of the Negro slaves of Haiti, the Revolution of 1848 in Europe, the Paris Commune. But it fell to the great revolutions of the twentieth century, those in which the proletariat, the peasants, and other national layers played a decisive role, to bring into the life of the peoples the revolutionary principles of the Jacobins of 1792. This is the case with the Cuban Revolution, brilliant inheritor of the first French movement of emancipation.

El Jacobino follows this observation with some thought-provoking remarks on the contrast between the problems of 1789 and those which the Cuban revolution faces today:

> The mission of the Cuban Revolution is more profound than that of Jacobinism at the end of the eighteenth century. The conditions in which it is developing, in an epoch of general crisis for Yankee imperialism, lessens the possibility of a ninth of Thermidor, the possibility of a victory of the counter-revolution. The Cuban Revolution goes beyond the simple formal equality of citizens before the law, since with the support of the great majority of the people, it is carrying out in depth political and social transformations which will give an intense impulse to new relations of production serving the interests of the nation as a whole. The Cuban Revolution takes on the political and moral characteristics which were the glory of the French Revolution during the Jacobin period: revolutionary audacity, unbreakable firmness in defense of principles, creative

energy, incorruptibility, shining faith in the creative forces of the popular masses. The Jacobins of Cuba, the Robespierres, the Marats, the Babeufs of our epoch, sharing with the people strong national roots, face vigorously the emigrés of the new Coblenzes [places where counterrevolutionaries mobilize abroad], the threats and aggressions of American imperialism.

Three great, closely interrelated problems of the Cuban revolution are indicated in El Jacobino's article: (1) How to defend democracy and extend it. (2) How to avoid a Thermidorian overturn. (3) How to assure definitive victory to a revolution in a country as small as Cuba against a hostile power as colossal as the United States.

That these problems occupy the minds of the revolutionary leaders can be deduced from many indications. But as men inclined more to action than to theory, whose instinctive reaction to a blow is a counterblow in kind, they have not clearly articulated the large-scale problems they face.

In this they are different from the leaders of the 1905 and 1917 upheavals in Russia, who deliberately brought theory to bear as a most powerful means of advancing and defending the revolution and mobilizing support for it. Through theory, the Bolsheviks sought to think problems through to the end, the better to mold action and direct it in the most fruitful way. As the first great leaders of the revolutions of the twentieth century, the Bolsheviks thereby demonstrated that they stood on the shoulders of the leaders of the French revolution, the revolution of 1848, and the Paris Commune.

Because of this, it would seem that the theories and experiences of such men as Lenin and Trotsky would hold unusual attraction for the Cuban revolutionaries. Yet they did not turn in that direction in the beginning, and it remains to be seen to what degree they will search the writings of these great leaders for deeper insight into their own revolution and its future course in this epoch of world upheaval.

On the problem of democracy, for instance, Castro has put up a sturdy defense against the attack of American imperialism and its spokesmen. The imperialists, who backed dictator Batista, have no right to talk about democracy in Cuba, Castro points out; nor have they any right to talk about defects of democracy in other countries while the Negroes in the South, among other minorities in America, are denied the most elementary civil rights. Moreover, the Cuban government has put into effect a most radical measure of democracy—it has armed the population. Right now, a firm base for democracy in Cuba is being prepared through sweeping economic and social reforms, including a nationwide effort to eliminate illiteracy.

Excellent as Castro's stand is, it still remains a defense. The Bolsheviks went much further. They established a new type of democracy—proletarian democracy. Against the charge of Western imperialism that they had ended parliamentary democracy, the Bolsheviks responded "Quite true!" Then they analyzed parliamentary democracy, showed how narrow it was and how, in fact, it was based on the denial of democracy to the great mass of people. In contrast, the soviets—councils set up by the workers and peasants and soldiers—extended democracy to an unheard-of scale; and this new democracy was far superior to the limited democracy practiced by the capitalist powers.

The living example of a proletarian form of democracy was a most powerful means of winning support for the Soviet Union in the difficult early days, not only throughout Europe but in the United States.

That the democratic councils of workers, peasants, and soldiers were later smashed by Stalin in the Thermidor that befell the Bolsheviks does not invalidate their accomplishments in this field. It simply shows that the domestic and international forces of reaction were so strong that not even proletarian democracy, in the conditions of the time, could overcome them.

A rebirth of proletarian democracy on Cuban soil would add powerfully to the defense of the revolution. Few things would prove more convincing to the American workers that this revolution opens new, attractive perspectives. Elsewhere in the world it would give incomparable impulsion to the tendency to emulate the Cuban example.

The Bolsheviks, ardent students of the French as well as other revolutions, were well aware from the very beginning that Thermidorian reaction threatened their revolution. They did not foresee its exact form, and imagined that if it occurred, it would be through a violent overturn in a brief time. In their opinion this would prove inevitable if imperialism succeeded in isolating the revolution. Their policy, consequently, was to do their utmost to break the imperialist encirclement by extending the revolution; that is, encouraging revolutionary movements like their own in other lands. As we know today, the political reaction in the Soviet

Union was stretched out, taking the form of Stalinist degeneration.

Is El Jacobino correct in judging that the chances of Thermidor in Cuba, whatever its form, are rather remote? A lot depends on the course followed by the Cuban revolutionary leadership. The causes of Thermidor in the Soviet Union were quite complex. They included the exhaustion of the proletariat, the decline in revolutionary ardor among the peasantry, and the isolation of the revolution through the *cordon sanitaire* set up by the imperialist powers.

It would seem apparent that Cuba, taken by itself, is not guaranteed against an analogous fate. The peasant, having won a plot of land, wants to enjoy it; workers can be worn out by too prolonged sacrifices, especially if privilege seeking among official circles should develop to any significant extent; and Wall Street is obviously following the policy of seeking to isolate Cuba, suffocate it economically, and put another puppet government in power.

But the Cubans of 1960 do enjoy a much more favorable world situation than that faced by the Bolsheviks in 1917-21. The Bolshevik revolution made possible the establishment of planned economy and eventually the rise of the Soviet Union as a world power. Assistance—as already demonstrated—is available today from the Soviet bloc, and the Cubans have done well to seek it. In addition, colonial uprisings during the past fifteen years have helped alter world relations enormously to the disadvantage of the old imperialist powers, including the United States. The possibility of Cuba obtaining economic and moral aid from the People's Republic of China is proof enough of that.

With new revolutions breaking out, such as those now seething in Africa, it will not be easy for the big corporations and their political agents in Washington to isolate and destroy the Cuban revolution at their leisure. One of the most favorable conditions for the Castro government is the inspiration provided by these fresh revolutions, which counteracts the tendency to relax or to become discouraged over the difficulties imposed by American imperialism.

Despite these pluses, the Cuban revolution still remains in great danger. The Cuban revolutionary leaders realize this, as is clear from virtually everything they do and say. This realization, coupled with their repeated declarations that they intend to carry things through to the end, are highly encouraging auguries. But it remains to be seen how well they understand the ultimate logic of the Cuban revolution and how well they will succeed in fitting their action and theory to that logic.

*       *       *

The Cuban revolution is an event of major significance to North as well as South America. Not since the victory of the Chinese people over dictator Chiang Kai-shek in 1949 have the two continents been so stirred. The rise in fear among the reactionary, property-holding classes is registered in the preoccupation of the capitalist press and the State Department over the "menace" that has appeared on the tiny island in the Caribbean. In contrast, the rise in hope among the workers and peasants throughout Latin America is visible in constant trade union resolutions and popular demonstrations in support of Cuba. Moreover, the progress of the political, economic, and social overturn in what was formerly one of Wall Street's holdings has inspired fresh political currents.

But the victory in Havana is not yet definitive. Arrayed against the Cuban people is the richest oligarchy in the world—America's billionaire rulers. They are cunning and ruthless. They have decades of experience in suppressing or diverting popular movements. They have vast economic, financial, political, and military resources. To succeed against this formidable force requires strong nerves, the utmost determination, and—correct policies. A great responsibility rests on the leaders of the Cuban revolution— and not only them, as I shall try to indicate.

To successfully defend the gains made thus far, they face crucial tests in four areas: (1) Continuation of the revolution in Cuba. (2) Extension of the revolution into the rest of Latin America. (3) Connection of the revolution with the fate of the Soviet bloc, including the tendency in those lands toward revival of proletarian democracy. (4) Establishment of solid ties with the most advanced layers of the American working class.
How well will the Cuban revolutionaries meet these tests? Some partial answers are already in.

Under attacks from the American monopolists and their agents in Washington, the Castro government has indicated its capacity to go far in expropriating capitalists as well as feudalistic landholders. Some of the requisites of planned economy have been established and the government is already operating a considerable sector of industry in a planned way.

One of the most heartening manifestations has been the recognition, among the main leaders, that the revolution could not stand still; that it had to move forward even to maintain itself. Their acceptance of the need to take continually more radical measures is an object lesson for revolutionary-minded forces throughout the world. This growth in revolutionary consciousness is a good augury for the future.

They have done well, too, in inspiring defense of the Cuban revolution on the continent. From Mexico to Chile and Argentina, Cuba has become a key issue in public life. In all likelihood the next revolution in any of the Latin American countries will tend to follow the militant example of Cuba rather than that of Guatemala, where a compromising attitude toward the old ruling circles and their armed forces facilitated restoration of reaction.

As victims of exploitation at the hands of Wall Street, the Latin Americans have much in common. They are also united by language, by background and culture, and by similar economic and social problems. Such mutual interests clearly indicate the need to form a United States of Latin America. The policy of the new Cuban government to seek closer solidarity with sister countries in Central and South America would gain much greater force if it were tied in with the explicit goal of a mighty cooperative federation reaching from the Rio Grande to Patagonia. This perspective, long supported by Trotskyists, has yet to become part of the political armament of the July 26 Movement.

In respect to ties with the Soviet bloc, the Castro government has moved largely under compulsion from the blows rained on Cuba by the White House, Congress, and the State Department. Without economic aid from the Soviet Union, China, and the East European countries, the Cuban revolution might be speedily suffocated in the coils of Wall Street. It should be noted that the aid was not free. It took the form of exchange of commodities and was therefore of mutual benefit. Coming when it did, however, this economic aid may well prove to be decisive in saving the Cuban revolution.

It is unclear as yet what political concessions the Kremlin may seek from Havana and how the demand might be handled. So far, the Castro government has demonstrated a strong tendency to maintain the country's independence in relation to pressures from all sources. Che Guevara has publicly declared that independence will be defended in relation to the Soviet bloc no matter what the cost. His declaration undoubtedly reflected the thinking of most, if not all, of the leaders of the Cuban revolution. It may well turn out, as we have previously indicated, that the further development of the Cuban revolution will not strengthen dictatorial rule in the Soviet bloc but on the contrary, help to loosen it by further inspiring the forces working for restoration of proletarian democracy.

Where the Castro leadership has proved weakest is in its appeals to the American workers and farmers. Cuba's cause is directly connected with the interests of the working people in the United States, many of whom are exploited by the same companies that have bled the island since the turn of the century. But boldness of policy in this field has been lacking. Instead the main bid has been to restore the tourist trade. There is nothing wrong with this, of course; Cuba has much to offer as a vacationland, including low cost. But the case for Cuba's revolution and appeals for help against the common foe located in Manhattan and Washington have not been presented with the needed energy and thoroughness. It is singularly difficult, for instance, to find even such elementary items as English translations of the speeches and writings of the Cuban leaders.

Perhaps one reason for this is the fact that the Cuban revolution has not reached the socialist stage, where the international ramifications are clearly seen and followed. Its appeals have largely been nationalist in character. These can well serve to arouse the Cuban people for a time to heroic efforts and can serve as a stirring example to other countries in Latin America. But they are not sufficient to deeply move the American working class. Not even the far-reaching reforms already achieved in Cuba will catch the imagination of the American workers, although the Cuban fighting spirit may arouse enough sympathy and admiration to complicate Wall Street's effort to whip up a warmongering spirit against the small country.

The American workers would be much more inclined to respond to socialist appeals for international solidarity. They proved this after World War I when they rallied to the calls issued by Lenin and Trotsky. In 1919 the workers in Seattle even staged a general strike to protest American intervention against the Russian revolution.

It is quite true that the Stalinist bureaucracy succeeded in dissipating this good will; but the American workers are certain to respond with enthusiasm to a revolution that becomes socialist and clearly demonstrates that it is inherently opposed to everything dishonest, reactionary, and despotic. And the American working class remains one of the most important forces on this earth.

\*         \*         \*

Whatever course the Cuban revolutionaries take, politically conscious sections of the American labor movement should do everything in their power to support Cuba's struggle for freedom from American imperialism.

The Cubans have the right to choose whatever form of government they want. That's an elementary democratic right, the very right on which the organizers of our American revolution stood. We are duty bound to support that right no matter what kind of government the Cubans decide to establish.

Besides that, we have a lot to gain from defending any revolution that weakens the power of the monopolies riding on our own backs. The Cuban revolution has already struck these monopolies some stinging blows, and it is going to deal more. The Cubans are in much the same position as strikers who ask us to respect their picket lines in a tough battle. If they win we will be in much stronger position in our own battles with the same outfits.

Finally, no matter how well or how poorly the leadership of the Cuban revolution measures up to its great historic responsibilities, the revolution in its course tends to be socialist. Whatever help we can rally in the United States will strengthen that tendency. This has direct bearing on the greatest issues of our time—the struggle for enduring peace, the struggle to end poverty and insecurity, the struggle for democracy and a world brotherhood based on planned economy.

# THE CLASS NATURE
# OF THE CUBAN STATE

*In the early sixties, determination of the class nature of the Cuban state posed big theoretical questions for the Socialist Workers Party and the Fourth International. The leadership of the revolution was neither Trotskyist nor Stalinist, and it was not guided by a Bolshevik program. The Castro leadership proceeded empirically within the framework of a struggle for national liberation and democratic rights, mobilizing the workers and peasants against the Batista dictatorship and its imperialist backers. While defending the first socialist revolution in the Western Hemisphere and winning a new generation to revolutionary socialism, the Trotskyist movement was presented with an opportunity to test and enrich its theoretical arsenal.*

*The discussion in the SWP began in July 1960 with Joseph Hansen's document "The Character of the New Cuban Government." With the elimination of procapitalist representatives, the government was no longer a coalition that defended capitalist property relations and held back land reform. The new government encouraged mass mobilizations and carried out expropriations of land and industry.*

*As this process deepened, the SWP Political Committee drafted its "Theses on the Cuban Revolution," dated December 23, 1960. It characterized Cuba as a workers' state because of the transformation of property relations following the destruction of the old state apparatus and the establishment of a workers' and farmers' government. The new state was based on a monopoly of foreign trade, nationalization of the land and key sectors of industry, and the introduction of economic planning. Forms of proletarian democracy such as workers' councils were missing, but they could be developed without a political revolution because there was no hardened, bureaucratic caste in power. Joseph Hansen reported on the theses for the Political Committee at a National Committee plenary meeting January 14, 1961.*

*A common position on the Cuban revolution was part of the growing area of political agreement that led to the reunification of the Fourth International in 1963, after a split lasting ten years. Although the majority of each of the two public factions, the International Committee (IC) and the International Secretariat (IS), held that Cuba was a workers' state, there were differences of opinion on this. A tendency in the IC led by Gerry Healy of the Socialist Labour League in Britain insisted that the lack of a mass Trotskyist party in Cuba meant that the state was capitalist. A minority of the SWP led by Shane Mage, Tim Wohlforth, and James Robertson held a similar view, as did the French section of the IC. Their sectarian approach extended to the reunification itself, and they remained outside the reunified Fourth International. Hansen's polemics against this tendency and other views expressed in the discussion in the SWP are in "What the Discussion on Cuba Is About" and "Cuba—the Acid Test."*

*This discussion illustrates how Marxists approach new phenomena. Hansen applies the scientific socialist concepts of the theory of permanent revolution, the theses of the early Communist International on workers' and farmers' governments, and the Transitional Program to the facts of the Cuban revolution, using theory to illuminate the revolutionary process and at the same time enriching the theory itself in light of the new developments.*

*"Theory of the Cuban Revolution" (reprinted from the winter 1961 International Socialist Review) reviews two books: Listen, Yankee by C. Wright Mills, and Cuba—Anatomy of a Revolution by Leo Huberman and Paul Sweezy. The article adds to the material in the internal discussion and criticizes the position of the American CP that Cuba in 1961 was still in the "democratic stage" of a two-stage revolution.*

*"Stop the Crime Against Cuba!" (April 19, 1961) is a statement by the SWP Political Committee at the time of the Bay of Pigs invasion. It helps place the theoretical debate in its historical context.*

# The Character of the
# New Cuban Government
# (July 1960)

The Cuban revolution has proved to be deepgoing. Beginning with the simple political objective of overthrowing Batista's army-police dictatorship, it rapidly disclosed its tendency to revolutionize economic and social relations and to extend its influence throughout Latin America and beyond.

The main force opposing the logical development of the Cuban revolution is American imperialism. But the measures it has taken in attempting to stem the revolution and eventually suffocate it have had the opposite effect of spurring it forward.

The new Cuban government that took power in January 1959 has played a positive role up to now in the development of the revolution. First it secured its governing position by smashing the old armed forces and the police. It supplanted these with the rebel army, a new police largely recruited from the ranks of the revolutionary fighters, and later it set up a people's militia almost entirely proletarian and peasant in composition. It rapidly undertook a radical agrarian reform. This has two forms: (1) division of the land among the peasants on a limited private ownership basis (the land cannot be sold or mortgaged); (2) cooperatives closely tied to government planning. The emphasis has been on the side of the cooperatives. By last fall the government initiated planning of industry and control of foreign trade. A new stage was opened with the expropriation of land held by the sugar interests. Most recently, in response to the pressure of American imperialism, measures of expropriation have been extended to important foreign industrial holdings (principally American), and a virtual monopoly of foreign trade has been instituted.

A significant indication of the direction of movement of the Castro government is its tendency to establish friendly relations not only with the so-called neutral powers but with the Soviet bloc. This includes trade pacts that cut across the long-established trade pattern with the U.S. More important, however, is the tendency to emulate the planned economic structure of the Soviet countries.

The Castro government has proved that its responses to the mass revolutionary movement in Cuba and to the counterpressure from the U.S. are not simply passive. The new government has courageously defied American imperialism, resisting blandishments, threats, and reprisals. On the domestic side, it has repeatedly mobilized the Cuban workers and peasants in political demonstrations, in taking over landlord and capitalist holdings, in disarming the forces of the old regime, and in arming the people.

The direction of development on the political side has been demonstrated in the series of crises surmounted by the government since it took power. At first it put bourgeois democratic figures in key positions (finances, foreign trade, diplomacy, even the presidency). With each crisis induced by the interaction of imperialist and revolutionary pressures, these figures either turned against the government or were pushed out, being replaced by active participants in the preceding civil war, however youthful and inexperienced in their new duties.

The bourgeois outposts in such fields as the press, radio, and TV have suffered a parallel liquidation. On the other hand, workers' and peasants' organizations, including political tendencies, have been granted freedom of expression on the one condition that they support the revolutionary measures taken by the new government.

The Castro leadership began in 1952-53 as a radical petty-bourgeois movement, but one that took its revolutionary language seriously. It organized and led an insurrection. In power it sought (a) to bring the various revolutionary tendencies together in a common front by giving them due representation in government offices and by opposing any witch-hunting, and (b) to form a coalition with the remnants of the bourgeois-democratic movements that had survived the Batista dictatorship. The coalition, in which these elements were a minority unable to set policy, proved to be unstable. The defection of Miro Cardona a few weeks after he was appointed ambassador to the United States epitomized the instability of the coalition at the same time that it appears to have marked its end.

The Castro leadership has shown awareness of its own origin

and its own leftward evolution, including the stages through which it has developed. What is remarkable is its acceptance of this development and its repeated declarations of intent to follow through to the end, "no matter what," and despite its own surprise at the turns that open up. The constantly emphasized concept of the Cuban revolution as an example for Latin America, as the first link in a new chain of revolutions in Latin America against Wall Street's domination, is especially to be noted as an indication of awareness that the leadership of the Cuban revolution faces great historic responsiblities.

The dynamic rather than static character of the Castro leadership, of extraordinary interest to the revolutionary socialist movement, is undoubtedly ascribable in large part to the world setting in which the Cuban revolution occurs. It has the examples of the Soviet Union, China, and Yugoslavia, as well as the examples of colonial insurgency in a series of countries. These examples, plus the material aid and moral encouragement to be obtained from such sources, plus the feeling of participating in a worldwide revolutionary upsurge, have had a powerful effect on the outlook of the Castro leadership.

In addition, this leadership is close to the mass movement of both the peasants and workers, who have solidly and militantly supported each revolutionary measure and inspired their leaders to go further. The popular response throughout Latin America has had a further effect in the same direction.

All this points to the conclusion that the new Cuban government is a workers' and farmers' government of the kind defined in our Transitional Program as "a government independent of the bourgeoisie."

This does not signify that a workers' state has been established in Cuba. What has been established is a highly contradictory and highly unstable regime, subject to pressures and impulses that can move it forward or backward. Enjoying the support of the workers and peasants, having led them in a political revolution, faced with the imperative need to carry the revolution forward to its culmination by toppling bourgeois economic and social relations and extending the revolution throughout Latin America and into the United States, the regime lacks the socialist consciousness (program) to accomplish this. Even if it carries out extensive expropriations, these, precisely because of the lack of socialist consciousness, are not so assured as to be considered a permanent foundation of the state. In its bourgeois consciousness, the regime falls short of the objective needs of the revolution. (Whether the decay of capitalism and the example and influence of planned economies elsewhere in the world can make up for this lack—and to what extent—need not concern us here.)

Insofar as such a government takes practical measures against the bourgeoisie—that is, begins to resolve its contradictory position in the direction of socialism—it warrants support. And insofar as it grants democratic rights to revolutionary socialists, it warrants a fraternal attitude. Against imperialism, it must, of course, be supported unconditionally.

Whether the Castro regime, or a section of it, will evolve until it achieves socialist consciousness remains to be seen. As a petty-bourgeois formation it can retrogress. Its direction of evolution, however, has certainly been encouraging up to now.

By recognizing the new Cuban government as a workers' and farmers' government, we indicate its radical petty-bourgeois background and composition and its origin in a popular mass movement, its tendency to respond to popular pressures for action against the bourgeoisie and their agents, and its capacity, for whatever immediate reasons and with whatever hesitancy, to undertake measures against bourgeois political power and against bourgeois property relations. The extent of these measures is not decisive in determining the nature of the regime. What is decisive is the capacity and the tendency.

The concept *workers' and farmers' government* is not at all a new one. At the Fourth Congress of the Comintern in 1922, it was discussed at some length and included in the "Theses on Tactics" document that was adopted. In view of the encouraging prospects then facing the Third International and the known characteristics of such formations as the Mensheviks, the possibility was not considered great that a petty-bourgeois government in opposition to the bourgeoisie would actually appear. But it was considered a possibility and some of its characteristics were delineated. These offer us criteria by which to measure the new Cuban government. For instance, the "Theses on Tactics" declares:

The overriding tasks of the workers' government must be to arm the proletariat, to disarm bourgeois counter-revolutionary organizations, to introduce the control of production, to transfer the main burden of taxation to the rich, and to break the resistance of the counter-revolutionary bourgeoisie.

The document continues by declaring that "such a workers' government is only possible if it is born out of the struggle of the masses, is supported by workers' bodies which are capable of fighting, bodies created by the most oppressed sections of the working masses."

The new Cuban government has obviously met these criteria, even if we include an item not stated by the authors of the theses: the task of resolutely opposing imperialist rule.

It is true that the Bolsheviks had before them the petty-bourgeois organizations of their time and not a government formed by something as revolutionary-minded as the July 26 Movement; but then in discussing possible forms of a workers' and farmers' government they left room for variants which they could not predict and which it was fruitless to speculate about.

The main value to be derived from thus classifying the new Cuban government is not simply to be able to use a correct designation but in the possibility it opens—from the viewpoint of consistent theory—to apply the politics suggested by the Fourth Congress and by our Transitional Program in relation to such governments.

Trotsky was one of the guiding, if not the chief guiding spirit at the Fourth Congress in 1922. He considered its main documents, like those of the previous three congresses, as part of the programmatic foundation of the Fourth International. He clearly had the discussion at the Fourth Congress in mind when he wrote the section on workers' and farmers' government in the Transitional Program in 1938. This section, consequently, becomes much richer in content and implication if the previous discussion in 1922 is borne in mind.

Trotsky repeats one of the main points—that one of the uses of the formula of workers' and farmers' government was as a pseudonym for the dictatorship of the proletariat, first in the agitation of the Bolsheviks in preparing to take power, later as a popular designation for the proletarian dictatorship that was established. Trotsky emphasizes this in order to contrast what Stalinism did with the pseudonym after usurping power. Comparing what Trotsky says with the declarations of ·the "Theses on Tactics" adopted at the Fourth Congress, we see that Stalinism supported those types of "workers'" governments opposed by the Bolsheviks as masked forms of bourgeois power. In this way, Trotsky brings the "Theses on Tactics" up to date on this point by including the historic experience with Stalinism in relation to the concept of workers' and farmers' government.

As for a different use of the formula workers' and farmers' government—the one that concerns us here—to designate a regime that is neither bourgeois nor proletarian but something in between, he generalizes the entire experience since 1917 in an exceedingly condensed sentence:

> The experience of Russia demonstrated and the experience of Spain and France once again confirms that even under very favorable conditions the parties of the petty-bourgeois democracy (SRs, Social Democrats, Stalinists, Anarchists) are incapable of creating a government of workers and peasants, that is, a government independent of the bourgeoisie.

This appears to rule out the possibility, discussed at the Fourth Congress, of the actual formation of such governments. However, Trotsky refused to make an absolute out of his generalization of some twenty years of historic experience. Instead he affirms the position of the Fourth Congress in the following well-known paragraph from the Transitional Program:

> Is the creation of such a government by the traditional workers' organizations possible? Past experience shows, as has already been stated, that this is, to say the least, highly improbable. However, one cannot categorically deny in advance the theoretical possibility that, under the influence of completely exceptional circumstances (war, defeat, financial crash, mass revolutionary pressure, etc.), the petty-bourgeois parties, including the Stalinists, may go further than they themselves wish along the road to a break with the bourgeoisie. In any case, one thing is not to be doubted: even if this highly improbable variant somewhere, at some time, becomes a reality and the workers' and farmers' government in the above-mentioned sense is established in fact, it would represent merely a short episode on the road to the actual dictatorship of the proletariat.

In explaining the political value of the formula as a slogan, aside from the question of its actual historical realization, Trotsky stands on the position of the Fourth Congress: (1) It is an extremely important weapon for exposing the treacherous character of the old petty-bourgeois leaderships. (2) It has tremendous educational value, for it "proceeds entirely along the line of the political development of our epoch (the bankruptcy and decomposition of the old petty-bourgeois parties, the downfall of democracy, the growth of fascism, the accelerated drive of the workers toward more active and aggressive politics)."

Trotsky does no more than suggest the historic conditions that might convert the possibility of a workers' and farmers' government ("a government independent of the bourgeoisie") from something "highly improbable" into something quite probable and even into a reality. Some twenty years later we can see that the main historic conditions turned out to be the continued crisis in the leadership of the proletariat (the long default, due to Stalinism, in taking advantage of revolutionary opportunities) coupled with the continued decay of capitalism and the mounting pressure of popular movements seeking a way out, plus the survival of the Soviet Union in World War II and the subsequent strengthening of its world position.

Trotsky did not deal with the tactical problems that would face our movement should such a government actually be formed. The reasons for this are clear enough: (1) On the eve of World War II the possibility of such a government actually appearing was remote. (2) The basic strategy from which to derive tactics was well known, involving no more than the application of the Leninist attitude toward petty-bourgeois formations in the two possible variants of their development—toward or away from Marxism. (3) The Fourth Congress in its "Theses on Tactics" had already specified the conditions under which such a government would be supported or opposed. (4) The main issues confronting such a possible government would be the same in general as those for which key transitional slogans were proposed; these could be modified to fit whatever specific case might arise.

\*　　　　\*　　　　\*

In conclusion, whatever the particular circumstances were that gave rise to a government of the type now seen in Cuba, the possibility of the appearance of such a government was foreseen long ago by the Bolsheviks, its relation to the world revolutionary process was anticipated, and a general concept of how to approach it was worked out even down to specific slogans. In the abstract form of a transitional slogan we are, in fact, thoroughly familiar with it.

Its appearance in the form of a living reality does not overthrow our theory. On the contrary, the actual appearance of a government like the one in Cuba would seem to offer a most brilliant confirmation of the lucidity of Marxist thought and its power to forecast. It would also seem to constitute the most heartening evidence of the grand possibilities now opening up for revolutionary socialism and the party that has kept its theoretical heritage alive.

# Draft Theses on the Cuban Revolution
## (December 23, 1960)

1. The Cuban revolution began under the leadership of the July 26 Movement, a radical petty-bourgeois political tendency centered around the leadership of Fidel Castro. The initial program of the July 26 Movement was largely bourgeois-democratic, but promised thoroughgoing agrarian reform and industrialization.

It was distinguished by its clear recognition that the Batista dictatorship could be unseated only by revolutionary means, by its insistence on this as a principle in its relations with other groupings, and by its resolution in carrying the struggle against Batista through to the end no matter what the consequences.

2. In the Sierra Maestra phase of the revolution, the Castro leadership succeeded in mobilizing the *guajiros* and the agricultural workers, the decisive sector of the Cuban working class, to overthrow the Batista dictatorship. The outlook of the young revolutionary leaders became modified by these social forces. The city workers, under a trade union leadership imposed on them by the Batista dictatorship, were unable to bring their power to bear in the early stages, but with the victory they rallied in their overwhelming majority behind the revolutionary leadership.

3. The July 26 Movement came to power in January 1959 in a popular political revolution that at first appeared to be limited to democratic aims.

4. The revolutionary leaders enacted such immediate reforms as an increase in wages and reduction of rents, electric rates, and food costs. They set up a coalition government, granting such important posts as the presidency to the bourgeois-democratic elements.

5. The American monopolists and their agents were hostile to the July 26 Movement from the beginning, although they also sought to use flattery on its leaders. With the institution of

sweeping agrarian reform measures, the Castro leadership met with a belligerent response from American big business and the bipartisan Democrats and Republicans. Wall Street counted on the bourgeois-democratic elements in the coalition government as points of support for its counterrevolutionary objectives. Increasing strains appeared between the two sides in this government as Washington stepped up the pressure.

6. The conflict between American imperialism and the Castro forces precipitated a political crisis in Havana. This was resolved by a decided turn to the left, signaled, among other things, by the expulsion from the government of such figures as Urrutia and Pazos; and the coalition came to an end in the fall of 1959.

7. The fact that Cuba now had a workers' and farmers' government was indicated by its firm resistance to imperialism and its Cuban agents, the resoluteness with which it went ahead with the agrarian reform, disarming of reaction, arming of the people, and "interventions" of capitalist holdings. The lack of respect which this government displayed toward capitalist property relations was coupled with bold projects to meet the needs of the masses in employment, housing, education, recreation, and culture.

8. The interacting process between American imperialism and the Cuban revolution swiftly deepened after the end of the coalition government. The measures undertaken by the Castro regime in the interests of the Cuban people met with ever more unbridled attacks from Wall Street, its political agents, propagandists, and counterrevolutionary agents. The blows of these counterrevolutionary forces, in turn, compelled the Castro government to resort to increasingly radical measures.

9. These included the establishment of a monopoly of foreign trade, the nationalization of the latifundia, and, in August-October 1960, the virtual expropriation of the American and Cuban capitalist holdings; that is, the key sectors of Cuban industry.

These steps necessitated economic planning. This started in the fall of 1959, developed concomitantly with the nationalization of industry, and is now firmly established.

All these measures were taken with the examples of the Soviet Union, Eastern Europe, Yugoslavia, and China available for study. Thus, in the final analysis, the overturn in property relations in Cuba is an echo of the October 1917 revolution in Russia.

10. When the capitalist holdings in the key sectors of Cuban economy were taken over by the government, Cuba entered the transitional phase of a workers' state, although one lacking as yet the forms of democratic proletarian rule.

11. The Castro government had already smashed part of the old state structure in coming to power, liquidating the old army and police force in order to assure Batista's defeat. But the failure of the Castro leadership to proclaim socialist aims showed that the subjective factor in the revolution remained unclear and along with it the possible course of the revolution.

In the two years since then the state structure has undergone a cleansing out of holdovers whose basic loyalty was to the former, capitalist power. Upon nationalization of the key sectors of industry, the new state structure became so committed to a planned economy that only civil war can now restore capitalist property relations. A civil war could not succeed without a counterrevolutionary invasion far bloodier than that engineered by Washington in Guatemala in 1954.

12. The Cuban government has not yet instituted democratic proletarian forms of power such as workers', soldiers', and peasants' councils. However, as it has moved in a socialist direction it has likewise proved itself to be democratic in tendency. It did not hestitate to arm the people and set up a popular militia. It has guaranteed freedom of expression to all groupings that support the revolution. In this respect it stands in welcome contrast to the other noncapitalist states, which have been tainted with Stalinism.

13. If the Cuban revolution were permitted to develop freely, its democratic tendency would undoubtedly lead to the early creation of proletarian democratic forms adapted to Cuba's own needs. One of the strongest reasons for vigorously supporting the revolution, therefore, is to give the maximum possibility for this tendency to operate.

At the same time, revolutionary socialists advocate forms of this general character for Cuba because they would greatly strengthen the political defense of the revolution, help safeguard against possible retrogression, and, by setting a new world example, speed revolutionary developments inside the imperialist countries and in the colonial areas they still dominate.

The appearance of democratic forms of proletarian rule in Cuba would also have enormous repercussions in the Soviet bloc, aiding the revolutionary socialist tendency in those countries, which seeks the revival of Leninist democracy.

14. In search of allies in its defense of the revolution, the Cuban government turned to the Soviet bloc. It met with a favorable response from both Moscow and Peking. The material aid which it received may well prove decisive in its defense against the American-supported counterrevolution.

The overturn in property relations makes it feasible in principle for Cuba to tie its economy in with that of the Soviet bloc, including Yugoslavia, thus strengthening the planned economies in Europe and Asia as well as gaining life-saving support from them.

This does not conflict with the fact that it is in the interests of the Cuban as well as the American people to resume the trade with the United States which was cut off by Eisenhower.

15. The Cuban revolution constitutes the opening of the socialist revolution in Latin America. The Castro government has won tremendous support throughout the entire area below the Rio Grande and in turn has inspired millions of oppressed people with the desire to emulate the Cuban revolutionary success. The Cuban question has become the key question dividing all tendencies in Latin America.

16. The Stalinists were bypassed by the July 26 Movement. This is a fact of worldwide significance, for it shatters the illusion that revolutionary victories can be won only through the Communist parties. In turn, the success of the July 26 Movement adds to the ferment visible in many Communist parties in the past few years, giving fresh weight to the tendencies seeking to break through the crust of Stalinist bureaucratism.

17. The Cuban Communist Party is not exempt from this ferment. The American capitalist propagandists have built a fantastic bogeyman about a "take-over" in Cuba by the Communist Party. They leave completely out of account the effect of the revolution and its development on the thinking of the Cuban Communist Party, above all its ranks.

The fact is that the Cuban Communist Party supports the revolution. If a rift were to occur between Cuba and the Soviet Union, it can be taken for certain that the loyalties of a decisive section of the Communist Party, if not the party as a whole, would remain with the Cuban revolution. The experience in Yugoslavia speaks eloquently for such an outcome.

With free access to the views of all radical currents, as is the case in Havana today, the Cuban Communist Party can be expected to undergo considerable transformation, no matter what the ups and downs of the diplomatic relations may be.

18. The Cuban revolution has had a stimulating effect on the radical movement in many countries. It can play a powerful role in reviving hope and confidence in the socialist goal, in demonstrating that Stalinism is not inevitable and thus helping to pave the way for construction of mass revolutionary socialist parties. In the United States it has already opened up new opportunities for revolutionary socialists, as is evident in many areas, particularly the campus, Spanish-speaking minority groups, and the Negro people.

19. Whatever one may think of the Castro government and the new property relations in Cuba, it is our duty to defend this small country from the attack of the giant American corporations, their government, and their counterrevolutionary agents. The Cubans have a right to decide their own form of government and property relations, free from pressure.

It is especially in the interest of the American trade union movement to defend Cuba, for the monopolists now seeking a counterrevolutionary overturn there are the same ones that have long sought to cripple and smash the union movement in the United States.

The general slogans that should be advanced are "Hands Off Cuba!" "End the Blockade!" "Help the Cuban People!"

20. Despite the colossal power of American imperialism and its counterrevolutionary ruthlessness, plus the grave dangers and sacrifices these signify for the Cuban people, the perspectives for the defense of the revolution are most promising. It occurs in the general context of colonial uprisings beyond the capacity of the imperialist powers to contain, and it derives strength from this vast upheaval. The Cuban revolution occurs, in addition, in the context of the rising world power of the Soviet countries, whose interests coincide with the defense of Cuba. Finally, the workers and peasants of the small island appear as the vanguard of the Latin American revolution and therefore enjoy mass support on a continental scale.

Born under the influence of these forces, the Cuban revolution quickly established connections with them. It began influencing them in turn. A highly dynamic revolution, it can, by following the natural lines of its defense through revolutionary policies on the international scene, add qualitatively new force to the colonial revolution, to the defense of the Soviet countries against imperialist attack, and to the struggle for worldwide socialism.

# Cuban Question:
## Report for the Political Committee
## (January 14, 1961)

In your folders you have a document, "Draft Theses on the Cuban Revolution." The line of this has been adopted by the Political Committee. There is a disagreement in the committee; and a minority has a separate viewpoint which will be presented here. The majority is simply asking the plenum to vote on this one document—not for every sentence in it or every phrase or how it's phrased but for its line. That's all we want today.

We need this in order to give our party press and our spokesmen throughout the party a guide for some very important developments which have occurred in the Cuban revolution. There are in addition a number of complexities about this revolution and a number of implications on which I'm sure there is considerable disagreement and maybe many nuances. And on these differences I am sure that we will have to have an extensive discussion, a discussion which will probably go on for some time in our party, to go into the ramifications of all that is implied by the Cuban revolution.

Now I hope that we can have this discussion in the most objective kind of way, in a cool way, in a way that is in the tradition of our party when we handle questions of this kind—without heat, without epithets, and without any of that pulling together and defending each other's positions because of special relationships in other parts of party work. We want to have an objective, free discussion, and I think that one of the advantages of that will be that it will enable us to cooperate in clearing up these differences that we have among us or that can develop among us.

I think that's the freest kind of discussion because it enables us to take an opposing viewpoint and study it and size it up from the viewpoint of seeing where it reflects a weakness in our own position. If I have a position and someone is opposed to it, I'm very interested in his position because I'm sure he's a capable, reasonable person and that he's seeing certain weaknesses in my position to which I should pay the utmost attention to preserve the party's interests.

Now our approach on this whole question of the Cuban revolution is from the party-building viewpoint. I think this was manifested yesterday in the discussions that we heard from any number of comrades after Comrade Farrell [Dobbs] had finished his report. Each of the branches and each of the areas has reported how the Cuban revolution affected their work. And this is perfectly normal and perfectly in order. This is the way we approach all these big events.

Now it may have seemed in a certain way that we were approaching the question narrowly. We were seeing what factional interests the SWP had in the Cuban revolution and how we could capitalize on it as a party. But I think if you look a little further than just this surface aspect of things, what's involved is a broad sense of the party's historic role and how the Cuban revolution can help us, the class-conscious vanguard on an international scale, in building the party that is needed in taking us past capitalism and into the socialist world of the future.

Now this broad, party-building viewpoint has been characteristic of all our discussions on all the big questions in the past decades. This is the approach that we took when we came to the big events in Germany in 1931 to 1933. The main question was the role of the party and how the role of the party was affected by events there. The same thing was true when we approached Spain—the Spanish revolution and our discussions revolving about that. And it was true in the forties when the war broke out and we were faced with the problem of defending the Soviet Union. There again it was the role of the party that came first in our thinking. It was true in our discussion on Eastern Europe, on the character of the state there, on Yugoslavia, and again in China.

In every one of these discussions the question that was dominant was the role of the party. Now this is in the heritage of the Left Opposition, the heritage that goes back to the very first days, when Trotsky first organized against the Stalinist counterrevolution. And I must say that this is a great tradition of our party, one that we are fully conscious of and one with which we approach all these questions.

I say this in turning to the Cuban revolution to indicate that when we approached this question it was with our tradition fully in mind and with the attitude of utmost seriousness towards the questions involved in theory and in politics in relation to the Cuban revolution. It was with full consciousness of the responsibilities that rest on us in approaching these questions.

The reason for this is that the Cuban revolution is a great revolution. It's a revolution that can prove decisive for the development of our party and our cothinkers in Latin America for years to come. We already see how the Cuban revolution has become a pole of attraction in the radical movement in the United States, separating the various tendencies, cutting through them, beginning a new combination of forces in the United States. This is much more so in Latin America itself. The Cuban revolution has now become a key issue in all political discussions in South America, forcing every party from the extreme right wing of the bourgeoisie over the whole spectrum into the working class, forcing them to take a position on Cuba. The Cuban revolution is having the same effect in Latin America, as a key issue, as the Russian revolution had in its day. The Cuban question now is comparable in Latin America to the Russian question some decades ago.

In the United States, besides becoming a question differentiating the different tendencies in the radical movement, it has also become a key issue in foreign policy. There's no party now that takes a stand on foreign policy in the United States that can avoid the question of Cuba. So this is a very, very important question for us.

Now how did we begin our approach to the Cuban revolution? We did not begin it from a theoretical level. We began it from a political level. The first thing we did was to determine what our attitude would be toward the Cuban revolution as a whole, what our policy would be toward it. This was reflected immediately in our press, in the *Militant*.

Now we had no difficulty whatsoever reaching a political position on Cuba. Because no matter what the specific characteristics of the revolution might be, as a whole it obviously was a part of the whole colonial revolution that had been sweeping the Far East, the Middle East, Africa, and Latin America. Therefore, we supported it, as an automatic reflex. We supported it with all the more energy because it involved American imperialism, our own enemy right here at home. That's the approach on a political level.

Now similarly, as this revolution developed, in each of its crucial stages, we had no difficulty in finding what our attitude would be, determining our policy toward each of these turns, and expressing it in the *Militant*. For example, in January of 1959, when the people of Cuba moved in and took power in all the cities of the country and in Havana and they held the tribunals, citizens' tribunals where they put these criminals, these butchers of the Batista regime, on trial, we had no difficulty in stating where we stood on those tribunals. On the opposite side, the Democrats and Republicans and all the spokesmen of the bourgeoisie also had no difficulty in stating where they stood, and we were on opposite sides of class lines. We had no difficulty there.

We had no difficulty taking a stand on the agrarian reform, which began very early but which became codified in the law of May 17, 1959. We were all for that agrarian reform, the bigger the better, and it turned out to be a pretty big one.

We had no difficulty in determining our attitude toward the bourgeois ministers who were in the Cuban government. Fresquet, Pazos, Urrutia, and the others. We were glad to see them dismissed and kicked out. We had no difficulty whatsoever in taking a political position on these ministers and what should be done about them. I might say in passing that every one of these are now part of the counterrevolution; they are in one or another of the groupings that are located in Florida.

Well, we had no difficulty in determining our political attitude toward the July 26 Movement taking full responsibility in Cuba as the government. That was easy to determine. We said, "Yes, we're all for that, because this is something quite different from the bourgeois ministers, from those who seemed to be a facade for the revolution for a time." And we were all for them replacing the ministers in the various posts.

We had no difficulty at all regarding the nationalizations in Cuba. We were a bit doubtful in the beginning whether they would go that far, we would wait and see what would occur. But when they occurred we did not have the slightest difficulty in stating exactly where we stood: "We're for those nationalizations, every bit of them, and the bigger the better." And they were plenty big.

We had no difficulty on such key questions as the monopoly of foreign trade when it was done, first in the form of controls by the government over foreign trade. It became established, and we were for that because it was part and parcel of our whole traditional program as to what a country of that character should do as it moves forward—to establish a monopoly of foreign trade.

We had no difficulty taking a position on the planned economy that began in Cuba in an early stage in very tentative forms and which is now rolling ahead. We had no difficulty saying, "Yes, we're for a planned economy. We have been for a long time. We think planned economies are a good thing."

And we had no difficulty taking a position on the relations with the Soviet bloc. We said, "That's very good. Cuba has found a possibility here for saving its revolution from being crushed by American imperialism and we're all for that." We were for the aid that they got. And from the Soviet side, we were glad that they would give aid to the Cuban revolution. We had no difficulty taking a position on that.

And we had no difficulty taking a position on the extension of the Cuban revolution into South America. Even in the tentative forms with which it was begun by the Castro forces, the July 26 Movement, as they went to the various countries in South America, to Mexico and all the Latin American countries, and appealed to them for aid and for help, and suggested to these countries that they should imitate the Cuban revolution. "That's wonderful, that's a good way to defend the Cuban revolution." All we could say is that we want more like that and stronger and better organized.

On all these questions, which were key political questions, we had to take a stand. As the key situations developed we had no problem at all in reaching political positions.

Now on the theoretical side, the story is a little bit different. Besides the political side, the revolution has its theoretical side and these are rather closely interconnected. Because it is very difficult to take a political position that is consistent without relating it to theory, to your most general positions. And even if you don't develop and discuss your theoretical positions publicly, still you have to have them in mind as you study the politics and decide what your political positions will be. They're very closely interconnected.

Now we have let that side, so far as our press is concerned, remain rather in abeyance, and I will explain to you some reasons why in a moment.

At this point, still looking at things from a political viewpoint, it has become politically necessary to make a theoretical assessment. We can't just remain on the level of political events as they occur, we now have to turn to the theory of the Cuban revolution because there is a political need for it. Let me explain that.

First of all, there is a tremendous campaign being waged against Cuba by American imperialism. And one of its components is to picture Cuba as having gone "communist," as having gone "socialist," as having gone "Stalinist." This is in all the bourgeois papers; the most responsible of them as well as the most yellow has this estimate. Now that faces us with the problem, what do we say? Do we agree or disagree with them, and if so, why? You're faced with a political problem here. You have to answer it.

The same is true in relation to the radical movement. Other tendencies are characterizing the revolution, beginning with the July 26 Movement. The July 26 Movement characterized their movement in the beginning as "humanist." But it doesn't take much reading now of the Cuban press to see that they are shifting and giving this humanism a socialist content and talking more and more about Marxism and about socialism and planned economies and of the example of the Soviet Union and of China.

And if the July 26 Movement is shifting this way, we are faced with a political duty to say if we agree or disagree. Are they wrong or are they right, and why? And it's not only the July 26 Movement in Cuba—which forces us in any case, even if no one else said anything about it. There are figures like Sartre, very important intellectual figures, that have a position. Is he right or is he wrong? And C. Wright Mills. I'm sure all of you have read *Listen, Yankee.* At least all those in this room have read *Listen, Yankee.* All right, is he wrong, or is he right? A big, important figure in the academic world in the United States has made an estimate of the Cuban revolution. We are now faced with a political need to answer where we stand on this. Huberman and Sweezy have taken a stand on it. Do we agree or disagree? The Communist Party has a stand on the character of the revolution. Where do we stand—do we agree or do we disagree with them?

In other words, we feel a political pressure now to reach a definite decision as to the main characteristics of this revolution. It finally boils down to this question: Should we intervene in the dispute that's going on among all these currents, all these figures, or should we abstain from this dispute and wait still longer before we take a position? If we do, we suffer political damage. Political necessity forces us to turn to the theoretical side of the revolution.

There's another consideration that is even more important in my opinion. Enormous changes have taken place in the relationships of the classes in Cuba and in the relations between Cuba and the United States. First of all, inside Cuba it is obvious that there has been a complete turnover in class relationships. Between the United States and Cuba—this should be obvious to anyone who can read the headlines in the daily press—relations have completely altered from what they were even a short time ago. The relations between Cuba and the Soviet Union have completely altered. And the relationships between Cuba and Latin America have completely altered.

Now our policies, our political policies, are determined by these changes. We have to take positions on them, relate them to our own goals, say where we stand in relation to them, and determine our policies in relation to these changes. To do that, we must size up these changes, see what they are, see what has occurred, name them, label them so that we can see where we are at. We have to do that in order to either maintain our policies or to alter them if it is necessary.

Now we could let this go and just take political positions on current stuff, and give some reason or another, let the theory go for a while. But it is highly dangerous to let such a gap occur between your theory and your politics. We know that from theory—that theory itself at a certain point demands that we take cognizance of its needs too. And the reason for that is that theory links us with the past. It links us with all our past experience in revolutions, all our past experience with parties, and points the way in the long-range sense to the future; so at a certain point we have to take a position insofar as the theoretical side is concerned.

Now I am bringing these questions up because I want to stress one point. Our interest in this theoretical discussion is not primarily terminological. We're not interested in this label or that label or simply in slapping a label on the Cuban revolution. The real question that's involved here is to trace the actual stages of that revolution, to trace the actual shifts in the class relationships, the actual shifts in the political power in Cuba. That is very important.

On the other hand, I don't think we should be afraid of labels— especially if they are correct labels. Labels, you know, are sometimes a very advantageous thing. I've noticed that many times at the bar. Put a bottle of Old Pap up and a bottle of White Horse and you usually reach for the White Horse—although it might be mislabeled.

Labels can be very useful. Above all they are useful in indicating analogies. For example, we call Cuba a workers' state; we are immediately presented with the analogy of Yugoslavia and China. The mere label itself forces you to compare the two and see how they connect. And this means also that a label tends to indicate continuity of processes. By labeling the state— whether the label is correct or incorrect—it turns us, it forces us in the direction of previous manifestations of the same phenomena.

For example, has the October revolution in one way or another been extended or reflected in Cuba? Do we have a Soviet-type economy here or not? These are all indicated as soon as you come to the question of labels.

Finally, on the continuity of theory. How does this relate to similar theories on similar questions? It immediately points to the discussions we had on Eastern Europe, on Yugoslavia, on China. And it points even further back, as soon as you enter the field of theory, because there's direct continuity to the very beginning of our movement in Trotsky's Left Opposition and even before that in the Bolshevik period, which laid the very foundations of theory in our movement on the basis of what Marx and Engels had achieved.

Now in this case I think that the label should not give us cause for vexation. I think in this case the label should be rather a cause for rejoicing because what we are naming here, if we are correct, is the first workers' state in the Western Hemisphere. And it's a pretty good-looking one. Everybody that's been down there will agree with that. Cuba is the most auspicious opening for the socialist revolution in Latin America. I think anybody that's been there, really experienced it and felt it and seen these people and talked with them, will come back completely reinspired if they've been dragging a little bit because of the slowness of things in the United States. An auspicious occasion. So we shouldn't be so much afraid of labels.

If the Cuban revolution is such a favorable event, such an important thing, why did we wait until now to take up the question of naming it? I indicated that I would explain the reasons.

First of all, as you've probably gathered from the report that Farrell made yesterday, we did not have the full opportunity to discuss this question from the theoretical side. We were so busy defending that revolution and so busy organizing an election campaign that our personnel here became extremely limited. Key comrades were outside of the city. Others became sick at a crucial time. And consequently it was very difficult for us to discuss this question with thoroughness, with the amount of thought that's needed.

But I think that even if we had had greater opportunity to discuss the Cuban revolution, to probe into the theoretical sides of it, I doubt very much that we would have labeled Cuba a workers' state before now. In my opinion the reason for this was the absence of a manifest socialist consciousness on the part of the leadership of that revolution. We simply could not give them a blank political check when they came to power and say, "Well, obviously because of the mentality you have, your program, your consciousness, you're going to make Cuba into a workers' state. Therefore we're ready to call it a workers' state now." It remained to be seen in the struggle itself what the final course would be in Cuba. And therefore we had to be very, very cautious about it.

This test of the Cuban revolution, the test in struggle, was passed between August and October in 1960, three months ago, when industries were nationalized throughout the entire island. Castro said at one point they were going to nationalize them down to the nails in their shoes. This turned out to be correct. He meant *all* the nails. Cuba is one of the most thoroughly nationalized countries in the world. They took about two and one-half billion dollars worth of property down there. Most of it American. All that's left, according to the United States embassy in Cuba, before they had to leave too, was about $100 million of U.S. property. That was all that was left. That was their estimate. I don't know if they're figuring it on the tax levels or what. This consists mostly of properties like Western Union, Radio Corporation of America, communications outfits, small businesses, completely minor stuff. If you view this from the viewpoint of expropriation, it's hard to expropriate one end of a telegraph line. You've got to have both ends to really make it operate. Whatever the reasons, there's not much left down there.

Now this attitude on our part, of waiting until we saw what happened, of waiting until the nationalizations actually occurred, if they were going to occur, is a conservative approach. And this conservatism was due to our concern for theory, our realization of the importance of theory. It's a result of the long experience we have had in our party with improvisations and the dangers they lead to, with the dangers that come from failing to think things through. We want in questions like this to be absolutely sure.

Now the conclusions that we have reached are not speculations, they're not projections, are not based on any political confidence in what the regime down there is going to do. Our characterizations simply reflect the facts. The fact that the capitalists have been expropriated in Cuba. The fact that a planned economy has been started there. The fact that a qualitatively different kind of state exists there. No matter what you call these things, they are the facts that everyone has to start with. That's the situation.

Now we may be clear enough to put some labels on them.

I don't want to repeat what's in the theses you have before you because I expect everybody will have read and studied them. But what I would like to place before you are some considerations, some of which I am sure you will agree with, others which you may or may not agree with, and some considerations that I present as personal opinions. So first of all, let me indicate where I think you will all agree on the question of Cuba before I come to the speculative side, if it is speculative. It is very important in beginning a discussion to understand what we agree on. It makes the discussion a lot easier. This is true whatever the nuances may be in all the various positions that are taken.

The first fact I think we can all agree on is this: That the revolution began under a petty-bourgeois leadership, whose program was largely bourgeois democratic. That's one of the things I think everyone will agree with, one reason being that the leadership itself recognizes that. The Castro leadership says that. Now there are two special things about this leadership. One is that it was extremely radical. It believed in armed revolution. They practiced it, they advocated it. And let me add that it's completely legal in Cuba. I don't say it's legal here, but in Cuba it's legal to advocate the armed overthrow of the government.

This leadership had one more characteristic that I think everyone will agree with. Its first appeals were directed to the population at large—workers, peasants, everybody—in the expectation that there would be a spontaneous uprising in response, some actions that would dramatize the appeals. Then after they found that this did not work, they set about organizing an armed force consisting largely of the peasantry and of agricultural workers. I think those are facts that are so clear that no one would deny them. Certainly in our movement everyone will agree with them. I think we also have agreement among all of us that this is an extremely profound revolution, one that has gone to far-reaching economic and social measures. Everybody will agree on that, even though they won't agree on what to call them. I think everyone will agree that the revolution began with the support of the peasantry and of the agricultural workers, that it had the sympathy or quickly won the sympathy of the urban workers and finally their active support. That's the present stage of the revolution, and I think everybody else who has been there and studied there will agree on that point.

Finally, I think everybody will agree that the Cuban revolution has displayed strong democratic and socialist tendencies. It's much more democratic than anything we've seen in a long time.

That's where we have agreement so far as the main facts are concerned.

I think we will also have agreement on what our main tasks are in respect to the Cuban revolution, and that's of key importance for our party. Also for the discussion we want to have, an agreement on that score is of key importance.

The first main task is to defend this revolution against imperialism. That's our main preoccupation as a party in relationship to the Cuban revolution.

I think we have agreement that we should defend all institutions that have been created in Cuba, like the planned economy, the expropriation of the bourgeoisie—that we defend these revolutionary institutions against the counterrevolution. That's a big area of agreement.

I think we all agree that we should do our utmost to rally the American labor movement to the Cuban revolution and rally the students and intellectuals, whoever we can get together to defend that revolution. And I think we agree on certain tasks inside Cuba no matter how we name these various things that occurred there. First, that we follow a policy aimed at expanding and developing the proletarian democracy. That's our Number One. Second, that we follow a policy aimed at building a revolutionary socialist party. In other words, that we follow a policy of deepening, extending the socialist consciousness which has already begun in Cuba. And that we follow a policy aimed at extending the Cuban revolution throughout Latin America. We all agree on that no matter what we call these different things. And thus we have a very wide area of agreement.

I want to stress that again and again—the wide area of agreement that we have. I do that because in a discussion, there's a natural tendency to emphasize differences, emphasize even nuances that appear much larger than they really are. The fact is that our areas of agreement are so wide, so solid that we can afford to take things fairly easy on the other side.

Now we come to the theoretical questions that there may be some differences on. One of these key questions is what the Cuban revolution implies in theory about the role of the party.

I said that on the practical side, at least for the SWP, there's been a new opportunity. This is visible to every one of us. This is one of the consequences of a revolutionary victory. There it stands in great contrast to the defeats that were suffered in the revolutions of the thirties, in Spain and Germany and so forth. We are now experiencing, as a party, a revolutionary victory with immediate impact on the United States. That's a tremendous thing for us.

But we're still left with the question, How are we to explain this victory in Cuba in the absence of a party like the Socialist Workers Party? Let me explain that. There's no Socialist Workers Party in Cuba. But how can they have a revolution down there in Cuba without the SWP? Isn't there great danger involved in this? Doesn't this imply that no party is needed? Can you have a revolution without a party?

Now I will admit that there is a danger here. A danger that some comrades can reach such a conclusion. This was the case in our previous discussions on similar questions. It was the case in Eastern Europe. One of our fears was that this could lead to a revision among some comrades on the importance of the party. The same thing was true in our discussion of China. It was a foremost consideration in our discussion. Before that we had a manifestation in a different form in earlier years where certain comrades reached the conclusion that since in theory a party is absolutely essential to have a revolutionary victory, therefore since all the Trotskyist parties are very small, this signifies that the perspectives for the revolution are very dim.

To answer this question regarding the role of the party in Cuba and how it was possible to have a revolution there, a successful one, without a party like the SWP, you have to find the answer not inside Cuba but in the international situation in which Cuba is locked and which affects Cuba from all sides. Cuba is not an isolated country. It is affected by the international situation. And the main factor impinging on Cuba is first of all the decay of imperialism, which has reached such a state as to impel people after people in country after country towards revolutionary uprisings. The second factor is the strength of the Soviet bloc, which stands as a great, enormous example in their minds, a revolutionary example. They realize at least vaguely how the Soviet Union was started; they can see the revolutionary import of its institutions; therefore it stands as a constant revolutionary source of ideology, which tends toward a revolutionary direction.

And finally I think the other main factor in world politics which explains this is the default of the Communist Party in assuming revolutionary leadership for many decades. It has finally reached the point where people pressing toward revolution, which can no longer be delayed, revolutions which grow imperative, which are needed right now, put forward any leaderships which happen to be at hand.

And so we have these revolutions, with varied successes. One after another of these situations. I think what these situations indicate is not only the ripeness for revolutions but also the ripeness for the formation of a revolutionary party. It shows that side, too. That's quite evident if you stop long enough and think how rotten-ripe this world is for the birth of a revolutionary party.

Let me state once again what our concept of a party is, because I'm afraid that sometimes we tend to look at the SWP as it is— that's what we mean by a party, a revolutionary party. On that question, I think we have to say, "Yes, the SWP is what we mean by a revolutionary party, but also it's not what we mean by a revolutionary party." A yes-and-no answer. In program and in aim, yes. It's revolutionary socialist to the core. Personnel? Well, looking around here I can see a lot of people whose personalities need improvement. Mine's all right, of course. And I see a certain lack of forces here. We don't have a great mass party. You see there's a lot of room for improvement in this party both on the personalities that make it up, that's qualitatively, and also in the quantity of forces that we have at our disposal. So our tendency, therefore, is to take a very narrow conception of the party because it's what we see before us, the SWP. But even if we achieved a great mass base in the United States—which I'm sure would be a considerable step forward—even if we achieved that, we would still have a tendency, I think, towards a certain narrowness in our concept of the party.

Now when we talk about a party, we mean an international party, one that is commensurate with tremendous international goals. We mean a party that is capable of taking the world working class and leading it forward to overthrow capitalism, which is an international system. From then on, leading the world out of capitalism to the socialist world of the future. That's what we mean by a revolutionary socialist party. A tremendous thing. One that is of the greatest historic importance. It's probably the greatest task that has faced humanity, the building of such a party.

Now let me say right now that such a party has never been built yet. Marx didn't build one. Lenin didn't build one. They started the core of it. Their aim was absolutely clear—where they were headed. But they never conceived this party as simply a narrow, national party. They conceived it as an international one, one that is capable of the greatest task that has faced humanity, taking us from capitalism to socialism.

When we say that capitalism is rotten-ripe for revolution, we also say that the conditions on an international scale are rotten-ripe for the construction of such a party, a tremendous international party that has all the knowledge and capacity, both political and theoretical, for accomplishing these great tasks. How are we going to build such a party? Will it be built in advance of the revolution? It would be very good if it could be—at least that's what the Cubans themselves say now—it would be good to have such a party in advance. The fact is that such a party has got to be built in the very process of revolution as revolutions occur with varying degrees of success. That's the fact that faces us. In some countries I think we will be able to build national sections of the party before the revolution occurs, and in some countries, like ours, I think that is an absolute condition for success. In other countries the revolution forges forward faster than the party. That's an evident fact of politics now. So, when we say a revolutionary party, a revolutionary socialist party, we don't just mean a revolutionary socialist party in little Cuba or in little Guatemala or in little Costa Rica or in little Nicaragua. Those will be important sections of it. We are thinking of an international party on a major scale, in which these are component parts.

Thus we come to the conclusion that there is great unevenness in the growth and development of this party. Great unevenness. Some countries can forge forward faster than others. In some cases the action can transcend the political consciousness of it. Given this great unevenness in the development of an international party, we have to ask ourselves this question: Does this signify that it is impossible for the masses to overthrow a capitalist power in certain countries until the international party appears in full force and completeness? That's the question that faces us. We probably wouldn't even have asked this question if we hadn't already gotten certain answers. The answers are that in certain countries it is possible. Yugoslavia, China, and Cuba. That's the fact sheet. We have to look at it and say that's what it is. I would say that in the light of those three facts, we would have to conclude that it is possible in certain situations, in certain countries, under certain conditions—it is possible for the masses to go as far forward as establishing a workers' state.

Having said that, we immediately come to the question of limitations. These are tremendous. Let's just take the case of Cuba. First of all, there were great and costly errors committed in the Cuban revolution. Great and costly ones. The revolution established a coalition government with bourgeois democrats. That didn't help the revolution any. It led to a very ragged differentiation between the revolutionary forces and those that were counterrevolutionary—a process that's still proceeding in Cuba. That's the reason for all these "defections" that take place in Cuba; it's the flight of the counterrevolutionaries.

There was a great error made in the relations between the Cuban revolution and the American workers. One of the first things they did down there was to immediately break off all connections with the trade union movement in the United States. And George Meany said, "Thank you." He couldn't have asked for anything better than such an error on the part of the Cuban revolutionaries. Cut off their relations with the American trade unions.

They've made considerable errors in the extension of their revolution in Latin America. They realized the general importance and need of it, but so far as actually carrying it out in a coordinated, organized way, it has been very, very slipshod, with any number of errors. We can see that in a practical way in our experience with the Fair Play for Cuba Committee. The thing never seemed to get off the ground. It operates in a way that is completely alien to all our concepts—not only our concepts, but alien to the needs of the Cuban revolution. That's one of the problems that has arisen because of the lack of a revolutionary party in Cuba.

Take it from the economic side. Look at the delays that occurred down there in the process of the revolution, in expropriating the properties; they had to wait until they were pushed into it by American imperialism, slapped around, then there was a response, a defensive reflex to these blows struck by American imperialism. They were stumbling, fumbling, losing all kinds of valuable time which the bourgeoisie in the United States utilized in order to prepare the ground psychologically for their counter-revolution. Two years of time—a year and a half at least—was wasted almost, while the bourgeoisie in the United States, step by step, got prepared psychologically for the counterrevolution.

Finally, we come to this big error in the Cuban revolution, its big limitation; and that is the lack of the development of democratic forms of rule. To any Trotskyist, any revolutionary socialist, it jumps out before your eyes, the weakness of the revolution on that side. And that weakness derives primarily from the weakness of the leadership, of its consciousness. All these things tell us the limitations of this workers' state that has appeared in Cuba. And this side is just as important as the other side. That is, the recognition of what is positive about that revolution.

So, a success like the one in Cuba demonstrates not that a party has become superfluous—instead, what it demonstrates is just the opposite. It brings forward with new imperativeness the need for an international party of the kind I've tried to indicate in just a few sentences. That is, the need it has demonstrated is the need for Marxist political consciousness that takes the organized form of a party.

If you view that revolution as uncompleted, it's very easy to see then that this is the big need of the moment. An uncompleted revolution in transition—and what it needs for completion is a revolutionary socialist party. But if you view that revolution as completed, as being finished, then you can say, "Well, what do you need a party for? You can have a completed revolution without a party." So it depends how you view that revolution what conclusion you will come to about the party.

Well, we come to this question: What kind of consciousness has appeared in Cuba? What occurred down there? What are the perspectives for the development of revolutionary consciousness, revolutionary socialist consciousness in Cuba? The fact is that the consciousness is beginning to appear in Cuba. Dick Garza called my attention to the magazine *Verde Olivo*, the official publication of the armed forces. There's an article in there by Che Guevara, and there are others in the Cuban press, if you follow it closely enough, in which he takes up the question of Marx and Marx's contributions. A very interesting article. He says Marx foresaw the laws of the Cuban revolution. He says these laws exist objectively. Marx didn't just bring them out of his head. Marx was reflecting a reality. Marx saw these laws long ago; we were hazy about these laws but we discovered them in practice.

That indicates how the consciousness of this revolution is developing in the mind of one of its leaders. There are many interesting things in that article. For instance, he says,

They ask me if I'm a Marxist. That's like asking a physicist if he is a Newtonian, or a biologist if he is a follower of Pasteur. This has all become part of the body of human knowledge. You can't operate in world politics without knowing something about Marx. In a vague way, everybody has this consciousness.

He is talking, of course, about the intellectuals that you find in other countries, in Latin America; he wasn't talking about the United States and the workers here and the intellectuals in the United States. It's a reflection of a political culture that you find much more advanced in other countries than you find in the United States.

This process that occurred in Cuba, this action of the revolution, was bound at a certain point to have a reflection in consciousness. They did actually follow the laws of the revolution in practice. But that had an effect on their minds. What's impressive and important is that some of the leaders at this point are aware of this interconnection. They state this publicly. Now as soon as I mention this, let me qualify it. When they state this publicly, they also include references to Stalin. This is a very important consideration. It may be that this is due to diplomacy, their relations with the Soviet Union. It may be a political price they are paying for the political aid. It also may be a stage in their development. They may have to go through this development in their own mind of really probing Stalinism. Their first assumption may be that it is revolutionary.

We hope that it won't mean a retrogression. But under the oppression of American imperialism and the demands of the Soviet bureaucracy the Cuban revolutionary leadership can retrogress in their thinking. We hope that they won't. We struggle very, very hard, as much as we possibly can, to prevent it. That's one of the key questions with us—to fight for the soul of the Cuban revolution.

We have on our side this fact: we do know that the central

leadership in the Cuban revolution is aware of Stalinism in general and does not like it. Mills's report is a very accurate one on the thinking of the leadership in the Cuban revolution; that is, the anti-Stalinism. But they are under tremendous pressures, with American imperialism on one side and the Soviet bureaucracy on the other, and they make some very unwarranted concessions.

But besides the leadership there are also the masses in Cuba, the workers and the peasants. They are learning Marxism in the class struggle. They are learning it in the class struggle with the United States, and Eisenhower has given them some very eloquent lessons in it, and I think Kennedy will follow up his predecessor in giving them even more advanced lessons in the class struggle. Besides this, there is the alliance with the Soviet bloc, which is having a big impact on the thinking of the masses there. The example of what's been done in the Soviet Union, its culture, its achievements, science, planned economy, all of that is now making a big impact on Cuban thinking.

Finally, there's the publicity in the press that's now appearing about Marxism, even though it is tainted with Stalinism; it is having an impact on the thinking of the masses in Cuba. It, too, is a reflection of the thinking, of the shift toward revolutionary consciousness.

Thus, I would say that the conditions are becoming very favorable now in Cuba for the development of revolutionary socialism; that is, formation of a contingent or section of this big international party we are thinking about.

I am coming to my conclusion now. This is the opening stage, in my opinion, of the socialist revolution in Latin America. One small island off the coast of that tremendous land mass. And there are certain lessons we can already draw, I think, about the revolution, what this revolution shows us about what's going to happen in Latin America.

First of all, that in Latin America, the democratic tasks that face all those countries speedily pass into socialist ones. In Cuba, the gap was about a year and a half. The terrific speed of that revolution shows what the speed will be in the other countries of Latin America.

Another lesson, I think, is this: some very crippling myths have been dispersed through the Cuban revolution. The first myth is this: These countries, with their monocultures—one-crop or one-product countries—their poverty, which follows as a consequence of that kind of economy, so distorts and twists and cripples them that it dooms them if they should try to break out of the imperialist grip. This has been a crippling myth in Latin American politics for decades. You couldn't make a revolution in Bolivia because it's only got tin, and if isolated by American imperialism, what can it do but collapse? So therefore, why make a revolution? That kind of thinking has been in our own movement and in circles around our movement. That myth has been ended by the experience of the Cuban revolution.

The second myth that has been ended is that imperialism is so powerful that it would be absolutely futile in these countries to try to overthrow the state. Absolutely futile to overthrow the rule of the imperialists. Cuba, by existing as long as it has, only ninety miles from Miami, has demonstrated the fallacy of that view. And that can have tremendous consequences in Latin America.

Now there are some other items that have been disproved. One is that the revolution can be accomplished only by Communist parties. That was an illusion in many, many parts of this world— that you have to wait for the Communist Party. And if they happen to be off beam now, you have to wait until they are on beam. And let me just ask in passing: What does this do to the theory of entrism *sui generis*? Where would the Cuban Trotskyists have been in Cuba? They would have been in the CP, wouldn't they? What they needed was twelve guys to go up on the Sierra Maestra. If you go by that experience, that's literally what happened. It shows the importance of an independent organization as contrasted to the policy of burying yourself in some organization that's not so revolutionary.

Look what it's done to the theory of peaceful coexistence. Cuba can solve this peacefully with the United States? Every time you pick up a newspaper the headlines show you what a completely wrong, fraudulent policy that is.

And look what it's done to popular frontism, the policy followed by the CP and other organizations. Knocked it into a cocked hat. Popular frontism won't win revolutions. To win a revolution you've got to be very serious and organize from the bottom with the masses and move towards power.

There are many questions of the utmost importance, I think, that have been raised, theoretically and politically, and the comrades who have these special viewpoints are to be thanked for bringing them forward.

Let me indicate a few areas now where any comrade can make

a contribution who wants to in the field of theory. First of all, the character of the slogans that were used by the July 26 Movement. How many of them, what their character was, and how the masses responded to them. There's a lesson in that for a revolutionary socialist party, too. At a certain stage of the revolution, slogans become very simplified and condensed and very well worth studying from that one viewpoint alone in looking forward to the struggles of the future.

Another question: the importance of the struggle for democratic rights. We sometimes think of democratic rights as something you struggle for because you need room for the party to move in, to breathe in, to stay out of jail, and so on. But in this struggle in Cuba, the struggle for democratic rights against oppression turned out to be a key issue of the socialist revolution. That's a very revealing fact that's worth very serious study.

Another area: the immense importance of an agrarian program. Our tendency here in New York is to leave the agrarian problem to those out in Minnesota. In the Twin cities, they say, "What are you talking about? I was born in the Bronx. Or in Scandinavia, and I've become an American." Here I think we can go back and get a new appreciation of why it was that Lenin paid so much attention to the agrarian program, and why we, too, even in the United States, should be turning in that direction.

Another area is the true nature of this humanism in the Cuban revolution, its real content.

What was the true nature of the rebel army? Was it just an armed force, or did it have an ideology, a certain political character? Was it something more than an army? Was it partly a party? An armed party. A very interesting phenomenon, and the same goes for the militia today in Cuba. Is it just a militia that marches with arms, or does it have a political character, does it play a political role, and have a political consciousness? Those are areas we need to know more about.

Finally, let me give one for the students who go to Cuba. What's the structure of the political life in that country? I mean its real political life. Where's its political life occurring? In the unions? In the militia? In the army? In the cooperatives? In the government organizations? In the political formations like the CP? Exactly how does the political life of that country occur? We know they've got a lot of democracy there. We know there's a lot of discussion. But what are the forms exactly in which that is occurring down there? This is very important information for us in determining our political line in the sense of influencing the discussion of revolutionary socialism down there. As a matter of fact, that question alone can be decisive in the way in which we move along our policy of constructing the revolutionary socialist party.

# What the Discussion on Cuba Is About
## (May 25, 1961)

It can scarcely escape anyone who has been closely following the development of the discussion on the Cuban question that it has sharpened considerably since it began. Most, although not all, of this sharpness is to be found on the minority side. The tone of their documents, the unbridled accusations and provocative language they employ have not been seen in our party for a good many years. The reasons for this, however, remain obscure.

It is possible that this way of arguing was learned in the Shachtmanite school of polemics and is not easily unlearned by the comrades who became accustomed to its use and really intend no more harm by it than a seaman stating his frank opinions in a waterfront bar. It is also possible that the minority is caught up in the momentum of a somewhat factional position and does not know how to disengage.

Still we cannot be certain of such surmises and it would be a political mistake not to notice that the increase in sharpness has paralleled the increase of imperialist pressure on Cuba on the one hand and the deepening of the revolution on the other. We cannot forget for one moment that every bourgeois propaganda medium in the country is pounding day in and day out against the "menace" of the Cuban revolution. The party membership, like everyone else, is subjected to this incessant barrage of lies. Despite their best intentions, those who live in petty-bourgeois circles, or who have not been steeled by going through similar campaigns in the past, or who have lost their tempering, can begin to entertain doubts, to give a little, to feel that there is some, if not much, truth in the avalanche of filth. The feeling can grow that something about the Cuban revolution should give us pause in approaching it; that it might be advisable to pull away from it a bit. These hesitations and doubts can be transformed into hesitations and doubts about the wisdom of the positive course the party has been following toward the Cuban revolution. Rationalization can then convert all this into its opposite—that everyone is softening up except the doubters and skeptics.

One wonders if there is not something of this in the rather shrill accusations voiced by the minority that the leadership has brushed aside the importance of proletarian democracy, has given up the concept of the need for building a Leninist party, is conceding to "Pabloism," to "Kautskyism," to "Stalinism," even to "bourgeois nationalism"; in brief, is "betraying" Trotskyism.

If such social pressures are operating, then it will be more difficult for the minority to reconsider the untenable position they find themselves in. If the pressure of bourgeois public opinion is not involved, many of us hope that the minority leaders, in case of future differences, will carefully assess the bad impression made by the tone and style of polemics they have indulged in.

So far as the record reads in the discussion bulletin, the differences began over the "Draft Theses on the Cuban Revolution," submitted by the Political Committee. These are dated December 23, 1960, and were approved by the plenum of the National Committee on January 14, 1961. The ostensible answer to this document is "The Cuban Revolution and Marxist Theory," submitted by Shane Mage, Tim Wohlforth, and James Robertson. This is dated August 17, 1960.

Evidently something is askew. In what crystal ball was Comrade Shane Mage, the main author, able to read and criticize the draft theses . . . five months before they were written? Even more remarkable—read and criticize them before the particular events in Cuba which caused them to be written? The fact is that these three comrades make no claim to such prescience. Their article was a reply to a piece I wrote in July, "The Character of the New Cuban Government," which I submitted for the consideration of the National Committee. Apparently the three authors considered their reply to this analysis of the character of the government so much to the point and so solid that it was also an adequate reply to the subsequent analysis in the "Draft Theses" of the character of the state—after it had changed qualitatively.

Let us consider a little more closely the differences as they stood last August, almost a year ago. Cuba did not yet have a workers' state. But it did have the Castro government, a government that emerged with the disintegration of the coalition government that had been brought to power by the revolution after Batista fled. The Castro government was of extraordinary interest from the viewpoint of Marxist theory. It was clearly a petty-bourgeois government but it was carrying out measures which affected the structure of the state, such as smashing the old army and police force, and which, if continued, would inevitably lead to a qualitative change—the displacement of the capitalist state by a workers' state.

This government, only ninety miles from Florida, and inviting inspection by anyone interested, was available for first-hand study. The fact that it was not headed by either a revolutionary socialist or a Stalinist party made it all the more important, for it provided, if that is possible, a virtually pure case of this kind of government as a type. Any interested Marxist theoretician could have analyzed it on a strictly empirical basis. We did this; but we also checked the records to see whether anywhere in Marxist literature this type, as a type, had been anticipated. We found such an anticipation in the documents of the first four congresses of the Communist International, which Trotsky included as part of the programmatic foundation of our movement.

The aim of this research work was not only to arrive at a correct understanding of the nature of the Castro government but also to provide a sound theoretical base for a political approach to it. This was especially necessary, for there was no way of knowing in advance how far the Castro government would go in changing the character of the state or at what pace. The correct transitional slogans applicable to such a government had to be selected. Not much original work was required for this; they had been outlined in the main by the Bolsheviks at the Fourth Congress and indicated again in the 1938 Transitional Program.

In view of some of the misapprehensions that have appeared in the subsequent discussion, I want to call sharp attention to the fact that in analyzing the character of the Castro government, I abstracted from the character of the state. Obviously a contradiction existed between this government and the state structure it then rested on. Our main problem, however, was not simply to analyze this contradiction but to determine what political attitude to take toward the government to help resolve the contradiction in the favorable direction of establishment of a workers' state. The contradiction was resolved at breakneck speed, thanks to the help of American imperialism, and sooner than we might have expected we were able to analyze the development after it occurred and with the mighty assistance of empirical facts.

Turn now to the reaction of Comrades Mage, Wohlforth, and Robertson and note how ill-considered their August 17 response was. They attempted to analyze the character of the state, which I had not brought up; but on the character of the government, excepting for the label, they agreed!

This is easily proved.

By recognizing the new Cuban government as a workers' and farmers' government, [I wrote in my July article] we indicate its radical petty-bourgeois background and composition and its origin in a popular mass movement, its tendency to respond to popular pressures for action against the bourgeoisie and their agents, and its capacity, for whatever immediate reasons and with whatever hesitancy, to undertake measures against bourgeois political power and against bourgeois property relations.

The government is specified as "petty-bourgeois" with descriptive particularizations. A month later Mage-Wohlforth-Robertson wrote: "The Cuban government is a democratic middle-class regime basing itself on, and under continual pressure from, the workers and peasants." They specify "middle-class," noting it is under continual popular pressure.

Having agreed in essence, the authors berate the label used by the Bolsheviks for this type of government. "Is this self-evident description," they say, referring to the sentence quoted above about a middle-class regime, "any less useful than the abstract, arbitrary and false label 'workers' and farmers' government'?" With this keynote, they have been delivering moralistic lectures ever since on the evils of a fetishistic attitude toward labels. Perhaps this freedom from fetishism in such matters will permit them eventually to compromise and accept the label used by the Cubans: "Revolutionary Government."[1]

\*             \*             \*

So much for the preliminary discussion on the character of the government, which involved but a single aspect of the revolution,

---

1. A real curiosity is Comrade Wohlforth's later intimation, on reading Trent Hutter's contribution, that the designation *workers' state*—leaving aside the difference he would still hold on "tempo" and all that—would not be too bad if the right adjective could be found to put in front of the

although one of considerable importance at the time. The basic document of the minority was completed on the eve of a truly immense event. The increasingly heavy blows which American imperialism dealt the small republic were answered by a series of counterblows that toppled capitalist property relations both foreign and domestic in the commanding sectors of industry in August-October 1960. There could be no doubt about it. Cuba had become a workers' state.

The minority comrades, however, scarcely raised their eyebrows. They evidently felt that they had anticipated this with the arguments they had advanced in their August 17 document. It is true, I admit, that they did include a discussion of the character of the state in Cuba. It is also true that since they had not distinguished carefully between state and government in their analysis, what they had said about the state as it existed before the overturns could be stretched to fit the state that came into being after the overturns. Although they were talking about the state as it existed before August, and not after October, it was all one and the same thing so far as they were concerned.

Even under prodding from the majority, the minority comrades did not shift on this. Comrade Mage in fact sought to bolster the August 17 document by further arguments in "The Nature of the State in Cuba," an article dated April 14-18, 1961. He affirms, "We have thus termed the Cuban state neither a *capitalist state* nor yet a *workers' state*, but call it a *transitional state*." (Previously the adjective was "developing.") This novel type of state can shift towards either a capitalist state or a workers' state without a civil war, the minority comrades inform us. It can become a workers' state through institutionalizing workers' democracy. On the other hand capitalism can be restored in various ways, Comrade Mage holds. He seems most intrigued by the possibility that the Castro government might restore capitalism without denationalizing a single peso of state property. As he

---

noun on the label. "Deformed" is not quite right because it has been used to specify Stalinist domination and that "degree of Stalinist influence" doesn't exist in Cuba. This tempts one to call attention to the solution suggested by the majority in the "Draft Theses"—a workers' state "lacking as yet the forms of democratic proletarian rule." However, Comrade Wohlforth has reminded us a sufficient number of times that he finds this unacceptable. Shall we conclude that he really wants a "self-evident" label, not a useless "abstract, arbitrary and false" description?

visualizes it, through "large annual dollar payments for 'compensation,' 'interest' and 'debt amortization,' state property would in essence constitute *a means for the extraction of surplus value from the Cuban proletariat and peasantry and its transfer to U.S. capitalists.*" Comrade Mage declares that this would make it a capitalist state.

It would be bizarre to debate today whether surplus value extracted at gun point from this hypothetical state would make it capitalist. On such grounds it can be argued that the Soviet bureaucracy is capitalist because it robs the Soviet workers or because the Soviet Union in some fields has an unfavorable relation with the world market. Meanwhile we are faced with the real question: what is the character of the state in Cuba today?

"Developing" or "transitional," responds Comrade Mage. "*The answer will not be found in Cuba,*" the August 17 document emphatically declares. "It is clearly too early to answer in terms of finished categories, *for the nature of the Cuban Revolution itself is not yet decided by history,*" the same document continues just as emphatically. Comrade Mage affirms this once more just as emphatically in his April 14-18 article: "*the nature of the Cuban state is not yet determined by history.*"

With such labels and such arguments the minority leaders evade the problem of characterizing the state in Cuba. The state is quite real and must serve definite class interests, but our minority leave it floating above classes in defiance of everything taught by Marxism.

The neatest evasion is to refuse to consider the state in relation to the economic base on which it rests and to demand that it meet a political criterion. Proletarian democracy, they contend; more specifically the organization of workers' councils as the basis of control over the government, or the institutionalization of proletarian democracy, must appear before the state in Cuba can be characterized as "workers'."

No real political difference exists in the party over the necessity of jelling proletarian democracy in Cuba in institutional form—despite the highly articulate doubts of the minority on this point. Disagreement exists only over how to go about it tactically. But there is a difference, and a big one, over whether or not proletarian democracy is decisive in determining the character of the state.

What the minority seeks to do is chop off Cuba from all linkage with China, Yugoslavia, Eastern Europe, and the Soviet Union of today; that is, all linkage with the criteria used by the Trotskyist movement in determining the character of these workers' states as they exist. Here is how Comrade Wohlforth breaks the linkage in his article "In Defense of Proletarian Democracy":

Workers' power is not something that evolves—you've either got it or you don't. [There's dialectics!—J.H.] It is not something that is tacked on to the state at a later date by bits and pieces. *There is no such thing as a workers' state where there does not already exist a form of proletarian democratic rule and it is impossible to establish a form of proletarian democratic rule without the vanguard role of the Marxist party.* To say otherwise is to destroy the whole theoretical system of Trotskyism. [Wohlforth's emphasis helps distract attention from the very next sentence, where he is forced to contradict at least half of his underlined assertion.—J.H.] There is of course such a thing as a deformed-degenerated workers' state but this concept has been so far used by our movement *only* to apply to the Stalinist thermidor and the extensions of this thermidor into Eastern Europe and parts of Asia. [The "parts of Asia" include China with its almost 700,000,000 people.—J.H.]

Comrade Mage makes the same point more clearly in his article "The Nature of the State in Cuba." It is worth quoting at length, for it constitutes the main pillar of the minority position:

Originally Marxists identified a workers state as the *political* instrumentality of the democratic rule of the proletariat subsequent to the smashing of the capitalist state apparatus. It involved three main points: replacement of the army and police by the armed workers; all officials, without exception, elected and subject to recall at any time; salaries of officials reduced to the level of workers' wages. "Workers state" was simply another name for "workers democracy."

However, of the several existing countries that the Marxist movement considers to be "workers states," not one conforms in any way to the original criteria established by Marx and Lenin. The degeneration of the Russian revolution, followed by the extension of that revolution in deformed guise throughout Eastern Europe, China, and parts of Vietnam and Korea, forced us to develop a new theoretical category—that of the "degenerated" or "deformed" workers state.

To this new category corresponded a new norm: in the absence of workers' democracy these states are, for us, defined as deformed workers states by their basic property forms. Nationalization of industry, economic planning, the state monopoly of foreign trade—these economic institutions were established by the October revolution, and their survival and extension indicate the survival and extension of the state created by the October Revolution.

Thus we have two norms, *and the distinction between them should be kept clear.* One applies to the *victory* of the socialist revolution, the other to its degeneration or extension in distorted form. Our primary norm, the norm for a revolutionary workers state, is and must remain *proletarian democracy* as set forth in "State and Revolution." *Nationalized property is the norm for the degeneration of the revolution,* the norm that tells us that despite Stalinist totalitarianism the major historical conquest of the October Revolution continues to exist and therefore the state remains a workers state, bureaucratically degenerated.

In stating that Cuba became a workers state with the nationalization of industry in August-October 1960, the draft theses make the mistake of mechanically applying the criterion for the *degeneration* of the revolution to a revolution still in its ascending phase. This, to be sure, is a very easy mistake to make—why, after all, should we have much more rigorous standards for Cuba than for China, say, or Albania?

Two things leap out. (1) If the Stalinists had been thrust into power in Cuba, Comrade Mage, making obeisance to the label "deformed," would be forced, if he went by his criteria, to recognize Cuba as a workers' state. This is the Marcyite position: Stalinism in power = a workers' state. (2) Both Comrade Wohlforth and Comrade Mage, by attempting to use different criteria in Cuba from those used in the other workers' states, compel us to reexamine our previous positions.[2] The reason for this is that the Cuban leadership did not find their ideas in a patch of royal palms. They drew from the world in which Cuba exists. They themselves state their awareness of the example of those "parts of Asia" known as China and Indochina. If we are using the wrong criteria in Cuba then we must ascertain whether they were

---

2. At the opening of the discussion in the New York Local, I observed in passing that this would occur if the discussion went deep enough. Other comrades of the majority made the same forecast. Evidently mis-hearing what I said, Comrade Martha Curti wrote in "Stalinism and the Cuban Revolution" that "Comrade Hansen said that in the course of the discussion now unfolding it would be necessary for the party to reassess its whole attitude toward China, Yugoslavia, Eastern Europe, and the Soviet Union itself. Let us hope that this reassessment will lead to a reaffirmation of the present position of the SWP as put forth in the 1953 plenum resolution, 'Against Pabloist Revisionism'. . . ." This would not be worth mentioning were it not that some of the comrades in Britain took the report, along with its somewhat dim hope about my getting straightened out on Pabloism, as accurate.

not wrong for related parts of the world where similar phenomena occurred.

The minority comrades themselves in their own way recognize the intimate connection between Cuba and the other workers' states when they argue: "Look how long it took the SWP to recognize China as a workers state. Surely we can afford to wait similarly in the case of Cuba."

The delay was not felt at the time as a virtue. It was occasioned in part by precisely the same consideration that Comrade Mage raises in the case of Cuba. Is it correct to use the same criteria for an "ascending" revolution as one in decline? Isn't there a qualitative difference? If we recognize China as a workers' state doesn't that "destroy the whole theoretical system of Trotskyism"? It is an amazing fact—in Cuba, some of the comrades are in reality feeling for the first time the impact of China. This seems particularly true of those in Britain who are looking aghast at the Cuban revolution.

If ever there was a revolution that called for the category of "ascending" it was the Chinese. A quarter of the human race participated in it. The element of direct Russian participation, which loomed large in Eastern Europe, was relatively minor in China. It involved turning over captured arms to the Chinese armies. True, Russian forces were in occupation in Northeast China but they did not oversee an upset in property relations as they did in Eastern Europe. Instead they carted off a good deal of equipment, including entire factories, as was the case in the first stage in the occupation of Eastern Europe. An indication of the difference in the setting was the ultimate withdrawal of Russian forces from China, something that has not yet occurred in Eastern Europe. The scope of the forces, the depth of the revolution, its relative independence—all were in striking contrast to Eastern Europe. It was completely clear to us at the time that so far as "rise" or "decline" was concerned, the Chinese revolution came much closer to the 1917 upheaval in tsarist Russia than it did to the overturn in Eastern Europe.

While defending this revolution to the best of our ability and resources inside the United States, we watched its development on the Chinese mainland with the most absorbed attention. The character of the Mao leadership was no mystery—petty-bourgeois, Stalinist variety. The formation of a coalition government with the bourgeois-democratic elements came as no surprise. The proclamations promising to preserve capitalist property relations were not unexpected. Neither the promulgation of the "four-bloc" theory nor the overtures toward American imperialism astounded anyone.

Then Truman took a hand. He not only spurned the overtures, he plunged the United States into Korea and American troops went up to the Yalu. Truman ordered a tight economic and diplomatic blockade and stationed the Seventh Fleet in the Formosa Strait.

The People's Republic of China responded with counterblows. These included not only military measures, but the toppling of capitalist economic relations in China. The petty-bourgeois government power set up a qualitatively different state structure, based on the expropriation of the bourgeoisie and the institution of planned economy.

Did we automatically slap a label on that? We are not fetishists about nomenclature, but we hesitated. This petty-bourgeois government had come to power at the head of an insurgent peasantry through the medium of peasant armies that surrounded the cities and took them like fortresses. Neither the working class nor a revolutionary socialist party stood at the head of the revolution. It was an ascending revolution, not one in decline. It was bound to have immense repercussions, not only indirectly by altering the world relation of forces, but directly as an example. By labeling this a workers' state, not only were we faced with the problem of seeing how it fit in with Trotskyist theory, but we were faced with the problem of whether it might not be repeated to one degree or another.

But not to call it a workers' state offered no satisfying solution. If we left the label *capitalist* on it, we had to admit that it was certainly a faded and badly tattered bit of paper. It left us with the question whether or not this type of capitalist state was an advance over the old type and whether or not we would defend it against all efforts to replace it with the old type. We did not have that much concern over retaining a label. We decided that it was better to recognize the reality and call it a workers' state. To indicate that it was dominated by Stalinists, we used the same qualification as in Eastern Europe, "deformed." This was not a too satisfactory adjective but no one came up with a better one. Whatever credit is to be granted for first using it goes, I think, to Pablo, although he was not the first to designate the Eastern European countries as workers' states.

And how was such a turn in history to be accounted for? By the international setting in which the Chinese revolution occurred—the decline of world capitalism, the victory of the Soviet Union in World War II, its influence over the Chinese leadership, and the blows dealt by American imperialism, which, by arousing counterblows, forced through the far-reaching changes.

Having taken our time on China, any need for delay in the case of Cuba was eliminated. The main problem was already solved. If the great big pill of China tasted bitter to anyone, Cuba should have proved a welcome chaser. It not only confirmed our analysis of China, but Cuba contrasted most favorably in many respects, not least of all in the sincerity, honesty, and humanism of the Castro leadership. Despite the strong centralism of its underground organization and its extreme reliance on the will of a single leader, its innate tendency has been demonstrably democratic.

The efforts of Comrades Wohlforth and Mage to save their position in Cuba by breaking its continuity with the postwar revolutions elsewhere and by forcing an unbridgeable gap between a "rising" and a "declining" revolution does not even hold in the case of Eastern Europe. As we discovered in analyzing Yugoslavia closely, a revolutionary movement existed. A revolution occurred. Peasant forces, mainly guerrillas, were very prominent, and the leadership was petty-bourgeois, again of the Stalinist variety although with sufficient difference—perhaps due to the strength of the revolution itself—to avoid the fate of Rajk and the other victims of Stalin and to strike an independent course when Moscow attempted a crackdown.

Even in the bureaucratically managed overturns in Czechoslovakia, Hungary, etc., the revolutionary element, although highly distorted by the Kremlin's direct control, could be traced.

For that matter the smashing of the cordon sanitaire in Eastern Europe was never regarded by us as a mere extension of the counterrevolutionary Soviet bureaucracy. The extension also brought with it Soviet property forms. Their extension constituted not a decline but a rise in the revolution both in Eastern Europe and in the Soviet Union.

In all these cases, the criteria that guided us were (1) the smashing of bourgeois property relations, (2) the nationalization of economy, (3) the establishment of a monopoly of foreign trade, (4) the establishment of planned economy, and (5) the establishment of a state committed to the preservation of these gains.

Although the minority persistently leave out the first criterion in discussing this question, I rather think that they will give up trying to saddle the majority with the simplistic position of standing on nationalizations alone as the decisive criterion for a workers' state and grant that the smashing of bourgeois property relations is the primary criterion in determining the character of the state in every instance.

But this combination was also decisive in the Bolshevik revolution in determining the character of the state. It was contained in the program of the Bolsheviks, and if Russia was called a workers' state in 1917 it was because everyone knew that the contradiction between the government power and the capitalist state it took over would be resolved by the establishment of a new state structure conforming to the Bolshevik program. Let us not fail to observe, however, that the promissory note did not in itself wipe out the contradiction. This was only resolved in life itself, as Trotsky was to point out when he came to study the contradiction between the petty-bourgeois Stalinist power and the workers' state it rested on.

What was it that Comrade Mage said? "Thus we have two norms, *and the distinction between them should be kept clear.* One applies to the *victory* of the socialist revolution, the other to its degeneration or extension in distorted form." Note what happens now under this artificial double standard: "Our primary norm, the norm for a revolutionary workers' state, is and must remain *proletarian democracy* as set forth in 'State and Revolution.' *Nationalized property is the norm for the degeneration of the revolution.* . . . " (That emphasis is Comrade Mage's.) All our analyses of China, Yugoslavia, and the rest of Eastern Europe are held useless in the case of Cuba. All Trotsky's contributions in connection with the degenerated workers' state, the great contributions that made possible our analyses in the postwar revolutionary period, are likewise held useless. The board is wiped clean.

That's not all. Our theoreticians have us setting up "norms" for a socialist revolution in degeneration or extension. What we have actually done in Trotskyist analysis up to now, however, is to ascertain what socialist-type institutions were detectable in the degeneration or extension of a socialist revolution. (To call them workers' states, we have demanded more than nationalized property, as I have indicated above.) And these institutions are not different in principle from those of a socialist revolution in its rise. They are less or more healthy or strong, but not different in principle.[3]

As an exercise in the practical application of theory, let's go to Cuba and try out the simplistic norm which the minority leaders insist upon, leaving aside all we have learned in analyzing the other workers' states. A quick check reveals no workers' councils in Cuba, in fact no institutionalized forms at all of workers' democracy. Therefore, in accordance with this method of analysis, we are forced to conclude that no workers' state exists in Cuba.

It didn't take us long, did it? Short, sweet, and not very wordy. No danger either. No danger of conceding to Pabloism, or Kautskyism, or Stalinism, or bourgeois nationalism. Not much need to study either. Just bone up on the text of *State and Revolution*, a short pamphlet, and you've got it. And not much need to follow events closely. They took over a couple of billion dollars of capitalist property? So what? They didn't set up soviets. Let that August 17 reply to Hansen stand. And Comrade Robertson, giving the comrades of the New York Local the benefit of his familiarity with obscure texts, adds: The stuff about a workers' and farmers' government is "irrelevant"—a misapplication of some weird discussion or other at the Fourth Congress way back when in 1922. . . .

Unfortunately for this peaceful world of the doctrinaire, Cuba still exists—and only ninety miles from Florida. Tell us, please, do bourgeois property relations still exist in the key sectors of Cuban economy? Yes or no? Have the property holdings of the big capitalists and landlords been nationalized? Yes or no? Has a monopoly of foreign trade been established? Yes or no? Has a planned economy been instituted? Yes or no?

We shouldn't bother you with questions like this about the real world of today? Why not? Can't you find something on them in at least a footnote in the text of *State and Revolution*?

And what about the Revolutionary Government in Cuba deciding after considerable delay that the revolution is socialist in character? Does this have no meaning? No connection with the tremendous revolutionary changes in Cuba? No connection with

---

3. Lest some comrade of the minority mis-hear me, let me add that I agree that "the norm of a revolutionary [meaning healthy, I take it] workers state, is and must remain *proletarian democracy*."

the other workers' states? No relation to the increasing number of articles about Marxism and socialism, about the achievements of China and the Soviet Union appearing in the Cuban press?

Please, comrades, tell us what we are to think of all this, what we are to say about it to the rest of the world, how we are to answer the charge of Wall Street that Cuba has gone Communist, of other radicals that it has gone Stalinist, of the belief of the leaders of the Cuban revolution that it has gone socialist? Above all, tell us where we may find the criteria that will enable us to deal with this strange phenomenon unprovided for in the text of *State and Revolution.*

We have not yet finished. If workers' councils were set up—and we know this is possible even where a relatively strong capitalist state exists—what program would you suggest that they carry out to establish a workers' state? Smash the capitalist army and police? Already done. Nationalize the holdings of the big capitalists and landlords? Already done. Set up a monopoly of foreign trade? Already done. Establish a planned economy? Already done. We know there are tremendous political tasks for workers' councils in Cuba, but just what would you propose they do on these social and economic questions? When the workers' councils appear, how do you propose to explain the key tasks that they would normally assume in establishing a workers' state were performed before they appeared? How explain this inversion of sequence?

Of course there is an alternative. You may hold that since the discussion of such unheard-of things is not to be found in the text of *State and Revolution*, the doctrine gives us no choice but to conclude that the tasks normally assumed by workers' councils have all been carried out by petty-bourgeois democrats on the basis of a capitalist state. But if this is so, shouldn't we write Castro and tell him he is wrong in calling the Cuban revolution socialist? Perhaps we should add a P.S. admonishing him for light-mindedness and undue haste in such matters, a particularly reprehensible weakness when it can all be done under a capitalist label.

At this point let me consider one of the most forceful arguments advanced by Comrade Mage in behalf of his neither-here-nor-there state:

Is the idea of a "transitional state" something hitherto unheard of in history and Marxist theory? Not as far as our movement is concerned, at any rate, even if we haven't specifically used the term. We have adopted the position that China became a workers state sometime between 1951 and 1953. But the Chinese state was definitively established in 1949, and had in essence existed for 18 years before then. *What was the Chinese state before it became a workers state*, if not a transitional state? For that matter *all* participants in the present discussion on Cuba use this category, at least implicitly. The Draft Theses place the origin of the Cuban workers state in August-October 1960. Other comrades prefer the date of October *1959*. But the *violent revolution* that established the Cuban state was victorious in *January 1959*. Unless one maintains the completely anti-Leninist position that what was established in Cuba, China, and Eastern Europe were *capitalist* states which were converted into workers states by gradual reforms, one must recognize that they were *transitional states*, at least for a certain time ["The Nature of the State in Cuba"].

Has Comrade Mage forgotten? Only three pages previously in the same article he advanced the powerful argument that the Trotskyist movement has "two norms," one for a revolution in degeneration or extension and the other for an "ascending" revolution. He insisted that *"the distinction between them should be kept clear."* By not doing this, "the draft theses make the mistake of mechanically applying. . . ." Remember? It is instructive to see how mechanical Comrade Mage's two-norm machine proves to be. In order to try to maintain his case about a "transitional state" he finds himself compelled to illustrate what he means in Cuba by turning to China and Eastern Europe.

Thus he himself joins us in demonstrating that the mechanism of "two norms" doesn't work. Instead of coming under a qualitatively different set of criteria, making it impossible to compare Cuba with the other workers' states, Cuba can be understood only by using the same criteria. But if the case of Cuba is comparable to the cases of China and Eastern Europe, as Comrade Mage surely must agree at this point since he compares them, he has no alternative but to conclude that Cuba, like the states in those areas, is a workers' state. By attempting to illustrate what he means by his "transitional state," he proves that his basic methodological approach, his artificial division of criteria into two sets, is untenable.

However, let us consider the comparison made by Comrade Mage still further, so as to explore at least tentatively as many of the relevant points raised by him as possible. "We have adopted the position that China became a workers state sometime between 1951 and 1953. But the Chinese state was definitively established in 1949, and had in essence existed for 18 years before then. *What was the Chinese state before it became a workers state, if not a transitional state?*" To make the analogy accurate, let's put these statements in a setting of royal palms and malanga fields. "We have adopted the position that Cuba became a workers state sometime between August and October 1960. But the Cuban state was definitively established January 1, 1959, and had in essence existed three years before then. *What was the Cuban state before it became a workers state*, if not a transitional state?"

In their basic document, dated August 17, 1960, Comrades Mage, Wohlforth and Robertson told us that the "Cuban state is a *developing* state, scarcely more than a year old. . . ." Now the age has been abruptly changed and we discover that this prodigious infant was born in December 1956 when twelve men unfurled the flag of revolt on the Sierra Maestra.

All right, it's Comrade Mage's argument by analogy. By "transitional state" in Cuba, he means, obviously, a state that included both the capitalist state headed by Fulgencio Batista and the whatchumacallit state on the Sierra Maestra headed by Fidel Castro. In brief, his "transitional state" is broad enough to include a civil war of several years duration between a dictator and a popular political force. It is also broad enough to cover the downfall of the dictator, the smashing of his army and police, and the toppling of the property relations which the dictator was defending. Since this "transitional state" still exists today in 1961, according to Comrade Mage, it is not only five years old but has maybe years to go yet. God knows what new developments it is broad enough to cover.

What Comrade Mage has done here is commit the methodological error of dissolving the concrete into the abstract. His "transitional state" has become a meaningless label. The confusion all this engenders is not indescribable, but I don't think I care to meet the challenge. Among other things dual power is reduced to a hash along with governments and states. However, from the viewpoint of methodology it is a rather elegant error, and I have marked it for inclusion in a textbook I hope eventually to write, *Logic and How to Avoid It.*

One final observation: Comrade Mage asked us, "Is the idea of a 'transitional state' something hitherto unheard of in history and Marxist theory?" The correct answer is, "No, it is not something hitherto unheard-of in history and Marxist theory. Still more it is not just an idea. We have been living with a real one for more than four decades and a series of them have appeared since the end of World War II."

What label do we put on such a state to indicate that it has a definite class character as well as a condition of flux? *Workers' state*. We are so well aware of its transitional character that we noted it in the "Draft Theses." If you will read thesis no. 10 carefully, you will observe that it says, "Cuba entered the transitional phase of a workers' state. . . ."

Do you like that word "transitional"? Do you insist on it? Then you can vote for the "Draft Theses" with a perfectly easy conscience.

*         *         *

In his article "The Nature of the State in Cuba," Comrade Mage lists what he considers to be the seven basic contradictions determining the shape that the Cuban revolution has taken, the concrete forms in which we see it today. Analyzing these during the discussion in the New York Local, Comrade Rosemary Stone made some cogent criticisms.

Comrade Mage, she pointed out, does not weight the two sides of the various contradictions, indicating which is the more decisive. Still worse, he gives no indication of the development of the contradictions, their movement in one direction or the other. Thus, in reading "The Nature of the State in Cuba," we are left in the dark as to the general trend. This criticism is, in my opinion, completely valid. Comrade Mage's theoretical position collapses at the first touch of a dialectical logic. Trying to maintain that the Cuban state is like a weathervane, he cannot proceed with the contradictions he lists and follow their development in the Cuban reality.

Comrade Mage does not maintain that his list is exhaustive, but he does believe it "sets forth at least the most essential points on which our analysis of the Cuban state should be based." It is with some surprise, consequently, that we note he does not include as an essential point the contradiction between the state and the government in Cuba. Is it because such a contradiction does not exist? But obviously the Castro leadership found itself in contradiction with Batista's army and police. It smashed them. In coalition with the representatives of the former bourgeois-democratic parties, it found itself in contradiction with a state structure that resisted the agrarian and urban reforms. A major step was to bring the coalition to an end. The Castro government, which succeeded the coalition, continued making deep inroads in the state structure. Between ousters and defections, the personnel of the civil service, of the foreign service, of the judiciary was altered beyond recognition. The old commitment of the state to preserve bourgeois private property was shattered through a series of steps: "intervention" (a form of control) of ranches, businesses and industries; nationalizations and outright expropriations; workers' management. The emerging new state rested on the unions, cooperatives, INRA, and finally became committed to putting up the structure of planned economy. To repress the old ruling classes and defend the new property relations it relied on the Rebel Army; the Revolutionary Police; the militia; G-2, the secret service; and a renovated judiciary.

It was in relation to the development of this contradiction that all political currents, whatever their views, took their primary positions. Necessarily so because in this contradiction was expressed the heart of the revolution—property relations and political power.

The fact that the minority could overlook this contradiction tells us many things about their politics; above all, their inadequacy in orienting themselves in the Cuban reality.

The majority began by following the events with the utmost attention, gathering facts from all the sources at our disposal, including following at least one of the major Havana dailies obtainable by airmail in New York. We thus assembled the major facts now at the disposal of both sides in the internal dispute in the party. The minority, perhaps because they are somewhat disdainful of "empiricism," contributed little in this.

At first, basing ourselves on declarations by the revolutionary leadership about maintaining private property, we followed a quite critical approach, although we hailed the Cuban revolution with great enthusiasm. As it became clear that the Castro tendency was prepared to follow through to the end, no matter how this disrupted their previous ideology, we adopted a more and more friendly attitude. There was nothing particularly noteworthy about this shift on our part; it was nothing but the application of the ABC's of politics, particularly as we have learned them in the school of Trotsky. In the rich experience of the Socialist Workers Party, it has been applied again and again in relation to tendencies moving in a radical direction.

The political approach of the minority was quite different. During the first stages when we were judging Castro in the light of his declarations about private property, they remained silent. We were doing all right, apparently. But as the revolutionary forces began differentiating out and Castro took the road toward extreme radicalization of the revolution, the minority started to voice doubts, hesitations, and criticisms of the tactics being followed by the party leadership.

This was their democratic right, of course. We do not dispute that. In fact we welcome criticisms and discussion on this as all other questions involving the life of the party. But a critic must be prepared to face criticism of his criticisms. Are they right or are they wrong?

In this case the criticisms were dead wrong. The political course of the majority was to accept the Cuban revolution as it is, plunge in fully and completely, attempt to form relations with the revolutionaries and cement those relations if possible. The minority line, if adopted, would have kept us at arm's length from the Cuban revolutionaries, and by flinging doctrines and texts at them without regard for tactical considerations, we would have driven a wedge deeper and deeper between us and the revolution as it was actually developing. The Socialist Labor Party followed a doctrinaire course like that. The results were disastrous—for the SLP.

A striking example of Comrade Wohlforth's doctrinaire approach is available in his article, "In Defense of Proletarian Democracy." As he sees it, "in the three and a half months since the National Committee approved the general line of the "Draft Theses," the *Militant* has "*not once* called for the deepening of the revolution through the establishment of 'the forms of democratic proletarian rule.' I want the comrades to explain why this decision of the party has not been carried out." He continues with a passionate defense of proletarian democracy and ends up: "The failure of the *Militant* to *campaign* for proletarian democracy in Cuba is a criminal act of sabotage against this revolution—and it will be so recorded in the history of our movement."

Have a glass of ice water, Comrade Wohlforth. What was happening in the past "three and a half months"? Nothing less than a counterrevolutionary invasion of Cuba. By whom? The most colossal military power on earth, the most colossal the world has ever seen. And against a tiny country it could crush with a twist of the thumb. What was the main cry of the counterrevolution? The imperative need for democracy in Cuba. And what was the main need of the defense? Maximum central-ism. That military giant needed the sensation of having put his thumb on a tack.

Had the *Militant* opened a *"campaign"* for proletarian democ-racy at that precise time, it would not only have made it difficult for us to differentiate our position from that of the counterrevolu-tion; it would have facilitated the slanderous charge that we were acting as a "left cover" for the counterrevolution; and, as a matter of fact, in view of the need for centralism in facing the attack, the Cuban workers would have had good cause to consider such a campaign at that precise time as a "criminal act of sabotage against this revolution." They would have been doubly convinced of this, I am afraid, on reading the translations of the slogans which Comrade Wohlforth insists we should have cam-paigned for in New York: No "uncritical apologia." "In the present fluid situation the middle-class leadership of the Revolu-tion presents the greatest internal danger to the advance of the revolution." "Supplant the present petty-bourgeois leadership with a true working-class leadership." "Prepare for the next revolutionary wave." "Now is *precisely* the time to struggle for workers power."

Our task was to demonstrate our capacity, a genuine capacity, to participate smoothly in a centralized defense. In the Cuban revolution, military necessity for the time being took precedence over all other considerations. To anyone inclined to mis-hear, the word was *precedence*.

That is the way we have sought to proceed from the beginning—to seek in Cuban events themselves the points where our program, our politics, our methods are applicable and under-standable; and to show that we are willing to learn from others and to act in concert in a disciplined way. We considered it better to say nothing when the facts were not clear or the time not right than to make the gross error of injecting doctrinaire slogans or making doctrinaire explanations.

For some comrades this amounts to intolerable restraint. After all, what did they buy a typewriter for and why did they train themselves in oratory? They are like badly trained medical students who want to brush the surgeon aside during a delicate and critical operation. "Let me at that patient. Nurse, forceps . . . scalpel . . . No, make that a bread knife."

That Comrade Wohlforth can even entertain the line of thought he argues for demonstrates lack of touch with political realities. That he could display some emotion over the party's refusal to follow such a suicidal course indicates a certain responsiveness to the pressure of the Social Democracy.

No, I am not giving way to the pressure to use an epithet. Read the following footnote by Comrade Wohlforth in his article "On the Revolutionary Party":

> It is sad to see the anti-Marxist Draper so effectively destroy with Marxist methodology the arguments of the purported Marxists Huberman and Sweezy and to do so in the interests of imperialism. What makes it even sadder is that so many of our comrades are so enamored with Huberman and Sweezy. For instance, Draper notes Castro's Electrical Workers speech in which he urged the workers to take political power. He then queries as to why it was necessary for Castro to urge the workers to take power if Cuba was already a workers state? The majority comrades could do well to think that one over. Interested comrades should read this latest Draper article which can be found in the March *Encounter* or the March 21 *New Leader* under the title "Castro's Cuba: A Revolution Betrayed?"

What is sad is that Comrade Wohlforth thought Draper scored a point. Apparently he accepted Draper's interpretation without bothering to check the text of Castro's speech. But that speech excludes Draper's anti-Marxist interpretation. Castro was explaining to a group of backward workers that they should subordinate immediate material interests which could be improved only at the expense of lower-paid fellow workers. He sought to give them a broad vision and an understanding of the meaning of and need for worker's power. And he cited as a model example of this understanding the members of Cuba's most powerful working-class organization, the Sugar Workers Union. Comrade Wohlforth could do well to think that one over.

Let me add again to avoid any mis-hearing: I do not think that Comrade Wohlforth is "betraying" by displaying a bit of softness toward Draper. He just didn't think. So far as Comrade Wohlforth thinks things through I am sure he seeks a policy of unyielding opposition to the Social Democracy.

We come to the clamor about the leadership of the SWP buckling to "Pabloism," "Kautskyism," "Stalinism," and "bourgeois nationalism."

Only once since 1935 have charges so fantastically at variance from reality been heard in the party. This was during the recent regroupment period. An Oehlerite rejoined after some twenty-three years brooding on the sidelines. For several months he maintained a tactful silence. Then as the Marcyites began orating on the "implications" of our regroupment policy, he pulled the Oehlerite banner out of his underwear and unfurled it on high. "Cannon is betraying. Cannon has given up the Leninist concept of building an independent combat party." It was a historic occasion that will long be remembered by the New York Local. This political coelacanth thereupon joined with the Marcyites in a bit of Oehlerite action to save the concept of the party; namely, walking out, and is now back again brooding on the sidelines. I suppose he undertook all this effort to prove that revolutionary politics is not without its comic relief.

As for debating these wild accusations of the minority, I move instead that they be recorded in history as nonsense. Do I hear a second?

*          *          *

Let me turn now to a different variant of opposition to the majority line.

Comrade Trent Hutter's contribution to the discussion, "Danger Signals in Cuba," has aroused concern among those who know him. For some years he has faithfully sought by precept and example to teach the American Trotskyists a Marxist appreciation of bourgeois culture and, in passing, the need for amiability and good manners toward opponents, no matter what their failings. To this not small chore he has now added the aim of instructing them on the need to defend proletarian democracy. Can one man really hope to carry two burdens of such weight? Particularly if in assuming this new task he finds himself no longer able to set an example in the first?

There is not a milligram of independent or original thought in Comrade Hutter's arguments. Here is a typical example:

> And I wonder whether Fidel or Che will take the time to study the classics of Marxism. I am not under the impression that they will do so. They are no theoreticians. Their theoretical thinking is confused. And Fidel's willingness to learn has gradually been replaced by megalomania. A man who regularly engages in three- and four-hour speeches is not a man who will patiently listen and study.

This judgment reveals a good deal more about Comrade

Hutter's state of mind than it does Castro's. Whoever has patiently listened to or read Castro's speeches and studied their role in the Cuban revolution will find anything in them but megalomania (or "ranting and raving" as the bourgeois commentators put it). Each speech serves a definite political purpose connected always with mobilizing support for the defense or deepening of the revolution. Each point in each speech is logically placed. Every explanation and every illustration is admirably chosen to drive the points home. The appeal is to the best emotions, not the worst, and the predominant relation between the speaker and audience is intellectual.

Among other things, the role of Castro's speeches is of enormous interest for what it reveals of the power of a new medium of communication in a revolution—television. This is part of the explanation for Castro's ability to concentrate such great political weight in so few organized forces. Through the TV screen, the revolution's most attractive and able spokesman can step personally into homes throughout Cuba whenever necessary to explain the latest developments, where they fit in with the aims of the revolution, and what must be done about them. Castro does this in a way that stirs the most illiterate and backward, awakening them to political consciousness and bringing them into participation in the great world issues of our time. That's why even grandmothers in Cuba, devoutly religious homebodies all these years, suddenly display clear comprehension of the role of American imperialism in the economies of Latin America and voice decided opinions as to what should be done about it. Hutter, searching in his own way to understand the significance of all this, and not to be left behind by the grandmothers, gives us his decision—the man is off his rocker.

Let us take another argument: that the "giant mass meetings and four-hour television speeches" do not constitute workers' democracy. Instead of explaining the very useful role that the speeches and rallies do play, and continuing from there to indicate their relation to the Trotskyist norms of proletarian democracy. Comrade Hutter equates them with something qualitatively different. "It corresponds," he tells us, "to the classical methods of demagogic dictatorships." According to him, "these propaganda tactics were used by Dr. Goebbels in his speech at the Berlin Sports Palace after Stalingrad to rekindle German morale. . . ." Comrade Hutter recognizes that the great majority of the Cuban people support Castro. "That does not mean his regime is democratic." And then he informs us that "Hitler also used the argument: 'What regime could be more democratic than mine, since the overwhelming majority of the German people are behind me?'"

What a cesspool Comrade Hutter finds himself in. The argument is lifted with little change from such "theoreticians" as Theodore Draper and the authors of the State Department White Paper on Cuba. It is based on pure sophistry. The fascist Hitler, who sought to preserve capitalism, crush the first workers' state, and obliterate everything even vaguely associated with socialism, used mass rallies and claimed he had majority support. The revolutionist Castro, who led the Cuban workers and peasants in overthrowing capitalism and founding a workers' state and who has declared for the socialist revolution, uses mass rallies and claims he has majority support. Therefore, Castro = Hitler. What a truly vile slander! What could have brought Trent Hutter to such a state of mind that it becomes necessary to remind him that a reciprocal relationship exists between ends and means and that it is logically impermissible to equate means without consideration of the ends they serve?

"The case of Commander William Morgan, the handling of 'revolutionary justice' in Cuba clearly are symptoms of beginning degeneration," Comrade Hutter affirms, "and I refuse to go along with the *Militant*'s policy of either endorsing unreservedly the Castro propaganda line or refraining from comment. The *Militant* reads on the Cuban question like a New York edition of *Revolución*." Of everything he finds bad in the Cuban revolution, and that's quite a bit, the fate of Morgan disturbs Comrade Hutter the most. "If there still existed doubt as to the Castro regime's moving toward Stalinism, the frame-up trial and execution of Commander William Morgan ought to have dispelled it. For a frame-up trial it was: Not a shred of convincing evidence was offered by the prosecution."

Perhaps Comrade Hutter is right in this. However, he is not really sure. "It is very probable that Morgan never supplied anti-Castro rebels with arms or anything else." In addition to the "very probable," Comrade Hutter argues that Morgan could scarcely have been so unrealistic as to believe he could succeed at helping the counterrevolutionaries. Moreover, "why should he have wished to help overthrow a regime in which he had so big a stake?"

This scarcely constitutes evidence of a frame-up. The *Militant*—

in my opinion at least—could not take the responsibility of asserting on the basis of such probabilities and deductions that a frame-up had occurred. On the other hand, it is true that the press accounts of the trial did not give a clear picture of the evidence on which the court's verdict was based and Morgan did assert his innocence to the very end.

If this was a case of grave injustice, we should of course expose it. But before leaping to premature conclusions about the Morgan case or making a sweeping judgment about Cuban justice in general and what it might have to do with Stalinism, we should be clear about Morgan's background and the political circumstances in which the execution occurred, neither of which is mentioned by Comrade Hutter.

Morgan was an adventurer, a former paratrooper. He is said to have joined in the fight against Batista out of motives of revenge over the death of a friend. He did not fight in the Sierra Maestra with the forces of Fidel Castro but with one of the small bands in the Escambray Mountains. His social consciousness went as far as unionism, but in politics he was primarily anti-Communist—not anti-Stalinist but *anti-Communist*. In belief he was a devout Catholic. The Escambray front did not play a big role in the struggle against Batista; in fact it proved troublesome due to its lack of social consciousness, as Che Guevara has explained. When the counterrevolution sought to establish guerrilla forces inside Cuba around July 1960, the Central Intelligence Agency selected the Escambray Mountains as the main base of operations.

Did Morgan with his rabid anti-Communist bias and his close relationship with Catholic priests, who constitute part of the counterrevolution in Cuba, see that he had such a big stake in the regime that he deliberately refused to help the counterrevolutionaries? I would not condemn him without tangible evidence; yet it seems to me hazardous at the very least to give a person of such doubtful views a vote of confidence on the clarity of his vision.

With the establishment of the Escambray base of operations in the countryside, the CIA also began supplying counterrevolutionaries with explosives and incendiary mechanisms to be used in the big cities. By November popular anger was so high over the arson, bombings, and indiscriminate killings that the government, which had abolished the death penalty, felt forced to reinstitute it. The organization of an effective secret police—about which Comrade Hutter displays such indignation and alarm—

was another consequence of the terrorism waged under Washington's auspices.

Whether innocently or otherwise, Morgan fell victim in these developments. Comrade Hutter concludes that this is evidence of the degeneration of the Cuban revolution and its succumbing to Stalinism. Whatever gains Stalinist elements may have made temporarily, the real guilt lies with American imperialism. It is sad that Trent Hutter displays a certain blindness in this direction.

What is really eating Comrade Hutter? Is he developing unhappy doubts? Talking about the danger of bureaucratization in Cuba, he declares: "There are other forms of corruption than material corruption, and it is above all those other forms that I am thinking at this moment." He then refers cryptically to Lord Acton's aphorism: "Power tends to corrupt; absolute power corrupts absolutely." This is followed by a dark thought: "—and I am afraid that Fidel, Raúl and Che Guevara are becoming somewhat power-drunk."

Comrade Hutter falls prey to such gnawing suspicions while the youthful leaders of the Cuban revolution are moving heaven and earth to prepare their country for an attack plotted by imperialist rulers who hold the most absolute power on earth. (By ironic coincidence, "Danger Signals in Cuba" is dated April 17, the day of the invasion.) Lord Acton, who was a political adviser of Prime Minister Gladstone, undoubtedly had an unusual opportunity to observe tendencies that led him to make his famous comment about the power of power. But how much is there to it from the Marxist point of view, which relates the exercise of power to social and economic forces? Or from the psychoanalytical point of view, which finds deeper sources for the corruption of the human mind than the wielding of power? Perhaps Comrade Hutter will choose to enlighten us further.

It is possible that something different is involved. This may be alluded to in the following remarks:

When I wrote for our magazine an article on Puerto Rico's economic, social and political situation based on personal experience and a lot of research, it was rejected because it did not fit into the preconceived patterns of those who prefer to believe *Revolución* rather than a comrade who, after all, can speak of Puerto Rico with a certain amount of authority, knowing that island probably a little better than our Cuba specialists know Cuba. Unfortunately, the irrefutable facts I told about

Puerto Rico displeased some comrades: The facts did not fit into their mental image based on a situation that actually existed twenty or fifteen years ago. Nor did they fit into the Fidelista propaganda stories. Hence those comrades did not even care to discuss my article with me. It was simply buried.

Not buried. The first word was right—rejected. Comrade Hutter's article was very disappointing. A Marxist analysis of Puerto Rico today would be extremely valuable, since the State Department is displaying the captive island as the alternative to revolutionary Cuba, and Luis Muñoz Marin is among the foremost in the pack baying at Castro. But Comrade Hutter sought to prove the alleged exceptionability of Puerto Rico. His warm appreciation of what has been accomplished under the puppet government of Muñoz Marin stands in perfect symmetry to his coolness toward the revolutionary example of Cuba under the socialist-minded government of Fidel Castro. It would have been a scandal, if not worse, to print such an article as a Trotskyist view. The editor, no matter how much he appreciated the contributions Comrade Hutter has made on other topics, had no choice in this case but to make the unpleasant decision of declining it as politically unacceptable.

Instead of reconsidering his position on Puerto Rico or presenting his view in the discussion bulletin for study by the membership or simply forgetting his venture into Caribbean politics, Comrade Hutter let it rankle. This is not a very auspicious sign.

Another inauspicious sign is Comrade Wohlforth's praise of this unfortunate article as "quite good." Hutter agrees that Cuba is a workers' state. Wohlforth is in principle opposed to this view. Nevertheless, cutting across the disagreement in basic principle, he searches for common political ground. If the Cuban revolution were sufficiently degenerated, that is, had fallen under Stalinist control to the degree that Hutter believes it has, then Hutter could "make at least some sort of case for viewing Cuba as a deformed workers state." Wohlforth thinks Hutter "tends to exaggerate the degree of Stalinist influence"; therefore, in his view, Cuba is in healthier condition than Hutter maintains. So—according to this tortured reasoning—it isn't a workers' state at all and Hutter and Wohlforth have a lot in common!

Since agreement on the question of principle is excluded, what makes Wohlforth think Hutter's article is "quite good"? What is the source of attraction? What does Wohlforth really have in common with Hutter? It seems difficult to avoid the conclusion: responsiveness to the bourgeois clamor for "democracy" in Cuba.

*          *          *

It is with relief that I turn from Comrade Hutter's poorly conceived arguments to Comrade Bert Deck's discussion of the problem of dating the origin of the workers' state in Cuba. Here we have the pleasure of working out a difference with a comrade who is in solid agreement on the need for a vigorously positive attitude toward the Cuban revolution.

The gist of Comrade Deck's position is that the formation of the militia marked the qualitative change making Cuba a workers' state. I take it, although he is not explicit about this, that he is not utilizing by way of analogy our position on China, where none of us took formation of a people's militia as the decisive point. Consequently, he must view the Cuban revolution as qualitatively different from the Chinese revolution; and, even more clearly, qualitatively different from the other workers' states.

If this qualitative difference exists, why should October 1959 be taken as *the* date? Why not January 1, 1959, when the Rebel Army won its victory? The Rebel Army, constituting at that point the "bodies of armed men, a special repressive force," which is advanced by Comrade Deck as his criterion, was sufficient to oust Batista.

An even stronger case can be made for fixing the date as January 1, 1959, if to the criterion of "bodies of armed men" representing the people, is added the criterion—crushing of the special repressive force of the capitalist class. As all of us are aware, both the army and the police representing the capitalist interests in Cuba were smashed long before October 1959.

The reason Comrade Deck does not take January 1, 1959, is that the revolution at that time lacked socialist consciousness. It was thus not qualitatively different from the Chinese revolution *in that respect*. The absence of socialist consciousness made it impossible to call Cuba a workers' state on January 1, 1959, even though "bodies of armed men, a special repressive force," did exist then.

If we consider the "bodies of armed men" in the relation of means and ends, which is how they should be considered, it is even clearer how incorrect it would be to take January 1, 1959, as the decisive date. The Rebel Army at that point served three conscious ends, predominantly political in nature: (1) to topple Batista, (2) to prevent a Guatemala-type counterrevolution, (3) to defend the coalition government, which was committed to safe-guarding private property (with redistribution of land and rectification of abuses in other fields). It remained to be seen how the deepening of the revolution would alter these aims. To take a different view would force us into such misjudgments as Comrade Deck's conclusion that a "terrible backsliding" occurred with the victory when the fact is that the victory, marking a certain level of development, made possible a surprisingly swift advance.[4]

Once we are forced by the reality itself to reject January 1, 1959, as the point of qualitative change, we are compelled to await either the appearance of socialist consciousness or of economic institutions that in and of themselves are socialist in principle. Neither of these had appeared by Ocober 1959. What did appear was a quantitative increase in the "bodies of armed men"; that is, the extension of the Rebel Army, so to speak, on a wider and more popular basis. The formation of militias was very important, a development which we warmly greeted, but in itself it was not qualitatively different from the "bodies of armed men" already existing in the Rebel Army and the Revolutionary Police.

To my way of thinking, this is sufficient to invalidate October 1959 as the date of qualitative change. I do not see that this conclusion can be escaped unless the quantitative increase of the "bodies of armed men" can be equated to a qualitative difference.

---

4. The April 2, 1961, *Bohemia* quotes the following interesting observation by Fidel Castro on this point: "The revolution was not sectarian; if the revolution had been sectarian, it would never have put into the ranks of the government such gentlemen as Rufo López Fresquet, Miró Cardona or Mr. Justo Carrillo and some others of that kind. We knew how those gentlemen thought; we knew they were men of plenty conservative mentality. But the fact is that the government itself of the republic, in the first days of the triumph, was not in the hands of the revolutionaries; the government itself of the republic was not in the hands of the men who had spent many years struggling and sacrificing; it was not in the hands of the men who had been in prisons and had fought in the mountains; it was not in the hands of the men who lit that revolutionary spark and knew how, even in the moments of greatest uncertainty and skepticism, to carry aloft the banner of the revolution, and with that the faith of the people, to bring them to the triumph."

This would make the mere quantitative difference equivalent to the appearance of socialist consciousness or of economic institutions that are socialist in principle. Does a solution exist along these lines? Comrade Frances James, seeking a theoretical foundation for Comrade Deck's position, offers an attempt in her article "The Question of Criteria and the Cuban Revolution":

> True, in certain concrete historical situations developing after World War II, we considered nationalization the decisive criterion. But in other concrete historical circumstances it certainly *was not* the decisive criterion—for example in Russia in Oct. 1917 when a workers state was established and no nationalizations occurred for months. The criterion in 1917 was conquest of political power by the Bolsheviks. However, even within the Soviet Union itself the criterion changed. With the growth of Stalinism and the defeat of Bolshevism, the criteria for determining the USSR as still being a workers state became nationalized property, state monopoly of foreign trade, national planning, etc.

This suggestion, if adopted, would certainly rescue Comrade Deck. You want to make it come out October 1959 in Cuba? It's simple. Change the criteria for that country.

Is that date that important? Why not change the criteria to make it come out January 1, 1959? It at least has the advantage of being an easier date to remember—and to celebrate.

Comrade James's proposal really gives us something to ponder. By what criteria do you change the criteria? In other words, how do you tell when and where to use one set of criteria and when and where to use a different set?

It is plain that both Comrade Deck and Comrade James approached the criteria as a series of items, some of which can be put to use or left on the shelf, according to the occasion. But they leave us with no criteria whatsoever to determine the occasion. The error in methodology is precisely the same as that made by Comrades Mage and Wohlforth when they break the criteria into two sets of norms and arbitrarily assign one set to ascending revolutions and the other set to the extension of degenerated or deformed revolutions. The criteria, handled in this unscientific way, become disconnected, losing their own interrelations and therefore their reliability. This will become clearer, I hope, if we consider our criteria in their historical development.

*State and Revolution*, excellent as it is in bringing together the teachings of Marx and Engels as the foundation for everything that followed, does not contain the final word on how to determine the character of a state. It lacks the refinements introduced as a result of subsequent experience and subsequent development of Marxist theory. Written in August-September 1917, it lacks in particular a consideration of what the Bolsheviks discovered in life after they came to power. It tells us nothing, for instance, about the experience of the Bolsheviks in facing the contradiction between government and state and resolving it. Not a word appears in it about the contradiction between government and state in the case of degeneration of workers' power. We need not lament this limitation in Lenin's famous pamphlet. Trotsky brought the criteria presented in *State and Revolution* up to date as he followed the development of the first workers' state. In fact everything Trotsky wrote in relation to the character of the workers' state is built on the foundation of those teachings. *Built on.*

It was on the basis of this amplified and enriched body of theory that we were able, following World War II, to analyze the deformed workers' states as they appeared and characterize them successfully. No doubt Comrade Mage and Comrade Wohlforth, as well as Comrade Deck and Comrade James, will grant that it would have been impossible to reach correct conclusions about the deformed workers' states by simply using *State and Revolution*. We had to use the refinements of the criteria which had been developed by Trotsky for the Soviet Union.

We were on our own, of course, because these were new phenomena and Trotsky was no longer with us to offer guidance. Yugoslavia was the most difficult from the theoretical point of view, because it had more that was new than the others. But Yugoslavia was only a foretaste of China. As we noted earlier, China presented much that was unexpected and completely new, and the implications were far more sweeping. But by relying on the criteria as they had been refined in applying them to Eastern Europe and Yugoslavia, we succeeded in handling the case of China. Our success in the truly difficult case of China, let me repeat, enabled us to approach Cuba with relative ease. From the point of view of the historical development of the theory of the state, the greatest importance of Cuba was the *confirmation* it offered of our analysis of China. Cuba proved that China, like Yugoslavia, was not an exception, not a freak case. Or, looked at from the level of methodology, China proved once again that there are no exceptions; the so-called exception signals the appearance of new phenomena that require further refinement of already discovered basic laws.

At this point I see the alert finger of Comrade Wohlforth: "But you labeled China a 'deformed' workers' state like Yugoslavia; and you didn't put that label on Cuba."

True. An accurate observation. But then we try not to make a fetish of labels.

Besides, Cuba has something new to offer. Something different from China, different from Yugoslavia, from Czechoslovakia, from Bulgaria and the Soviet Union. Stalinists do not head the Cuban revolution. They were bypassed. This newness and this difference require recognition. This is registered in a refinement in the qualification of the characterization *workers' state.*

This brings us back to the difference in results flowing from the difference in Comrade Deck's method and ours. Comrade Deck gets the date October 1959. We get August-October 1960. Perhaps more careful analysis would also reveal that Comrade Deck puts no (or exceedingly minute) qualification on the characterization *workers' state* while we qualify it as "one lacking as yet the forms of democratic proletarian rule," meaning that while it is not "deformed" in the sense of having Stalinists in power, the state is not under the democratic control of the workers and peasants (but may develop such forms with relative ease).

A not unimportant additional difference flowing from this is that Comrade Deck, to find empirical confirmation for his way of determining that Cuba is a workers' state, is compelled to make out that forms of proletarian democracy already exist in Cuba. This leads him to some idealization of the reality which in turn points to political difficulties. What does he propose that is qualitatively different from the forms he already sees in existence?

The majority position, on the other hand, is able to see a workers' state in Cuba without the existence, as yet, of formal institutions embodying workers' democracy. This is an accurate reflection of the reality. As a consequence, our theoretical appraisal offers firm support for a Marxist political line in Cuba.

Comrade Deck, I am afraid, has to see more than actually exists in Cuba today and perhaps credit the revolutionary leadership with more revolutionary socialist consciousness than it has yet exhibited. Objectivity requires us to note, I think, that the minority, despite their exaggeration, scored a telling point against Comrade Deck on this.

From the methodological viewpoint it is quite instructive to see how the same fundamental error in using criteria leads to symmetrically opposing positions under the influence of political considerations. The negative attitude of Comrades Wohlforth, Mage, and Robertson led them to underrate the consciousness of the Castro leadership and the amount of democracy in Cuba. The positive attitude of Comrades Deck and James led them to overrate both. The two attitudes, of course, are not politically equivalent. A negative attitude today is dangerous and could be suicidal. But the opposite position, if carried out logically, could be troublesome in the stage ahead.

The difference in dates seems minor—a bit of hairsplitting—but in one case it represents the application of an entire body of historically developed, interrelated criteria and in the other a reversion to the theory as it stood before October 1917.

The Cuban revolution, I submit, is occurring in the context of the world situation of today and under the influence not only of imperialism and the colonial revolution of today but of the other workers' states of today. It is not possible to tear the Cuban revolution out of this context which has shaped it, attempt to measure it by a pre-October 1917 yardstick, and expect to come up with fully accurate results. To cope with the complexities of this ultramodern event with the utmost precision we need the theory of the state as developed in all its power by our movement.

# Cuba—the Acid Test
## A Reply to the Ultraleft Sectarians
### (November 20, 1962)

It is written: "In the Beginning was the *Word*."
Here I am balked: who, now, can help afford?
The *Word*?—impossible so high to rate it;
And otherwise must I translate it,
If by the Spirit I am truly taught.
Then thus: "In the Beginning was the *Thought*."
This first line let me weigh completely,
Lest my impatient pen proceed too fleetly.
Is it the *Thought* which works, creates, indeed?
"In the Beginning was the *Power*," I read.
Yet, as I write, a warning is suggested,
That I the sense may not have fairly tested.
The Spirit aids me: now I see the light!
"In the Beginning was the *Act*," I write.
—Goethe.

As the mainstream of the world Trotskyist movement heads toward healing a split that has lasted an unconscionable eight years, some ultraleft currents in various areas are pressing in an opposite direction, seeking to perpetuate the old rift, to deepen it if possible, and even to precipitate fresh ruptures. The Latin American Bureau of J. Posadas, ordering an end to discussion before it was even initiated, bolted from the International Secretariat last April under guise of "reorganizing" the Fourth International, and raised the banner of a program that goes so far in its deviation to the left as to include a but thinly disguised appeal to Moscow to start a preventive nuclear war. On the side of the International Committee, the top leaders of the Socialist Labour League, under guidance of Gerry Healy, have chosen to interpret the efforts of the Socialist Workers Party to help unify world Trotskyism as a "betrayal" of the basic principles of

Marxism which they intend to fight tooth and nail; and, to emphasize their dedication to this course, they have hardened a posture on Cuba the only virtue of which is to lay bare an astonishing lack of the most elementary requisite of revolutionary leadership—ability to recognize a revolution when you see one.

How are we to explain this curious turn? Obviously it was precipitated by the unification process. A series of practical problems surged to the fore. How can you unite with the opposing trendency even if they do consider themselves to be Trotskyists? The question is asked by groups on both sides. After years of bitter factional war, how can you collaborate and live in the same organization? Didn't the public positions of the other side damage the cause as a whole? How can you work with leaders whose records provide grounds for deep suspicion? How can you find areas of agreement? A far easier, more "Leninist," and therefore more "principled" tactic is to simply continue firing at them, no matter if differences have to be magnified. Prestige, pride, bullheadedness, personal eccentricities, all these came into play at the prospect of unification. In the case of the Latin American Bureau, for instance, a factor may have been fear that pretensions as to size and influence, which were actually declining, would be exposed by unification, or that habits of paternalistic centralism would have to give way to democratic controls. Nevertheless, however weighty they may be—and in a small movement they can loom large—such factors do not explain the political differentiation.

The same fundamental cause that brought fresh impulsion to unity sentiments in the past couple of years is also responsible for the flare-up of resistance. At bottom lie the mighty forces of the colonial revolution and the interrelated process of de-Stalinization. These are having an effect on the radical movement roughly comparable to that of the Russian revolution some forty years ago. Cutting across all formations, they are shaking them and regrouping them, dividing them to right and to left. If the repercussions among radicals began with the victory of the Chinese revolution and speeded up with the famous Twentieth Congress and the Hungarian workers' uprising, it came to a crescendo with the Cuban revolution. When the massive nationalizations took place, and the Castro government expropriated both American and Cuban capitalists, every tendency had to take a stand. The imperialists left little room for equivocation.

The Trotskyist movement has not escaped the general shake-up either. The Chinese victory, de-Stalinization, the Hungarian uprising were reflected in both capitulatory and ultraleft moods as well as strengthening of the mainstream of Trotskyism. What we have really been witnessing in our movement is the outcome of a number of tests—how well the various Trotskyist groupings and shadings have responded to the series of revolutionary events culminating in the greatest occurrence in the Western Hemisphere since the American Civil War. The move for unification and the symmetrical resistance to it are no more than logical consequences to be drawn from reading the results, especially those supplied by the acid test of the mighty Cuban action.

The fact that differences, even sharp differences, exist among the ultralefts who were turned up by the latest and most decisive test does not invalidate this conclusion. Posadas, for example, after initial opposition, came around to the view that Cuba is a workers' state, thus making a rather better showing than Healy on this crucial issue. Yet he is, if anything, even more truculently opposed to any moves toward unification of the Trotskyist movement. Advocating a line that bristles with inconsistencies and extravagances, Posadas is nevertheless compelled to adapt himself to one of the main realities of politics in Latin America today. Throughout that vast region, it is political death among radical workers to voice a position on Cuba like the one on which Healy insists. Posadas, for all his flights of fantasy, was able to recognize this reality after discovering it the hard way. Healy, unable to agree to so grim a conclusion from anything he has seen in insular British circles, is more nonchalant about the prospect of such a fate overtaking the Latin American Trotskyists.

As is typical among ultralefts, elaborate justifications "in principle" are offered for their sectarian course, along with dire prophecies about the consequences of the "betrayals" being committed by those following in the real tradition of Lenin and Trotsky. Like similar rationalizations of ultralefts before them, these offer little resistance to critical appraisal. I propose to demonstrate this by examining the main thread of argumentation about Cuba as presented in SLL material, above all the document "Trotskyism Betrayed." I will then take up briefly the related considerations offered by the leaders of the French section of the IC in "Draft Report on the Cuban Revolution," a document that discloses substantial differences with the SLL leaders on

Cuba while maintaining a united front with them on the question of unification.

## Should Marxists Go By the Facts?

The world Trotskyist movement has waited now two long and crowded years for the SLL to recognize the facts about the Cuban revolution. The SLL leaders have refused to listen to the American and Canadian Trotskyists who have followed events in Cuba with close attention from the very beginning. They have refused to listen to the Latin American Trotskyists who have firsthand acquaintance with the development and results of the revolution in both its home base and the rest of the continent. They scorn the conclusions reached by other Trotskyists throughout the world. Why this obstinate refusal to admit palpable events? Strangest of all, the leaders of the SLL have come to recognize that they are refusing to acknowledge the facts; they have converted this into a virtue and even elevated it into a philosophy. The reasoning is very simple: To recognize facts is characteristic of empiricism; Marxism is opposed to empiricism; therefore, as Marxists, we refuse to recognize facts. Here is how this reasoning—included as part of the package in a review of Lenin's Philosophical Notebooks—is presented by Cliff Slaughter in the original academic language which has proved so entrancing to the editors of [the SLL theoretical journal] *Labour Review* in recent years and which, we are sure, will prove just as entrancing to readers of this article:

Lenin's Notebooks on Hegel might appear obscure and a not very pressing preoccupation, when big things are happening all over the world. However, it is exactly on the theoretical front that the sharpest and most uncompromising struggle must be waged. A mistaken conception here can mean a whole mistaken method, the relations between the facts becomes totally misunderstood, and disastrously wrong conclusions will be drawn. For example, some "Marxists" assume that Marxist method has the same starting-point as empiricism: that is to say, it starts with "the facts". It is difficult to understand why Lenin and others should have spent so much time on Hegel and the dialectical method if this were true. Of course, every science is based on facts. However, the *definition* and *establishment* of "the facts" is crucial to any science. Part of the creation of a science is precisely its delimitation and definition as a field of study with its own laws: the "facts" are shown in experience to be objectively and lawfully interconnected in such a way that a science of these facts is a meaningful and useful basis for practice. Our "empiricist" Marxists in the field of society and politics are far from this state of affairs. Their procedure is to say: we had a programme, based on the facts as they were in 1848, or 1921, or 1938; now the facts are obviously different, so we need a different programme. For example, the spurious "Fourth International" of Pablo's group decided some years ago that the Stalinist bureaucracy and its counterparts in various countries were forced to act differently because of changed objective circumstances ("facts"). New "revolutionary currents" were abroad in the world, more recently particularly in the colonial revolution. The consequence of this "mass pressure" would be to force the bureaucrats to act contrary to their wishes and to lead the workers to power. The great scope of the colonial revolution, the "liberalization" of the Soviet regime, and the exposure of Stalin by Khrushchev, were taken as the "facts" in this case. Then again, the revolutions in Algeria, Guinea, and particularly Cuba are said to be yet a new kind of fact: *socialist* revolutions, even *without* the formation of revolutionary working-class parties [*Labour Review,* Summer 1962, p. 77].

Study of this shining passage is worth the effort, for it reveals the theoretical method used by the SLL leaders in approaching the Cuban revolution and much else in today's world. We note the qualifying sentence, "Of course, every science is based on facts." The author is to be congratulated on admitting this; it is a favorable indication of at least a certain awareness that a material world does exist. We can even pin a medal on him for the sage observation that the various sciences cover different fields, that in these fields facts have various orders of importance and that it is the job of science to reveal their significance and the significance of the relations between them so that we can put them to use. But let us examine more closely the two sentences that stick up like bandaged thumbs:

For example, some "Marxists" assume that Marxist method has the same starting-point as empiricism: that is to say, it starts with "the facts". It is difficult to understand why Lenin and others should have spent so much time on Hegel and the dialectical method if this were true.

So "Lenin and others" spent so much time on Hegel and the dialectical method in order to avoid starting with the facts? Or to be able to bend them with philosophical sanction to fit preconceived notions? Or to avoid sharing any grounds whatsoever with empiricism, especially in the precise area where it is strongest? But Hegel did not teach that. He was more dialectical in his appreciation of empiricism than Slaughter and others. Hegel recognized that empiricism is much more than mere observing, hearing, feeling, etc., and that its aim is to discover scientific laws. "Without the working out of the empirical sciences on their own account," he observed, "philosophy could not have reached further than with the ancients." As was his method with all views which he considered to have philosophical merit, he sought to include what was valid in empiricism in his own system. It is worth noting, for instance, that "Being," the opening category of his logic, corresponds on this abstract level to an empirical beginning.

Hegel criticized empiricism on two counts: (1) In place of the a priori absolutes of the metaphysicians, which it rejects, empiricism substitutes its own set of absolutes. Thus it is arbitrary, one-sided, and undialectical. (2) Its basic tendency is to oppose the idealism of which Hegel was an ardent exponent:

> Generally speaking, Empiricism finds the truth in the outward world; and even if it allows a super-sensible world, it holds knowledge of that world to be impossible, and would restrict us to the province of sense-perception. This doctrine when systematically carried out produces what has been latterly termed Materialism. Materialism of this stamp looks upon matter, *qua* matter, as the genuine objective world [*The Logic of Hegel*, translated from the *Encyclopedia of the Philosophical Sciences*, p. 80].

I would submit that "Lenin and others" did not bring from Hegel his opposition to empiricism on idealistic or religious grounds. On the other hand Marxism does share Hegel's position that vulgar empiricism is arbitrary, one-sided, and undialectical. But empiricism "systematically carried out"? This is the view that the "genuine objective world," the material world, takes primacy over thought and that a dialectical relationship exists between them. What is this if not dialectical materialism?

Slaughter's error is to establish an absolute gulf between empiricism and Marxism, leaving out what they have in common. In brief, he is guilty of rigid, mechanical thinking on this point. However, we plead that the culprit be let off with a light sentence in view of the novel circumstances. How often are we privileged to see a British metaphysician demonstrate that the heavy machinery of academic learning can be so finely controlled as to prove a mere trifle like facts don't count? And with Lenin's *Philosophical Notebooks* fed as information to the machine! It's better than cracking a walnut with a pile driver.

An additional error is involved. Slaughter finds it "difficult to understand why Lenin and others would have spent so much time on Hegel and the dialectical method" if it were true "that Marxist method has the same starting-point as empiricism: that is to say, it starts with *'the facts.'"* Our utilitarian must easily understand then that the practical benefit which "Lenin and others" got out of Hegel and the dialectical method was the view that a scientific system of thought like Marxism—unlike empiricism—takes precedence over facts. True, in its origin, the Marxist system of thought was admittedly built on a foundation of facts, but once in existence it became—thanks to Hegel— relatively free from the need for further contact with facts. Thus the time spent on Hegel and the dialectical method was more than compensated for by the saving made possible in disregarding current facts. The primary task of a Marxist theoretician today, consequently, is not to apply the dialectical method to analysis of reality—this is subordinate since the job has been done and we know from the system of thought what the reality is like and what it is going to be like. The primary task is to study the books and become adept at expounding the texts so that the system is promulgated in all its purity. Facts are of practical value in this task as illustrations and confirmation of the correctness of the system but are of not much import on the theoretical level.

But this is dogmatism, not Marxism. Marx and Engels did not simply take over idealist dialectics and assign it a chore such as it performed for idealism; namely, helping to dig up material to prove the validity of a philosophical system. From that point of view dialectics is devoid of methodological interest.

In the Marxist world outlook, dialectics does not serve an auxiliary role. It is central. To understand what this means and to appreciate its relevancy to the issue at hand—our attitude toward facts—we must go back to the origin of materialist dialectics, which is to be found in Marx's solution to the chief contradiction of Hegel's dialectics. This contradiction, as Slaughter will certainly agree, was its failure to provide for self-criticism, for dialectical self-adjustment. The impasse was inevitable, since the Hegelian system excluded anything more fundamental than thought itself and there was thus nothing for thought to be adjusted against. The material world was viewed as a mere inert and passive "other" created by the activity of thought. Research thus centered on the nature of thought, the "nuclear energy" of the Hegelian system. Marx brought dialectics out of this blind alley by empirically taking matter as the fundamental source of motion. He thereby turned things around drastically and opened the way in principle for adjustment of his own theoretical system; that is, by checking it against the primary source of all movement, the material world. In place of thought spinning on itself as in the Hegelian system, Marx found the way to a genuine feedback. Through this revolution the dialectical method became self-consistent. It, too, is open to change. A major characteristic of materialist dialectics, consequently, is supreme sensitivity to facts. Any work that fails in this respect will not stand up as an example of materialist dialectics. It is an apology or an academic exercise such as abounds in the Stalinist school of pseudodialectics.

Does this feature of materialist dialectics have any practical consequences or is it simply a curiosity among splitters of hairs? We are at the very heart of Marxist politics! An evolving material world, moving in a time sequence, inevitably forces rectifications in the thought that hopes to reflect it in close approximation. This holds with even greater force if that thought aims at active intervention, for it must seek genuine and not illusory points of support in a reality that is in movement. The primary task of a Marxist theoretician is to analyze reality with the best tools available—those of dialectics—so as to provide the most accurate guide possible for revolutionary action in the world as it actually exists at a given stage. This requires us to start with the facts.

The point is crucial. The type of thinking exemplified by Slaughter's contribution, which has brought the National Committee of the SLL to the sad position of refusing to acknowledge the facts in Cuba, has inspired a flood of arguments like those found in the previously cited paragraph from *Labour Review*:

1. Years ago some people of a "spurious 'Fourth International'" decided that there were new facts about the Stalinist bureaucracy which required Trotskyism to make adjustments. They were wrong. Today the same "spurious" sources assert that new currents in the colonial revolution can force bureaucrats to act contrary to their wishes and lead the workers to power. Wrong again. We leave aside the crude simplification and consequent distortion of opponents' views and also the merits of the real points involved in order simply to call attention to the logic: Bad people were wrong before; *therefore,* they are wrong again.

2. These same "spurious" characters, or perhaps some "'empiricist' Marxists" whom Slaughter does not name, also say—in obvious error—that "the revolutions in Algeria, Guinea, and particularly Cuba are . . . yet a new kind of fact: *socialist* revolutions, even *without* the formation of revolutionary working-class parties." Again we leave aside the distortion of opponents' positions in order to call attention to the hidden syllogism: What is not provided for in the program of Marxism cannot occur; this possibility is not provided for in the program of Marxism; therefore, it has not occurred.

In place of the problem of finding points of support for our program in the world in which we live, the SLL method is simply to assert the necessity for our program *despite* the reality.

There is nothing wrong, of course, with asserting the need for revolutionary socialism, including the need for party building, but this is only "A." Agreeing on that, we wish to proceed to "B"; how is this to be accomplished in a given situation? The SLL leaders display little interest in "B." For them "A" seems sufficient. Here is a typical example of their thinking that indicates this:

> In practice, however, both the Pabloites and the SWP find themselves prostrate before the petty-bourgeois nationalist leaders in Cuba and Algeria, which they have chosen to regard as the touchstone of revolutionary politics. Our view of this question is not opposed to that of the SWP simply in terms of who can best explain a series of events. It is a question rather of the actual policy and program of Trotskyist leadership in these backward countries.

But no revolutionary socialists "choose" what shall be regarded as the touchstone of revolutionary politics. This is done by much bigger forces; namely, classes in conflict. Cuba and Algeria happen to be the two areas in the world where this conflict has reached revolutionary proportions at the moment. This was not determined by any decision of ours. It was determined by revolutionary mass actions. Nor did we choose the current leaderships of the colonial revolution. They are the result of objective conditions of vast sweep. What we did choose was to study the facts and, in these facts, seek openings for *effective* application of our program. If we may express the opinion, it is an overstatement to say that anyone finds himself "prostrate before the petty-bourgeois nationalist leaders in Cuba and Algeria" because he refuses to follow the SLL National Committee in thinking that a Trotskyist can clear himself of any further responsibility by putting the label "betrayal" on everything these leaders do. It is an error of the first order to believe that petty-bourgeois nationalism = petty-bourgeois nationalism, has no internal differentiations or contradictions, and cannot possibly be affected by the mass forces that have thrust it forward. To avoid the political prostration that follows the method practiced by the SLL, revolutionary socialists seek to go beyond simply repeating the words about the need for a party. By joining in the action of the revolution, they seek to help build a revolutionary socialist party in the very process of the revolution itself instead of arguing with the revolution that it would have been better to delay things until the party had first been constructed.

Slaughter states, we recall, that "Part of the creation of a science is precisely its delimitation and definition as a field of study with its own laws: the 'facts' are shown in experience to be objectively and lawfully interconnected in such a way that a science of these facts is a meaningful and useful basis for practice." We welcomed that statement. Now we must protest what followed, if Slaughter was by some remote chance thinking of us when he said, "Our 'empiricist' Marxists in the field of society and politics are far from this state of affairs. Their procedure is to say: we had a program, based on the facts as they were in 1848, or 1921, or 1938; now the facts are obviously different, so we need a different program."

In the case of Cuba, proceeding by the Marxist method, we sought to establish the facts and then determine how they are objectively and lawfully interconnected with our previous analysis of China, Yugoslavia, and the buffer countries. Our conclusion was not to say, "We need a different program." Quite the contrary. We stated that the case of Cuba confirmed our previous analysis and thus confirmed the correctness of Trotsky's analysis of the Soviet Union and of his theory of permanent revolution. From this we derived a meaningful and useful basis for finding our place in the Cuban revolution.

In contrast to this, the SLL leaders approach Cuba as if the problem boiled down to illustrating the correctness of Lenin's norms for a healthy workers' state. The correctness of these norms is not at issue. We believe in them, advocate them, and seek to advance them as always. The SLL leaders, however, stop at the mere assertion of these norms and try to force them to do work for which they are insufficient. This leads them into a series of glaring errors and even into disastrous policies, as we shall see.

To anticipate what we shall attempt to prove in detail, the SLL leaders, following the method indicated in Slaughters' article, do not show how the facts in Cuba are objectively and lawfully interconnected with the preceding Trotskyist positions. Instead they commit a very common but also very basic mistake: they dissolve the concrete into the abstract. They do this in two steps. First they refuse to link the facts in Cuba with the criteria used in analyzing China, Yugoslavia, and the buffer countries. They then quite illogically stop at Lenin's norms. The result of going this far, however, is to leave them with only Lenin's norms to determine the character of a workers' state. The *criteria* for determining a workers' state have been dissolved into the *norms* which, since Trotsky's time, have been recognized as valid only for determining a *healthy* workers' state. By dissolving Trotsky into Lenin in this way, the SLL leaders are left without the tools of theory necessary to assess anything except what would have been considered a workers' state in 1917. What will not fit the norms is given a *capitalist* label, since no grays exist in the SLL's world of solid blacks and solid whites. Thus, incapable of correctly analyzing the Cuban revolution, they end up by refusing to accept as noncapitalist anything that deviates from Lenin's norms. The correct label for that position is ultraleft sectarianism. This method compels them, as an odd final consequence, to contend that "Lenin and others" brought from Hegel the view that facts are not primary. They provide their own ultimate absurdity and seek, appropriately enough, to find sanction for it in the philosophy of idealism.

With such reasoning the National Committee of the SLL determines its policy in a revolution that is shaking the Western Hemisphere. Thus in much of what they write about Cuba one gets the impression of a thought process little above that of medieval times, when the experts determined what the world was like through fasting, meditation, prayer, and pious reference to the Holy Scriptures.

## Who Has Lost Touch With Reality?

An instructive example of what this type of thinking can lead to is provided by the document to which the National Committee

of the SLL appended its joint signature, "Trotskyism Betrayed."
For instance:

> Does the dictatorship of the proletariat exist in Cuba? We reply
> categorically NO! The absence of a party squarely based on the workers
> and poor peasants makes it impossible to set up and maintain such a
> dictatorship. But what is even more significant is the absence of what the
> SWP euphemistically terms "the institutions of proletarian democracy" or
> what we prefer to call soviets or organs of workers' *power.*

To substantiate this stern decision handed down by the SLL
court, we are referred, in accordance with the method of thought
we have discussed above, to the writings of Lenin; and the
appropriate texts are cited as if the leader of the Bolsheviks had
the Cuban situation before him.

So what exists in Cuba? We are given it, straight from the
bench, without any ifs, ands, or buts:

"In our opinion, the Castro regime is and remains a bonapartist regime resting on capitalist state foundations."

As for Castro, he is taken care of with similar crispness: "The
regime, however, is a variety of capitalist state power. The Castro
regime did not create a qualitatively new and different type of
state from the Batista regime."

According to these experts in what the law books say, who
cannot find any mention of Cuba in Lenin's *State and Revolution,* not even dual power exists in the island:

> The "militia" [the quotation marks on "militia" put those half million
> armed Cubans in their place!—J.H.] is subordinate to Castro's state—not
> to soviets, not even to a constituent assembly. In this sense they do not
> constitute workers power or even dual power.

And all those happenings in Cuba, about which the papers
have been making such a fuss, are explained as easily as digging
up an appropriate citation from Lenin:

> Despite or rather because of [that "rather because of" is good!—J.H.] all
> the economic and social changes that have taken place in the last two-
> three years, Cuba has witnessed, not a social revolution which has
> transferred state power irrevocably from the hands of one class to
> another, but a political revolution which has transferred power from the
> hands of one class *to another section of that same class.* . . . Where the
> working class is unable to lead the peasant masses and smash capitalist

state power, the bourgeoisie steps in and solves the problem of the "democratic revolution" in its own fashion and to its own satisfaction. Hence we have Kemal Ataturk, Chiang Kai-shek, Nasser, Nehru, Cárdenas, Peron, Ben Bella—and Castro (to mention a few).

There you have it—in all its baldness—the judgment of the National Committee of the SLL on the Cuban revolution and its achievements.

But a puzzle remains. How come the Republican Party, which is fairly aware of Wall Street's thinking, doesn't recognize that Castro is just another "Batista"? Why the dragging of feet among the Democrats, who know Wall Street's thinking just as well as the Republicans but who take a longer view of the interests of capitalism? Above all, how explain the anomalous reaction of the Cuban capitalists who poured out of the island like rats from a burning cane field and holed up in Florida, the way Chiang and a section of the Chinese capitalists holed up in Formosa? How was it possible for the entire capitalist class of the United States to unite, without a single fissure, against Cuba and risk bringing the world to nuclear war in the effort to topple the Castro government? How come they refuse to recognize that their properties could not be in safer hands than those of a Cuban "Chiang Kai-shek"? How are we to assess this strange new phenomenon of Wall Street losing touch with reality in the one area where it never misses—its property interests?

Another mystery. How come the Soviet people, the Chinese people, the Koreans, Vietnamese, Yugoslavs, Albanians, and people of the East European countries all consider that Cuba has become noncapitalist and now has an economic system like theirs? How explain that they, too, have lost touch with reality on such a decisive question?

For that matter, what about the Cubans? Here a whole population is apparently suffering from a manic-depressive psychosis. The capitalists and their agents think they have been overthrown and it's a disaster. The rest of the population agree and think it's wonderful. They have raised the banners of socialism, and tens if not hundreds of thousands are assiduously studying Marx, Engels, and Lenin. Isn't that going rather far in failing to recognize that "capitalist state power" still exists in Cuba?

We have still not come to the end. There are ten countries, including the United States, in which Trotskyists sympathize with or belong to the IC. In all these countries, only the SLL holds this curious position on Cuba. Not a single other group agrees with them—not even those in France. Have the other nine, then, lost all touch with political realities? How is this to be explained? Have all of them "degenerated" and "betrayed" Trotskyism except Healy and his staff?

Let us also add that the Posadas group in Latin America would not touch the SLL position on Cuba with a ten-foot pole. Nor, for that matter, would a single solitary Trotskyist in all of Latin America, whether with the IC or the IS, so far as I know. Can't any of the Latin American Trotskyists recognize a "Batista" when they see one? How can they be so far out of touch with the real world?

Since I mentioned the IS, the ultimate horror of "Trotskyism Betrayed," let me concede that there the National Committee of the SLL can draw some comfort. In their next solemn session they might have Slaughter or Healy read as encouraging news the following declaration by a prominent member of the IS:

Fidel Castro is at present the latest "hero" discovered by the Communist Parties of Latin America, to whose regime they attribute the revolutionary gains of the Cuban masses. Fidel Castro, however, is only the Bonapartist representative of the bourgeoisie, who is undergoing the pressure of the masses and is forced to make them important concessions, against which his bourgeois teammates are already rising up, as has just been clearly shown by the opposition set going inside his own government against the—timid enough—agrarian reform.

The author of that statement, which the SLL position so obviously echoes and amplifies, is Michel Pablo. It can be found on page xiii of his pamphlet *The Arab Revolution*. Unfortunately, the authors of "Trotskyism Betrayed" cannot expect to build too much on this, since it was Pablo's position in June 1959, before Castro broke up the coalition government with the representatives of Cuban bourgeois democracy. Pablo long ago dropped that position, if position it was and not just a premature assessment. Pablo, whatever else you may think of him, has enough wisdom and ability not to insist on a position which is *that* untenable in face of the facts.

It seems, consequently, that the NC of the SLL has succeeded in finding an abandoned niche where they are doomed to complete isolation. It is theoretically possible that Healy and his closest collaborators are the only ones who have not lost touch with the Cuban reality. But the force of the facts makes this most unlikely.

## A New Type of Capitalism?

There still remain some vexatious theoretical problems of lesser order, all of which are opened up by the position of the National Committee of the SLL on Cuba, but of which not a single one is discussed in the document they submitted despite all the boasting and arm-waving about how the SLL leaders intend to bring theoretical clarity to the very much muddled world Trotskyist movement. First on the agrarian movement:

A basic criterion for a workers state in the economic sphere in an underdeveloped country is the *nationalization of the land* and thorough political measures by the ruling power to prevent the growth of the kulaks. Neither in Egypt nor in Cuba has this been done. On the contrary, in Cuba, Castro has recently promised (under the impact of the food crisis) to give the land back to the peasants. So long as land remains alienable, so long will petty commodity production continue and so long will Cuba remain a capitalist nation.

Such a tangle of errors is included in this paragraph that one can scarcely decide which loop to pick up first. But let us be patient, for this is all the National Committee of the SLL has to say about Cuba's agrarian reform. To begin with, let us pull out the misleading reference to Egypt since we are dealing with Cuba. Second, it is not true that so long as petty-commodity production continues, the economy of a country will remain capitalist. Petty-commodity production and capitalism are not synonymous. That is why a workers' state, on replacing a capitalist state, can safely call on the peasants to take the land. It is also the fundamental reason why Engels, and all genuine Marxists after him, have stood firmly on the principle that the peasants must not be forced into collectivization. That is also why nationalization of the land, while a very important and indicative measure, is *not* a basic criterion for a workers' state and was *not* considered as such in designating Yugoslavia, the Eastern European countries, and China as workers' states, a position for which the National Committee of the SLL voted. Third, the addition of the criterion "thorough political measures by the ruling power to prevent the growth of kulaks" sounds queer as a basic criterion for a workers' state in the *economic* sphere. In any case this new "criterion," in this unexpected association, was never even suggested in the discussion on Yugoslavia, Eastern Europe, and China. Is the National Committee of the SLL perhaps thinking of revising the Trotskyist position on the character of these states by demanding that this new "basic criterion" be added?

Not much is left of the SLL position on Cuba's agrarian reform; but, in compensation, the tangle is just about unwound. Only a snarl or two is left. Instead of giving "land back to the peasants," the main course of the agrarian reform in Cuba is just the opposite. It is true that the Cuban government has proved quite sensitive to the will of the *campesinos* in this respect, contrasting wholly favorably to the course followed in all the countries where Stalinist methods were applied either directly by Moscow or under its influence. Thus the deeds to many farms have been handed out, especially in the Sierra Maestra. Some cooperatives, too hastily formed, may have been dissolved, but the general line of development is clearly in the direction of a bigger and bigger state role. Thus, the most important cooperatives have now been converted into state farms. Good, bad, or indifferent, that happens to be the case.

On the *alienability* of land in Cuba, which is beside the point in this discussion, the National Committee of the SLL simply displays an ignorance in perfect harmony with the pattern of thinking which permits them to close their eyes to more important facts that stare them in the face. It so happens that the agrarian reform law specifies that the "vital minimum" of land, to which a *campesino* gets a deed, "shall be inalienable." Exempt from taxes, this land cannot be attached and is not subject to contract, lease, sharecrop, or usufruct. It can be transferred only by sale to the state, or through inheritance by a single heir on the death of the owner, or, in the event there is no heir, by sale at public auction to bidders who must be *campesinos* or agricultural workers. There is only one way in which the owner can even mortgage his land in Cuba and that is by mortgaging it to the state or to its specified institutions. Now that they have learned these facts, will our British comrades still maintain that nothing essentially new has occurred in Cuba?

We come to the theoretical problem, which is our reward for having opened up this tangle of errors. However you assess the agrarian reform in Cuba as a criterion in determining the character of the state, it was the swiftest and most thoroughgoing by far in the history of Latin America. How was such a radical reform possible under a regime that the SLL leaders allege is not qualitatively different from the Batista regime? Is this provided for in the classics of Marxism? How are we to explain it? Finally, are we for or are we against this agrarian reform? The National Committee of the SLL maintains a painful silence on this that is truly scandalous in leaders who consider themselves to be Trotskyists. But if, after a collective democratic discussion, they decide to vote yes, must they not also add that we should begin reconsidering our attitude toward "capitalist" regimes capable of such far-reaching measures?

We come to a related question. Castro's insistence on a thoroughgoing, radical agrarian reform blew up the coalition government in July 1959. The representatives of bourgeois democracy hastily stuffed stocks, bonds, dollars, and pesos into handbags and followed the representatives of the oligarchy and the imperialist interests into exile in Miami. Thus a new government came into being that proved capable of acting in a qualitatively different way from the previous one.

Let us note what this government did, so that the National Committee of the SLL will understand better what we mean by "the facts." It carried through, as we have noted, the swiftest and most radical agrarian reform in the history of Latin America. It did this against the combined resistance of the Cuban landlords, Cuban capitalists, and American imperialists. This resistance was not simply verbal. The counterrevolutionaries fought with rifle and bomb and whatever the CIA and Pentagon could give them.

Against this powerful landlord-capitalist-imperialist resistance the new government armed the people of Cuba. Not just with speeches but with mass distribution of guns and the organization of a powerful militia. Against the mounting military measures taken by American imperialism, the new government turned to the Soviet bloc for comparably effective defensive military hardware. While this was going on, the new government initiated sweeping economic measures such as the establishment of controls on foreign trade and controls over capitalist management. Still more important, it continued the process begun in conflict with Batista's army and police of smashing the old state structure. Finally, some two years ago, in defiance of the wrath of the mightiest capitalist country on earth, it expropriated capitalist holdings "down to the nails in their boots." This same new government proceeded with astounding speed to expand state controls into state planning; and when the imperialists brought an axe down, cutting all major economic ties between the United States and Cuba, this new government, responding in a heroic way to the emergency, tied its economy in with the planned economies of the Soviet bloc. Can such a government be described as differing only *quantitatively* from a Batista regime? Accurately described, that is.

All right, have it your way. Let us grant that the difference is only quantitative and—for the sake of the confusion on which the National Committee of the SLL insists—let us stubbornly refuse to grant this quantitatively different government even a quantitatively different label. Our theoretical problems are only worsened—and in a qualitative way. We must then admit that reality has so changed that it has now become possible for a Batista-type regime to carry out such revolutionary actions in a series of countries. What has happened to capitalism to give it the possibility of taking such self-destructive measures? Has it suddenly become rejuvenated? Has the death agony of capitalism really turned out to be a fountain of youth?

As in the case of Cuba's agrarian reform, we are also faced with a political issue that cannot be evaded—unless, of course, you counsel that we abandon politics. Are we for or are we against all these measures? If we approve them, are we then not compelled to admit that such governments are capable of a progressive role? Does it not follow, if they are "a variety of capitalist state power" as the SLL leaders assert, that capitalism has not yet exhausted all its progressive possibilities? If this is so, a still more thorny problem arises. Does any barrier exist to prevent a capitalist government in an industrially advanced country from playing a similar progressive role? If a barrier does exist is it qualitative or simply quantitative? What, inside this new capitalist reality, determines the character of the boundary? On all these questions, which are raised in principle by the document flung so vehemently on the table, the National Committee of the SLL maintains the most discreet silence.

Let us consider for a moment the character of the Cuban economy today. "The nationalizations carried out by Castro do nothing to alter the capitalist character of the state," the National Committee of the SLL claims. Good; for the sake of argument let's see what happens if we agree not to change the label, whatever else has changed. We note that these nationalizations were not undertaken by either the capitalist or imperialist supporters of Batista. Nor were they undertaken by the representatives of bourgeois democracy. The bulk of the Cuban capitalists, such as they were, most of the landlords, and the corrupt assemblage of politicians who served as their agents are now to be found in Florida or any other land of the palm save Cuba. Thus we must add to the fact of "mere" nationalization, the fact of expropriation of the Cuban and American capitalists and landlords. The National Committee of the SLL may stoutly deny this. None of the former property holders will. In addition, I think that, roughly speaking, 999.9 out of 1,000 observers who have taken the trouble to visit Cuba or study the events will put these two items down as incontrovertible facts.

To this must be added the fact that a planned economy has been installed that extends so far as to completely embrace the principal agricultural sphere—sugar. True, the planning may not be efficient. It may be hampered by lack of competent personnel, poor balancing, some bureaucratism, breakdowns, and other faults. These are due not only to lack of experience but to the direct sabotage of counterrevolutionaries and to the enormous pressure of American imperialism, which seeks to throttle in the cradle this effort at planning. Nevertheless, in principle the planned economy is operative in Cuba, has already achieved remarkable successes, and has clearly displaced private capitalism in all the key sectors of the economy. This is a fact, too.[1]

Putting these three main facts together—expropriation of the bourgeoisie, nationalization of industry, and the institution of a planned economy—and adding to this combination the "capitalist" label on which the National Committee of the SLL insists, what do we end up with? It's inescapable: *state capitalism.* But, again, what is gained by such a label save indescribable theoreti-

---

1. Perhaps this is the place to file an objection to a declaration in the statement of the SLL, where the nature of the state in Cuba is considered, that nothing essential was changed by the Castro government: "What it did do was to clear out the old judges, administrators, bureaucrats, diplomats and policemen and replace them with people who supported Castro. The old institutions were filled with new personnel." This is dead wrong. The old institutions, including their personnel, were committed to the preservation of private capitalist property interests. The new institutions, in contrast to the old, are committed to the preservation and administration of nationalized property.

cal confusion and the admission that capitalism still has great and progressive inherent possibilities despite all that has been said about its death agony? Moreover, we are not saved thereby from taking a political stand. Is this so-called state capitalism in Cuba better or worse than the private capitalism which it overturned? Yes or no? If it is superior, in what respect is its superiority apparent?

Finally, exactly what does the National Committee of the SLL propose on the *economic* level which, if enacted, would entitle us to cross out the "capitalist" label? Our haughty theoreticians disdain to answer in their document. We would appreciate, if it's not asking too much, a plain and simple reply to that question.

## China, Yugoslavia, and Eastern Europe

Two whole years after the event, as we noted above, the National Committee of the SLL still refuses to recognize Cuba as a workers' state. In their efforts to establish theoretical grounds for the dogmatic view that nothing has changed in Cuba and that it's all a malicious, "revisionist" invention about the Batista regime being overthrown, they inevitably tear gaping holes in basic theory.

Not openly and boldly, but in a covert way, they strike at the entire continuity of our theory since the time of Trotsky, insofar as it relates to assessing the character of a workers' state. They begin with Trotsky's analysis of the Soviet Union, attempting to cut that theoretical foundation away from the problem before us. "But it is ridiculous to think," they argue, "that the question of the Cuban state can be resolved abstractly by 'criteria' from this earlier discussion (with Shachtman and Burnham) even at the end of which Trotsky was still saying that the last word had still to be said by history." What do they mean by that cryptic last remark? That Trotsky doubted or was not sure of the character of the Soviet Union? Or that the National Committee of the SLL has now become shaky about it? What do they mean by the epithet "ridiculous"? Ridiculous by whose standards and on what grounds? The criteria used by Trotsky, abstract though they may be, happen to be the concrete theoretical grounds for every succeeding step in Trotskyist analysis concerning the problem of the character of the Soviet Union and the workers' states that have appeared since then. To sever this connection prepares the way for revising everything accomplished in theory in this field since then—and also prepares the way for revising Trotsky's theory of the degenerated workers' state. The National Committee of the SLL is taking here a most revealing step.

The mechanical thinking that feels an inner compulsion to cut the link with Trotsky's analysis, reveals itself in still another way. On page 12 of their document "Trotskyism Betrayed" they seek to summarize Trotsky's position: "The bureaucracy which usurped the government power in the social economy of Russia was a parasitic group and not a necessary fundamental class." That sounds correct on first reading, but something is missing. What kind of parasitic group? What was its class coloration? We search the page in vain for an answer. Yet this is one of the most distinctive features in Trotsky's analysis. The parasitic layer is *petty bourgeois,* a reflection of the peasantry, the remnants of the old classes, the elements who switched allegiance from tsar to the new regime—all these and the political-military administrative levels of the new government who, under pressure from the capitalist West, drifted from the outlook of revolutionary socialism or came to prominence without ever having genuinely understood or accepted it. What was new in this situation—and this is the heart of Trotsky's position on the question—was that a reactionary petty-bourgeois formation of this kind could, after a political counterrevolution, wield power in a workers' state and even defend the foundations of that state while being primarily concerned about their own special interests.

We come now to the question of why this point is important—of decisive importance, in truth—in solving the central problem posed by the spread of Soviet-type economies in the postwar period. However, let us first listen to the National Committee of the SLL:

The states established in Eastern Europe in 1945 were extensions of the Russian revolution by the military and bureaucratic methods of the Stalinist leadership. They were possible under the circumstances of special difficulty for imperialism and the chaos in Europe consequent on the defeat of German capitalism. In fact the betrayals of international Social-Democracy and Stalinism restricted the advance of the revolution to Eastern Europe (and later China). This perpetuates the essential conditions of the survival of the bureaucracy in the workers states. There was by no means the same dynamic in the foundations of the deformed "workers' states" as there had been in Russia in October 1917. Our movement's characterization of all these states was not simply a question of applying "criteria" like nationalization to the finished product.

These six sentences constitute all that seems to have registered with the National Committee of the SLL of that rich collective effort of our world movement to solve the complicated problems posed by "the facts" in those areas. Yugoslavia, a special case which gave rise to considerable discussion in the world Trotskyist movement, is not even mentioned. We will not cavil, however, in view of the fact that China was brushed off with three words (inside parentheses).

What is remarkable about this capsule treatment of an important chapter in the preservation and development of the theory of our movement is that although it concerns the decisive links of theory between Trotsky's analysis of the Soviet Union and the world Trotskyist movement's analysis of Cuba today, it does not contain a milligram of theory, not even by way of historical mention! Such references as "chaos," "betrayals," "circumstances of special difficulty," "by no means the same dynamic," etc., indicate the general setting to which theory must relate but not the points of the theory itself. The six sentences constitute in fact a shamefaced way of completely disregarding the theory of the character of these states. Thus, if we combine the previous operation of cutting away Trotsky's position on the Soviet Union by declaring it has no relevance to the Cuban discussion, we stand where? The answer of the SLL is to leap across all the intervening links to Lenin's abstract formulations of the *State and Revolution* period. None of the arguments used against the pertinence of our referring to China, Yugoslavia, and Eastern Europe apply to the pertinence of the SLL referring to Lenin! Why? Well, these are texts written by Lenin himself, you see, and you don't want to be against Leninism, do you? Now do you? This methodology is, of course, the correct means for accomplishing one end—the conversion of Lenin into a harmless ikon.

Leaving nothing undone to make sure that the confusion is twice confounded, the National Committee of the SLL states on page 13 of their document,

Our essential differences with the SWP on this question is, therefore, not over the "criteria" of workers states. We do not accept such a framework for the discussion; if, in fact, we had defined a workers state by the existence or non-existence of Trotskyist parties then this *would* be a lapse into "subjectivism," but we have not done this.

A few lines further down on the very same page, however, we have done this. We read:

Does the dictatorship of the proletariat exist in Cuba? We reply categorically NO! The absence of a party squarely based on the workers and poor peasants makes it impossible to set up and maintain such a dictatorship.

The latter sentence, then, excludes Cuba from being a workers' state—and also China, Yugoslavia, and the Eastern European countries. It even excludes the Soviet Union, since you cannot "maintain such a dictatorship" in the "absence of a party squarely based on the workers and poor peasants."

Listen again to the National Committee of the SLL on why Trotsky's analysis of the Soviet Union is not relevant to Cuba: "At every stage of his eleven-years-long work towards a 'definition' of the USSR, Trotsky insisted on a rounded, critical perspective and not simply on the 'normative' method of applying definition criteria." Are we in a kindergarten? It was precisely because Yugoslavia, the East European countries, and China did not follow the norm that we could not use the "normative method." That was the big difficulty, if we may remind the National Committee of the SLL, and why we sought an adjective like "deformed" to indicate that these workers' states were not according to norm.

The SWP method is the opposite, taking certain "criteria" from the discussion of one particular manifestation of the revolutionary struggle in one part of the world as a unique stage in the development of the world revolution. They apply this criteria to another part of the world a generation later, to a particular sector at a particular stage of the struggle. Thus nationalization and the existence of workers militias are sufficient to make Cuba a "workers state" and to make the Cuban revolution a socialist revolution.

We protest! And not just over the misrepresentation of our position in the last sentence. It is the SLL method that is normative. They refuse to consider either the individual or the particular. They go back *two* generations to *the most general* norms of the workers' state as defined by Lenin in the light of the writings of Marx and Engels. They then apply these *norms* to the individual case of Cuba. Since Cuba does not fit, their conclusion is that Cuba is not a workers' state. It is this method of thought which we claim is now represented in the positions that the SLL is pressing for adoption by the entire world Trotskyist movement. It is undialectical and completely mechanical. It measures facts by norms, and if they do not measure up, too bad for the facts.

What are the particular threads of theory to which Cuba must be related if we are to proceed dialectically? In the case of the Eastern European countries, we held that the petty-bourgeois layer which had usurped the power in the Soviet Union could, under certain conditions, export both their own rule and the property forms on which they were a parasitic excrescence. To do this they had to overthrow capitalist property relations as well as capitalist regimes. (At a certain stage they also liquidated native revolutionists who might have led independent currents.) The physical presence of Soviet armies in the occupied countries made it not too difficult to grasp the theory that reflected this process. In Yugoslavia, as has been pointed out before, it was more difficult. Partisans played the predominant role, and in place of Soviet generals and Soviet secret political police, the Yugoslav revolutionists came to power. They were, however, of the Stalinist school with a strong nationalist coloration. Can a workers' state be established by petty-bourgeois figures such as these? Without the intervention of a revolutionary socialist party? The National Committee of the SLL voted yes. The theoretical position they approved was that a petty-bourgeois Stalinist leadership can take power and establish a workers' state—not because it is a *Stalinist* species of petty-bourgeois leadership, but because it is at the head of a revolution involving both peasants and workers, a revolution that is of even greater relative strength because it occurs in the time of the death agony of capitalism and after the victory of the Soviet Union in World War II.

The next link was China. This particular case displayed even more novel features: years in which the Mao leadership existed as a dual power in which guerrilla warfare played a prominent role, eventually paving the way for full-strength regular armies, the march on the cities, and so on. With all its differences, the key problem again was like the one in Yugoslavia, save that the direct role of the Soviet Union was even more remote. Could a revolution be led by a petty-bourgeois formation—without prior organization of a revolutionary socialist party—to the successful formation of a workers' state in a country as vast and populous as China? There was long hesitation about this, but the facts, which the National Committee of the SLL so lightly wave aside today in the case of Cuba, spoke so powerfully that the world Trotskyist movement had to accept the reality. The National Committee of the SLL, be it noted, did not contribute much to that discussion, but they made up for the slimness of their writings by the alacrity with which they voted to call China a workers' state. Perhaps it is only now that they are beginning to consider the implications of what they voted for? The strange part is that this difficulty in taking a cuba libre chaser after downing China in a single gulp arises over the fact that the Cuban leadership is in every respect superior to the Chinese, unless you consider Mao's Stalinism to be a virtue. Perhaps, with the help of Alcoholics Anonymous, the SLL leaders have learned to put up a hand with firm resolution, "Thanks, but we don't drink!"

The position that Cuba is a workers' state rests on the extension of the theory, as it was developed in the previous particular cases, to this new case. A contrary position must demonstrate either that the previous positions were fallacious or that nothing has really happened in Cuba. A halfway position, with which the National Committee of the SLL may be toying, is to hold that each individual case calls for its own special criteria—one set for Cuba, another set for China, etc. This would signify the complete breakdown of any scientific approach, not to speak of dialectics, and the enthronement of the most vulgar empiricism. The National Committee of the SLL has chosen the alternative of denying the facts. It has, however, gone far, as we have shown, in preparing the ground for shifting to the other main alternative; namely, that everything must be revised back to 1940, if not back to Lenin.

On the other hand, the theory with which we were able to provide a rational explanation for the appearance of such unforeseen formations as workers' states deviating widely from the norms laid down by Lenin has proved its worth—and quite dramatically in the case of Cuba. I refer not only to its help in defending and extending the Cuban revolution but in understanding why the Cuban issue is of such extraordinary explosiveness in world politics.

The position of the National Committee of the SLL utterly obscures this role, in fact denies it, for Cuba is seen as only one particular "unique" case, unconnected with anything save the colonial revolution in general and perhaps the American elections in particular; hence incapable of playing any great or even unusual role. They overlook what is absolutely basic—the fact of a socialist revolution in the Western Hemisphere. In place of the revolutionary action which flared in the powder house of imperialism, the SLL leaders substitute the most barren academic schema: "A Marxist evaluation of any movement insists upon an analysis of its economic basis in the modern world. This must begin from the international needs of imperialism." How do these most generalized economic abstractions apply to the blaze in the Caribbean? "We have tried to understand and discuss the Cuban question," the National Committee of the SLL answers, "in terms of our own analysis of the economic position of Cuba and the evaluation of the present struggle in Cuba and the rest of America." This approach, worthy of a dogmatic instructor in an economics department, has led them to constantly underestimate Cuba politically; and the many painful surprises have taught them nothing.

Once you see Cuba for what it is, a workers' state and the opening stage of the socialist revolution in the Western Hemisphere, as is made possible by linking it to the revolutions in Yugoslavia, Eastern Europe, and China (the Cuban leaders are well aware of the latter tie), then it is quite clear why it plays such a spectacular role. The extension of the October 1917 revolution into the Western Hemisphere is a *revolutionary action* far more decisive in the scales than the weight of Cuba's economy in North and South America. This revolution has something *qualitative* about it as a culmination of the overturns that began in Eastern Europe. With its signal that the stage is now opening for non-Stalinist revolutionary leaderships, it even appears as a major turning point in the whole postwar period. Wall Street, quite understandably from the viewpoint of its class interests, is not excited over the weight of Cuba as a particular country but as a bright flame burning amidst crates of high explosives. It can absorb the economic losses in Cuba. It cannot absorb the political consequences of long continued existence of the revolution that caused these losses. Cuba, in its eyes, to change the metaphor, has the peculiar shape of a fulcrum offering a point of support for a lever from the land of the October 1917 revolution. Wall Street knows very well that not much weight is required on that lever to lift the entire Western Hemisphere, and with it the world.

Thus U.S. imperialism views Cuba as of first-rate importance. This being the view of the most powerful capitalist class, the heart and center and main support of all the other capitalist sectors, its moves in relation to Cuba inevitably reverberate in every country. For all the weaknesses inherent in its size and economic and military position, Cuba thus occupies the center of the stage and becomes a general problem for all of humanity.

This is not all. By bringing forward a leadership of non-Stalinist origin, the Cuban revolution has visibly hastened the eventual closing of the whole chapter of Stalinism. By impelling this leadership toward revolutionary socialist views, the Cuban revolution has increased in a marked way the actuality of Lenin's general norms. This would seem so graphically evident that the blind could see it in the measures taken by the Castro regime against Stalinist bureaucratism and in the debates resounding in the Soviet bloc over the meaning of "peaceful coexistence" and how to best fight imperialism. "Unique" Cuba, following the particular pattern of the buffer countries, Yugoslavia, and China, has become a general concern for capitalism and the Soviet bloc, and given fresh inspiration to the partisans of Lenin's norms. Dialectics has provided us with a beautiful example of the interrelationship between the individual, the particular, and the general.

In maintaining and developing in this way the theoretical positions staked out by Trotsky, we have not engaged in "revisionism," as Healy and his closest collaborators charge. We have conceded nothing in our program, which continues to be based on the fundamental positions laid down by Lenin. We have, on the contrary, found it easier to find our way in the complex course of the revolutions that followed World War II. Our analysis enabled us to work out more skillful ways of finding points in these revolutions from which to bring the norms of Lenin to bear. We prefer to believe that this was Lenin's way both in spirit and in method.

## The Proof of the Pudding.

As the National Committee of the SLL can undoubtedly prove a thousand times over by quotations from "Lenin and others," theory and practice are intimately interrelated. A bad theory is bound to be reflected in practice; and vice versa. Thus from the highly erroneous theory of the Cuban revolution which the SWP holds, as the SLL leaders see it, certain disastrous consequences must inevitably follow. Prominent among these is a pro-Castro attitude and a vast overrating of the importance of the Cuban revolution. These sickening symptoms, in the opinion of the National Committee of the SLL, show the cancerous "degeneration" which the SWP has suffered. The alleged decline of the American Trotskyist movement is in turn to be explained as a product of the unhealthy environment of economic prosperity and political witch-hunting in which the SWP has had to operate throughout the postwar period.

It really is a curious dialectic, isn't it? The SWP displays its tendency to capitulate to American imperialism by standing in the forefront against all the witch-hunting of the American imperialist pack howling and clamoring for Castro's blood and the downfall of the Cuban government! On the other hand the National Committee of the SLL shows how much better it resists the imperialist pressure of Wall Street's junior partners in the City [London] by sneering at the importance of the Cuban revolution and calling Castro just another "Chiang Kai-shek." This proves that the freer and easier environment provided by British capitalism is more conducive to Leninist intransigence since the temptation to stray into sin is higher and the opportunities for it more numerous than in the U.S.A., and these challenging objective conditions offer on the subjective side greater scope, under wise Leninist guidance, to stiffen and improve the character and consciousness of the cadres . . . or words to that effect.

Despite "or rather because of" this sour, bilious attitude toward the goings on in Cuba—whatever they may be—the National Committee of the SLL is convinced that it is putting up a model defense of the Cuban revolution. Following a paragraph reaffirming the need for the "construction of a Marxist party based on the working class and armed with the finest and latest [What are the latest?—J.H.] weapons from the arsenal of Marxism," the Committee declares:

In conclusion we state that such a policy does not inhibit the struggle for the defence of Cuba against imperialist attack, nor does it prevent episodic alliances with the Castroite forces in the struggle against the latifundists. On the contrary, it would immensely facilitate the tasks of defending Cuba and defeating landlordism.

The defense of Cuba and Castro against imperialism is a *tactic*. Our strategy remains the overthrow of capitalism and the setting up of a real workers' state with *real* workers' power. This task still remains to be done in Cuba.

Should we begin with the end and work back through this

tangle? "A real workers' state." Then some kind of workers' state now exists in Cuba and the task is to make it "real." But that means capitalism has been overthrown. Our authors scramble to the alert. "That's not what we mean!!" All right, let's skip it and take a look at how your reduction of the defense of the Cuban revolution from a principle to a "tactic" has worked out.

Before their policy had crystallized into a hardened sectarian dogma of refusing to recognize the victories of the Cuban revolution, the British comrades organized a demonstration in behalf of Cuba that brought immediate response in Havana. The papers there gave it top-bannerline coverage and reproduced big photos of the demonstrators with their placards. This action undertaken by the SLL proved to be only a flash in the pan. In place of sustained action, a literary campaign was substituted. Perhaps the SLL was too weak and uninfluential to do more. But the literary campaign has to be read to be believed. Utilizing as object lessons what it took to be the crimes and betrayals of the Castro government, it sought to provide, apparently, a healthy offset to the supposed deviations of the SWP. The theme of this educational material was "Cuba Sí, Humbug No." This was the headline over what was passed off as a fundamental contribution, setting the tone and line of the press for the ensuing period. This key article took us everywhere in the world—to Siberia and Bolivia, through time and space—everywhere but Cuba. As I noted elsewhere, some of the American defenders of the Cuban revolution thought that a typographical error was involved and that the title was really intended to read, "Humbug Sí, Cuba No."

As late as a year or so ago, the SLL might possibly have recovered from the heavy penalties that were being paid for its ultimatistic abstentionist course. But they took a step that could scarcely be better conceived to block recovery of lost ground. They turned down an invitation from the Cuban embassy to attend a reception. This rejection was couched in the form of an ultimatum and put in such an insulting way as to signify that the occasion was being utilized to slam all doors and to hell with any Cubans, Trotskyist-minded or otherwise, who might be extending a hand in their direction. The excuse for this ultimatum was a report that appeared in some South American newspapers of an attack on the Cuban Trotskyists (members of the Posadas group) which Guevara made at Punta del Este in the summer of 1961. The SLL did not inquire at the Cuban embassy as to the accuracy of the newspaper account. It did not then inquire—if the account had turned out to be accurate—whether Guevara would still stand on these remarks.[2]

It did not even leave open the possibility that there might be differences among the Cubans over the question of Trotskyism and that the opening of a door in Britain might be due to pressure in our direction. The National Committee of the SLL acted as if by reflex—not to explore, but to slam the door. That's what openings are for, ain't they?

Later, in response to suggestions from the SWP, the leaders of the SLL organized a campaign for aid to Cuba. This was very tardy, but it still might have opened some possibilities if it had been accompanied by a positive turn in the SLL press. This was not to be so. The campaign itself was conceived and executed in such unilateral, isolated fashion that not even the Cubans were consulted, despite the talk about "episodic alliances with the Castroite forces." Thus the SLL campaigned for "food" for Cuba, without coordinating the campaign with the international one launched in consultation with the Cubans for "medicines." The result was that the SLL got its reply to the diplomatic note that had been sent the Cuban embassy: disavowal of the isolated, unilateral SLL campaign for "food." The Cubans did not go for the "*tactic*" of the SLL. The SLL leaders felt, in consequence, that they had no choice but to abandon their campaign. In this they were wise to recognize the reality: they had proved incapable in Britain of either leading or inspiring so much as a modest concrete campaign to aid the Cuban revolution. Thus a departure from the *principle* of defending Cuba and Castro against

---

2. On one occasion, Guevara attacked the newspaper of the Cuban Trotskyists over TV. News of this attack was quickly disseminated, since there are many forces, including Stalinist-minded, who are interested in driving a wedge between the Cuban revolution and Trotskyism. Only months later did we learn accidentally that on TV, the very next night after this episode, Guevara apologized to the "Trotskyist comrades" for the misrepresentation of their views and said that he had been mistaken in his interpretation of what they had said. Even at Punta del Este, Guevara met with leading representatives of the Posadas group, and they gave banner lines to this interview, paying no attention to the alleged attack on them, as if this were inconsequential or had been garbled by the reporter who included it in his dispatch. Experiences of this kind taught us quite early in the Cuban revolution how cautiously any reports in this area must be handled. Such considerations, of course, are meaningless to Healy. They don't show up in the crystal ball he reads in London.

imperialism—the principle of unconditional defense—had been paid for to the damage of the SLL as well as the Cuban revolution.

The SLL defense efforts were, consequently, reduced to their press. But here any campaigning was not only cut down in size, it was made to carefully reflect their theoretical concept of the Cuban revolution. To read the *Newsletter* on Cuba is like exploring an empty vinegar barrel. Not much there and not very enticing.

How the centering of attention on the texts of Marxism, coupled with refusal to admit and to weigh facts, can separate a leadership from some of the main realities of world politics can be seen in vivid fashion by following the pages of the *Newsletter*. We need not go far back in the file; some fresh examples are available for study.

As American imperialism began its preparations for the naval blockade, the *Newsletter* handled the news in perfunctory fashion. The issue of September 8 reports the new aggression planned and correctly calls for "assistance of the Cuban people in every way possible." However, the temptation to spoil this with a jibe is irresistable: "The true friends of the Cuban Revolution are not the 'radical tourists' flying back and forth across the Caribbean, but the working class movement throughout the world." Among the "radical tourists" happen to be revolutionists from the working-class movement all over the world, especially Latin America, for Havana has become a kind of revolutionary crossroads of the world. The SLL leaders, of course, can be excused for not knowing this since it is within the realm of "facts" about Cuba; moreover, they are not inclined to be "radical tourists," especially in a hot place like Cuba.

In the September 15 issue Cuba gets a few inches on page 3. It seems that the "U.S. State Department has been pressing other governments, including the British [that's alert reporting—J.H.], to stop ships from taking goods to and from Cuba, in an effort to tighten the stranglehold of their economic blockade of the island." This brief item gets the very correct but very perfunctory headline: "Labour must counter U.S. Cuban plans." Labor must, of course, but the *Newsletter* is not much excited about it. Even the heavy pressure for the U.S. State Department on the Macmillan government fails to kick off a sharp reaction in the phlegmatic editor. Has this counterrevolutionary pressure, then, no meaning for British politics? Is the Labour Party to draw no lessons from the despicable role played by the Macmillan government in the Cuban crisis? Are the Labour Party ranks supposed to regard complacently how the bureaucrats knuckled under?

The September 22 issue gave Cuba a real break: a signed front page story—but modestly at the bottom. "Any resemblance between a real war danger and the present crisis in Cuban-American relations must be seen as pure coincidence." The analyst presents his reading of the situation: "The U.S. government, and Kennedy in particular, are still smarting from the Bay of Pigs fiasco last year. Moreover this is election year in the U.S. and Kennedy knows only too well that the only way to stay in the White House is by staying out of Cuba—and concentrating on Berlin."

The author correctly notes that "the State Department has a long-term plan whose sinister implications are becoming clearer every day. It hopes to starve Cuba into submission by intensifying the blockade and threatening sanctions against West European nations who continue to trade with and aid the Cuban nation." These excellent sentences are, however, completely spoiled by the ultraleft prescription which is proferred to the Castro government: "Any attempt to establish normal relations with the U.S. government would undermine the Cuban liberation movement irretrievably in the eyes of the Latin-American masses." The headline for this illuminating article is "Cuba: hot air and wine."

The commentator who wrote this, Michael Banda, is not to blame. He is only very faithfully and very logically applying the line developed by the National Committee of the SLL, giving a practical demonstration of how thoroughly steeped he is in its method of thinking.

The September 29 issue of the *Newsletter* apparently did not consider the continuation of Kennedy's new aggressive moves to be newsworthy despite the mounting world tension. The editors have their own way of gauging the importance of "the facts"; and, as we have seen, this does not necessarily coincide with the views of the rest of the world or even anyone else.

The October 6 issue continues to rate the Cuban revolution and its defense as unnewsworthy. Perhaps it was just as well.

In the October 13 issue, Cuba managed to fight its way onto page 2. Someone, obviously bored with the assignment, notes that "The past few weeks have seen a stepping up of the U.S. efforts to tighten the economic stranglehold on Cuba." It appears that the

State Department is going to place a naval blockade on Cuba. The British government may get involved in this, but it's not too clear from the article just how. The abstract formulas about the vital need for "assistance from the International Labour movement" are repeated. Finally we come to the section where we must bare our flesh to the needle. The plunger is pushed to the bottom. We are inoculated against the danger of placing the slightest confidence—not in the British, but in the Cuban government.

> The aid, both military and economic, which the Cubans have received from the USSR, has enabled them to defy the attacks of U.S. big business. But increased dependence on these supplies carried with it the danger of political pressure from Khrushchev for more "responsible" policies to be followed.
>
> The UN speech of Cuba's President Dorticos is a warning of the possibility of such moves. Dr. Dorticos declared his government had no intention of spreading revolution to the South American mainland, or of taking action against the U.S. naval base at Guantanamo.

In the following issue, October 20, Cuba did pretty well in the *Newsletter*. A column on the front page noted that the pressure was being stepped up, a Cuban patrol boat having been sunk "by a large exile ship." The main danger was correctly seen to be "the strength of American imperialism," not the "small groups of counter-revolutionary exiles." Another danger was well handled by the author, Eric Neilson; that is, the readiness of the Soviet bureaucracy to compromise with the American imperialists. With almost prophetic insight the author wrote probably the two best paragraphs in many an issue of the paper:

> This compromise could mean that Khrushchev is considering cutting off the supply of arms to Cuba, arms vital to the defence of that country against U.S. imperialism.
>
> Any such compromise must be firmly opposed by all those who claim to support the Cuban revolution against the reactionary forces which now threaten it.

When Kennedy had completed the mobilization of troops for invasion of Cuba, stationed the fleet in the Caribbean, put bombers in the air carrying nuclear weapons, and readied rockets and submarines for the attack, he issued his ultimatum to the Soviet government. The world teetered at the edge of nuclear destruction. For once the National Committee of the SLL decided that the facts outweighed their texts. Reality broke into the columns of the *Newsletter*. The top headline in the October 27 issue was awarded to Cuba. "SAY *NO* TO YANKEE WAR." A map even was printed on the front page showing that there is an island named Cuba and that it lies off the tip of Florida and between the Bahamas and Jamaica, which are of special interest to British readers.

Even more, a big section of page 2 was used to reprint extracts from the speech by President Dorticos about which readers of the *Newsletter* had been warned in the October 13 issue. Now the *Newsletter*, veering completely around, praised what Dr. Dorticos had said: "This very clearly exposes the preparations for war which have now entered a stage of open and undisguised aggression not only against Cuba but against the Soviet Union."

In the main article Gerry Healy became so enthusiastic over the Cuban revolution that he ventured to say these welcome words:

> The Cuban revolution is a continuation of the great colonial revolution. Its defence cannot be organized within the framework of "co-existence with world imperialism."
>
> To defend the Soviet Union is to fight for the extension of the revolution which gave rise to it in the first place.
>
> The Cuban revolution is just such a revolution. That is why U.S. imperialism wants to destroy it, and in doing so has now decided to attack the Soviet Union itself.

Splendidly stated! The existence of a workers' state in Cuba, extending the October revolution into Latin America, is an unbearable challenge to U.S. imperialism. That is why Wall Street is willing to risk nuclear war to crush it.

You would never know it from the pages of the *Newsletter*, since such facts are of little concern to them, but the British working people acquitted themselves well in this emergency. Hundreds of spontaneous and hastily organized demonstrations flared up throughout Britain. These became a significant factor in causing Kennedy to hesitate in reaching for the red telephone.

This impressive response of the British working people to the crisis over Cuba was a convincing demonstration that they are not nearly so insular in their outlook as the National Committee of the SLL. Our "Leninists" were so far behind events that they could not even be said to be "tail-ending." To be a tail-ender you at least have to run after someone who does something or try to catch up with actions that are occurring. The National Committee of the SLL was dreaming about a different world than this one.

To close this gruesome chapter, we place in evidence the November 3 issue of the *Newsletter*. The Cuban crisis still rates a prominent place but the leaders of the SLL have obviously relaxed. The opening sentence of the front-page article by Gerry Healy reads: "The defence of the Cuban revolution against U.S. imperialism is now the acid test for the world Trotskyist movement."

In a newspaper addressed to the British workers, it may be taken as eccentric to open the main article with a sentence of such narrow focus. Actually the audience which Healy specifies is too broad. It would have been sufficient to cite the National Committee of the SLL. That's the public Healy has in mind anyway, isn't it? This strange article does not go after British imperialism for the treacherous role it played in the crisis. Instead it attempts to illustrate the thesis that "Cuba is another grim warning of the predominantly reactionary nature of the Soviet bureaucracy and its politics." Much of the article is a plodding repetition of the basic Trotskyist explanation of the nature of this bureaucracy and its opposition to the revolution. When he gets to his point, however, on how the Cuban situation illustrates his abstractions, the author runs into trouble. "In the case of Cuba, Khrushchev has provided Castro and his people with food supplies although in inadequate quantities." On this, Healy's view of the situation is a little awry. Some of the shortages faced by the Cubans, such as pork and lard, could probably not be made up in the Soviet Union. In general the poor people in Cuba are eating better than in Batista's time, the children are certainly, and hunger is not the main problem as of now. Where the Soviet role has been decisive is in supplying oil, tools, vehicles, machinery, and military goods. The Cuban cause is very popular throughout the Soviet bloc, and it is a considerable error to think that quite substantial aid has not been given.

However, Healy rests his case not on this but something rather unexpected:

The establishment of rocket bases in Cuba could not possibly defend the Cuban revolution. This can only be done in the immediate future by the struggle to win over the solidarity of the American working class and to extend the revolution in Latin America.

Of course the Cuban government had every right to accept these rocket bases and sign such agreements as it wished with the Soviet Union.

But it was most inadvisable that it should have exercised this right by permitting Khrushchev to place under the control of Russian technicians rocket bases which were plain for all to see on the small island.[3]

Having a right and exercising it are two different things. One does not necessarily follow from the other.

Like the hero in the novel by Victor Hugo, Healy deserves to be decorated for that sentence about winning the solidarity of the American working class and extending the revolution into Latin America. And then summarily shot for his advice to the Cubans: "Having a right and exercising it are two different things. One does not necessarily follow from the other." If he objects to such a harsh penalty, the military court can well reply: "Having a right to advise the Cubans and exercising it are two different things. One does not necessarily follow from the other." We can hear Healy's immortal reply as he refuses a blindfold: "What kind of right is it if you can't exercise it?"

The irony of his advice is that only a few weeks before, the ultraleft spurs were being dug into Dorticos for declaring that his government had no intention of exporting revolution or of taking action against the U.S. naval base at Guantanamo. A couple of weeks before that, the *Newsletter* shook its finger warningly against the Cubans considering "any attempt to establish normal relations with the U.S. government." And only two issues before Healy's article, in the number that went to press on the eve of Kennedy's ultimatum, the *Newsletter* warned that Khrushchev might cut off Cuba's supply of arms, "arms vital to the defence of that country against U.S. imperialism." The *Newsletter* alerted its readers to the evident dangers in that quarter: "Any such compromise must be firmly opposed by all those . . . ," etc., etc. Apparently Gerry Healy didn't get around to reading the column on Cuba that week. Or perhaps by "arms vital to the defence of that country against U.S. imperialism," with its stockpiles of nuclear "deterrents," the *Newsletter* had something only quantitative in mind, like 40,000 tons of bows and arrows and flint

---

3. How microscopic does Healy think the island is? The U.S. resorted to U-2 spy planes and the violation of Cuban air space to discover them.

tomahawks. Thus the Kremlin betrayed by sending defensive equipment of too superior a quality.

Perhaps Healy is right, but the fact that the White House chose the rocket bases as the excuse for pushing to the brink of nuclear war was partly accidental. Before that they obviously weighed seizing on Soviet aid in building a fishing port as a cause for going to war. As I write this, the stationing in Cuba of planes capable of carrying bombs is the pretext for maintaining the blockade. If this today, then tomorrow in a new crisis something else. In every case it will be an instance in which the Cuban government exercises its sovereign rights. The real reason, of course, is that Cuba is a workers' state, a fact which Healy cannot bring himself to admit. U.S. imperialism, more realistically, has recognized its existence and consciously and calculatingly made it a major policy to end this standing affront, challenge, and threat to the capitalist system. If a plausible pretext is lacking, one will be manufactured. The facts are absolutely conclusive on that.

Healy's position is a concession to the pacifist view: don't provoke the warmonger! As if they are not always provoked by their intended victims, if for no other reason than by their weakness.

The major lesson to be drawn from this is that in an acid test what looked like 24-carat ultraleftism can reveal some surprising opportunist streaks.

## Position of the French Section of the IC

The leading comrades of the French section of the International Committee share with the National Committee of the SLL the view that Cuba is not a workers' state. They differ on two fundamental points, however. Unlike the British comrades, they believe that dual power exists in Cuba; and they hold that the Castro regime constitutes a workers' and peasants' government. Moreover, in contrast to the SLL's top leaders, they recognize the logic which has compelled the majority of the world Trotskyist movement to consider Cuba to be a workers' state. Their criticism is not against the justifiability of extending to Cuba the same basic approach that was used in the case of China, Yugoslavia, and the East European countries. What they maintain is that since Cuba is not a workers' state—according to their estimate—something must have been wrong in the preceding position. We must, therefore, dump all the work done up to now in estimating the character of the state in China, Yugoslavia, and Eastern Europe and start over again. What they propose as a substitute, they have only intimated; perhaps they will soon offer us something more substantial.

In a certain sense they have thus proceeded in a more sophisticated and methodical way than the National Committee of the SLL. They are prepared to acknowledge most of the facts which the British comrades consider to be an unbearable or indecent sight. They are willing to admit the consistency of the workers' state position. Thus they rectify the most repelling crudities of the SLL position. With the same sharp eye for avoiding what is grossly absurd, they take what they consider to be valid in the views of their allies—that Cuba is not a workers' state—and insist that it be carried to its obviously necessary conclusion; namely, revision of the hard-won theory of the world Trotskyist movement back to 1948 and earlier. They state this quite frankly:

> And we rejoice that the discusssion on Cuba inevitably entails return-ing to this former discussion and the elaboration of a new analysis of the nature of the buffer states, of Yugoslavia and China, questions on which we are "revisionists" insofar as—the discussion on Cuba demonstrates it—these comrades today, in basing themselves on the characterizations adopted in 1948, at times place in question the very principles that served as the foundation structure of our international movement.

We, for our part, acknowledge that this methodology is inher-ently superior to that of the National Committee of the SLL, since it recognizes in principle the preeminence of reality; and we will add that the British comrades might profitably study the coher-ence and lucidity with which their French allies argue their case in "Draft Report on the Cuban Revolution." It is regrettable that the authors of the "Trotskyism Betrayed" document chose to brush this contribution rudely aside, not even referring to it, still less discussing its views in their opus. However, the French comrades may, with good reason, have felt grateful for this lack of consideration.

As I see it, the position developed in the "Draft Report" rests on four main errors: (1) Substitution of "Workers' and Peasants' Government" for "Workers' State"; (2) refusal to recognize a qualitative change in the character of the state in Cuba; (3) misunderstanding of the main criteria used in characterizing the buffer states; (4) abuse of an analogy with the Spanish revolution of 1936-39. I will consider these in order.

The authors of the "Draft Report" agree that the breakup of the coalition government in Cuba in July 1959 marked a change of decisive character in the regime; it was qualitative. This position, in my opinion, is unassailable. The turn proved to be an essential link in the chain of Cuban events. The new regime that replaced the coalition undertook a series of measures directed against the interests of the landlords, native capitalists, and imperialists, that clearly advanced the class interests of the Cuban *campesinos* and workers. These measures took effect in all fields, economic, social, and political. Their outstanding characteristic was disarmament of the bourgeoisie and armament of the masses. Deep inroads were thus made in the old state structure. The correct label for such a government is *workers' and peasants'*, a petty-bourgeois formation foreseen long ago by Marxists. Our Transitional Program noted the possibility of such governments appearing in our epoch, as well as the possibility of their going much "further" than they originally intended. When the Cuban workers' and peasants' government, in reply to the aggression of U.S. imperialism, expropriated landlord and capitalist properties on a major scale, in September-October 1960, then instituted a planned economy and completed the destruction of the old state apparatus, it obviously went beyond anything foreseen in any of the theoretical or programmatic writings of Marxism in the period before World War II, including the writings of Trotsky. Whatever label may be put on the resulting state, we are up against a hard fact which Marxism must account for on pain of confessing incapacity to deal with reality. If our opponents will concede for the moment that what we have before us is a workers' state of some kind or other, then what is new in life, and what must therefore be reflected in theory, is that a workers' and peasants' government—that is, a petty-bourgeois government—can go so far as to establish a workers' state.[4]

---

4. The conditions under which this has occurred, together with the limitations of the resulting workers' states, that is, their "deformation," have been discussed concretely in the cases of the buffer countries, Yugoslavia, and China. The conditions which made possible a similar development in Cuba have been discussed, but it is still too early to draw final conclusions on the limitations. As for what the particular pattern of

This is the precise point which the authors of "Draft Report" balk at. And recognizing very clearly that this conclusion cannot be avoided in view of the fact that it involves the same principle operative in China, Yugoslavia, and even Eastern Europe, they very logically extend their negative position backward to include those cases.

By doing so, however, they at once involve themselves in a self-contradictory stand. They insist—properly so—on "underlining the importance of the rupture of the coalition between Castro and the bourgeois figures installed in the government after the flight of Batista." This qualitative political change marked the appearance of a new kind of government. On the other hand they underline the importance of *not* recognizing any qualitative change in the economy or the state resting on that economy at any point up to now in Cuba.

It requires considerable dexterity to justify this self-contradictory stand. To the natural question that at once arises—"What kind of state exists, then, in Cuba?"—they offer an ingenious answer. If it is not a workers' state, then it must be a capitalist state. Since this is scarcely demonstrable, the authors of "Draft Report" maintain that what we have before us is a "broken-down, decomposed, phantom bourgeois state, controlled by the group of men around Castro" ("un état bourgeois, délabré,

---

these overturns of capitalism signifies for the general necessity in our epoch of constructing a revolutionary socialist International, this question was raised at the time of the discussion over the buffer countries—most sharply, if I remember correctly, by leading comrades in the SWP. The general conclusions drawn at that time remain completely valid. First of all, it is far easier for the proletariat to come to power in a backward country than in an imperialist center. This was well understood by the Bolsheviks, but it is still truer today. The relative decline of world capitalism in relation to the rise of the Soviet Union, plus the enormous revolutionary ferment on a global scale, has made the grip of capitalism much weaker in the backward areas than it was even a few decades ago. Experience has demonstrated that forces which are socialist-minded but not Bolshevik can come to power and undertake a series of measures that in certain circumstances go so far as to transcend private capitalism, providing the base for a workers' state. Such a state, however, testifies to its specific origin  by deviating from the Leninist norms. These new possibilities, however, have not eliminated the need for revolutionary socialist parties. What they really demonstrate is the richness of revolutionary openings and therefore the bright perspective facing revolution-

décomposé, fantomatique, controlé par le groupe d'hommes qui entourent Castro").

What import this novelty has for Marxist theory is not discussed in "Draft Report." Perhaps the authors will return later to the profound meaning which phantom bourgeois states hold for our epoch. Meanwhile we are inclined to jog along with what the Castro government has succeeded in accomplishing, having at its control such a phantom in Cuba.

There might be dialecticians who would contend that if you break down and decompose something until nothing but the ghost remains, it is no longer the same, having really undergone a qualitative change. The authors of the "Draft Report," to forestall such a criticism, argue that alongside Castro can be found the "elements of workers' power," still appealing to the same leadership but "in reality always increasing their pressure toward more radical measures." As in Spain in 1936-37, the "Draft Report" contends, dual power exists in Cuba.

Even if this were so, we would still be left with the phantom bourgeois state, this formless plasma of the spirit world. If, as materialists, we eliminate this wraith from consideration we are left with only a "Workers' and Peasants' Government" to which the "Draft Report" thus assigns the functions of a state. And this despite their recognition that it is a "serious error in method to

---

ary socialism in these areas. Could anything be more instructive than the turn of the Castro leadership towards Marxism-Leninism in the very course of revolution and its acknowledgment of the need for a revolutionary socialist party?

Likewise valid is the conclusion drawn in the 1948 discussion of the absolute necessity for construction of revolutionary socialist parties in the advanced capitalist countries. In fact experience would seem to indicate that the difficulty of coming to power in the imperialist centers has increased if anything since the time of the Bolsheviks. This is due not solely to the perfidious role of the Stalinist, Social Democratic, and trade union bureaucracies, but also to the lessons learned by the bourgeoisie in the defeats they have suffered. Consequently, to win in the imperialist centers, construction of a revolutionary socialist party has become even more imperative. None of this, of course, is of much concern to the ultraleft sectarians, whose politics consists of little more than parrot-like repetition of a stock of revolutionary phrases. To repeat these phrases in Cuba with a semblance of plausibility, they are forced to deny reality. In a country like Britain they make up for this by repeating them thrice.

confound the nature of the state and the nature of the government."

We come now to the second error, which, of course, flows from the first one. If Cuba is now a workers' state, when did the qualitative change occur? In the SWP, the majority view is that the date was fixed by the massive nationalizations. This was the point of qualitative change. But the authors of the "Draft Report," holding that no qualitative change has occurred, are compelled to dispose of all possible dates. Those involving power are rejected on various grounds without specifying the real one, which is that revolutionary socialists could not in advance grant political confidence to the Castro leadership in view of the limitations of its declared program. Fundamental economic criteria are likewise rejected, two grounds being advanced for this: (1) they are not sufficient in themselves; (2) even if they are sufficient in themselves this is true only if they are operative over a long period of time. These arguments really beg the question. Implied in them is the premise that the most drastic overturn of an economy has no qualitative meaning in itself, only a quantitative one. The admission that a long period of time would ultimately bring qualitative considerations to bear alters nothing in the hidden premise, since it is not specified what economic measures, accumulating bit by bit, would lead to the qualitative change, nor what would constitute, *on the economic level*, the point of decisive change. Thus the protagonists of this view are left without a program specifying what they demand in Cuba in the economic sphere that would mark the clear emergence of a workers' state. All their demands are of a political character, involving the nature of the power, the lack of institutions of proletarian democracy such as workers' councils, etc. Consequently they end up like the National Committee of the SLL and the minority in the SWP, with a mere political definition of the workers' state. To justify this in Marxist theory they are forced to fall back to the generalized *norms* stated by Lenin before further concretization was made possible by study of the reality in a degenerated workers' state.

This completely unhistorical approach calls for its payment in the history of our movement. It forces our French comrades to demand complete revision of our position on the series of deformed workers' states. They argue that the destruction of the capitalist economy, the nationalization of the key sectors of industry, and the introduction of planned economy were not sufficient to prove that the bourgeois state had been smashed and that it had been displaced by a workers' state. They contend that two more essential criteria must be added:

We think that it is precisely here that one of the weaknesses of our analysis of 1948 becomes evident, and we will return to this later. However, undeniably, in the case of the European buffer countries, the criterion of "nationalization" is inseparable from the criterion "cultural assimilation" with a "degenerated workers' state": it is because the bonapartist state of the buffer countries is the instrument of the bureaucracy of a degenerated workers' state that the Trotskyists were able to consider it as a deformed workers' state, and the criterion "nationalization and planning" is not, by itself, sufficient.

Precisely what is meant by "cultural assimilation" is not indicated. Do they mean "structural" assimilation? But that is just a condensed way of saying expropriation of the capitalists, nationalization, and planning. Perhaps by "cultural" assimilation they mean liquidation of independent political trends, a process brought to its culmination in the purge trials of 1949 and again in the suppression of the Hungarian uprising in 1956? Or is it something as vague as a phantom bourgeois state?

On the other point, the authors of the "Draft Report" are, quite logically from their point of view, adding a political criterion to those we used in 1948; and, just as logically, making it *the decisive criterion*; "it is because the bonapartist state of the buffer countries is the instrument of the bureaucracy . . . ," they say. Not so. We rejected the criterion of power in 1948 since it would have signified that we considered the buffer countries to be workers' states *because* of Stalinism and not *in spite of it*. Otherwise we would have ended in a position inconsistent with our position on the Soviet Union itself. We specified that labeling the buffer countries as workers' states did not thereby imply political confidence in the bureaucracy. We opposed its bureaucratic measures. We conceded absolutely nothing to Stalinism.

Had the criteria now advocated by the authors of the "Draft Report" been adopted, what slippery footing we would have found! For example, so long as the Tito leadership remained a docile instrument, we would have had to call Yugoslavia a workers' state. When it fought for political independence and broke diplomatic relations, thus no longer serving as the "instrument" of the Soviet bureaucracy, we would have had to switch and say: "Sorry, but a bourgeois phantom state is again haunting

Yugoslavia." And when Yugoslavia was able to resume relations, we would have had to report: "Thank God, that ghost has been laid again."

As for China—that would have been a spiritualist's paradise. When is a phantom not a phantom? Can you have half phantoms and quarter phantoms and so on ad infinitum?

The big advantage in such juggling of criteria, of course, is that you can avoid calling Cuba a workers' state. I would agree that in some instances, at least, the authors of the "Draft Report" hit the nail on the head with their observation: "The disagreements go beyond words. It is in fact in setting up a conception of the Cuban Revolution as a whole that each one chooses a definition which, at bottom, epitomizes his politics." Of course, to maintain their novel position, the French comrades have to prove that no Soviet "cultural assimilation" has occurred in Cuba and that the Castro regime is not an "instrument of the bureaucracy of a degenerated workers' state." Unfortunately, here our authors, seeking to establish a close analogy with the Spanish revolution, depart from their admirable consistency and try to prove that the Castro government has gone a long way in succumbing to Stalinism; that is, in taking the road to a workers' state, according to the criteria they now advance.

The fourth major error in the "Draft Report" is a concession to the Healy-Slaughter school of thought which can scarcely win our praise. For some obscure reason the French comrades insist on looking at Cuba primarily through the dark glasses of the defeated Spanish revolution. An analogy has its uses but it inevitably breaks down if carried too far. Since the limitations of the analogy are not stated by the authors we are forced to determine them ourselves.

First of all, how can the countries themselves and the major situations confronting them be compared with much meaning? A key question in Spain was the colonies. The failure of the republican government to grant freedom to the Moroccans was more decisive in strengthening Franco than the military aid he received from fascist Italy and Nazi Germany. Cuba, on the other hand, belongs to the colonial world and has just won freedom from an imperialist power. The situation is not one of a civil war involving a fascist threat but of an attempt by imperialism to crush a workers' state and restore colonial rule.

The analogy between the counterrevolutionary forces is thus not very close. In Spain, Franco was fighting for power. In Cuba, the native Franco, Batista, has been overthrown and the native counterrevolutionaries, as the Cubans have scornfully said many times, could be handled by the children if it were not for the U.S.

Cuba has a revolutionary-minded leadership, which the Spanish workers and peasants lacked. This leadership came to power in revolutionary struggle, proving itself in action. It demonstrated that it had drawn correct lessons from the experiences in Guatemala and Bolivia and that it was capable of learning from the experience of the Chinese revolution. Finally, this leadership has proved its awareness of the duality of the Soviet bureaucracy as a source of material aid and as a source of political danger. When such a leadership proclaims that it has become "Marxist-Leninist," its words must be taken with the utmost seriousness even though it may not yet measure up to our norms.

To this we must add that the world setting today is completely different from what it was in 1936-39. In place of the entrenchment of European fascism, the Soviet Union has consolidated a position as one of the two primary world powers. The Soviet economic structure has been extended deep into Europe. China has become a workers' state. The colonial revolution has brought hundreds of millions to their feet. De-Stalinization has altered the capacity of the bureaucracy to impose its will in flagrant fashion as in the thirties. The analogy breaks down here especially in leaving out of account such experiences as the rebellion of the Yugoslav CP, the uprising in East Germany, the attempted political revolution in Hungary, and the current differences between the Russian and Chinese CPs. Where does the parallel to the breakup of Stalinism exist in the Spanish situation? The revolutionary stream today is not running in the direction of Stalinism. In all of Latin America to one degree or another the Communist parties are in deep crisis over the Cuban revolution—above all in Cuba. All these differences in conditions point unquestionably to the validity of the conclusion that the outcome of the revolution in Cuba is far more promising politically than it was in Spain.

An analogy cannot substitute for analysis of reality itself. It is a gross error in methodology to conclude that because the Spanish Republic was not a workers' state, *therefore* Cuba is not. To determine the general characteristics of the Cuban or any other revolution we must begin by considering it individually; that is, ascertain the facts; for, as we learn from Hegel, the individual is a combination and manifestation of the general. On doing this, we see at once that the analogy between the Spanish and Cuban revolutions is destroyed by the different outcomes of the two, which in turn confirms that different means were operative in the two revolutions. The Spanish revolution was defeated for internal reasons, primarily the counterrevolutionary role of Stalinism. The Cuban revolution was victorious, sealing its victory in the establishment of a workers' state. A revolutionist must be able to tell the difference between victory and defeat! The immediate future of this workers' state does not hinge on the outcome of a civil war in the face of native fascism, but on successful resistance to the diplomatic, economic, and military aggression of a foreign imperialist power. Is that not so? For additional light on how best to meet this threat facing Cuba, the Spanish revolution offers little. We must turn to other analogies such as the comparison with the Russian workers' state when it was battling imperialist intervention.

As for the subsidiary points in "Draft Report," these can be safely left aside. There is much quibbling about "nationalizations" in general, for instance, which is beside the point in considering the specific nationalizations in Cuba. Undue credit is given Miró Cardona for actions taken while he was in government and their real import is missed. Other errors of this kind could be cited. A major one, the alleged take-over of Castro's forces by the Cuban Communist Party, has been sufficiently exploded by events. The meaning of the attacks on the Cuban Trotskyists is exaggerated and placed at the wrong door, besides not being properly balanced against the ideological influence which Trotskyism exercises in a significant sector among the Cuban revolutionary vanguard.

The accusation that the appreciation of Cuba as a workers' state has led the SWP to adopt "centrist, opportunist and liquidationist positions" is a premature announcement of our death. It also displays a rather disturbing lack of appreciation of the political logic flowing from the conclusion that a workers' state has been established under a non-Stalinist leadership. This has opened up fresh and most encouraging perspectives for party building in both Latin America and the United States, although it has also brought some new and difficult tactical problems. The first experiences in this respect have already been favorably recorded both by the SWP and the Latin American Trotskyists. If our French comrades are doubtful about the favorable reports on what has been gained in the main bastion of world imperialism, perhaps they will listen with more open minds to what our comrades in Latin America have to say about their experiences. These are much more pertinent to the discussion on the Cuban revolution than the highly questionable analogy with Spain. The Latin American Trotskyist view may also provide a good antidote for the ill-considered policy that would have us undo everything since 1940.

## Cuba and Reunification

I have tried to demonstrate that the National Committee of the SLL proceeds in the Cuban revolution from assumptions hardened into dogmas; that is, they brush aside or disregard facts that cannot be fitted into their preconceived framework and throw out of focus those that do seem to exemplify their preconceptions. Elevated into a principle, this subjective approach turns everything upside down—the Notion is made supreme over the mundane world of material events. We are not surprised that the same method is applied to the problem of reunifying the world Trotskyist movement. Nor are we surprised that the SLL leaders even take pride in their methodological consistency: "The SWP criticism of the SLL starts from the Cuban revolution," they observe. "In doing so, it reveals its whole mistaken method. We must begin from the need to establish Leninist parties in every country, and in the first place to defeat revisionism."

Let us pause a moment right there. We are given a blueprint in which the subjective side is listed first; moreover, not program in general but the "defeat" of a challenge to the program; still further, a specific variety of challenge—"revisionism," by which they mean revisionism in the opportunist direction, not the ultraleft. (The SLL leaders seem to work from a revised copy of the general blueprint which conveniently leaves out the need to defeat ultraleftism.) Next in order comes general application of the general blueprint for establishment of "Leninist parties" in "every country." (Granting them the benefit of the doubt, we assume that they mean concretely by this the construction of the world party of the socialist revolution, the Fourth International.) Only after descending this ladder do we come to the need to establish the concrete development of the revolution, which in reality must constitute the foundation for everything else in Cuba.

This methodology is rigorously applied even in the structure of the SLL manifesto, "Trotskyism Betrayed." The Cuban revolution, which constitutes the acid objective test for every tendency that proclaims itself to be revolutionary, is subordinated and relegated to the mere level of one example among many, an example of minor importance in view of Cuba's relative economic weight in the world. On the other hand, the struggle against revisionism, as interpreted by the leaders of the SLL, is given first place in the document both qualitatively and quantitatively. To justify putting the real problems that face the world Trotskyist movement upside down in this way, it is necessary to magnify the danger of "revisionism" in direct proportion to the reduction of the importance of the Cuban revolution. In turn this necessitates construction of a kind of demonology inside the world Trotskyist movement symmetrical to the Holy Scripture they make of Leninism. Disregarding or misinterpreting facts—in perfect parallel to their approach to Cuba—the SLL leaders picture the relationship between the IS and the IC as if absolutely nothing had changed since 1953. Well, not absolutely. The SLL leaders acknowledge that some change has occurred. As they see it, the differences have—deepened!

To prove this they would have to demonstrate that the IS, instead of satisfactorily clearing up the political differences that appeared to us to lie behind the organizational dispute of 1953-54, had developed them into a system or at least gone far down that road. It is promised that this will be done in the course of the projected discussion, but as yet little has been forthcoming beyond repetition of the points of difference of almost a decade ago.

A weakness of such glaring proportions in the SLL position requires compensation. Thus our dead-end factionalists picture the IS today as a monolithic group committed to revisionism but also committed to covering up its revisionism with diabolical cleverness. However, since theory and practice are intimately related, as we know from Lenin and others, it is possible to expose these revisionists. Hence every sentence written by anyone adhering to the IS is scrutinized under the microscope for evidence of the hidden revisionist concepts which must lie behind them. Not even leaflets put out by this or that group of comrades in this or that local situation escape the sleuths. A phrase torn from a leaflet distributed at the Renault plant in Paris in defense of Cuba against U.S. imperialism serves for elevation to front-page attention in the *Newsletter* in London, so hard-pressed are the leaders of the SLL to find evidence of the revisionism of the IS.

In this fantasia of ultraleft sectarianism, the course of the SWP takes on sinister meaning. The plain truth is that the SWP noted the facts concerning the declared positions of the IS on the important issues of the day. It noted its stand on the Hungarian uprising, on political revolution in the USSR, on de-Stalinization. It noted especially that the IS had assessed the main stages of the Cuban revolution in the same way as the SWP, the Canadians, and the Latin American Trotskyists; that is, by utilizing the basic conclusions made in the particular cases of the buffer countries, Yugoslavia, and China. Thus the real situation in the world Troskyist movement was that the political differences had been narrowing for some time and new grounds for common action had appeared. Most important of all, the IS in its majority and the IC in its majority had passed the acid test of the Cuban revolution. This opened a highly encouraging possibility for healing old wounds and reuniting the world Trotskyist movement on the most solid basis in its history. Whatever differences remained could surely be contained in a common organization under normal rules of democratic centralism. It was impossible to escape the conclusion that objectively the correct course was to press for reunification. The dispute over who was right in 1953-54 should not be permitted to stand in the way of joining forces in common assault on the problems of today. To proceed in a less responsible way would constitute a default in leadership. These simple, elementary considerations, which are ABC to Leninists, are given a different explanation by the leaders of the SLL.

According to their interpretation, the SWP, drifting into the wake of Pabloism, has decided to accept its revisionist views; that is, in the Cuban revolution, for instance, to acknowledge the facts and assess them in the light of the Trotskyist analysis of the buffer countries, Yugoslavia, and China. But this course, with its logical consequences, constitutes "betrayal" in the eyes of the SLL leaders. How is such a miserable end to be explained in the case of the SWP, which in its entire long history has never betrayed but always upheld the program of world Trotskyism? The explanation can only be that the SWP has "degenerated"; otherwise the SLL leaders are proved to be in error, and how can that be, since they *begin* with the need to defeat revisionism? Thus the SWP is crossed off; or virtually crossed off. That is why members of the SWP are now privileged to read in the factional documents of the SLL, perhaps with some astonishment, that their party is racked by a deep crisis, having made opportunist concessions to the imperialist environment, above all in its approach to the Cuban revolution. Not by accident, consequently, the SWP wants to unite with "Pabloism"; and that, as the SLL leaders see it, is the real explanation for the present efforts of reunification.

The logical concomitant to the SLL view that "revisionism"—as represented chiefly by the IS—constitutes the main danger facing the world Trotskyist movement, is that unification of the Fourth International is excluded. It is excluded until such time as the SLL view sweeps the ranks of the world Trotskyist movement and wins a majority. This confronts the SLL with a rather sticky contradiction. The elevation of anti-Pabloism into the First Commandment blocks unification. On the other hand, the desirability of winning a majority of Trotskyists to its views forces the SLL to consider how to gain a favorable hearing. Thus, while it bridles at the prospect of unification, it wants discussion. To get such a discussion, the SLL leaders are forced to recognize that the overwhelming sentiment in the world Trotskyist movement is in favor of unification. They must go even further and appear to bend with this sentiment. Hence the initiative they took in the IC to go to the IS and propose formation of a Parity Committee. In doing this the SLL leaders had to admit the eventual possibility of unification; more concretely they had to recognize the need and advisability of engaging in common actions with the IS, whatever may be the views of unification—early, delayed, or never at all.

In the process of reunifying the world Trotskyist movement, the proposal for a Parity Committee was objectively called for. The SWP did not look into what subjective motives the SLL leaders might have had in making this proposal, but weighed it on its objective merits, attempting in this case as in all others, to utilize the Marxist method of beginning with the reality of the situation. The IS responded in similar fashion to the initiative of the SLL leaders. Thus the Parity Committee was born.

No sooner did this committee meet, however, than the top leaders of the SLL began raising among IC adherents the ugly question of a new split. Naturally they point an accusing finger at the SWP and the IS. It is typical of dead-end factionalists to begin preparations for a split by raising the issue in the form of an accusation. In this case it also reflects the consistency with which the SLL leaders apply their methodology of inverted thinking.

The accusation has two variants: First, "the Pabloites consider their participation in the Parity Committee as a maneuver to obtain the support of the SWP." That is, they "are using the Parity Committee as a means to get closer to the SWP in order to drag it more rapidly into their orbit." The "Comment" containing this charge was "approved unanimously" by the National Committee of the SLL after the very first meeting of the Parity Committee. Why then did the SLL leaders open the way to such a deadly maneuver? Why did they propose a Parity Committee if it would help the Pabloites in their Machiavellian scheme to "get closer to the SWP"? Or did the well-meaning but bumbling leaders of the SLL fail to see such a possibility when they proposed the Parity Committee? They can scarcely argue that they failed to receive friendly notification. The SWP hailed the initiative as an important step toward reunification. The IS accepted it with the statement that it would participate in accordance with its declared aim of seeking early reunification.

Second, that the SWP has in mind maneuvering to present the discussion to be conducted under Parity Committee auspices "as one which promises early unification, but that this is prevented by the attitude of the SLL and its co-thinkers." Moreover that the SWP leadership is prevented from pressing for early reunification by its members and its past tradition; therefore it regards the Parity Committee proposals as a means of making an official approach to the Pabloites without appearing to break from the IC. However, according to this inside dope, the SWP has been preparing the political ground for such a break. Once again, then, why did the top leaders of the SLL obligingly facilitate such a dastardly move by proposing formation of the Parity Committee?

The fact is that most Trotskyists throughout the world, including the SWP and the IS, hailed the formation of the Parity Committee in good faith as a big step in the direction of reunification. Why the initiators of the Parity Committee should suddenly present it at its very launching as the vehicle of splitting maneuvers cooked up by the SWP and the IS is difficult to conceive, unless we are again being presented with an example of inverted thinking.

What is most ridiculous and unbecoming in this pose is that the SLL top leadership has been developing political positions which in the key case of the Cuban revolution are completely at variance with the rest of the world Trotskyist movement, including their closest allies in France. It is quite doubtful that they would seriously contend, in the light of the evidence, that their position on Cuba represents that of the majority of the IC. They are thus preparing the political ground for anything but an attempt to bring harmony among the adherents of the IC. On the contrary they have been placing the SWP, and anyone in the IC who thinks that the stand of the SWP on Cuba and unification has merit, under increasingly heavy fire. They have proclaimed that the SLL represents a separate tendency, one even that has declared war on all opponents to its positions. "The Socialist Labour League," they say, "is not prepared to go any part of the way with this revisionism, and will fight it to the end." And, "It is in the construction of the revolutionary party in the USA itself that the necessity of defeating the SWP leadership's revisionism is most urgent." In short, the political split has already been carried out by the SLL. As for relations between the SLL and the IS, it is superfluous to speak of a break, since the SLL leaders openly proclaim their hostility in the face of comradely overtures from the IS and are scarcely diplomatic about indicating that they visualize no reunification so far as they are concerned unless it takes place on the basis of their ultraleft sectarian views. But since this is unrealistic, what course remains open but to go it alone and to begin as early as possible to prepare the grounds for it?

It is in the light of such considerations that we must evaluate their language, which, while it scarcely displays much originality, carries not a small ballast of epithets, especially in relation to the SWP. We are offered the curious paradox of furious intensification of ultraleft factional war against all who hold the position that Cuba is a workers' state, the SWP in the first place; while, bending to the pressure for unity, Healy, with commendable civility, sits down with the representatives of the IS in the Parity Committee. By this public show, you see, he makes a kind of record in favor of reunification.

Is someone's duplicity showing? I do not think so. Deviousness is hardly the explanation. Comrade Healy happens to be a superb fighter who has been in many a bout. At the sound of the bell he has learned to start swinging at once with savage jabs and hooks, cunning counterpunches, and deceptive weaving. Sometimes this occurs when his opponent is not in that corner of the ring; sometimes, even, when Healy himself is not in the ring. One's admiration for such delicately poised reflexes is tinged with a certain pity. Please, won't the National Committee of the SLL consider adopting a very simple course to stymie the enemy's treacherous maneuvers, which they unwittingly facilitated? To save the SWP from being dragged away from the SLL into a fate worse than death, let Healy patiently stand by the American comrades. You, too, all of you, stay with them in their mistaken enterprise of trying to unify the world Trotskyist movement. As loyal friends and comrades, who have shared many vicissitudes over the years, go through the experience with them, painful as it may be. Block the splitters by the easy, sound tactic of accepting their offer to unify!

Even from the viewpoint of the narrow factional interests of the SLL this would seem much the wiser course. Certainly you have a much better chance of winning a majority of Trotskyists to your views by persuasion inside a united movement than by attack from the outside. You are doubtful about respect for your democratic rights in a united movement? But this betrays a feeling of extreme weakness in relation to the IS. Does this reflect the reality in regard to numbers or is it lack of political confidence? Or perhaps the internal regime of the SLL cannot be offered as a model example of what you mean by the "democratic" part of democratic centralism? In any case, as the unification process continues, the problem of democratic guarantees for minority tendencies will certainly come up under the proper point in the agenda. From a realistic assessment of all that has been learned by both sides since the experience of a decade or so ago, there can be little question that this demand will be satisfactorily met within the general principle of adherence to democratic centralism. The conditions of 1951 or 1953 no longer exist.

On the other hand the leaders of the SLL may decide that they can best preserve the texts of Lenin in all their purity—the texts in which Lenin fought revisionism—by drawing all the necessary organizational conclusions from their present isolationist political course. There are precedents for this in the British Marxist movement, including British Trotskyism. However, not one of these ultraleft experiments makes very happy reading today— that is, if you judge them by the facts. A repetition at this time of day could scarcely prove any happier.

In the school of Leon Trotsky and James P. Cannon—which is also the school of Lenin—I was taught that important as the books are and for all the time that must be put into mastering them, what is decisive is the revolution itself. A revolutionist who misses the test of revolution is a failure no matter how well he or she can quote the texts. That is why the Cuban revolution, not the ultraleft preoccupations of the National Committee of the SLL, provides the yardstick by which to measure their pretensions to Leninist leadership.

We suggest that the National Committee of the SLL take another look at the Cuban revolution. "'In the beginning was the *Word*' . . . The *Word*? . . . 'In the Beginning was the *Act*.'"

# Theory of the Cuban Revolution
## (1961)

*"No revolution has ever anywhere wholly coincided with the conceptions of it formed by its participants, nor could it do so."—Leon Trotsky.*

In the first stages of the Cuban revolution, not much appeared about it in the way of searching analysis. Publicity was largely agitational, whether for or against. Consequently the worth of most early writings hinges largely on the accuracy of the reporting and the extent to which documentary material is included. This is especially true of some items, highly laudatory of the revolution and its leaders, by authors who have since gone over to the counterrevolution.

The situation today is quite different. The character and meaning of the Cuban revolution, of the government that displaced the Batista dictatorship, and of the state now in power are under intense discussion throughout the radical movement on an international scale. The theoretical questions have come to the fore.

This reflects the course of the revolution itself. It began as an ill-reported and ill-understood revolutionary democratic movement on a small island ruled by one of a dozen strong men in Wall Street's empire. Today it stands as a colossal fact in world politics—the opening stage of the socialist revolution in Latin America, the beginning of the end of American capitalist rule in the Western Hemisphere.

The two books under review are among the best in a new literature appearing about the Cuban revolution, a literature written by serious thinkers accustomed to probing for the deep-lying forces and trends in modern society. These thinkers are fascinated by what this revolution has revealed, for they feel that perhaps here may be found clues to titanic revolutionary events now drawing near. As Huberman and Sweezy express it: *"In Cuba they are actually doing what young people all over the world are dreaming about and would like to do"* (Emphasis in original.)

Let's begin with *Listen, Yankee*. In writing this book C. Wright Mills displayed considerable courage. The author of *The Power Elite* and *White Collar*, to mention his best known books, staked a big reputation and high standing in academic circles when he decided to support the Cuban revolution with such forthrightness. That he weighed the issues is evident from the following statement:

> Like most Cubans, I too believe that this revolution is a moment of truth, and like some Cuban revolutionaries, I too believe that such truth, like all revolutionary truth, is perilous.
>
> Any moment of such military and economic truth *might* become an epoch of political and cultural lies. It *might* harden into any one of several kinds of dictatorial tyranny. But I do not believe that this is at all inevitable in Cuba. And I do believe that should it happen it would be due, in very large part, to the role the Government of the United States has been and is continuing to play in Cuban affairs. . . .
>
> The policies the United States has pursued and is pursuing against Cuba are based upon a profound ignorance, and are shot through with hysteria. I believe that if they are continued they will result in more disgrace and more disaster for the image of my country before Cuba, before Latin America, and before the world. [Emphasis in original.]

To help enlighten his fellow Americans and as a service in countering the hysteria, Mills presents the Cuban revolutionary case. As a succinct presentation of the main facts that led to the revolutionary explosion, of the achievements since then, and of the aims, attitude, and outlook of the main rebel forces, the book is a remarkable accomplishment. I cannot recommend it too highly to anyone seeking a quick briefing, particularly as a knowledgeable Cuban revolutionist, leaving aside diplomatic considerations, might give it to you on a visit to the island.

The salient feature of *Listen, Yankee* is the clarity with which it presents the anti-Stalinist aspect of the Cuban revolution. Most readers of the *International Socialist Review* will understand at once, I am sure, that this has nothing to do with the anti-Communism of the House Un-American Activities Committee or similar bodies of witch-hunters and counterrevolutionaries. Even in most Communist parties, where the cult of the late dictator was once the First Commandment, it is generally accepted today—since Khrushchev's Twentieth Congress revelations about Stalin's crimes and paranoia—that to be anti-Stalinist does not automatically put you in Hitler's camp.

An understanding of the attitude of the Cuban revolutionists toward Stalinism is particularly important. The Cuban Communist Party supports the revolution. The government, in turn, has respected its democratic rights, as it has the democratic rights of other radical groupings. It has refused to engage in any witch-hunting and has denounced anti-Communism as a divisive weapon of the counterrevolution. This, plus the aid solicited from the Soviet bloc countries (which undoubtedly saved the Cuban revolution from going down), has been utilized to falsely picture the Cuban government as having succumbed to Stalinism.

The issue happens to be crucial in the United States for winning support for the Cuban revolution in sectors of the trade union movement, among intellectuals, and on the campus. It is not just a matter of attempting to overcome hysterical Stalino-phobia. In these circles the truth is widely known about Stalin's suppression of proletarian democracy, his frame-ups of working-class political opponents, mass deportations, and assassinations of socialist leaders. Many rebel-minded people in the United States who offered their support to the Soviet Union felt betrayed on learning the facts about Stalinism. Consequently, out of fear of being burned again, they are cautious. On the other hand, the appearance of a genuinely democratic socialist revolution could reanimate them. Besides constituting the only sectors of the population ready at present to give a fair hearing to the Cubans, they are an essential link in rebuilding a mass socialist movement in America.

Mills gives the question the importance it warrants, citing many facts to indicate the profoundly anti-Stalinist nature of the revolution. Among these he notes the stress placed on immediate benefits for the people, the readiness to listen and learn in all fields, the freedom that makes Cuba so exhilarating to radicals, above all those on vacation from the stifling atmosphere of McCarthyland.

On the decisive political fact of leadership, Mills has his Cuban protagonist write an entire letter (No. 5), explaining why the Communist Party is not in power in Cuba and why it is highly unlikely even to seek power.

The plain fact is, our revolution has outdone the Communists on every score. From the beginning up till today, always at every turn of event and policy, the revolution is always faster than the Cuban Communist Party, or individual Communists. In all objective facts, then, we are much more radical, much more revolutionary than they. And that is why we *are* using them, rather than the reverse; they are not using us. In fact they are being very grateful to us for letting them in on the work of the revolution.

In fact, this is the case generally with local Communist parties in Latin America. In a real revolution today, in Latin America at least, the local Communists are to the right of the revolution. Here in Cuba, certainly the revolution has outpaced them and does on every front. They always arrive too late and with too little. This has been the case in Cuba and it still is the case: they lag behind our revolution. [Emphasis in original.]

The truth is that Stalinism proved to be an insuperable handicap for the Communist Party of Cuba, no matter how revolutionary-minded its ranks were; and it was bypassed by Castro's July 26 Movement.

On the theoretical assessment of the Cuban revolution as it stands today, Mills offers some interesting opinions. "The Cuban revolution," he observes, "has swiftly destroyed the economic basis of capitalism—both foreign and Cuban. Most of this power was foreign—in fact, North American. It has now been destroyed with a thoroughness unique in Latin American history."

In his sociological estimate, Mills says:

The Cuban revolutionary *is* a new and distinct type of left-wing thinker and actor. He *is* neither capitalist not Communist. He is socialist in a manner, I believe, both practical and humane. And if Cuba is let alone, I believe that Cubans have a good chance to keep the socialist society they are building practical and humane. If Cubans are properly helped— economically, technically and culturally—I believe they would have a *very* good chance. [Emphasis in original.]

As to political power, in Mills's opinion, "The Government of Cuba is a revolutionary dictatorship of the peasants and workers of Cuba. It is legally arbitrary. It is legitimized by the enthusiastic support of an overwhelming majority of the people of Cuba." In letter No. 6, the Cuban spokesman specifies that it is not a Stalinist-type dictatorship:

In the most literal sense imaginable, Cuba is a dictatorship of, by, and for the peasants and the workers of Cuba. That phrase "dictatorship of workers and peasants," was turned into a lie by Stalin and under Stalinism. Some of us know that. But none of us is going about our revolution in that way. So, to understand us, you must try to disabuse yourself of certain images and ideas of "dictatorship." It is the pre-Stalin meaning of the phrase that is accurate to Cuba.

It is in the political area that Mills expresses the greatest worry for Cuba. "I do not like such dependence upon one man as exists in Cuba today, nor the virtually absolute power that this one man possesses." However, Mills believes that "it is not enough either to approve or to disapprove this fact about Cuba. That is much too easy; it is also politically fruitless. One must understand the conditions that have made it so . . . for only then can one consider the prospects of its development." The conditions include the form of struggle needed to overthrow Batista, the enormous counterrevolutionary pressure of the United States, and the fluidity of the present situation, in which democratic forms have not yet been worked out in the living experience of the revolution.

Castro's leadership in the difficult revolutionary struggle brought him this exceptional personal power, but it is Mills's conviction that Castro is opposed to any leadership cult, is aware of the danger, and will help the revolution to pass through it. "In my judgment," says Mills, "one must take seriously this man's own attempts to shift roles, even in the middle of his necessary action, and his own astute awareness of the need to develop a more systematic relation between a government of law and the people of Cuba."

*      *      *

Let us turn now to the book by Leo Huberman and Paul M. Sweezy, the editors of the *Monthly Review*. They wrote this after a three-week visit to Cuba in March 1960, publishing it as a special edition of their magazine. Events soon dated parts of it. The authors took another trip to Cuba and have now published a supplement, "Cuba Revisited" (December 1960 issue of the *Monthly Review*), which, I understand, is to be included in a new edition of the book.

The strong side of *Cuba—Anatomy of a Revolution* is its emphasis on economics. The authors do a good job of summarizing the main facts about Cuba under Batista, available in such books as Lowry Nelson's *Rural Cuba,* then turn to current problems, where they offer the results of their own investigations on the scene. The facts they have assembled are encouraging indeed. Instead of collapsing, as the capitalist press has been predicting, the Cuban economy has grown stronger. Consider, for instance, the main crops, which have been the center of a planned expansion drive:

> *Their total volume increased by almost one third in the first year of the Revolution, and there is no doubt that a comparable rate of expansion is being maintained this year.* China, it seems, is not the only country capable of "big leaps forward"! But what other country has ever staged such a leap forward in the very first year of a Revolution and in the midst of a far-reaching agrarian reform? It can be said without exaggeration: in the Cuban Revolution the world is witnessing a process of socio-economic transformation and vitalization that is in many important respects without *any* precedent. Let the world look hard and draw the appropriate conclusions! [Emphasis in original.]

When the agrarian reform was put through, predictions were freely made in the big press that the Cubans, with their "lack of know-how," would speedily bring the cattle industry to ruin by slaughtering the breeding stock, some of it of top quality. The spiteful forecasts of the dispossessed cattle barons were not borne out. Huberman and Sweezy cite a representative of the United Nations Food and Agriculture Organization who said that while no figures were available for the island as a whole, Havana was eating 60 to 70 percent more beef in March 1960 than the previous year while the supply of beef cattle had also been sharply stepped up, "chiefly owing to better feeding methods." The authors conclude: "There could be no better evidence than this that (1) the Revolution has already transformed the standard of living of the Cuban masses, and (2) this new and higher standard of living has come to stay."

In political matters, Huberman and Sweezy in general leave much to be desired, in my opinion. A few indications:

They manage to "credit" the administration of Franklin D. Roosevelt with having "abrogated" the Platt Amendment. They also criticize the same administration for withholding recognition of the Grau government and granting it to Batista; but the political necessity of tipping their hats to the FDR myth blocks them from seeing Roosevelt's role in establishing the foul Cuban dictator and maintaining his brutal rule.

In lauding the readiness of the Cuban peasantry to go directly to agricultural cooperatives, Huberman and Sweezy refer to the views of bourgeois land reformers who have aimed at breaking up large landed estates into small peasant holdings.

More radical thought, at least from the time of Marx, has generally rejected this aim on the dual ground that small-scale peasant cultivation of the soil is hopelessly inefficient and that a small peasantry is inevitably a reactionary, counter-revolutionary force. However, the Russian Revolution showed the difficulties which confronted any attempt to go directly from a system of latifundia to some form of collective agriculture. In spite of themselves, the Russian Bolsheviks were forced to distribute the land to millions of small peasants, and it was only much later after fierce and bloody social struggles and frightful agricultural losses that they succeeded in establishing the system of collective and state farms.

Thus they amalgamate Lenin's adherence to the political position of Engels with its direct opposite, that of Stalin. Engels held that collectivization in agriculture, despite its obvious economic advantages, could proceed only in accordance with the will of the peasants themselves. A revolutionary government could seek to convince them by argument and examples but in no case force them. That was how Lenin proceeded. Stalin, after first pandering to the rich peasants, collectivized Soviet agriculture by force. The catastrophic consequences still plague the Soviet Union. If a real lesson is to be drawn from the Cuban experience, it is the advantages to be gained by following the method worked out in theory by Engels and put into practice by Lenin, in contrast to the brutal method used by Stalin. Huberman and Sweezy credit Cuba's success to Castro's knowledge of the peasantry and sensitivity to their deepest wishes. If Castro is not aware of the theoretical and historical background, the confirmation of the Marxist view is all the more notable.

A serious political error which Huberman and Sweezy themselves admit in their postscript to the book was the estimate that Washington would not slash the Cuban sugar quota. We remain uncertain as to why they made the error. Did they calculate that it was not in the best interests of capitalism to do this and that the powers that be would recognize this? Or did they underestimate the deeply reactionary character of both the Democratic and Republican machines? Fortunately, the politically astute Cuban leaders were not caught by surprise. As Castro indicated in his speech at the United Nations, they are well aware of the true relationship between "the shark and the sardine."

I mention these items with no thought of disqualifying *Cuba— Anatomy of a Revolution.* They are minor, if annoying, flaws in an excellent report and strong defense of the Cuban revolution. My intent is to suggest that if the authors have any predilection it is in the direction of the Communist Party. This gives certain of the things they say about Cuban politics much greater weight than they would otherwise have; for, representing a break with their predilection, these views were undoubtedly pondered many times over before being expressed.

From the origin of the July 26 Movement in 1953 until the rebel army was well on the way to victory, Huberman and Sweezy declare, "the Cuban CP was cool to and sometimes critical" of Castro's organization. The leadership of the revolution "owed absolutely nothing to the Communists. . . ." Only Castro, if he should join the Communist Party, could persuade any of the others to follow him. "Since no responsible observer, to the best of our knowledge, has ever suggested that Fidel has done any such thing, we conclude that the hypothesis of Communist infiltration of the leadership is a pure figment of the anti-Communist imagination."

Can the Communists get into position to "wrest the leadership of the masses, of the revolutionary movement itself, out of the hands of Fidel and his colleagues in the army and government?" Huberman and Sweezy ridicule the possibility, pointing to the smallness of the Communist Party and its lack of standing as against the size of Castro's following and their revolutionary record.

The authors go even further:

In our judgment, for what it is worth, the Communists could make no bigger mistake, now or in the foreseeable future, than to challenge Fidel and his close associates for the leadership of the Revolution. They would lose, and in losing they might easily do irreparable damage to the cause of the Revolution, which of course is also their cause. On the other hand, if they continue to pursue their present course, they may play an important, and in some repects perhaps an indispensable, even if subordinate, role in the building of socialism in Cuba.

To make their meaning still clearer, they compare the Cuban Communists with the American Communists in the New Deal period.

They worked hard and often effectively, trying of course always to push matters somewhat further to the Left than they would otherwise tend to go. While they won control in some unions, they were never in a position to make a bid for political leadership in the country and never caused any serious problems except in the minds of the right-wing lunatic fringe.

In short, although the authors do not say it, since the thirties neither the Cuban nor the American Communists have played the role of *revolutionists*.

All the charges and accusations concerning the alleged Communist character of the Cuban government and/or Revolution tend to hide what may turn out to be historically one of the most important facts about the Cuban Revolution: this is the first time—ever, anywhere—that a genuine socialist revolution has been made by *non-Communists!* [Emphasis in original.]

Castro and the rebel army, "calling themselves neither socialists nor Communists, in fact without any clearly formulated ideology, seized power in Cuba after two years of bloody civil war and proceeded with élan and dispatch" to do what needed to be done. "No one can now foretell the full implications of this startling fact," Huberman and Sweezy believe, "but no one need doubt that it will open up new vistas not only in the realm of social thought but also in the realm of revolutionary action."

Although there is considerable difference in the angle of view, in emphasis, in political inclination, and in the way they express what they observed, it is clear that the impressions which the revolution made on C. Wright Mills on the one hand and Huberman and Sweezy on the other were not greatly different. The similarity extends to other fields.

What kind of social order does Cuba have? "For our part," declare Huberman and Sweezy, "we have no hesitation in answering: *the new Cuba is a socialist Cuba.*" (Emphasis in original.)

How did it get that way? After the seizure of power, "the aspect which the Cuban Revolution first presented to the world was that of a quite respectable middle-class regime." This gave rise to many misunderstandings. However, the real power remained in the hands of Castro. "A sort of dual system of government began to emerge, with Fidel on one side and Urrutia and the cabinet on the other." The "paradox between the essentially revolutionary character of the regime and the predominantly liberal-to-

conservative personnel which represented it before the world"
was resolved by March 1960. Two of the landmarks were Castro's
resignation in July 1959 to force the resignation of Urrutia, and
Che Guevara's assumption of the presidency of the National
Bank in November in place of Felipe Pazos. The Castro regime
carried the revolution through to the establishment of a planned
economy.

*         *         *

*Cuba—Anatomy of a Revolution* was saluted with vexed
criticism from spokesmen of both the Cuban and American
Communist parties. (At this writing they have not yet got around
to reviewing Mills's book.) The CP finds it obnoxious to think
that the label *socialist* should be applied to Cuba. It's a national
democratic revolution, you see, in which the national bourgeoisie
still plays an important role and in which the need for "unity" is
foremost. In addition, Huberman and Sweezy slight the role of
the Communist Party in the revolution, and the increasingly
important role it will play after the proletarian stage opens.

The two derelict authors answer the criticism somewhat disre-
spectfully with a footnote in their postscript:

Now that the big majority of the means of production are in public
ownership, and the regime is rapidly developing a consciously socialist
ideology, the Communist argument against classifying Cuba as socialist
appears more and more clearly as mere verbal gymnastics. The reason for
the Communists' adopting this position, however, is straightforward
enough: they don't want to admit that it is possible for socialism to be
built under non-Communist leadership.

One wishes that Huberman and Sweezy would venture to
analyze this reluctance of the Communists. The question would
seem not unimportant and very definitely related to their own
belief that the Cuban revolution has opened up "new vistas not
only in the realm of social thought but also in the realm of
revolutionary action." Isn't the failure of the Cuban Communist
Party central to this far-reaching conclusion? Wouldn't a knowledge of the reasons for the failure be of considerable value to
other Communist parties—to the revolutionary-minded rank and
file, if not to leaders who never cause "any serious problems"?

In the dispute between the Communists and the editors of the
*Monthly Review*, it appears to me that Huberman and Sweezy

have the stronger case. In fact they hanged the Communist Party theoreticians with their own terminology. If each of the countries in the Soviet bloc, including Albania, is "socialist," then why should this term be denied Cuba, which now has a planned economy—and far greater freedom than any of them?

The fact is that "socialist" was used by Stalin in the years of his psychosis as a mislabel for Soviet society. It was a way of proving that you can build "socialism in one country." This played into the hands of the worst enemies of the Soviet Union, for they never tired of agreeing and even emphasizing that socialism was what the Soviet Union had all right and therefore Stalinism and socialism were one and the same thing and if America went socialist you'd lose democracy and get frame-up trials and concentration camps here, too. To confer the badge "socialist" on Cuba may thus—unfortunately—be taken as a somewhat dubious honor.

In the early days the Soviet Union was called a workers' state; "with bureaucratic deformations," Lenin added. It was socialist in *tendency*: that is, it was a transitional formation on the road to socialism but not there by a long shot. Nor could it reach socialism on its own resources—such a concept, had anyone suggested it in Lenin's time, would have been dismissed as self-contradictory. The Soviet power was a working-class conquest in the international struggle for a worldwide, scientifically planned society built on the foundation of capitalism as a whole, or at least on the combined resources of several industrially advanced countries.

The concern the Bolsheviks felt for terminology was not due to an aesthetic pleasure in splitting hairs. Precision in applying labels reflected their concern over knowing exactly where they stood in relation to the goal still to be achieved. It was a good tradition, well worth emulating, like much else in Leninism.

If Cuba is not socialist and is highly unlikely to achieve socialism by itself on one small island, what is it?

The Cubans themselves have been reluctant to say. Professing some disinterest in abstruse questions of theory, they have politely invited those of their supporters and well-wishers who are better informed in such matters to have at it. Meanwhile they propose to move ahead, with or without labels, to work out problems that permit no delay and that have kept their limited personnel going twenty-four hours a day. As their own guide, they find it sufficient to follow the broad generalizations of a humanism concerned with the fate of the humble. If you can tell a *guajiro* from an imperialist and hold government power, it seems to work out all right.

This pragmatic approach has added to the theoretical puzzle. If the Cubans don't know whether Cuba is socialist or not, how is anyone else to know? Jean-Paul Sartre, on visiting Cuba, came away with the conviction that the world was witnessing something completely novel—a revolution impelled by blows from an imperialist power to respond with counterblows, each more radical than the previous. Would a revolution driven forward by such a process create its own ideology? That remains to be seen. In any case, Sartre found it a refreshing contrast to what he considers the sectarian approach—applying a preconceived ideology to a revolution.

Others, stimulated like Sartre by the Cuban revolution, have decided that even Marxist theory breaks down before such phenomena. What provisions are there in Marxism for a revolution, obviously socialist in tendency but powered by the peasantry and led by revolutionists who have never professed socialist aims; indeed, who seem to have been limited to the bourgeois-democratic horizon? It's not in the books!

If Marxism has no provisions for such phenomena, perhaps it is time provisions were made. It would seem a fair enough exchange for a revolution as good as this one. On the other hand, what books do you read?

The Cuban revolution is not the first to have given the theoreticians something fresh to consider. The Russian revolution exceeded it in that respect. In 1917 the entire world socialist movement was caught by surprise, including the Bolshevik Party—not excepting even Lenin. Socialists wielding power at the head of the workers and peasants in a backward country like Russia! It wasn't in the book. Well . . . most of the books.

The Russian revolution was fortunate in having a leadership as great in theory as in action. Four decades ago it was common knowledge in the socialist movement that one at least of the Russian leaders had accounted in theory for the peculiarities of the Russian revolution in all its main lines—*some twelve years before it happened.* His name was Leon Trotsky.

Trotsky's theory of the permanent revolution greatly facilitated the Bolshevik victory by giving the revolutionary cadre the clearest possible conception of the import of their action. But if Trotsky had not been there, had not made his great theoretical contribution, we may be sure that Lenin, consummate socialist politician and man of action that he was, would have led the Bolsheviks to power just the same, and an accurate reflection in theory of the revolution would have come later.

I mention this not only to defend the right of the Cuban revolution to have its own peculiarities but to draw from Bolshevik theory to attempt to explain certain of these peculiarities.

The main power in the Cuban revolution was the peasantry (as in Russia). But this peasantry shaded into the powerful mass of agricultural workers, which, because of the role of the sugar industry, constituted the most dynamic section of the Cuban proletariat. The agricultural workers solidly backed the revolution. The city workers favored the revolution but were not in position to head it (unlike Russia) for two reasons. (1) The unions were strapped in the straitjacket of *mujalismo*: that is, a bureaucracy tied directly to the Batista dictatorship. (2) The political leadership was held by the Communist Party, an organization devoted to "peaceful coexistence," "people's frontism," and the cult of Stalin; an organization which, as Huberman and Sweezy put it diplomatically, "never caused any serious problems." The CP leaders actually went so far in avoiding causing any serious problems for Batista that they pictured him as a man of the people and took posts in his government.)

The main demands of the peasantry were an end to hunger, an end to Batista's savage killings, and agrarian reform. (In Russia: Bread! Peace! Land!) These demands became the slogans of the July 26 Movement.

By all the criteria of origin, aims, and social following, the July 26 Movement was a petty-bourgeois formation, but an extremely radical one. It had one plank in its program which separated it from all similar groupings and which was to prove decisive. It made a principle of armed struggle without compromise against the Batista dictatorship. To carry out this aim, it organized a peasant guerrilla movement that has been compared to Tito's and Mao's. Parallels can also be found, however, in the rich revolutionary experience of Latin America, including Cuba itself. Its formation was not as novel as its success.

On coming to power, the July 26 Movement set up a coalition government that included well-known bourgeois-democratic figures—and not in secondary posts. In retrospect these may have seemed middle-class decorations or mere camouflage, hiding the real nature of the government. It is more accurate, I think, to view this government as corresponding to the political aims of the revolution as they were conceived at the time by its leaders.

But such a government stood in contradiction to the demands of the insurgent masses and to the commitment of the July 26 Movement to satisfy these demands. The revolution urgently required far-reaching inroads on private property, including imperialist holdings. As Castro and his collaborators moved toward fulfillment of the agrarian reform, they met with resistance from their partners in the coalition—a resistance that was considerably stiffened by support from Wall Street, which viewed then as the "reasonable" elements in a regime packed with bearded "wild men."

As Huberman and Sweezy correctly observe, "a sort of dual system government began to emerge." The displacement of Felipe Pazos by Che Guevara in November 1959 marked a decisive shift and the resolution of the governmental crisis, whatever hangovers from the coalition still remained. The government that now existed was qualitatively different from the coalition regime.

Its chief characteristics were a genuine interest in the welfare of the bottom strata of the population, readiness to entrust the defense of the revolution to them by giving them arms, clear recognition of the identity of the main enemies of the revolution, and resoluteness in disarming and combating them. It was even free from fetishism of private property. Yet it did not think of itself a socialist. It did not proclaim socialist aims.

What should we call such a strange government?

Among the great discussions organized by the Bolsheviks in the first four congresses of the Communist International was one precisely on this question. Deeply buried under landslides of Stalinist propaganda, the minutes and resolutions of that discussion are not readily available. When you unearth them, your feeling is one of shock at their timeliness. Did the Bolsheviks really discuss such a question four years before Castro was born!

The Bolsheviks analyzed several varieties of "workers' and peasants' governments"—that is, radical petty-bourgeois governments—indicating differences that would cause a revolutionary socialist party to offer support or to refuse support. They also left open the possibility in theory of variants they could not readily foresee at the time. The general label they used for such regimes was *workers' and farmers' government.* Here we must expostulate a bit with the Bolsheviks; they also called the dictatorship of the proletariat a workers' and farmers' government. A representative from theoretically backward America might have asked for distinctive labels so he could more easily tell them apart. But the Bolsheviks discussed this point, too, and felt that it would not be confusing so long as everyone was clear on the difference in content, since the first kind of government would likely prove to be only a transient form preliminary to the latter type.

Of course, the Communist delegates in 1922 could not visualize such a change without the helpful presence of a genuine revolutionary socialist party such as the Russian workers had in the Bolsheviks. A key question requiring our attention, therefore, is the absence of this factor in Cuba. To find the answer we must turn to the world situation in which Cuba is locked.

The most prominent conditioning force in international politics today is the deep decay of the capitalist system. Leaving aside the effect of such general threats as another major depression or atomic annihilation in a third world war, Cuba has experienced the decay of capitalism in two specific ways: (1) the deformation of national life through imperialist domination—monoculture, superprofits, hunger, disease, ignorance, dictatorial rule, etc.; (2) the economic and diplomatic strangulation a power like the U.S. applies to a colonial nation seeking independence. The moves of Wall Street and the State Department, as many observers have noted, powerfully accelerated, if they did not make inevitable, the radicalization of the Cuban revolution. Eisenhower "lost" Cuba much the way Truman "lost" China.

Next in importance to the death agony of capitalism is the existence and the growing power of the countries where capitalist property relations have been transcended and planned economies constructed. Showing what can be achieved in economic, scientific, and cultural progress, not to mention sovereign standing, these countries serve as practical object lessons. Their tendency to magnetize attention, especially in the underdeveloped areas, has become an active political factor that is now powerfully strengthened by the possibility of securing material aid from this source. The Soviet Union, by its mere existence, has always been—even in the terrible years under Stalin—a radicalizing force among oppressed peoples. The attraction was enormously increased by the Chinese revolution and the fresh example which China has provided of how to break out of age-old stagnation and imperialist oppression. Cuba has been affected by all this in the most vivid and concrete way.

The third feature of world politics is the long default of the

Communist parties in providing revolutionary socialist leadership to the working class. For decades this signified betrayal and defeat in the most promising of revolutionary situations. Today it has finally begun to signify the emergence of alternative leaderships—the masses in the underdeveloped areas, having lost fatalistic acceptance of hunger, misery, ignorance, and ruthless exploitation, have become impatient and are pushing forward whatever leaderships are at hand. Nationalists have filled the vacuum at least temporarily in many areas, but the tendency is toward much more radical currents. Nowhere is this to be seen with greater clarity than in Cuba.

Finally, there is a tendency among the nationalist movements and newly emerging countries in the Far East, the Middle East, Africa, and Latin America to seek mutual encouragement and support. The Cuban revolutionists, for example, are in close touch with the Algerian freedom fighters. They have diplomatic relations with Yugoslavia, India, Ghana, etc. Sékou Touré and Sukarno have been honored guests in Havana. Lumumba is a hero in Cuba. A radical move taken by any of them that proves successful has big impact on all the others. For instance, Nasser's seizure of the Suez Canal, when Egypt suffered the combined attack of Britain, France, and Israel, made a lasting impression.

In the light of this international background, the series of countermeasures taken by the Cuban government under pressure from the State Department are seen to have an ideological origin that does no violence to Marxist theory; in fact these countermeasures are explainable only by a theory grounded in the international class struggle.

Whatever the consciousness of the Cuban revolutionists may have been, not a single major measure undertaken by them was unique. "Intervention" of the latifundia and domestic and foreign capitalist holdings was undoubtedly as Cuban as the royal palms, but it finds a precedent in the "control" exercised over private enterprises under the Bolsheviks prior to the establishment of workers' management of industry. A similar stage appeared in the Chinese revolution. The expropriations and nationalizations are likewise far from novel. A government monopoly of foreign trade is in the Russian tradition; and the planned economy which Cuba has now begun is, of course, recognized by everyone as in the pattern initiated by the Russian workers and peasants.

In the October 1960 issue of *Political Affairs,* James S. Allen, a spokesman of the Communist Party, labels these as "measures of a state-capitalist type." This effort to avoid the label "socialist," as advanced by Huberman and Sweezy, is not very satisfactory. Are the measures of similar kind in the Soviet Union, Eastern Europe, Yugoslavia, Albania, and China also to be labeled as "of a state-capitalist type"? Evidently not.

Aside from this, Allen's position has another flaw. What about the state? Is it capitalist? Can a capitalist state carry out such measures and still remain capitalist? Judging from the shrieks of the counterrevolutionaries and the froth on Wall Street's mouth, it is not possible.

The fact is that the state structure began to undergo alteration upon Castro's coming to power, January 1, 1959. For good and valid political reasons, Castro insisted on smashing both the old army and the old police force. The lesson of Guatemala had been well absorbed by the July 26 Movement. A new army and a new police, based on the rebel forces, replaced the old. A nationwide militia was organized.

One could have decided that this was enough to require us at the time to call Cuba a workers' state. But the premise for such a conclusion is that the conscious aims of the leadership are revolutionary socialist, openly proclaimed, so that it remains only a question of time until the entire state structure is altered to conform to the needs of a planned economy. This political premise, of course, did not exist. It remained to be seen what course the pragmatic leadership would take and whether their proclaimed political aims would become altered as they sought to put into effect the reforms they advocated; or whether in sticking to their political positions they modified or gave up their social and economic aims. The outcome could be determined only by the struggle itself.

The results are now in. In the two years since the victory, the holdovers from the old state have been sloughed off in the key positions, although they may still hold authority in some sectors. With the completion between August and October 1960 of the nationalizations in the major areas of Cuban industry, a new state had come into being, so deeply committed to a planned economy that Cuba's course in this direction cannot now be changed save by an imperialist invasion and a bloody civil war.

Since the transcending of capitalist property relations and the construction of a planned economy correspond with the economic interests of the working class and are objectively socialist in tendency, we must, if we are interested in exact terminology, call this a *workers' state*, signifying that it is a state committed to the task of carrying Cuban economy and society forward through the transition from capitalism to socialism.

It is true that this workers' state lacks, as yet, the forms of proletarian democracy. This does not mean that democracy is lacking in Cuba. Far more democracy exists today in Cuba than ever existed under any previous regime. It does mean that a government based on workers', peasants', and soldiers' councils, or some form of councils in the democratic control of the government, has not yet been worked out. Mills's observations about the concentration of power in one person are accurate.

Marxist theory admits the possibility of situations in which no alternative exists save such concentration of power. However, it regards this as exceptional and dangerous to the revolutionary interests of the workers and peasants. It is a sign of weakness in the organization of the struggle. The norm is the extension of democracy into all phases of the nation's life. It is not just a question of democratic rights but of organizing the most powerful defense and bringing the maximum power to bear in carrying out the structural changes and constructing the planned economy. Consequently, while defending the present Cuban government from attack from all quarters, Marxists advocate the earliest possible development of proletarian forms of democracy in Cuba. It would seem self-evident that this would add greatly to the political defense of the revolution, above all as an example to be emulated in other countries.

This is the tendency in Cuba, as Mills notes, and one must join him in ardently hoping that the ferocious pressure from American imperialism will not lead to retrogression.

A new stage in the Cuban revolution of the greatest interest and importance is now opening up. The leaders have convincingly demonstrated that they really meant it when they said they were prepared to carry the revolution through to its necessary conclusion no matter where it took them. What have been the consequences in their thinking?

Looking back, they must note with some astonishment, I imagine, that it proved impossible to carry through simple humanistic aims, all of them long proclaimed by the bourgeois society that toppled feudalism, without taking measures that transcended capitalist property relations. Capitalism doesn't work for the poor. To fulfill their desire to turn the promise of a better life for the humble into reality, these men of powerful will found they had to put Cuba on the road to socialism. They discovered this through practical experience and not through preconceived notions. It is almost like a laboratory test. What theories did it confirm or disprove, or must we wipe the slate of theory clean and start fresh?

Is this experience not worth evaluation? Wouldn't the way be smoothed for revolutionists in other Latin American countries, for example, if they knew the reasons for the course that had to be taken in Cuba? Surely the experience will be similar elsewhere in Latin America and other continents as revolutionists follow the example of the Cuban vanguard and bring their peoples into the mainstream of history.

Up to now the Cuban leaders have appeared as great revolutionists of action. Perhaps some of them may now venture into the field of theory with commensurate contributions. It is time, we think, to attempt to bring the theory of the Cuban revolution up to the level of its practice. From such a development all the friends and supporters of the Cuban revolution stand to gain— not least of all in the United States, where the success of the July 26 Movement has brought new hope and inspiration to the radical movement.

# Stop the Crime Against Cuba!
## Statement by the SWP Political Committee
## (April 19, 1961)

The Kennedy administration has launched an undeclared war on Cuba. This is the brutal fact now facing the American people.

No less an authority than the *New York Times* felt forced to admit in an editorial April 18, the day after the invasion: "It is also no secret that the United States Government has been helping the Cuban exiles over a period of many months with arms, training and facilities on American soil and in Guatemala. This has been too well publicized to be ignored today."

Khrushchev has appealed personally to Kennedy "to put an end to the aggression." The Soviet premier warned that "any so-called 'small war' can provoke a chain reaction in all parts of the world." He reaffirmed a pledge to help Cuba "in beating back the armed attack." Once again he stressed the interest of his government "in a relaxation of international tension." "But," he added, "if others aggravate it we shall reply in full measure."

This restrained indication of the possible consequences must be taken with utmost seriousness. If the Kennedy administration persists in its armed aggression, it can set in motion forces that will inevitably plunge humanity into nuclear war.

Let there be no mistake about the guilt. The Central Intelligence Agency, first under Eisenhower and then under Kennedy, financed and trained thousands of counterrevolutionary mercenaries. They were armed with U.S. naval, air, and army weapons, including B-26 bombers and troop transports. Their invasion of Cuba was masterminded by American military experts in flagrant violation of the U.S. laws, including the Neutrality Act, and nonaggression treaties.

The crime against Cuba is also a crime against the American people. All Kennedy's talk about a "Peace Corps" and an "Alliance for Progress" in Latin America proved to be lying propaganda. It aimed at covering up the real plan of action—a new ordeal of terror and butchery for the Cuban people.

Kennedy's campaign promises about a "New Frontier" and world peace were directed primarily to the youth of America. But Kennedy is not teaching the ways of peace. The planting of phosphorous in the air-conditioning system of Havana's biggest department store is hailed as a heroic act. Corps of bombers are praised as champions of freedom and democracy. By this glorification of sabotage and indiscriminate terror, Kennedy is fostering in America's youth the type of mentality now on display in the Eichmann trial. Is this the "New Frontier"?

Like Eisenhower, Kennedy is acting for the economic and financial interests that stand behind the Democratic and Republican parties. These dealers in stocks and bonds bled Cuba for six decades, condemning the population to poverty, unemployment, illiteracy, and endemic disease. They want back their lucrative holdings—no ifs, ands, or buts. Besides that, they fear the Cuban example will inspire similar revolutions throughout Latin America. Their recipe is "Crush it in the bud."

The counterrevolutionary generals of the invasion army lie when they say they are fighting for "democracy" and the "liberation" of Cuba. Their sole aim is to make the island safe once again for the dollars of American investors.

This is proved by the key plank in their call for war against the Castro regime issued April 8 in Manhattan by Miró Cardona, head of the "Cuban Revolutionary Council" set up for recognition by the U.S. as the "government" of Cuba: "We emphatically assure those who have been unjustly dispossessed that all of their assets will be returned. . . . We shall encourage investment in private property, both national and foreign, and we shall give complete guarantees to private enterprise and to private property."

The Cuban revolutionists have followed an opposite course. In place of capitalist production for profit at the expense of human rights, they are building a planned economy.

In Cuba the long-standing army of unemployed has been greatly reduced and its liquidation is feasible in a year or two. Jim Crow was wiped out along with capitalism, its main supporting institution. Attractive, low-cost homes are being built by the thousands throughout the island in a great national effort to provide housing for everyone. Rents were slashed in half and now every tenant can become a home-owner, since rent is accepted by the government as installment payments on a house or apartment.

Landless peasants have received their own farms or else participate in cooperatives that have already made possible an impressive rise in national productivity. Illiteracy, which affected a third of the population in 1959, is now close to elimination, a two-year achievement no other country can match.

These are some of the gains in Cuba which Wall Street regards as a mortal threat. The money-changers are right. Why should any people endure the domination of big monopolies when by kicking them out they can win such enormous improvements?

Wall Street's scheme is to correct things by overthrowing the government of Cuba the way the Central Intelligence Agency overthrew the lawfully elected government of Guatemala in 1954.

What is this mysterious CIA? What does it do with its enormous funds? To whom is it accountable?

All that the American people have been permitted to know is that the head of this spy agency is Allen Dulles and that it carries on "cloak and dagger" operations. Spying, it turns out, reaches the level of undeclared wars.

One courageous journalist, I. F. Stone, has asked why Allen Dulles is not indicted. A congressman alive to his responsibilities to the American people would go further and demand impeachment of Kennedy.

Many voices have demanded investigation of the CIA—investigation of its U-2 spy operations, its sinister efforts to get us into war in Laos, its recruitment of Cuban mercenaries, its training of saboteurs and terrorists, its construction of military training camps and secret air bases in other countries, its access to the arsenals of the navy, the army, and the air force to outfit an entire expeditionary force and keep it supplied in a war.

The American people are entitled to know exactly how this agency assembles foreign troops on American soil, how it transfers these mercenaries to other countries, how it lands them on the beaches of Cuba and supplies them with the matériel of war; and who pays for all this.

The crimes committed by American big business against Cuba since 1898 make a somber list. Instead of capping these crimes with the horrors of invasion and war, we should in simple justice offer the Cuban people all the help in our power.

Let's resume normal diplomatic and trade relations. Let's send delegations to study the successes of the Cubans and see what we can learn from them. Instead of a policy of hatred toward Cuba, let's initiate a policy of friendship.

We firmly believe in the right of every people to choose whatever kind of government they want, free from any foreign pressure. We believe that the Cubans are entitled to exercise this basic democratic right. We call for solidarity with them in defending it.

We hope that every American who believes in the equality of nations will join in picketing and demonstrating for this right or will indicate to Congress and the White House by other means how he feels.

End the aggression against Cuba at once! End the economic blockade! End the policy of trying to isolate and crush the Cuban revolution! Hands off Cuba!

# THE CUBAN MODEL FOR
# REVOLUTION IN LATIN AMERICA

*The Cuban revolution's impact on Latin American radical politics was explosive. Young revolutionists were drawn to the Cuban example and they sought to repeat it. They broke away from the influence of the Communist parties in the direction of guerrilla warfare. The Cubans gave support to these movements, polemicizing against the electoralist CPs.*

*As an alternative to class collaborationism, the Cuban model had a positive thrust; as Castro put it in the "Second Declaration of Havana" (March 26, 1962), "the duty of every revolutionary is to make the revolution." The Organization of Latin American Solidarity (OLAS) conference of 1967 attempted to draw together the left-wing currents in opposition to the betrayals of the conservative CPs.*

*Joseph Hansen attended the conference as a reporter for the Militant. His article "The OLAS Conference: Tactics and Strategy for Continental Revolution" (November-December 1967 International Socialist Review) and part of his "Report on the International Situation" to the October 1967 SWP convention, "The Promising Developments at the OLAS Conference," excerpted here from the January-February 1968 International Socialist Review, outline the strengths and weaknesses of the Cuban strategy—its internationalism and revolutionary goals on the one hand, and, on the other, its lack of a clear political strategy for mobilizing the working masses and building a revolutionary party.*

*The experience of Latin American revolutionaries who tried to repeat the Cuban experience was negative; guerrilla movements across the continent were put down by armies trained and aided by the U.S. The CIA and the Pentagon learned the lessons of the Cuban revolution from their point of view and found methods to*

*block its repetition. The Cubans and other Latin American rebels
began to rethink their strategy.*

*The Fourth International's position on guerrillaism was chang-
ing in the late 1960s also—but in a different direction. Young
radicals in Europe were fired up by the revolt in France of May-
June 1968 and inspired by the example of Che; many of them
joined the Trotskyist movement with guerrillaist illusions. At the
Ninth World Congress of the Fourth International in 1969, the
majority voted for a guerrillaist perspective in Latin America. A
minority, including Joseph Hansen, held to the traditional
Marxist orientation of building mass revolutionary parties that
could lead working-class revolutions. The discussion of this issue
in the International lasted almost a decade, with agreement at
the end that experience had proved the guerrilla orientation to be
incorrect. In the course of that debate, the lessons of the Cuban
revolution were cited by both sides to support their arguments.
The excerpts from various reports and documents by Joseph
Hansen reprinted here give his assessment of the Cuban leadership's guerrilla strategy.*

*"Why Castro Ended Up in the Minority in Venezuela" is from
"Assessment of the Draft Resolution on Latin America." "The
Seven Errors Made by Che Guevara" is from "Report on the
Third World Congress of the Fourth International Since Reunifi-
cation," given at a New York SWP branch meeting June 4, 1969.
"The Cubans Pause for Reflection" is from "A Contribution to the
Discussion on Revolutionary Strategy in Latin America," June
26, 1970. These three articles are in Discussion on Latin America
(1968-1971), an International Information Bulletin published by
the Socialist Workers Party, June 1972.*

# The OLAS Conference:
# Tactics and Strategy
# of a Continental Revolution
# (1967)

The first conference of the Organization of Latin American Solidarity, which met in Havana from July 31 to August 10, was recognized from all sides as an event of worldwide political significance.

The international press gave top priority to the deliberations, 157 foreign journalists registering for credentials. The State Department paid the conference a high, if involuntary, tribute by postponing a scheduled meeting of the Organization of American States until September in order to place this reactionary body in better position to try to offset the decisions reached by the OLAS gathering. All of Washington's satellite governments in Latin America reacted to the conference with anger and apprehension, taking extraordinary measures to block delegates from attending. The Mexican government, under pressure from the Johnson administration, even staged a provocative witch-hunt on the eve of the meeting.[1]

It was the largest assembly of authentic representatives of the active guerrilla fronts in Latin America that has yet been held. Cuban sponsorship of the gathering, the sponsorship of a workers' state, gave it added significance. Delegations attended from ten other workers' states and from fourteen international

---

1. Government agents raided a Maoist bookstore in Mexico City to secure "more than twelve tons of evidence" that Mexican capitalism and its chief ornament, President Díaz Ordaz, were the target of a guerrilla "plot" involving fourteen followers of either Mao Tse-tung, Fidel Castro, or Leon Trotsky. Some of the fourteen became acquainted with each other for the first time in the torture rooms of the Mexican political police. On May 14, 1969, they were sentenced to two-, five-, six-, and nine-year prison terms.

organizations. (A conspicuous absentee was the People's Republic of China.) An outstanding feature was the presence of spokesmen of the Black Power movement in the United States. Stokely Carmichael, one of the leaders of the Student Nonviolent Coordinating Committee, was included among the top figures of the conference, being made an honorary delegate.

The apprehensions of the imperialists and their retinue were not misplaced, as could be judged from the way their press and even the U.S. Congress fumed as the conference proceeded. Among the leftist currents, reactions were mixed, ranging from the open displeasure and opposition voiced by right-wing Communist Party leaderships, as in France, to the gratification expressed by various guerrilla movements, the commendatory statements of spokesmen of the Black Power movement in the United States, and the recognition by leading Trotskyists that the conference represented an encouraging achievement and step forward for the world revolution.

The subjects considered by the delegates were of burning actuality:

1. The United States and Latin America, with particular emphasis on the place of the Cuban revolution in the struggle of the exploited continent for freedom from the imperialist metropolis.

2. The escalation of U.S. imperialist aggression in Vietnam, with its associated threat to other countries, including the People's Republic of China and the Soviet Union, and the increasing implication that the extension of U.S. military power in Southeast Asia will continue until it reaches the level of nuclear war unless effective countermeasures are taken in time.

3. The ghetto uprising in the United States and their connection with the colonial revolution and the international struggle for socialism.

4. The class struggle throughout Latin America, involving on the one hand the utterly reactionary oligarchies backed by Washington and on the other the worker-peasant masses and their revolutionary vanguard.

5. The betrayal of the revolutionary struggle in Latin America committed by the right-wing leadership of the Venezuelan Communist Party.

6. The class-collaborationist Kremlin policy of "peaceful coexistence" with world capitalism followed by the Kosygin-Brezhnev regime.

Throughout the proceedings, the main theme was the reactionary role played by U.S. imperialism in Latin America, particularly its maintenance of the most repressive military regimes. Considerable attention was paid to the depth of U.S economic, political, and military penetration on a continental scale. The delegates added graphic accounts of what is happening in their own areas and how the U.S. blocks the social overturns needed to lift their countries out of stagnation.

The indictment of U.S. imperialism began with the opening address made by President Osvaldo Dorticós Torrado and reached its most powerful expression in the closing speech made by Prime Minister Fidel Castro at the Chaplin Theater.

However, the most dramatic moments in the presentation of the case against the world's most colossal economic and military power came during two press conferences at which the journalists and delegates were given an opportunity to question agents of the CIA captured in Cuba while on counterrevolutionary missions. One of the groups had landed during the conference itself!

From the basic premise concerning the continental scale of the role of U.S. imperialism and its policy of intervening in any country in Latin America where it decides an active threat may exist to its reactionary interests, the conference drew a number of far-reaching conclusions.

First of all, it was obvious that the struggle for emancipation must itself be conducted on a continental scale. Heavy stress was placed on the identity of interests among the toiling masses in all the countries of Latin America. This was summarized at the conference in the words of Simón Bolívar: "For us, our country is America." Rephrased, this becomes the present-day slogan: "Latin America—one country."

Secondly, it was obvious in face of Washington's policy of blocking even modest reforms by bolstering or installing the most ferocious military dictatorships, that no road is left open to the peoples of Latin America but armed struggle. Moreover, it was affirmed that the objective of this struggle must be nothing less than a socialist victory.

These two conclusions—the hemispheric nature of the freedom struggle and the necessity of taking up arms in a battle for the socialist way out—were affirmed in speeches and resolutions that made headlines around the world. The position was graphically symbolized in two giant portraits, one of Simón Bolívar, the Liberator, as a backdrop at the opening session, the other of Che

Guevara similarly placed in the Chaplin Theater where the OLAS meeting came to an end. The meaning was unmistakable—what Bolívar began in the past century as a bourgeois-democratic revolution can be completed and carried to success today only as a socialist revolution.[2]

This outlook, it is clear, stands in sharp contradiction to the line of "peaceful coexistence," or class collaboration, followed by the right-wing leaderships of the Communist parties in Latin America. The experience with these leaderships, particularly the right wing of the Venezuelan Communist Party, which went so far as to publicly repudiate the guerrilla fighters, was placed on the agenda for special consideration. The Cubans, along with the

---

2. A curious sidelight was the reaction of the ultraleft sectarians to this. For instance, Mike Banda of the Socialist Labour League, describing the decor at OLAS as he saw it from London, said: "This conference significantly and unlike previous [?] conferences was adorned by portraits [?], not of Marx and Lenin, but of Simón Bolívar, the bourgeois-landlord-statesman."

Banda was silent about Che Guevara and his portrait, probably because of a blind spot in his binoculars. But an unsigned article in an adjoining column of the same issue of the *Newsletter* (September 2) supported the thesis of J. Posadas and the SLL that it was all a lie about the famous guerrilla leader having left Cuba, since he was presumably liquidated by Fidel Castro. The authenticity of Guevara's message on the need to bring massive aid to the Vietnamese people by creating more Vietnams and taking the road to socialist revolution is highly suspect, according to the same anonymous writer, who also remains unconvinced by Régis Debray's "unclear" statements about "some kind of encounter with Guevara" in Bolivia. It is not at all to be assumed from this that the SLL supports Guevara or his line. A subsequent article in the September 16 *Newsletter* declared that the OLAS conference drowned out basic Marxist concepts with "loud noises about 'armed struggle.'"

Whatever else may be said of Banda's views, it must be admitted that he adheres with flawless consistency to the SLL theory that Cuba is a capitalist state headed by "another Batista," who is itching to sell out to U.S. imperialism despite the resistance of the State Department to a deal, and who demonstrated this by caving in to the Kremlin's line of "peaceful coexistence," getting rid of the revolutionary Guevara as part of the betrayal. Thus it is not by accident, if we are to believe Banda, that Castro feels a natural affinity for the portrait of the "bourgeois-landlord-statesman" Bolívar, just as it is not by accident that Banda feels a natural affinity for the portrait, if not the thought, of the "manufacturer" Engels.

representatives of the various guerrilla fronts, called a showdown on the issue.

On the ground that they had betrayed the struggle in Venezuela, the Venezuelan CP leadership was not invited to the conference. It fell to a center group, headed mainly by the CP contingent in the Uruguayan delegation, to seek to avert or soften the showdown. They argued that it would be unwise to split with the right-wing Venezuelan CP leaders—they were good comrades who would see the error of their ways in time. The unity of the movement must be preserved at all costs. Even if the Cubans and the guerrilla fighters felt strongly about the actions of the Venezuelan CP leaders, definitive action should not be taken at the OLAS conference. The question should be referred to a subsequent conference of the Latin American Communist parties, where the Communists could settle their differences among themselves. Besides, it would be a mistake to make a fetish of armed struggle. In some countries, of course, no other means is open and it might well be that it will eventually prove to be a necessary stage in all countries; but the value of other forms of struggle should also be admitted. Criticism of the Soviet government for offering technical and financial aid to such dictatorships as the one in Colombia was considered particularly uncalled for and reprehensible.

These and similar arguments did not convince the delegates, and the conference ended by characterizing armed struggle as the only road to victory under the conditions prevailing in Latin America, all other forms of struggle being necessarily subordinate to this and of value only insofar as they further armed struggle.

In conjunction with this, the conference held up the experience of the Cuban revolution as a general model. Whatever mistakes were made in the course of the Cuban revolution and whatever modifications might be required due to specific circumstances in the various Latin American countries, the main lesson of Cuba remains valid—against a repressive military dictatorship of the Batista type, only armed struggle can assure victory. Moreover, the Cuban experience, it was maintained, also remains valid on the tactical level. The key to mounting an armed struggle with any hope of success is to launch guerrilla war.

The question of armed struggle was thus taken at the OLAS conference as the decisive dividing line separating the revolutionists from the reformists on a continental scale. In this respect it echoed the Bolshevik tradition. Seeking to pin things down still more tightly, the Cubans insisted on the key importance of guerrilla war as a method of moving toward armed struggle. They likewise insisted on the priority of the countryside over the city in initiating a guerrilla nucleus and advancing it. Certain modifications, nonetheless, were to be noted. For instance, it was reported that in Venezuela the guerrillas have shifted from a fixed center to a "moving column." Another interesting development was the distinction made between "revolutionary conditions" and "revolutionary situations." The former refers to the broad relationship of forces, the latter to a specific combination of circumstances such as Lenin had in mind in projecting the seizure of power. While revolutionary conditions hold for all of Latin America, in no country does a revolutionary situation in the Leninist sense exist at the present moment. Thus the perspective is for a long and difficult period with no easy success in sight.

While the delegates concentrated on problems of the Latin American revolution, the framework of their deliberations was much broader. They did everything possible to utilize the conference as a sounding board to express solidarity with the Vietnamese people. They did not limit themselves to hailing the heroism of the Vietnamese, but insisted on the need to support them in the most vigorous and effective way possible—by stepping up material aid, by opening up new fronts against U.S. imperialism, by revolutionists making the revolution in their own countries.

A similar attitude was displayed in relation to the struggle of the black people in the ghettos of the United States. When Stokely Carmichael spoke at the final plenum, he received a standing ovation; and throughout his stay in Cuba, the press, radio, and television featured him as one of the main luminaries. The uprisings in the ghettos in the U.S. going on at the time of the conference were given similar prominence; and after the conference a giant rally was staged in Havana on August 18 in commemoration of the Watts explosion. In this way the Cubans sought to call dramatic attention to the common ties between the colonial revolution and the struggle of the black people in the United States, and to draw the appropriate lessons.

The conference ended by setting up a permanent organization with a set of statutes. The aim of the new organization, OLAS, is to coordinate and advance the revolutionary struggle in Latin America along the lines specified in the main resolutions passed by the delegates. In this way, the conference not only drew a balance sheet on the experience with the right-wing leaderships of the Latin American Communist parties, it set up a new continental organization to challenge them in the field of struggle. This was probably the single most important outcome of the Havana gathering.

What was the line of political thought behind the OLAS conference? No documents are available on this, but it can be inferred with perhaps reasonable accuracy. I would say that the Cuban leaders have drawn certain broad conclusions concerning their entire experience up to this point.

To save the Cuban revolution from being smashed by American imperialism, they were compelled to turn to the Soviet Union. Without material aid from the Soviet Union, it would have been virtually impossible to survive without immediate extension of the revolution. Besides material aid, they also turned to the first workers' state for models in various areas. This also involved turning to the existing Communist Party in Cuba, particularly for cadres.

This course, from which the Cubans felt there was scarcely any realistic escape under the circumstances, also carried certain disadvantages. One of the worst was the undue impetus given to the growth of bureaucracy, which would have been a problem in any case. The danger was seen in time, and the Cuban leaders met it head-on in the famous Escalante affair. They drove ahead to completely restructure the party so as to further deprive the Escalantes of points of leverage.

In the international field, where the Cubans from the very beginning were committed to advancing the cause of world revolution, the experience was even more disturbing. Khrushchev's course in the missile crisis of 1962 showed the dubiousness of relying on the Soviet bureaucracy in a showdown with American imperialism. The doubts that arose, or were reinforced, at that time settled into firm conclusions in view of the policies followed by both Moscow and Peking in face of Johnson's escalation of the war in Vietnam. An Asian land war which ought to have led to an early defeat for American military power was permitted to drift into an increasingly dangerous threat without a single serious countermeasure being undertaken. The two powers have proved incapable up to now of uniting even at a government level in defense of a beleaguered workers' state and with their own countries marked as subsequent targets! The Cubans thus came to see in Vietnam a warning as to their own possible fate.

The conclusion was inescapable. The defense of Cuba rests primarily on the Cuban workers and peasants. The best defense is extension of the revolution.

As they came to realize this with fresh urgency, the Cubans went through another disappointing experience—the leadership of the Venezuelan Communist Party gave up the armed struggle to which it had committed itself and reverted back to the "electoral road," i.e., participating in the electoral field not as a revolutionary opposition party, but as a pressure group supporting the "progressive wing" of the national bourgeoisie.

And this betrayal received covert support from the Kosygin-Brezhnev government through cynical proffers of technical and financial aid to Latin American military dictatorships participating with all their counterrevolutionary energy in the U.S. blockade of Cuba.

To counter the Venezuelan betrayal and the Kremlin's treacherous maneuvers in Latin America, a vigorous new assertion of revolutionary principles and a fresh start in applying them was obviously required. The OLAS conference was designed to serve this objective.

Looking back, it can be seen that the Tricontinental conference, held in January 1966, represented a step in this direction. It ended in a compromise, however. Along with the assertion of revolutionary goals, formulas were agreed to that provided a cover for the right-wing CP leaderships and all those who were willing to pay lip service to armed struggle while in practice continuing to play the rotten game of electoral politics. This was capped with Castro's attack on "Trotskyism," which, however much it satisfied the right-wing CP leaderships, was taken by all vanguard elements with any real knowledge of the Trotskyist movement as at best a mistaken identification of Trotskyism with the bizarre sect of J. Posadas and at worst nothing but a belated echo of old Stalinist slanders, the purpose of which remained completely obscure. It was thus necessary to wait and see what the true outcome of the Tricontinental conference might be. The course followed by the Cubans quickly disclosed that the revolutionary side of that conference was the more important and it became clearer and clearer, particularly after the disclosures concerning the betrayal in Venezuela, that a public break with the right-wing CP currents was inevitable and imminent.

This was formalized at the OLAS conference. The right-wing CP leaders were branded as betrayers of the revolution, those who attempted to straddle the issue were compelled to line up, a clear declaration was made on armed struggle as the only road in Latin America. In this context, the political meaning of the OLAS conference is absolutely clear. It registered the fundamental differentiation of the Cuban revolution from the old Communist parties and their class-collaborationist politics.

Does this mean that the Cuban leaders have become Trotskyist? The answer is no. What they have done is assert their political independence in relation to both Moscow and Peking, or any other center for that matter. As the logical concomitant to this, they have decided on a policy of *nonexclusion* in relation to all other revolutionary tendencies. They will give a hearing to and collaborate with any revolutionary current. Whether or not a given tendency is actually revolutionary is to be determined by its attitude toward the Cuban revolution and the principle of armed struggle in Latin America.

The break with the right-wing CP leaderships consummated at the OLAS conference consequently opens the way throughout Latin America for an accelerated regroupment of revolutionary forces. How this will work out specifically remains to be determined in each country, of course.

A conference or congress, no matter how revolutionary it is in principle, cannot do more than draw a balance sheet on the experiences of the preceding period and project a course of action in accordance with the lessons that have been learned. The OLAS conference was no exception; in fact it did well in this respect, accomplishing what it set out to do.

Nevertheless, some very important questions, raised at least by implication, received little or no discussion. In the coming period they will undoubtedly occupy the attention of many of those who participated in the conference, and perhaps they will be brought up at a later stage in the regroupment process.

For instance, there is the problem of explaining the betrayal of the right-wing leadership of the Venezuelan Communist Party. It is scarcely sufficient to consider such a development to be a matter of individual weakness of character, inasmuch as an entire leading staff of a mass party with a strong trade union base was involved. Evidently the betrayal had social roots. These ought to be explored not only for the education of new revolutionary cadres, but also the better to avoid a repetition of such a disastrous outcome and the better to combat the betrayers in Venezuela itself.

Obviously associated with this are the international ties of these leaders, their political background, and particularly their formation in the school of Stalinism. All this should be brought out into the open and the lessons assimilated.

A related question is the failure of the Cubans in particular to anticipate the betrayal. To raise the question does not at all mean to indict the Cubans. In fact the integrity they have displayed makes it possible to raise it dispassionately. Study of the question will of itself eliminate the deficiency—which is lack of knowledge of the true history of the world Communist movement and lack of appreciation of what Stalinism did to that movement.

That this has a very practical side is indicated by a related question: How did it happpen that in the internal struggle in the Venezuelan Communist Party, the faction that stood for revolutionary principles ended up in a minority while the faction that stood for class collaboration ended in a majority? The question is all the more pertinent in view of Cuba's nearness, the impact of the Cuban revolution throughout the continent, and the fact that the revolutionary faction had behind it the weight of a workers' state. The course of that factional struggle ought to be studied closely in all its aspects, with a view to determining whether the defeat was objectively inevitable or whether perhaps avoidable errors were committed. If the defeat was due to a shift in the relationship of class forces in Venezuela, then the revolutionary movement must examine not only the causes of this but how it affects tactics and strategy. If it was due to blunders in leadership, the objective effect of these blunders must still be weighed.

A problem which some delegates were already pondering at OLAS demands the most intensive consideration. This is the problem of the revolutionary struggle in the cities. The key issue is what to do in situations where the masses are not yet prepared to engage in all-out combat but can be mobilized to at least some degree. Is leadership of the workers and the unemployed to be turned over to the right-wing betrayers? Without a battle for the allegiance of the masses? Are there partial struggles which the workers and unemployed might be prepared to engage in that could prove propitious to the revolutionary cause and which might serve at least to remove the right-wing betrayers from the field as a serious obstacle?

It is to be noted that the Venezuelan betrayers, in seeking to answer the damning charges leveled against them by Fidel Castro, have advanced as one of their strongest arguments precisely the question of the revolutionary vanguard maintaining its ties with the masses in the cities. They, of course, seek to utilize the masses as pawns in the electoral game and at the same time divert them from the revolutionary road; but their calculation that the Cubans are vulnerable on this issue should be weighed quite objectively. It is not only in chess that the moves of a foe can indicate weaknesses in one's own position that might otherwise be overlooked. The correct countermove would seem to be to step into the arena of the class struggle in the cities and seek to outflank the right-wing CP leaders to the left. The secret of success lies in the development of transitional slogans which in and of themselves are more realistic than the measures advocated by the reformists yet entail a logic that takes the masses along the road of revolution.

All this is associated with the question of developing a homogenous leadership and organizational structure capable of giving correct guidance to the revolutionary struggle in all its aspects. This is what revolutionary Marxists mean when they talk about the necessity of building a party of action. At the OLAS conference this question was colored by the Cuban experience, so that one heard such contradictory statements as "the revolution will be made with or without a party" and "the guerrillas constitute the core of the party." If the revolution can be made without a party, why advance the concept of a party being built around guerrillas or of guerrillas performing any political function at all? And while the possibility of making a revolution without a party was voiced, at the same time the necessity for absolute discipline in the struggle, the disciplined combination of the military and political aspects was insisted upon. The question obviously demands deep consideration, the elimination of misunderstandings arising from various sources—not least of all the bad impression created by the Stalinist and Social Democratic record in Latin America and elsewhere. A study of the Bolshevik experience could possibly prove of unusual interest if it were undertaken with due consideration for the peculiarities to be found in Latin America.

The correct relationship between revolutionary theory and practice can also be expected to come under examination in the coming period. There was an evident tendency at the OLAS conference to ascribe the failures and betrayals of the right-wing CP leaderships to wrong or outdated theories, or to "theorizing" divorced from reality. Deeper study of the whole phenomenon of Stalinism will disclose, however, that the policies of the parties affected by it did not flow from "theory" but directly from some very mundane and practical bureaucratic interests. The "theory" constituted little more than window dressing, although eventually certain theories that were advanced, such as the theory of building socialism in one country, had their own pernicious influence. The tendency noticeable at the OLAS conference to discount theory was one of the consequences of leaving out of account the role of Stalinism as a determinant in the betrayal of the Venezuelan Communist Party.

It should be added that the seeming bias against revolutionary theory in general derives in reality from a specific rejection of Stalinist, Social Democratic, and all other varieties of reformist ideology, just as the seeming discounting of the decisive role which a party can play as a revolutionary instrument derives from a specific rejection of parties of the Stalinist and Social Democratic type. This attitude, a necessary stage in preparing the way for the organization of genuinely revolutionary mass parties in Latin America and for a rebirth of revolutionary theory, is now coming to a close. The definitive break with the right-wing CP leaderships is a certain sign of this.

Finally it should be noted that while the black struggle and its Black Power phase in the United States was handled in exemplary fashion at the OLAS conference, the antiwar struggle and the dynamic movement shaping around it in the United States did not come up for attention and analysis. The oversight stood out all the more in view of the importance ascribed to it by the Vietnamese and the impact it has had throughout the world. Perhaps the Cubans misjudge the potential of the antiwar movement, considering it to be frozen in a pacifist pattern. In the coming period this wholly unprecedented development in the American class struggle will undoubtedly reveal new facets that will not fail to prove impressive to all Latin American revolutionists and to invite closer attention on their part.

The OLAS conference ended a chapter in Latin American revolutionary politics and opened a new one with very promising perspectives. For the imperialists, things have taken a decided turn for the worse. For the vanguard, a great advance has been registered. They are now in a much better position to carry out their duty, which is to make the revolution.

# The Promising Developments
## at the OLAS Conference
## (1967)

One of the most encouraging developments in the recent period—a development greatly accelerated by the war in Vietnam—has been the growing realization among sectors of the vanguard that have hitherto been influenced if not swayed by the Soviet or Chinese leaders, that these leaders are not to be relied on. The clearest manifestation of this centers around the Cubans, but it is also apparent among the Vietnamese, the North Koreans, among circles in and around certain Communist parties, and among sectors of the intellectuals in the Soviet Union and the East European countries.

The Cuban revolution is acting as a polarizing center for this critical sentiment. The Cuban revolution is serving in this way precisely because of the high level of consciousness of its leadership and the conclusions they have obviously drawn from the course of the war in Vietnam.

We very early came to the conclusion, it will be recalled, that the Cuban leadership represented something new. It was not shaped in the school of Stalinism. Its political consciousness had deepened in the very process of revolution, and it had independently developed revolutionary Marxist conclusions out of the practical experience gained in making a revolution. We foresaw that there were excellent chances for this leadership to go much further in its development. In any case, we were convinced that it marked the beginning of a new important phenomenon—the rise of a genuinely revolutionary-minded generation, free from the blight of Stalinism.

We are now able to state that these estimates were not wrong. In fact, the way the Cuban leaders have acted in response to the war in Vietnam has served to confirm our prognosis in the strongest and most striking way.

At the recent OLAS conference in Havana, this leadership

reaffirmed the need for the masses to take the road of armed struggle and condemned the decision of the right-wing leadership of the Venezuelan Communist Party to turn away from that road and to revert back to mere electoral politicking as nothing less than a betrayal of the socialist revolution. A new, influential voice was thus added to the long list of revolutionists who reached similar conclusions concerning the attitude and actions of the bureaucratic CP leaderships. But this condemnation represents a historic first. It is the first to come from the leadership of a workers' state since Trotsky began the struggle against Stalinism and in defense of the program of socialist revolution.

The condemnation of the right-wing Venezuelan CP leadership at the OLAS conference was another step in the process that began inside Cuba with the struggle against bureaucratism, a high point of which was the condemnation of Aníbal Escalante and his supporters. The showdown at OLAS, however, was a reflection of international and not domestic developments.

In relation to the Latin American revolution as a whole, the differentiation between the Cuban leadership and the right-wing CP bureaucrats has proceeded around the issue of armed struggle as the only means to victory where all other possibilities have been barred by dictatorial regimes backed by U.S. imperialism. Holding up the Cuban revolution as an example, the Castro leadership has exerted increasingly heavy pressure on this issue ever since the beginning of Johnson's escalation of the war in Vietnam. The right-wing CP leaderships did their best to evade the issue or to pay lip service to it while they actually sabotaged it.

We observed this struggle very attentively despite its muted nature until recently. Even Castro's attack on "Trotskyism" at the Tricontinental conference in January 1966, which we of course answered immediately, did not cause us, out of anger or resentment, to lose sight of the reality and turn away. We noted the very positive steps taken at the Tricontinental conference to reinforce the revolutionary struggle in Latin America. We realized that if the resolutions adopted at that conference were actually applied it could only facilitate the exposure of the pseudorevolutionists and help speed up the process of building a revolutionary leadership on a continental scale. The Cubans demonstrated that they meant what they said, and the differentiation with the treacherous right-wing CP leaderships speeded up accordingly. The showdown came at the OLAS conference in Havana in August.

The political meaning of the decisions taken at the OLAS conference is crystal clear. They represent a definitive break with the treacherous leaderships whose advocacy of "peaceful coexistence" really signifies a line of maintaining the status quo and doing everything possible to block the masses from taking the road of revolution. The OLAS conference thus represents an important ideological advance, offering the greatest encouragement to revolutionary Marxists throughout the world. One of its first consequences will be to facilitate a regroupment of revolutionary forces in Latin America and to speed up their development along programmatic lines. Even a setback as severe as the death of Che Guevara will not halt this process. The turn marked by the OLAS conference conforms with the political realities of Latin America and the imperative need to build a revolutionary leadership capable of correctly absorbing and applying the lessons of the Cuban revolution on a continental scale.

In some quarters it has been maintained that the Organization of Latin American Solidarity, which was set up at the Havana conference in August, represents the appearance of another International. For instance, John Gerassi, writing on the OLAS conference in the October issue of the *Monthly Review,* asserts that Castro has launched a "new, Fifth International."

A conclusion of that kind is hasty, to say the least. However well-intentioned and internationally minded such a conclusion may be, it indicates a serious underestimation of what a task it is to create an International; that is, a genuine, revolutionary Marxist International. The underestimation derives most likely from lack of study of the history of what has been done in this field. Above all, it reveals an underestimation of the role of program in constructing an International.

In this respect, the Organization of Latin American Solidarity has much to accomplish before the claim can seriously be advanced that it constitutes a new International. First of all, OLAS must consider the problem of the revolutionary struggle in the industrially developed countries, particularly the main power center of world imperialism, the United States. This is not an unimportant question since American imperialism is the principal prop of the oligarchies and dictatorial regimes that directly confront the revolutionary movement in the colonial and semicolonial world. The industrially developed countries are also where the final and decisively important battles will be fought in the struggle for world socialism.

Secondly, OLAS must consider the problem of the revolutionary struggle in the workers' states, the question of a "revolution in a revolution." Again, this is not unimportant, as is proved in the clearest possible way by the course of the Soviet and Chinese bureaucracies in the Vietnam War.

Thirdly, even in Latin America, the area of primary concern to OLAS, some very important problems remain to be worked out, particularly the problem of providing revolutionary leadership for the masses in the cities through the development of transitional slogans and partial struggles, breaking the way for broader and more decisive battles.

Fourthly, the immense problem of the internal life and functioning of an International must be considered. A rich experience testifies to the immense difficulty of constructing an international party—for that is what an International is—even with the most skilled and knowledgeable application of the principles of democratic centralism. But the statutes adopted by OLAS at the Havana conference show that these principles have yet to be grasped by the founders of the organization. This question, however, stands at the heart of constructing a viable International.

It is to be hoped that OLAS will take up these problems. I think that it is completely in the logic of the progress already made by the Tricontinental and OLAS conferences to turn toward serious considerations of these problems. I believe that significant contributions in these areas can be expected from the revolutionary figures who have assembled in the Organization of Latin American Solidarity. But it is certainly quite premature to credit them with already having established a new International, a claim which they themselves have not as yet ventured to assert.

The role of the war in Vietnam in nurturing the differentiation between the revolutionary orientation of the Cuban leadership and the right-wing CP leaders in Latin America can easily be followed. From the very beginning of Johnson's escalation of American involvement in the civil war in Vietnam, the Cuban leaders pointed out the need for vigorous countermeasures. As both Moscow and Peking permitted things to drift, the Cubans became more and more concerned. This was evident in the increasing stress they placed on the danger which the war in Vietnam signified for the Cuban revolution. If the Vietnamese should be defeated, then it is certain that the Cubans will be next. Another significant indication of the trend in their thinking was the alteration of the slogan, "Cuba does not stand alone," to a new slogan: "We Cubans must rely on ourselves." Along with this, heavier and heavier stress has been placed in Cuba on the heroic example of the Vietnamese.

Preparations for the armed defense of the island against a new invasion have been stepped up considerably so as to make any attempted invasion as costly as possible to the imperialist forces. All these developments are indications of the lessons which the Cubans have drawn from the course of the war in Vietnam.

On the international front the Cubans have vigorously advanced two themes: First, the need of the revolutionists in each country to make the revolution. Second, the need to bring effective aid to the beleaguered Vietnamese.

They state, quite correctly, that the best way to help the Vietnamese is to make the revolution in other countries. This is the meaning of the slogan advanced by Che Guevara: "Create two, three . . . many Vietnams." It was also the central meaning of Che Guevara's action in attempting to organize a guerrilla focal center in Bolivia. He wished to set another example, to provide a living contrast between the lip service being paid to the Vietnamese cause by Moscow and Peking and the resolute action which the situation requires.

The effect upon the outlook of independent-minded revolutionists like the Cubans is, in my opinion, the single most important consequence of the escalating war in Vietnam. The Cubans display this effect to a striking degree but it is also observable elsewhere, as we have indicated.

In a less conscious way, a similar effect is observable among broad social layers. The rebellious mood among the American youth, particularly on the campuses, is a good indicator of the radicalization being induced by the war in Vietnam. We are being provided with fresh proof of the inherent tendency of a reactionary war to inspire a progressive countertendency. As revolutionary Marxism noted long ago, a reactionary war tends to become converted into a civil conflict, into a civil war. It tends to sponsor mass resistance and to prepare the way for a new generation of revolutionary leaders capable of organizing this resistance so as to provide society with a road out.

We stand at the beginning of this development on an international scale. It is this which disconcerts and worries those in the capitalist class still capable of observing what is happening. It is this which gives our movement reason for the greatest optimism and confidence. The stream of history is turning in our direction.

# Why Castro Ended Up in the
# Minority in Venezuela
# (1969)

1. Guerrilla war in Latin America was not the invention of the Cubans. It has existed in the continent as a living tradition with a venerable history.

2. One of the most unexpected features of the Cuban revolution was that this tactic could prove sufficient to win. Our conclusion at the time was that this testified much more to the weakness of imperialism and the national bourgeois structure than to the discovery of something superior to a Leninist combat party.

3. More than a mere guerrilla band was involved in the Cuban struggle. The July 26 Movement had an extensive organization. Its petty-bourgeois program enabled it to secure financial assistance in a big way from Cuban bourgeois circles. It was also able to operate quite freely in the United States, where it was actively supported by a large Cuban colony.

4. The July 26 Movement proceeded to a considerable extent like a party based on a single issue—armed struggle against the Batista dictatorship. Its appeal cut across class lines.

5. The key leaders of this movement were of such high caliber that when the revolution reached the crossing point to socialism, they plunged ahead, splitting their own movement and transcending the program they began with.

6. In transcending their original program and declaring for socialism, they also transcended the tactic through which they had won. Just as every succeeding revolution in Latin America must take as its model *socialist* Cuba instead of the July 26 Movement as it was first formed, so in tactics it is compelled, if success is to be assured, to make an advance, developing means capable of achieving the mass mobilizations required to win a socialist revolution. This means putting politics in command. Technique, tactics, even armed struggle must be subordinated to political consciousness, to political direction, to a clear political

program. The key problem, consequently, is to build a combat party capable of seeing this and doing it.

7. The Cuban leaders, although the logic of their own revolution calls for it, have not proceeded along this line up to now. The reasons for this are plain. Dependent on aid from the Soviet Union, aid which was absolutely essential to the survival of the Cuban revolution, they were confronted with the problem of the Kremlin's policy of "peaceful coexistence" with imperialism and in particular its rabid opposition to Trotskyism. The course followed by the Cubans shows that they decided that if errors were to be made, they should be made on the side of caution so as not to jeopardize the flow of material aid. This explains why the Cuban Stalinists were not reproved for their gross attacks on Trotskyism and why Castro himself could make the kind of attack he did at the Tricontinental conference in January 1966. It explains, too, why the Cubans took such an ambiguous attitude during the May-June 1968 events in France and why to this day they refrain from publicizing the role of the Trotskyists in the French upsurge. And it explains why Castro—with very important reservations, it is true—came out on the side of the invaders of Czechoslovakia. In short, the Cubans have not yet settled accounts with Stalinism. Until they have done so, it is misleading to say without qualification, as the resolution does in point 11: "This leadership by its attitudes, its actions and generalizations has contributed in a decisive way to the maturing of a new vanguard."

8. There is an immense anomaly in this failure to settle accounts with Stalinism, inasmuch as the Castro team won their victory in Cuba in face of the default of the Blas Rocas and their active opposition. One of the main lessons of the Cuban revolution is that it is now possible to outflank the Stalinists from the left.

9. Instead of fostering an extension of this course elsewhere in Latin America, the Castro team sought to utilize the existing Communist parties. On the surface, it appeared feasible to repeat the political formula of the Cuban revolution—but with a different combination of political tendencies from those assembled in the July 26 Movement in the struggle against the Batista dictatorship. The formula was to suppress the political differences with the Stalinists and form a combination on the single issue of armed struggle against the indigenous dictatorships and their imperialist backers. The basic idea was once again to make

politics secondary to technique, to subordinate political strategy to the tactic of rural guerrilla war.

The results were hardly brilliant. No sector of the opposing camp was taken in by the camouflage. The lack of political clarity could only serve to sow confusion in the ranks of the revolutionists. Still worse, greater forces were now required to win; i.e., the masses in the urban centers. But the tactic itself was not designed to raise their political understanding, to organize and mobilize them. It banked on winning by pitting very small contingents in skirmishes remote from the cities. Moreover, the political confusion in the camp of the revolutionists involved a decisive issue in the new stage of the Latin American revolution—the role of Stalinism. Lack of clarity on this led to some very costly defeats.

The Cubans have made progress in overcoming this limitation, but only through very painful experiences. It is the beginning of political wisdom to insist that revolutions in Latin America, or elsewhere in the world where similar conditions exist, cannot be won along a "peaceful" or "democratic" road, or under the leadership of an alleged progressive sector of the national bourgeoisie. The issue, once considered in the radical movement to be a hallmark of "Trotskyism," proved to be of key importance in bringing the Cubans to understand that Stalinism and organizations dominated by Stalinists are not reliable instruments of revolution. But by confining the dispute with the Stalinists almost exclusively to the issue of armed struggle, and limiting it even further to the question of rural guerrilla war, the Cubans gave precious political ground to their opponents by default. Thus the Stalinist betrayers of the revolutionary struggle in Venezuela were able to advance telling arguments on why the workers need a revolutionary party. For the Venezuelan Stalinists, who cited Lenin in a completely abstract way, this was only a smoke screen; but the Cubans were not able to answer them effectively, and this could not fail to influence at least some good, revolutionary-minded militants. In the same way, the Cubans failed to offer an adequate challenge to the Stalinists in the urban centers, making it easier for them to retain a rather large following, which they, of course, are now seeking to use in their wheeling and dealing in the bourgeois electoral arena.

The Cubans likewise conceded the field of theory to the Stalinists under the hardly laudable guise of ridiculing the "theorists" as against men of action, who don't need to learn about revolution in books inasmuch as they are practicing it with guns.

The Cubans even made the mistake of posing the issue in terms of a conflict between the men in the mountains and the bureaucrats in the city over who should have final command. Arguments were adduced concerning the technical difficulties of urban guerrilla war—the helplessness of the masses, the corrupting influence of the city, the difficulties and dangers of maintaining liaison—to explain why leadership should be in the hands of the men in the rural areas. The political issue underlying this obscure debate was very simple: should the struggle be led by men committed to a revolutionary struggle for socialism or by men committed to Moscow's treacherous foreign policy of "peaceful coexistence" with imperialism? This was the key question no matter where the leadership was located under the exigencies of the struggle. But this issue, which should have been brought to the fore in order to clarify the dispute and to fight for a majority on the basis of it, was left in obscurity by the Cubans. The Stalinists took full advantage of the ineptness of the Cubans, or their hesitation at speaking out because of possible economic pressure from Moscow, to further obscure and bury the question.

The result of these mistakes was that even in such a favorable situation as the one in Venezuela, with the prestige of the Cuban revolution behind them, and the not immaterial advantages of state power, the Cubans ended up as a small minority in their factional struggle with the Stalinists.

10. Immediately after the Cuban victory, the Trotskyist movement held that one of the most important tasks facing the revolution there was construction of a revolutionary Marxist party. This has been borne out in the most decisive way by events and ought to be pointed out in the draft resolution on Latin America.

11. The key task facing the vanguard in Latin America, as elsewhere, still remains the construction of a revolutionary Marxist party. This takes priority over all questions of tactics and strategy in the sense that these must be directed to achieving this end as the decisive link in the revolutionary process. It is not enough to say, as the resolution does in point 19, that "the existence and functioning of a revolutionary party, far from being an outworn schema of outmoded Marxists, corresponds to the concrete and ineluctable needs of the development of the armed struggle itself. . . ."

The party is not a means to the armed struggle, as this sentence seems to say; the armed struggle is a means to bring the proletariat to power under the leadership of the party. Construction of the party must be viewed and presented as the central task, the main orientation, the almost exclusive preoccupation of the vanguard. And the explosiveness of the situation in Latin America does not lessen the need; it intensifies it.

# The Seven Errors Made by Che Guevara
## (1969)

In considering the limitations of the Cuban leaders, some points were brought out at the congress which have not been discussed before. Our view on the Cubans as we presented it at the congress was that the Cubans made an enormous break-through in their revolution. They succeeded in gaining a victory due to the default of the Communist Party, and the fact that they, as a young generation of revolutionaries, refused to follow the Communist party, and struck out on their own. Under the peculiarities of the situation in Cuba at that time, they succeeded, through guerilla warfare and its development, in gaining power. This was their great positive achievement. But this very achievement, in the peculiar form in which it occurred, also tended to set the subsequent course of this leadership along lines which they have not yet transcended.

First of all, in Cuba they utilized the Communist Party. They dismantled it, tried to put it together and make something new out of it. It was like using old bricks in a new building. They found the Cuban CP useful in this respect.

Then, in extending the Cuban revolution, thereby defending Cuba in the most effective way, they sought to repeat the Cuban pattern, that is, the pattern of the Cuban revolution. They sought to utilize the Communist parties in other parts of Latin America.

After a time, this effort to utilize the Communist parties in Latin America ended up in a real faction fight. Because the Cubans, in utilizing the Communist parties, did not try to build a combat party in any of these countries; instead they tried to utilize the Communist parties to build guerrilla forces. This proved not to be successful. So they ended up in a factional struggle with the CPs, in which the key issue became armed struggle versus peaceful coexistence.

On that issue, of course, all of us were on the Cuban side—against the concept of peaceful coexistence.

The faction struggle ended in a split with the important Venezuelan CP, and this was codified more or less at the OLAS conference in 1967. Here, one of the limitations of the Cubans showed up, that in splitting with the Venezuelan CP, they did not make any political accounting. No political accounting over what the role of Stalinism was, and they sort of buried the whole thing and ended up in a very small minority. Because of their incorrect political course, the Cubans ended up with a small minority not only in Venezuela but elsewhere in Latin America. Nowhere did they succeed in building, or putting together, forces of a size and quality capable of carrying out a revolution in the pattern of the Cuban revolution, or any other pattern.

At the OLAS conference, they projected a new course—that they would work with anybody. We interpreted that to mean, well, "anybody"—that includes Trotskyists. How else would you designate Trotskyists from the Cuban viewpoint?

The defeat of Che Guevara followed that. It had a dampening effect on the whole Cuban line, and its implementation. At the OLAS conference the OLAS had a definite structure, had a definite set of rules, and was projected as a definite organization. And if you'll recall what was said at the time, it was projected that the OLAS might even constitute the core of a new International. This appeared in different newspapers and magazines written by people who had very close contact with the Cuban leadership. Such an article appeared in *Ramparts,* for example. But Che's defeat had a dampening effect, and the OLAS began to wither. It eventually became more and more reduced, until, at the congress, the comrades who were closest to the situation in Latin America said, "OLAS does not exist. What does exist is a number of currents, or tendencies, who more or less agree on the necessity of armed struggle, or guerrilla warfare, who come under the general designation of OLAS, and that's all that remains."

Despite these bitter experiences, the line of the Cuban leaders—and this is primarily at the present time the course and the line of Fidel Castro—remains rural guerrilla warfare on a continental scale over a prolonged period. That's their line. But our assessment of it—we're talking now of the assessment we made at the congress in presenting a minority view—is that it is more difficult today to repeat that pattern than it was in 1958 and 1959. The enemy, that is, the imperialist enemy, has learned a bit, and there has been a series of defeats which have had their effect in Latin America.

In presenting these views, we asked, or rather called for, a drawing of a balance sheet on the whole experience of guerrilla warfare, as to what conclusions could be drawn from it, its weaknesses, whatever positive qualities it has, how far it should be included in the program of the Fourth International, just what assessment should be made of it.

In the process of this discussion, we brought up the question of Che Guevara and the lessons to be learned from the defeat of his undertaking in Bolivia. We drew some rather sharp political conclusions concerning Che Guevara's course in Bolivia.

First of all, we talked about Che Guevara as a symbol. He really is a very admirable figure. He is an admirable figure to all youth who are inclined in a revolutionary direction. He caught their imagination. For one thing, he was a man of action. That's a type of revolutionist coming into increasing prominence—revolutionists of action. Che Guevara's dedication is particularly impressive. He was second or third in the leadership of Cuba, had enormous prestige, an assured government career. He gave that up. He gave up his wife, his children—everything. He gave up all this in order to dedicate himself to a struggle that was very hazardous, a difficult, hard struggle. No wonder he caught the admiration of the youth everywhere. We share this feeling about Che Guevara. We share it very deeply, because to us, he's our kind. We're the kind who dedicate ourselves in the same way, really dedicate our lives to the revolution.

At the same time, we have to make an estimate of him politically, of what he did politically, and what happened politically.

First of all, on the points where we agree with Che Guevara.

We agree with Che Guevara on his overall goal of revolutionary socialism. But we disagree with him that this can be precipitated at any given moment by the will of a revolutionary.

We agree with him on the concept that the best aid that can be given to the Vietnamese revolution would be to create one, two, many Vietnams. But we disagree with him on its being possible to do this through the action of a small group that decides in a selected country that it will precipitate a Vietnam there.

We agree with Che Guevara on his internationalism, and particularly with his concept that the best way to defend Cuba is by extending the revolution. Here we disagree with him on one simple thing. We disagree with his concept that a revolution can be exported. In saying this we are taking into consideration more what he tried to do than what he may have said on this point. That's what he actually tried to do in Bolivia—export a revolution.

We agree with him on his opposition to Stalinism. What we disagree with him on is how to oppose Stalinism. Our concept is that in opposing Stalinism, we must work this out through political confrontation with Stalinism, through the elaboration of differences with Stalinism, through the assessment of the historical experience with Stalinism, so that the whole development of Stalinism and its meaning becomes understood to the core. It's not enough simply to be anti-Stalinist. Much more is required.

We agree with him in his opposition to the politics of peaceful coexistence. Our alternative to that policy is to construct a combat party in the Leninist tradition, and what we stress is the importance of political leadership.

We did not take up the technical side of Che Guevara's operation in Bolivia, simply indicating that very little has been said on this by experts. Fidel Castro only went so far as to say that Che Guevara had a tendency sometimes to be much too bold in these operations; but he might have meant that in the sense of throwing himself personally into sectors of the battle where he could easily have been killed.

What we were concerned about was Che's political errors. And these we listed as follows:

First, he assumed that a particular situation in Bolivia followed directly from a general situation on a continental scale. If all of Latin America is in an explosive condition and if the whole situation is prerevolutionary, then if you look at Bolivia, you must say that Bolivia is the weakest link in Latin America. And you can list all the reasons why it should be the weakest link. But what Che left out in making this estimate was that there are also ups and downs within a particular country, and that it becomes very, very important in a revolutionary struggle to know when the movement is actually rising among the masses, and when it is declining. This involves the question of timing—when to throw yourself into action, how to conduct yourself, what slogans to raise, what actions to engage in.

Second, Che Guevara left out the timing in relation to the Bolivian class struggle. Timing is a crucial question in an important revolutionary action. I should say that it's also a very difficult question for even a revolutionary party to determine. We know that from the Bolshevik experience. It is very difficult for even a revolutionary party to determine precisely the moods of the masses, the exact extent that they're moving forward, and to be able from this knowledge to undertake the correct action at the correct moment. It does not follow directly from a general situation and it requires a party in order to determine it. Che had no party. His timing was conceived in the light of a general continental situation and on the objective need to help the Vietnamese and to defend the Cuban revolution, not on a direct and immediate appreciation of Bolivian realities.

To be noted in this conjunction was his belief that a revolution can be precipitated through the action of a small force, even from the outside, because most of the people whom he brought into Bolivia in the beginning were from the outside. This whole approach of Che Guevara in this situation resembled a sectarian approach. Preconceived ideas. The general situation is explosive, you've got to help the Vietnamese, and the revolution can be precipitated by a small force. He proceeded almost dogmatically. He formed his concept of the situation in Bolivia in much the way sectarians do.

His third political mistake was that in place of relying on a combat party, in place of constructing that, or having it available to him in Bolivia, he depended on a very treacherous ally. In the first place, you shouldn't depend on an ally, any ally at all; you should have your own forces. But he didn't have his own forces—political forces—and he had to depend on an ally. And the ally was a very treacherous one—it was the Bolivian CP. Even with the Bolivian CP, his political preparations were inadequate. He did not work out his alliance with the Bolivian CP carefully. What he should have done, since they were treacherous, was to have a showdown with them in advance, before the operation was even engaged in. He had to have this showdown with them in order to determine how reliable they might be when the fighting began. It was absolutely essential for the success of his guerrilla operation in Bolivia to have good connections with the miners, and to have good connections with the masses in the cities, particularly in La Paz.

The fact that he did not undertake this showdown, but simply engaged in the action, made it much easier for the Bolivian Stalinists to shift their differences with Che Guevara from a political level—that is, the difference between the lines of peaceful coexistence and armed struggle—to shift it from the political level to organizational questions, which happens nearly always in a factional fight with an unprincipled group. They raised the organizational question against him. They were all for what he did, but they had organizational differences with him. First of all, they accused him of a lack of consultation. And, of course, they had a point there. He did not consult them about the operation. Next, they raised the question of who should have command. That's not a very good question to debate because it involves personal qualifications and the whole thing gets lowered to a very vulgar level. The Stalinists did this very deliberately to avoid the main political question. It was an error to permit this kind of situation to develop.

Che Guevara's fourth error, which I have already referred to, was to begin an armed action without a political party or even a nucleus of a party either in the countryside or the city. He did not even have any ties with the Trotskyists, who had a certain connection with the masses both in La Paz and in the mines, and he did not have any connections with the peasants, or any organized political forces in the countryside, so that when he began his action, he was faced with a situation in which, if the peasants did not rally immediately to his cause, then he would have to substitute for them. So he fell into a position where a small force substitutes for the masses, or tries to substitute for them. I'm quite sure that in the writings of Che Guevara you can find statements against this, against any substitution for the masses, statements that certain preconditions are required for guerrilla warfare; but the fact is that this is what he fell into in Bolivia.

His fifth error was that he made no advance political preparation among the peasants of any kind. Not the slightest of any kind whatsoever. Party or no party, simply no kind of preparation whatsoever with the peasants. So they were taken completely by surprise. All of a sudden, here are these guerrilla fighters, and it takes them some time to estimate this, and to judge what it may mean. Precious time was lost by that while the enemy mobilized.

Then, his sixth mistake was to underestimate the will, the readiness, and the technical capacities of the CIA and the Pentagon to initiate countermeasures against him. This he badly underestimated. They, on the other hand, did not underestimate him at all. When they learned about his action, we now know, they held a top-level meeting in Washington, involving all the forces around Johnson—the Pentagon, the CIA, the State Department, all their top men were involved with all their connections in Bolivia, their vast resources, technical apparatus, and we don't know how many millions of dollars were spent. They estimated Che Guevara as being a very serious person, one who required their special attention. In other words, they had a better appreciation of him than he had of them. That's a bad mistake for a political person to make. You've got to estimate the enemy very, very carefully.

His seventh error was to choose a position—and this involves a technical side, too—where it was difficult to break out or to receive aid. It may have been a very good area to practice the technique of guerrilla warfare, but it wasn't very good to receive aid, or to break out of. And he was actually caught when he tried to break out of that place. So this choice made it easier for the counterforces to isolate him when the peasants did not rally immediately, as he had hoped they would.

If we summarize all these errors, we come to the following general conclusion about them: that Che Guevara put guerrilla technique—armed-struggle technique—above politics. He put military action above party building. And I think that this is incontrovertible, that this is what he actually did.

The conclusion to be drawn from this, remembering that Che Guevara was a very important advocate and practitioner of guerrilla warfare, is that first of all, guerrilla warfare does not stand up as a general strategy, however well it may fit in as a tactic in certain situations when it is used by a well-constructed combat party.

A second conclusion to be drawn from this experience is that it presented fresh proof that the struggle in Latin America has become more difficult and requires a better instrument than previously—it requires the construction of a combat party to a much greater degree than, say, in 1958 or 1959.

# The Cubans Pause for Reflection
## (1970)

Since the last world congress, the configuration of the revolutionary vanguard has undergone significant alteration.

The most important development is undoubtedly the discussion opened by such figures as Héctor Béjar on the lessons to be drawn from the guerrilla experience. As thinking revolutionists, they cannot help wondering what has gone wrong. Why is it that more than ten years after the Cuban revolution not another success has been registered in the entire continent? It is surely not due to lack of courage or audacity, to lack of commitment to armed struggle, to failure to regard the Cuban revolution as the great model to be emulated.

As a first approximation in making an analysis, some of the revolutionists have sought to locate technical, or perhaps political, errors. Not a few, as was to be expected, have been found. But then the Cubans made not a few technical and even political errors, yet succeeded. The Cuban experience demonstrated that it is possible to commit considerable errors without ending in disaster. Nevertheless, throughout Latin America, attempt after attempt in countries of the most varied kind and with leaders of the most varied temperaments and skills has ended in defeat.

One of the reasons adduced is the more intensive repression exercised by U.S. imperialism. But if this were *the* reason, then it is clear that a more effective and powerful strategy than the one used by the Cubans is required.

Inevitably the most conscious revolutionists are haunted by the feeling that something is eluding them in their efforts to discover what has been going wrong.

It is very instructive to see how in their efforts they continually touch on questions directly connected with the problem of building a combat party. This stands out with the utmost clarity in Héctor Béjar's analysis, although he continually turns away from that road. Moreover, in their efforts they are drawn, despite themselves, toward reading Trotsky.

This search for the correct reasons for the defeats suffered by the Latin American revolution since the Cuban victory is a very positive development. It shows that some important sectors of the vanguard, or at least some important cadres, have come to realize that action alone is not sufficient. Correct concepts—a correct theory—are also required. This is in marked difference from the Cuban revolutionists, who got along without much theory and who even decried theory.

The Trotskyist movement has every reason to foster this discussion and to offer answers of its own. Unfortunately the majority line is not conducive to this. History has settled the question, if we are to believe Comrade Maitan. Che was right. Guerrilla warfare is the solution, and an alternative strategy, reducing guerrilla warfare to a tactical problem, is a priori virtually excluded, including the Russian strategy in 1917 of which Trotsky, following Lenin, was the great practitioner and exponent.

Another very important change in the Latin American situation is the current reluctance of the Cuban leaders to become involved in rural guerrilla warfare.

At the world congress, the majority counted on the Cubans continuing to do what they had done in the case of the guerrilla front opened by Che Guevara in Bolivia. This was a hazardous calculation, the minority maintained, because the full consequences of the defeat of Che had yet to be measured. In particular the Cubans might be in the process of reassessing their line in Latin America in view of the repeated setbacks that had been experienced. If the Cubans were to undertake a reorientation, the minority pointed out, then the resources available to the small groups still committed to carrying out the old line would become even more limited. To plunge ahead despite this change in the situation could prove to be exceedingly ill-advised.

It is now fairly clear that what the minority called attention to at the world congress (and much before that in the leadership of the world Trotskyist movement) turned out to be an accurate political assessment. The changed attitude of the Cubans has now become one of the key questions in the discussion going on in the vanguard over revolutionary strategy in Latin America and what course to take. This has had its repercussions inside the Fourth International.

In the resolution passed at the world congress, the first task assigned to the revolutionary Marxists in Latin America was:

"Integration into the historic revolutionary current represented by the Cuban revolution and the OLAS, which involves, regardless of the forms, integration into the continental revolutionary front which the OLAS constitutes."

The majority has now been compelled to modify this. In his article "Cuba, Military Reformism, and Armed Struggle in Latin America," Comrade Maitan writes:

First of all, it must be noted that not only has the OLAS, as an organization, failed lamentably but also that the role of the Cuban leadership in the Latin American revolution is being increasingly disputed. I already mentioned the public attack on the Cuban leadership by Douglas Bravo's movement. But others also are expressing criticisms that follow more or less the same lines. In fact, most of the groups linked to Castroism are increasingly taking their distance from Havana, accentuating their independence. They now have a tendency to consider the relations they establish among themselves more important than their relations with the Cubans and what remains of OLAS—more properly speaking, of the preliminary moves to establish this organization.

In order to maintain a correct attitude toward the Cuban revolution, it is of crucial importance to understand the pressures it faces and the courses open to the Cuban leadership. Some comrades in the Fourth International appear to be leaning to the opinion that a qualitative change has occurred and that Cuba ought now to be designated as a degenerated workers' state. Against this view, Comrade Maitan argues—correctly so, in my opinion—that while various things are disturbing, particularly the political influence of the Kremlin, the adverse developments have not reached the point of qualitative change.

It must be said, however, that Comrade Maitan's attempt to rebut the charge that Fidel Castro has given up internationalism is exceptionally weak:

Revolution in Latin America is still considered a necessary condition for the survival and development of the Cuban state itself. There is indisputably a turning inward on domestic problems and a pause for reflection. It is also probable that no initiative similar to Che's Bolivian campaign nor even like those previously in Venezuela will be attempted in the present stage. But there is nothing to support the assumption that in the event of the outbreak of a new wave of revolutionary struggle and armed struggle in a Latin-American country the Cuban leadership would adopt a reserved attitude or try to cool things down. Once again its active solidarity would be assured.

The guerrilla groups that charge the Cubans with having given up internationalism point precisely to the lack of "active solidarity" in operations designed to further the strategy of "rural guerrilla warfare." Their point is well taken if you agree with them that "the only realistic perspective for Latin America is that of an armed struggle" and that "armed struggle in Latin America means fundamentally guerrilla warfare." However, that is precisely the viewpoint of the majority. Comrade Maitan reasserts it in the most emphatic way in his article.

Were he to participate actively in the discussion now being carried on between the Cubans and their critics on this point, he would in all consistency have to agree with those who are "taking their distance from Havana." For what is their basic point? It is simply that they are attempting to continue in accordance with the line previously followed by the Cubans. It is the Cubans who have changed, not they.

Shouldn't Comrade Maitan come to their aid by at least polemicizing with the Cubans, marshaling arguments to convince them to stop drifting in such a crucial matter as "rural guerrilla warfare" and to resume their old line?

It would be wiser for our movement, of course, to emulate the Cubans in their "pause for reflection," even if our conclusions are not the same as theirs.

Since the defeat of Che Guevara in Bolivia, the Cubans have faced a crisis in their international revolutionary orientation. The basis of the crisis is the failure of "rural guerrilla warfare" to win any successes. It has met with defeat after defeat.

In addition, despite all the prestige of the Cuban revolution and the immense advantage of holding state power, the Cubans even appear to have come out second in their factional struggle with the Stalinists on the continent.

Precisely because of their success in Cuba, it was difficult for the Cubans to see the negative consequences of their orientation placing guerrilla warfare above party building. How could it be that what had proved successful in one instance should prove disastrous in a series of other instances? The outcome of Che's venture proved conclusively that it was not a question of experience or know-how. What, then, is the correct solution to the crisis?

It would be a big mistake for our movement to exclude the possibility of the Cuban leaders, or at least some of them, eventually arriving at a correct solution. It is true that the outcome is not guaranteed; the comrades who are ready today to write off the Cubans may have the satisfaction finally of being able to say that they were right. But one of the determinants in the outcome may well prove to be our own attitude toward the Cubans, particularly our explanations and the course we propose.

Thus both for the fate of the Latin American revolution and the immediate future of the Trotskyist movement it is of the utmost importance to fight for a positive outcome to the dilemma facing the Cubans in their international revolutionary orientation.

From this standpoint, Comrade Maitan's insistence on the sovereign virtues of "rural guerrilla warfare" is disorienting. In his article "Castro, Military Reformism, and Armed Struggle in Latin America," he reduces the key problem of the Latin American revolution to that of sketching "the concrete forms armed struggle will take." As a contribution, he sketches various forms, trying to put them into a kind of logical order and to assess the chances of their being seen in Latin America in the future. This is a barren exercise in view of the absence of the political context, particularly the party-building context. Above all, he is attracted to guerrilla warfare. "Guerrilla warfare," he says, "has proved at the same time necessary and effective in all kinds of experiences over the past fifty years in Asia and Africa, as well as in Europe itself during the Nazi occupation (above all in Yugoslavia, in Italy, and in France)."

The only conclusion the Cubans could come to on reading that, if they are utilizing their pause for reflection to really think things through, is that the Trotskyists have become more Cuban than the Cubans and that they are advancing arguments that hardly point forward.

What the Fourth International should do by every conceivable means is insist on the primary task *at the present stage*. This is to begin at the beginning—to assemble sufficient cadres to start serious construction of Leninist combat parties.

This requires a sustained polemic against all the tendencies that stand in the road or that threaten to divert the work. The main one, of course, still remains Stalinism, which has gained a reprieve in Latin America because of the persistence of the Cubans and others in seeking to lift rural guerrilla warfare into a strategy in opposition to the strategy of party building.

It also requires some concrete examples of what we mean when we talk about engaging in revolutionary politics. And some concrete examples, anywhere in the world, of what we mean when we talk about building a Leninist party.

This is so elementary that one feels embarrassed to have to insist on it more than three decades after the founding of the Fourth International. Yet this is the real situation, and there is no point in blinking at it. A few further words should be said about this in the interests of rearming our movement.

The most decisive turning point in the long ideological struggle against the pernicious influence of Stalinism was the Cuban revolution. Viewed in historic perspective, the leaders of this revolution represented the first contingent of a new generation that was able to appreciate the positive meaning of the Russian revolution and the existence of the Soviet Union, yet was repelled by Stalinism.

This contingent came to power in Cuba through means that had long ago been superseded in the arsenal of revolutionary Marxism. That this could actually occur was solely owing to the default of Stalinism in combination with objective conditions for revolution that were exceptionally favorable.

Our movement hailed this development, defended it with all our energy, and sought to further and to extend the Cuban revolution.

The absence of a revolutionary Marxist party in Cuba did not disconcert us because we understood the uniqueness of the combination of circumstances that had made the success possible. We considered that the logic of the revolution, if it were not to fall back, would impel the development of such a party in Cuba in the long run and that the same would hold true in Latin America as a whole. Our basic line therefore remained promulgation of the theory and practice of building revolutionary Marxist parties as the correct revolutionary strategy.

We faced some difficult tactical problems. While the Cuban revolutionists had succeeded in bypassing the Cuban Communist Party, they were forced into reliance on the Soviet Union for material aid because of the efforts of U.S. imperialism to crush the revolution. Without that aid the Cuban revolution, as a matter of simple fact, could not have survived. Nevertheless an overhead political cost was involved. The Cubans were undoubtedly made aware, if they did not sense it themselves, that one of the conditions for receiving material aid was to keep "Trotskyism" at a distance. Stalinism was thus able to play a certain role in Cuban affairs. The resulting unhealthy state of affairs reached its height under Aníbal Escalante.

A further complication was that the cause of the Cuban revolution was taken up with the greatest enthusiasm by the youth everywhere. This was an extraordinarily heartening development with its clear portent for the future. However, these revolutionary-minded youth did not understand the basic political reasons for the Cuban success; they sought the explanation on the side of skillful technique in the use of arms.

The Cubans fostered this lack of understanding, wittingly or not, since they never assessed their own revolution in the light of the default of Stalinism. To have done so, they would have had to settle accounts with Stalinism—to which the Kremlin would have responded by cutting off material aid.

Moreover, the Cubans in their own international revolutionary orientation insisted on the priority of skill in the technique of armed struggle. Their contempt for theory and hostility to party building were additional negative elements.

All of this fostered ultraleftism and even an antipolitical attitude among the youth drawn into the orbit of the Cuban revolution, particularly in Latin America. It should be added that, like many youth on first coming to revolutionary views, they were inclined toward ultraleftism to begin with. They thus evinced a strong predilection for sheer action, violent action, even by small, isolated contingents, without consideration for the political necessity to calculate everything they did and said in relation to the problem of reaching the masses and organizing and mobilizing them on the necessary scale.

This was where the revolutionary-minded youth were to be found, this was what they were like, and the Trotskyists, if they were not to lose contact with the new generation of revolutionists, beginning with the Cubans, had to go through the experience with them.

In taking this course, we made no concessions in principle. In the imperialist centers we stood on our own Trotskyist program in the first line of defense of the Cuban revolution. It is enough to recall what the Trotskyists in the United States and Canada did in helping to organize and advance the Fair Play for Cuba Committee. Our comrades in Europe and India and many countries in Latin America were similarly active.

# IS THE CASTRO GOVERNMENT STALINIST?

*The Cuban revolution was unique among the revolutions that have overthrown capitalism. Unlike the October 1917 Russian revolution, Cuba did not have a conscious, revolutionary socialist leadership or mass democratic workers' councils. Moreover, unlike the post-World War II overturns in Eastern Europe and Asia, the Cuban revolution was not led by a Stalinized Communist party. Yet Cuba's connection with Stalinism has been a central question for defenders of the revolution.*

*Months before the Cuban leaders adopted Marxist positions and proclaimed the revolution to be socialist in 1961, the State Department was red-baiting Cuba, trying to whip up public opinion in the United States with charges that Cuba had gone "Communist." Their charges that Cuba was antidemocratic were part of the preparations for a counterrevolutionary war—the 1961 Bay of Pigs invasion, the 1962 missile crisis—not an attempt to help the Cubans deepen the democratic roots of their revolution. The first two essays in this section answer these red-baiting attacks.*

*The threat to the Cuban revolution from capitalism can be defeated only by deepening and extending the revolution—establishing institutions of workers' democracy inside Cuba and encouraging revolutionary movements in Latin America and throughout the world. This was the course the Cuban leadership tried to follow; they armed the masses, organized the militia, carried out vast educational campaigns, and gave what aid they could to movements in other countries.*

*But the Stalinists in Cuba tried to implement another policy: collaboration with capitalism abroad, and fostering of bureaucratism inside Cuba. The first battle over bureaucratism was the Escalante affair of 1962. Aníbal Escalante, an old CP leader who held a leading organizational post in the Integrated Revolution-*

ary *Organizations (precursor to the unified Communist Party of Cuba), pulled together a clique of Stalinist functionaries who began to issue directives and assume authority as if they were the central leadership of the party and the government.*

*Fidel Castro denounced these corrupt, privilege-seeking, sectarian practices in several public speeches, asserting a revolutionary line of internationalism and workers' democracy ("the duty of every revolutionary is to make the revolution . . ." and "the revolution must be a school of unfettered thought . . .").*

*The Stalinists were unable to defend Escalante against Castro, but they found a way to attack revolutionary socialism on another front: Hoy, the newspaper of the old Cuban CP, opened an attack on "Trotskyism." In "Trotskyism and the Cuban Revolution—an Answer to Hoy" Joseph Hansen explains the essence of Trotskyism and the role of Trotskyists as defenders of the Cuban revolution, and exposes the class-collaborationist record of the CP.*

*In 1965 after extensive travels in Africa, Che Guevara left Cuba, leaving a message which Fidel Castro conveyed to the media. The mystery of Che's departure and whereabouts led to speculation in the bourgeois press about a split in the Cuban leadership; some ultralefts went even further, opining that Castro had capitulated to Stalinism and purged Guevara. In "'A New Field of Battle' for Che Guevara" Joseph Hansen discusses the changes in the Cuban leadership and the role of Che in continuing the internationalist policies of the revolution as part of the Castro team.*

*The Cuban Stalinists opened a new round of anti-Trotskyism after Fidel Castro at the Tricontinental Conference in early 1966 charged that "Trotskyism became . . . a vulgar instrument of imperialism and reaction." This throwback to the slanders of the Moscow trials was picked up by Blas Roca, a CP hack who had led the Stalinists' support for Batista in the thirties. He amalgamated some quotes torn out of context from the papers of tiny sectarian splinters from the Fourth International with repeated references to "Trotskyism" to "prove" that Trotskyists did not support the revolution. In "Stalinism or Trotskyism in the Cuban Revolution," Joseph Hansen dissects Roca's charges and his method of argument.*

*Castro's speech at the Tricontinental Conference also attacked Adolfo Gilly, a radical journalist whose articles on Cuba and Guatemala had been published in Monthly Review. In "Adolfo*

Gilly, Fidel Castro and the Fourth International" Joseph Hansen discusses the positions of Gilly and the editors of Monthly Review on issues raised by the Tricontinental speech, including the fate of Che Guevara, the reasons for the attack on "Trotskyism," and Sino- and Soviet-Cuban relations.

In 1968, Castro critically supported the Warsaw Pact invasion of Czechoslovakia. His position posed the question of whether the Cuban leadership was becoming Stalinized. "Fidel Castro and the Events in Czechoslovakia" analyzes Castro's position on the invasion, explaining the contradictory character of Cuba's foreign policy and the non-Stalinist nature of the Cuban leadership.

# Ideology of the Cuban Revolution
# (1960)

Jean-Paul Sartre relates that at the beginning of the year [1960] some Cuban friends came to see him. "They talked at length, with fire, of the Revolution, but I tried in vain to get them to tell me whether the new regime was socialist or not."

Sartre was prevailed on to visit Cuba and determine for himself. Upon leaving, he offered his impressions in an essay of unusual interest, "Ideología y Revolución" (Ideology and Revolution), which was published in the March 21, 1960, issue of *Lunes de Revolución*.

In it, he wrote:

What first surprises one in Cuba—above all if you have visited the countries of the East—is the apparent absence of ideology. Yet it is not ideologies that are lacking in this century; here too, they have representatives who from all sides offer us their services. Your leaders are not ignorant of them; they simply don't employ them. Their adversaries formulate the most contradictory reproaches. For some, this absence of ideas is nothing more than a trick; it hides the most rigorous Marxism, which does not yet dare name itself; some day the Cubans will remove the mask and communism will be installed in the Caribbean, a few miles from Miami. Other enemies—or, on occasion, the same ones—accuse them of thinking of absolutely nothing: "They are improvising," I have been told, "and after having done something they elaborate a theory." Someone adds politely: "Try to speak with the members of the government; perhaps they know what they are doing. As for us, I must confess that we know absolutely nothing." And a few days ago at the University, a student declared, "Autonomy becomes all the more indispensable since the Revolution has not defined its objectives."

In reply to all this, Sartre continued, he had heard a thousand times: "The Revolution is a *praxis* which forges its ideas in action." This reply, the French existentialist philosopher and playwright held, was logically unassailable, but a little abstract. Citing a practical interest in clearing up the question of the theory of the Cuban revolution, he declared: "It is necessary to understand, certainly, the uneasiness—sincere or feigned—of those who say that they don't know anything or who reproach the revolutionary movement with not having defined its aims." Mentioning his first query—is the Cuban revolution socialist or not?—Sartre recognized that the question was not well put, due to the fact that from a distance one tends to be a "little abstract, falling into those big words that today constitute symbols rather than programs." Nevertheless, "Socialism? Liberal economy? Many intellects ask; they are convinced in good faith that a Revolution ought to know where it is going."

Sartre believes they are wrong. The French revolution of 1789 was "totally blind." The same ones

who voted for the Republic were monarchists two years before. Everything terminated in a military dictatorship that saved the rich and reinstituted the monarchy. And, through the mirages of an inflexible rigidity, how many vacillations, how many errors, how many slips backward the Russian Revolution experienced during its first years!

A NEP imposed by circumstances, "failure to foresee" the wreck of the revolutionary movements in Europe or even its own isolation. "The new ideas were expressed within the framework of an ideology without flexibility, becoming converted into hernias: Socialism in one country, the permanent revolution; inventions which it was believed could be justified through quotations."

Sartre, presenting his credentials in this field, is clearly not to be taken as a serious theoretician of revolution. From his brief remarks about Europe's two greatest revolutions, it would be hard to escape the conclusion that revolutionary theory is of little use. Nevertheless, he finds it scarcely satisfying to reply in response to the question in Cuba, "Are you going to build Socialism?" that "*praxis* will define its own ideology."

Sartre found among the leaders of the Cuban revolution two conceptions which he at first thought were contradictory. One of the leaders told him that the revolution is unable to take a long-range objective "because it is a *re-action,* or if you wish, something that rebounds."

He meant by this that your people, placed before a too powerful neighbor, never had the absolute initiative and saw themselves obliged to employ every recourse of intelligence and energy to *invent* a counterblow. And he added: "How can we make long-range plans when we can find ourselves invaded tomorrow, or suffer the most intense economic pressure? Guerrilla war, resistance to economic blockade, would necessarily change the structure of our society. All we know is this: we will not be defeated. But the conditions of our struggle would change us: it will be *another* Cuba that sees the victory." I understood that he meant that your "improvisations" are not, in fact, anything but a defensive technique: the Cuban Revolution must *adapt itself* constantly to the enemy maneuvers. Perhaps the measure of *counterblow* will give birth to a counter-ideology?

However, other leaders talked about themselves.

I asked them questions about their lives, about the evolution of their thought. All of them told me that the Revolution had dragged them far beyond their first positions. Violent clashes had occurred and they had to confront severe realities: some of their old friends had not followed the movement; others, reluctantly in the beginning, had become *radicalized*.

The two concepts at first seemed incompatible to Sartre.

In the first case, I thought, one adapts himself, one temporizes, everything must remain fluid and principles must not constitute a hindrance. In the second, the revolutionary movement becomes more profound, in a sure and, as a whole, regular manner; there exist then an order of march, points of reference, a direction. Perhaps it would be too ambitious to call the discovery of an orientation an "ideology," but it must be admitted that the demands of *praxis* have changed the ideas of these revolutionary leaders.

Observing the reciprocal relation between Havana's masses and Castro, during the Cuban leader's speech following the blowing up of the freighter *La Coubré* as it was unloading munitions for the defense of the country, Sartre came to the conclusion that the two concepts "counterblow" and "radicalization" were actually interrelated and that they marked the entire course of the Cuban revolution. In the rest of his essay he sketches this interrelation, beginning with the appearance of bourgeois-democratic patriots who had to find a class base in the "agricultural workers" in order to build an effective movement, then take up the agrarian cause to carry through the overthrow of the Batista dictatorship, and finally undertake radical economic measures to consolidate the victory and defend the country against imperialism. Sartre sees as the possible end point of this development, should the foreign pressure prove sufficient, "self-radicalization" of the Cuban revolution and, as its economic counterpart, "radical socialization."

In April, a few weeks after the appearance of Sartre's observations, a book by Ernesto "Che" Guevara was published in Havana. Since he is one of the top figures of the Cuban government, anything that Guevara writes is, of course, to be studied. In the particular field covered in the book, guerrilla warfare, he is an undoubted authority, having proved this by his military leadership in the civil war. At present, as head of the National Bank, he is in charge of Cuba's foreign trade, a post of key importance in the defense of the country and in the development of economic planning. *La Guerra de Guerrillas* will undoubtedly be widely discussed in revolutionary circles throughout Latin America, where Cuba is now preeminent as a source of inspiration.

*La Guerra de Guerrillas* is largely a handbook; the author deals in considerable detail with the practical side of guerrilla warfare in a country like Cuba under the conditions of a dictatorship like Batista's. As Guevara stresses, virtually everything he presents is taken from the Cuban experience and may not be applicable in every instance to other countries—even those having much in common in the way of climate, topography, and socio-economic inheritance. I shall not deal with this aspect of the book save to note the striking portrait that emerges of the average Cuban guerrilla fighter.

Recruited from the countryside, chances were that he came to the Sierra Maestra barefoot and unable to read or write. He had gone through a period of testing, not least of which was to obtain his own gun and ammunition—most likely by a raid on a contingent of Batista's armed forces. He did not come with blind faith. Observing the guerrilla leadership in action he had become convinced of its honesty and fairness, the sincerity of its program of agrarian reform, and its will to carry the struggle through to the end.

The guerrilla's life was not easy—under constant threat of death, he was often like a hunted animal, scurrying from cover to cover. He had to make lightning marches by night, attack, and flee. Sometimes as much as three days went without food. He slept in a hammock at best, under a strip of nylon to keep off rain and insects. Tension was never absent. A bath, a shave were luxuries to dream of. (Guevara notes that each man could be told by his individual odor and the whole force by its acrid smell, repelling strangers.)

The firmest asceticism prevailed, the fighters living like monks or Spartans. An iron principle of the leaders was to lead by example: ". . . the chiefs must constantly offer the example of a crystal clear and self-sacrificing life." All, leaders and ranks, shared and shared alike—no exceptions. This included not only the occasional handouts of tobacco but the rugged fare, the hunger, the risks, and the worst hardships. As the guerrilla fighter's horizon widened under indoctrination, he became a revolutionary, charged with the conviction and fervor so characteristic of forces dedicated to a great cause.

The small guerrilla bands grew until they were able to hold considerable territory, where, as a power dual to that of Batista, they were able to give a demonstration of what their government would be like. The guerrilla forces developed into a full-fledged army of such force, hardness, and skill that nothing in the country could stand against it. Batista's forces melted away. The *barbudos,* the bearded ones, marched in triumph into Havana, many of them seeing the wonders of the nation's capital for the first time.

Is it possible to draw more general lessons from this experience than the best practical way to organize guerrilla forces and later convert them into an army? Guevara thinks so. He presents some rather far-reaching conclusions. It is these, of considerable ideological interest, rather than such items as a good recipe for making a Molotov cocktail, or how to trap a Sherman tank, that will undoubtedly arouse most interest. Here is how Guevera begins:

The armed victory of the Cuban people over the Batista dictatorship has been, in addition to the epic triumph recognized in the news of the entire world, a modifier of old dogmas on leading the popular masses of Latin America, demonstrating palpably the capacity of the people to liberate themselves from a suffocating government through guerrilla struggle.

We hold the Cuban revolution made three fundamental contributions to the mechanics of the revolutionary movements in America. They are:

(1) The popular forces can win a war against the army.

(2) It is not always necessary to wait until all the conditions are ripe for the revolution; the insurrectional center can create them.

(3) In underdeveloped America, the terrain of the armed struggle must be fundamentally the countryside.

Explaining his first two conclusions, the Cuban revolutionary leader says that they speak against

the quietist attitude of revolutionaries or pseudo revolutionaries who take cover and cover up for their inactivity, under the pretext that against a professional army nothing can be done, and some others who feel that they have to wait until, in a mechanical form, all the necessary objective and subjective conditions are ready, without preoccupying themselves about accelerating them.

Guevara recognizes, of course, that certain minimum objective conditions must ripen before the "first insurrectional center" can be set up. "Where a government has come to power through any form of popular consultation, fraudulent or not, and maintains at least an appearance of constitutional legality, it is impossible to precipitate guerrilla warfare since the possibilities of civic struggle have not been exhausted."

On the third point, which is of greater interest both in itself and as an indication of how at least this top leader views the Cuban revolution in its wider aspects, Guevara declares:

The third contribution is fundamentally of strategic import and must be a call to attention for those who attempt with dogmatic criteria to center the struggle of the masses in the movements of the cities, completely forgetting the immense participation of those in the countryside in the life of all the underdeveloped countries of the Americas. Not that struggles of the masses of organized workers are to be depreciated, the analysis simply chooses a realistic criterion to estimate the possibilities under the difficult conditions of armed struggle, where the guarantees that customarily adorn our Constitutions are suspended or ignored. Under these conditions, the workers' movements must be clandestine, without arms, in illegality and running enormous dangers; the situation in the open field is not so difficult, the inhabitants supporting the armed guerrillas and in places where the repressive forces cannot reach.

Developing his point further, Guevara specifies that since guerrilla action is best conducted "in wild and little populated places" the struggle for the demands of the people is centered

preferentially and even almost exclusively, on the plane of changing the social composition of land tenancy; that is, the guerrilla is above all an agrarian revolutionary. He expresses the desire of the great peasant mass to be owner of the land, owner of their means of production, of their animals, of all that they have dreamed of for years, of what constitutes their life and will also constitute their cemetery.

Of the two types of guerrilla warfare, Guevara sets aside the one which is complementary to the struggle of big regular armies "such as the case of the Ukrainian guerrillas in the Soviet Union."

What interests us is the case of an armed group which continues progressing in the struggle against the constituted power, whether it be colonial or not, which establishes a single base and which continues progressing in the rural surroundings. In all these cases, whatever may be the ideological structure that animates the struggle, the economic base is given by the aspiration to possess the land.

Seeking other examples to support his generalization, the Cuban leader points first of all to China:

Mao's China begins as an eruption of workers' nuclei in the South that is defeated and almost annihilated. It becomes established and initiates its ascendant march only after the long march to Yenan when it settles in rural territories and places as the base of demands the agrarian reform. The struggle of Ho Chi Minh in Indochina is based on the rice-growing peasants oppressed by the French colonial yoke, and with this force it continues progressing until it defeats the colonialists. In both cases there is an interruption of patriotic war against the Japanese invader, but the economic base of the struggle for the land does not vanish. In the case of Algiers, the great idea of Arab nationalism has its economic replica in the exploitation of almost the entire arable land of Algiers by a million French colons; and in some countries like Puerto Rico, where the particular conditions of the island have not permitted a guerrilla out-break, the national spirit, wounded to the depths by the discrimination committed daily against them, has as its base the aspirations of the peasantry (although in many cases it is already proletarianized) for the land which the Yankee invader seized; and this same central idea was what animated, although in different projections, the small holders, peasants and slaves of the haciendas of eastern Cuba who closed ranks to defend together the right to possession of the land during the thirty-year war of liberation.

Guevara does not rule out the action of the city proletariat altogether. But, since city terrain is the most unfavorable for guerrilla warfare, only limited acts are possible. In other words, reversing the situation of the Ukrainian guerrillas, the workers can only complement the struggle of the guerrilla fighters in the countryside. At a final point in the civil war, however, when the guerrilla forces have swelled into a peasant army capable of regular battle, the city proletariat can find it possible to engage in mass actions "whose final result is the general strike."

In the closing section of his book, "Analysis of the Cuban Situation, Present and Future," Guevara offers some additional considerations. After more than a year in power, it is necessary, he thinks, to take "the exact dimension" of the Cuban revolution. "This national Revolution, fundamentally agrarian, but with the enthusiastic participation of the workers, the people of the middle class and even today with the support of the industrialists, has acquired great continental and even world importance. . . ."

The agrarian reform, "extremely harsh" for those whom it displaced from ownership, put in motion INRA (National Institute of Agrarian Reform), which now "advances like a tractor or tank," breaking up the big landholdings. The agrarian reform was "antifeudal" but occurred in "capitalist surroundings" and against the monopolies. Thus it had to help the peasants and agricultural workers with credit and with machinery and "People's Stores."

Of all the characteristics distinguishing it from the other three great agrarian reforms of the Americas (Mexico, Guatemala and Bolivia), what appears most important is the decision to carry it through to the end without favors or concessions to any class.

Production of such important items as rice, grain, and cotton is developing rapidly, constituting "the center of the process of planning." Cuba's rich subsoil resources have been retrieved through petroleum and mining laws which may turn out to be "as important" as the agrarian reform. The profits of foreign monopolists have been limited. The small island of Cuba is leading the anticolonial struggle in the Americas and has been permitted to take "the heroic, glorious, and dangerous post of the vanguard."

Small countries have sought before now to maintain this position; Guatemala . . . which fell before the direct aggression of the colonialists; and Bolivia . . . which yielded before the terrible difficulties of the struggle despite having provided three of the examples which served the

Cuban Revolution in a fundamental way: the suppression of the army, the Agrarian Reform and the nationalization of the mines. . . .

Cuba knows these examples, knows the pitfalls and the difficulties, but knows also that we are in the dawn of a new era in the world; the colonial pillars have been swept down by the popular national struggle in Asia and in Africa. The tendency today toward unification of the peoples does not come from their religions, from their customs, from their appetites, racial affinity or lack of it; it comes from the economic similarity of their social conditions and from the similarity of their eagerness for progress and recuperation. Asia and Africa shook hands at Bandung; Asia and Africa will shake hands with native and colonial America through Cuba here in Havana.

Guevara notes the decline of the old colonial empires in face of the popular upheavals.

Belgium and Holland are two caricatures of empire; Germany and Italy lost their colonies. France debates in the bitterness of a war she must lose, and England, diplomatic and skillful, liquidates her political power while maintaining economic connections.

The United States has replaced some of the old capitalist colonial powers but knows that this is "transitory." Wall Street's main field is Latin America. But if "all the Latin American people raised the banner of dignity, like Cuba," the monopolists would tremble and have to accommodate themselves to a "new politico-economic situation and to substantial pruning of their gains." That is why the monopolists today attack Cuba as a "bad example." They accuse Cuba because of the road it has pointed out, "the road of armed popular struggle against the supposedly invincible armies, the road of struggle in wild areas to consume and destroy the enemy outside its bases, in one word, the road of dignity."

Guevara winds up discussing the possible variants of imperialist aggression against Cuba and the means of combatting it. For defense he counts heavily on "international solidarity" and guerrilla warfare.

Leon Trotsky remarked in 1940, "The life-and-death task of the proletariat now consists not in *interpreting* the world anew but in *remaking* it from top to bottom. In the next epoch we can expect great revolutionists of action but hardly a new Marx."

Cuba, it would seem, has done her share toward verifying this observation. In their pattern of action, the Cuban revolutionaries feel certain that they have pointed the way for all of Latin America. The proof is their own success. But when we seek to determine the exact meaning of their deeds, Marxist clarity is not easily found.

Are we to understand from what Guevara says that the peasantry has displaced the proletariat as the leading revolutionary class—in the underdeveloped countries at least?

If so, what does this signify for revolutionary perspectives in the highly industrialized countries? Must the perspective of proletarian revolution be considered unrealistic there? If so, how does this affect the defense of revolutions like the one in Cuba? And what does it signify for humanity on such an issue as the possibility of a third world war? Can the proletariat by revolutionary means hope to prevent a nuclear conflict, or must this possibility be relinquished as utopian—unless the farmers take the lead by mounting guerrilla warfare?

Guevara insists—quite correctly, the facts testify—that Cuba now stands in the vanguard of the Latin American revolution. This would seem to impose an obligation to examine the theories and programs affecting that revolution, particularly if Cuba has made a new discovery. Why did the others happen to go wrong? How did the Cubans happen to stumble upon the right road? If for no other reason, such an examination could prove fairly decisive for the defense of the Cuban revolution. Yet even Guevara seems to evade such questions, confining himself to a cryptic reference—the "quietist attitude of revolutionaries or pseudo revolutionaries." What revolutionaries or pseudorevolutionaries? The Stalinists? The Apristas? We are left in the dark.

It is quite true that the Cuban revolutionaries do not have any time for spinning fine theories. They are practical people, swamped with tasks. They scarcely have time to look up from the day-and-night schedules they have had to follow since they came to power.

Yet there are some questions about which the Cubans should be able to say a good deal. For example, how did it happen that the once-powerful Communist Party proved incapable of leading the revolution? How did it happen, instead, that a handful of dedicated students were able to build a revolutionary movement from virtually nothing and accomplish what the Communist Party failed to accomplish? The answer to that should prove instructive to all of Latin America, and the entire world for that matter.

Such topics, however, are not very high on the agenda of the Cuban revolutionaries. Their boldness and sureness of touch in the field of action have no corresponding reflection in the field of theory. Despite Guevara's sweeping conclusions, the theoretical lessons of the Cuban revolution have not yet been drawn.

By way of beginning this task, let us establish some preliminary points of departure.

The founders of the July 26 Movement started as petty-bourgeois democrats. Fidel Castro, for example, ran for Congress in the 1952 elections as a member of the Ortodoxo Party (Partido del Pueblo). After Batista's March 10 coup d'etat, Castro shortly set out on the road to insurrection. This led him within a year to the famous assault on the Moncada fortress and then to prison and exile. On March 19, 1956, he declared his disillusionment with the Ortodoxo Party and announced the July 26 Movement as an independent revolutionary organization. This proved to be primarily a party of action, dedicated to the overthrow of the Batista dictatorship. Although occasional blocs were made with other groups and parties, the essence of its politics was to remain independent and not to swerve from its primary objective. It was a revolutionary youth movement much closer to the campus in the beginning than to either the factories or the fields, although later it came powerfully under the social influence of the poorest peasants and agricultural workers.

Why weren't these youthful revolutionaries attracted by the Communist Party? The answer would appear to be quite simple and even obvious. The Communist Party was not revolutionary enough. In fact, it was not revolutionary at all. It was tainted by its support of the Batista regime. Moreover, neither Stalin nor his heirs were exactly magnets to youth burning with the will to smash the dictatorship. Among other things, Moscow's policy of "peaceful coexistence," i.e., maintenance of the status quo, which was faithfully echoed by the Communist parties throughout the world, was repellent to revolutionaries seeking above all things to alter the status quo.

The models and inspirational guidance they might have found in the early Soviet leaders were not available to them, or were at least obscured under the successive layers of Stalinist mud.

The Cubans turned to what was closest at hand—the leaders of the independence movement of the past century. These figures had a virtue lacking in the Stalinist movement: honesty. Implacable foes of tyranny of any kind, they were dedicated men capable of accepting martyrdom to advance the cause of freedom.

Thus it came about that the July 26 Movement marched under the banners of freedom, equality, and independence, as if the main problem of a modern revolution boils down to reenacting 1776, 1789, or—in Cuban history—1868 and 1895. The 1956-59 struggle closely paralleled the struggle of 1895-98, including the opening landing and the final advance of the guerrilla forces. Although they did not consciously plan it that way, the Cuban revolutionaries, with their beards, even bore close physical resemblance to the heroes of the past century.

Moreover, they took power, as Guevara stresses, not at the head of the modern proletariat but at the head of the peasantry, a class that is vestigial from the precapitalist era.

The pattern seems to defy the Marxist theory that the proletarian revolution has superseded the bourgeois. Yet does it really invalidate the main laws of the world revolutionary process as much as it appears to when you look at the Cuban revolution merely in isolation? If we connect it with the main international events of the past forty-odd years, two outstanding facts of contemporary history at once offer a key: (1) the deepening decay of capitalism, which impels revolutionary outbursts no matter what the barriers; (2) the decades of defeats of the proletarian revolution in the capitalist centers due to the pernicious influence of the Communist parties under control of the bureaucratic caste that usurped power in the first workers' state.

That the main thrust of the Cuban revolution from the beginning was against capitalist imperialism is well understood among those who overthrew Batista. When McKinley intervened in the civil war in 1898, the freedom fighters had virtually won independence from the Spanish colonial master. McKinley aimed at blocking Cuba's independence and bringing the island into the orbit of Wall Street. American capital soon became dominant in both the island's economy and politics. Under the State Department, Batista, like Machado before him, ruled in the style of a gauleiter. Consequently, it is not difficult to see that the main motor force in the Cuban upheaval was American capitalism.

It is perhaps not so easy to see that Batista's rule of a quarter of a century was no more necessary than the similar span of Chiang Kai-shek's rule in China. Had the Cuban Communist Party responded to Batista's seizure of power in 1933 with one-tenth the energy and singleness of purpose later displayed by the July 26 Movement, there can be no doubt that among Roosevelt's headaches would have been a socialist Cuba. Instead the Cuban Stalinists used their influence in the working class to rally support to Batista just as the American Stalinists utilized their influence among the American workers to spread the debilitating cult of "FDR."

The pattern was fundamentally the same as that followed by the Communist parties throughout the world prior to World War II. This is the true explanation for the fact that, more than forty years after the October 1917 revolution, not a single Communist Party has led a revolutionary struggle to success anywhere in the world save in China and Yugoslavia; and in both these instances the leaderships disregarded the line laid down by Moscow. *Stalinism proved to be the most powerful brake on revolution in the experience of the proletariat.* This was so not only in Germany, France, and Spain before World War II, to mention only the most outstanding examples where the workers could easily have taken power, but after the war, when millions of workers flocked into the Communist parties in France and Italy and other countries. If twelve determined men on Pico Turquino proved sufficient to start the avalanche that buried Batista, what couldn't the Italian Communist Party accomplish with its millions of members if it displayed similar revolutionary determination and devotion to the socialist cause which it claims to represent!

On a world scale, taking the entire span since the advent of Stalinism, it is the same default of leadership in the working class, due to Stalinist exploitation of the proletarian tendency to turn toward the first workers' state, that finally resulted in the extraordinary spectacle today of revolutions breaking out in dozens of countries—not under Communist, but under petty-bourgeois and even bourgeois nationalist leadership. One may imagine what Lenin might say of a Soviet Union capable of putting satellites in orbit about the sun and photographing the other side of the moon, yet incapable of giving direct inspiration to revolutionary socialist struggles in other lands; on the contrary, sabotaging them, and thus creating a vacuum in revolutionary leadership!

However, the extension granted capitalism did not remove the objective necessity for transcending the system. The great new fact in world politics is that neither Stalinism nor imperialism, nor the combination of the two, proved capable of suppressing the revolutionary process indefinitely. They could not prevent it from breaking out finally on democratic issues that might even mask the proletarian direction. They could not prevent the revolutionary process from finding leaders capable of at least making a beginning even though they might fail to meet the objective need—or oppose it—at the very next stage.

Unable to blast away the Stalinist obstacle, the revolution turned back a considerable distance and took a detour. The detour has led us over some very rough ground, including the Sierra Maestra of Cuba, but it is clear that the Stalinist roadblock is now being bypassed.

It is not necessary to turn to Moscow for leadership. This is the main lesson to be drawn from the experience in Cuba. And it is the lesson to be drawn above all by the working class in other countries, especially the underdeveloped ones where the revolutionary potential is high. Once this lesson sinks home we will witness an acceleration of the revolutionary process that will not leave the slightest doubt that the main power in society resides with the working class and that it will not forfeit its manifest destiny of leadership in the decisive battles now looming.

A single revolution under the guidance of the working class anywhere in the world today will reveal such energy and dispatch in breaking out of the old society that in retrospect even the dynamic Cuban revolution will appear drawn out and grossly out of proportion in toil and agony. That, however, will not detract from the debt the working people of the world owe the Cubans. To finally break the hypnosis of Stalinism, it became necessary to crawl on all fours through the jungles of the Sierra Maestra.

Men and women capable of that, will prove capable, we think, of transcending the bourgeois limits set at the beginning of the Cuban revolution. Already indications of this are visible. The July 26 Movement came to power not in 1898 but in 1959; and within a few months it became amply clear that not even the simplest democratic aims could be achieved without far-reaching alterations in the economy. Here the revolutionary models taken from the past century could offer little in the way of guidance. Their theory was inadequate.

But economic planning, thanks to the October 1917 revolution, is no longer a matter of theory. Models exist and a vast practical experience, both good and bad. To help solve their own problems, the Cuban leaders are evidently seeking to come abreast of modern times and are turning in this direction.

Thus the inherent tendency of the Cuban revolution to develop in the proletarian direction has been accelerated, and there is every possibility that in an indirect way the fate of Cuba will be profoundly affected by the proletarian revolution led by Lenin and Trotsky. As this pattern of action cuts its way to consciousness, we may hope that the influence of October will be reflected directly in the ideology of the Cuban revolution.

# In Defense of the Cuban Revolution:
# An Answer to the State Department and
# Theodore Draper (1961)

*"But," said Mr. Hennessey, "these open-shop min ye menshun say they are f'r unions if properly conducted."*

*"Shure," said Mr. Dooley, "if properly conducted. No strikes, no rules, no contracts, no scales, hardly iny wages and dam few members."*

The effort to overthrow the Revolutionary Government of Cuba proceeds on various fronts.

The Cuban counterrevolutionaries have set up a "government in exile" dedicated to restoring the nationalized properties to their former owners. They have projected an early invasion of the island. By way of anticipation, terrorists have been planting bombs indiscriminately in crowded areas of Havana. Others have sought to form guerrilla nuclei of a counterrevolutionary army inside Cuba. In military camps in Florida and Guatemala still other contingents are in training for the landing.

Behind these Benedict Arnolds and mercenary killers stand well-heeled henchmen of former dictator Batista, some giant U.S. corporations, and the sinister Central Intelligence Agency, which accounts to no one for the enormous funds it disburses. Behind them, too, stand the Democratic and Republican parties. By cutting off sugar imports and imposing a tight economic blockade on the small country, Eisenhower and Congress sought to starve the Cuban people into submission. Kennedy, since coming into office, has tried to tighten the screws still further.

On another front, the State Department broke off diplomatic relations and pressed all the Latin American countries to follow suit in a holy anti-Communist crusade against a rebellious people that dared lay profane hands on Wall Street's holdings. American tourists, whom the Castro government sought to attract to the tropical vacationland, were scared away by the State Department in order to cut down Cuba's income from tourism; and when a few went anyway to see for themselves what the truth might be, the State Department slammed down its own Iron Curtain, putting Cuba off bounds in violation of the democratic right of American citizens to travel any place they please for pleasure or education.

To this, add the media of mass communication in the United States. The press, radio, and TV payola boys and quiz geniuses are doing their utmost to prepare public opinion for the planned conversion of Cuba into another Guatemala or Korea, campaigning with ferocious intensity against the Castro government, picturing it as having gone "Communist," the more lurid ones talking darkly about Russian "spies" and Russian "rocket bases" a few miles off the coast of Florida.

In a key area, however, public opinion is far from that state of brainwashed stupor displayed at the opening of the Korean conflict. In fact, well-known figures who have taken the trouble to make firsthand investigations have spoken up forcefully in behalf of the beleaguered Cuban people and against Washington's reactionary designs. Their reports have had great impact, particularly among intellectuals. This has given the counterrevolutionary propagandists a problem somewhat beyond their customary skills. How do you win, or at least neutralize, thoughtful persons inclined to support the Cuban side because of facts they have read in *Listen, Yankee!* or similar sources? The matter is important because such people can articulate and lead public opposition to an armed adventure in the Caribbean.

This is where Theodore Draper comes in. As the author of *The Roots of American Communism* and *American Communism and Soviet Russia,* Draper has won a reputation for scrupulous concern for facts and for expert knowledge of the Communist movement. His reputation for factual accuracy in the two volumes is solidly based, whatever the final verdict may be on the correspondence between his general opinions and the truth. Draper has now entered the political struggle over Cuba, bringing to bear the reputation he earned as a historian. His contention is that Castro "betrayed" the Cuban revolution and is taking Cuba down the road to totalitarianism. This is a well-gnawed theme in the Cuban counterrevolutionary press; Eisenhower philosophized on it a bit between rounds of golf; and the State Department has adopted it as the official line for its propaganda machine. Draper offers it in a highly sophisticated version aimed at providing intellectuals with a perfect rationalization for abandoning any sympathy for the Castro regime.

*Castro's Cuba: A Revolution Betrayed?* appeared as the main feature in the March issue of *Encounter,* a British monthly, and has now been reprinted in New York by the Social Democratic *New Leader* as a supplement in pamphlet form to its March 27 issue. The pamphlet is advertised at 25 cents a copy, $20 for 100, or $175 for 1,000 copies—an attractive offer, it must be admitted, in case you feel strongly about that man in Havana, have dough to back your feelings, and want to help spread the anti-Castro gospel.

As his immediate targets, Draper takes the "myth makers"—namely, authors of favorable reports on the Cuban revolution. He singles out for special attention Jean-Paul Sartre, Simone de Beauvoir, C. Wright Mills, Samuel Shapiro, Paul Johnson, Leo Huberman, and Paul M. Sweezy. They get rough treatment.

For example, Draper admits that C. Wright Mills's *Listen, Yankee!* gives an authentic account of the way the Cuban leaders talk, which was what Mills set out to do. ("Sometimes the words in the book," says Draper, "were so close to those I had heard that I felt I knew the name of the source.") Yet Draper insists that a reader has "a right to expect" that a "sociologist would at least be able to give a reasonably accurate report of the social structure of the country," and he condemns Mills's effort:

> The book as a whole is just as honest and dishonest as any unrelieved propaganda is likely to be, and if Mills merely sought to be a front man for the Castro propaganda machine, he has succeeded brilliantly. But is that all that should be expected of C. Wright Mills?

To avoid having his own article appear as unrelieved propaganda, Draper also attacks *Red Star Over Cuba,* a book by Nathaniel Weyl that makes Castro out to have been "a trusted Soviet agent" since 1948. An audience that knows anything at all about Cuba will reject that out of hand as a product of the Batista propaganda machine. Draper, naturally, is severe with Weyl.

Draper combs the writings of his targets for inconsistencies (or seeming inconsistencies), inaccuracies, and muddleheaded theory. Not unexpectedly, he succeeds well in this enterprise, particularly in finding inconsistencies of interpretation and theoretical blunders among the various authors. The Cuban reality is complex; the reporters are variegated in background and outlook and ill-equipped in revolutionary theory. Draper finds Huberman and Sweezy, the editors of *Monthly Review,* especially vulnerable. He makes much, for instance, of such things as their conclusion from a "personal incident"—an interview with a few peasants through a translator—that the Cuban peasants are not "anxious to own their own plots of land" and "didn't understand the question at all until it had been repeatedly rephrased and explained." Draper acidly observes that "the Cuban peasants are truly unique, and no one apparently ever understood them before—certainly not Fidel Castro who put so much emphasis on giving them their own land in 1953 and after."

Yet this campaign in behalf of accuracy and consistency and theoretical clarity is not exactly free from tendentiousness. In the case of *Cuba—Anatomy of a Revolution,* for example, our historian, despite his reputation for objectivity, somehow manages to avoid challenging the main point made by Huberman and Sweezy—that the Cuban revolution is doing well economically and has already brought impressive benefits to the poorest layers of workers and peasants. Similarly, he appears to have concluded that for a politically minded research expert, silence is the best policy to adopt toward the critical opinion of the Cuban Communist Party expressed by Huberman and Sweezy. Discussion of that theme might conflict with picturing the CP as a monolithic juggernaut rolling toward totalitarian power in Cuba.

Rigorous as he is in the standards he imposes on the theses of others, Draper is a bit more relaxed when it comes to his own. One of his central contentions is that Castro is a "Pied Piper" bent on leading Cuba into the camp of Stalinism. The conclusion really follows from preconceptions Draper brings to his analysis, but he also tried to find facts to support it. Here is one which he presents like a prosecuting attorney, as a key piece of evidence in his case:

Events have also dealt unkindly with Jean-Paul Sartre's clairvoyance. In the introduction (dated September 12, 1960) to the Brazilian edition of his series of articles on Cuba, he wrote: "No, if Cuba desires to separate from the Western bloc, it is not through the crazy ambition of linking itself to the Eastern bloc." He also communicated his certainty that "its objective is not to strengthen one bloc to the detriment of the other." On December 10, Major Guevara was "crazy" enough to announce publicly in Moscow: "We wholeheartedly support the statement adopted by this conference [of 81 Communist parties]." It would be hard to imagine any way of linking Cuba more closely to the Eastern bloc or of strengthening that bloc to the detriment of the West than the wholehearted support of this statement.

Guevara was in Moscow in December as head of a mission seeking trade relations that could prove decisive in preventing American imperialism from strangling the Cuban economy. He would have been a strange human and still stranger diplomat not to have felt gratitude for the timely aid the Soviet bloc countries granted Cuba. So that the reader can judge how "crazy" Guevara actually was in expressing his gratitude, here is the relevant section of a report he made over the air on his return:

Mr. Gregorio Ortega: Major, in your trip through the socialist countries you happened to be at the meeting of eighty-one Communist and workers' parties. They issued a declaration and an appeal. I understand that you made some statements about this historic meeting which reached us only in part over the cables.

What can you tell us about this declaration and this appeal?

Dr. Guevara: Well, the truth is that I didn't speak about the declaration, but only supported with enthusiasm the part in which Cuba was mentioned and cited as a shining example for the Americas. And, in addition, the fact that it was mentioned four times in this declaration, of the capital importance which an event of this character has: the meeting of the Communist countries of the whole world.

For us, really, it was an important happening, a thing worthy of pride, to see the importance which was given to the Cuban Revolution, which is considered one of the most outstanding phenomena of the world today and perhaps, after the Chinese Revolution, the most important event that has occurred in the world in the struggle against the imperialist powers.

There was simply a gathering at the Hall of the Trade Unions of the Soviet Union, a traditional hall where foreign visitors can speak. We didn't develop anything but the theme as to why, in our estimation, Cuba was the example for the Americas. . . .

We said there at that time that Cuba was an example because of the form in which it had developed its struggle and because it had interpreted the situation perfectly when the time came to bring forth the Revolution. We believe that there are three fundamental contributions which the Cuban Revolution has already made, things that are not new, which have taken place in other countries, too, but which we put into practice for the first time in the Americas and which we rediscovered, not having had an exact, theoretical understanding of what others had contributed.[1]

---

1. *Obra Revolucionaria,* January 6, 1961, p. 25.

The "three fundamental contributions," according to Guevara, are the creation of an "insurrectional focus," the basing of revolutions in Latin America "fundamentally on the peasant classes," and, on coming to power, the destruction of the armed forces constructed by the ruling classes.

Did Guevara do wrong in Moscow to speak of the Cuban revolutionary experience along such lines and to expound its significance, as he saw it, for other countries, particularly those in Latin America? As a politician of completely different stripe, Draper is, of course, entitled to take a dim view of the pride Guevara displayed in Moscow over the Cuban revolution, but doesn't a reader have a right to expect at least a reasonably accurate report of what the representative of the Cuban government said in Moscow?

Theodore Draper's analysis of the course of events in the Cuban revolution suffers from a defect that has no rational explanation if you consider his approach to be objective and scientific—he leaves out the role of American imperialism as a cause for the radicalization of the revolution.

Our learned historian might be dealing with the world as it was before Columbus discovered America, for all you will learn from him about such provocative actions as the slashing and then ending of the sugar quota, the imposition of an economic blockade on Cuba, the crescendo of insults, proddings, and aggressions under auspices of the State Department and Central Intelligence Agency, and the ominous current preparations under American military advisers for armed invasion of the small island.

What political ends does this singular omission serve?

In seeking the answer, I suggest a careful comparison of Draper's pamphlet, *Castro's Cuba: A Revolution Betrayed?* and the State Department "White Paper" on Cuba, which was released April 3 and reprinted in next morning's *New York Times*. The State Department document was drafted by Arthur M. Schlesinger, Jr., former Harvard historian, with the "cooperation of Richard Goodwin," according to E. W. Kenworthy of the *New York Times,* and was "written in the White House under the close direction of President Kennedy." James Reston reports in the April 5 *New York Times* that Kennedy "approved the State Department's White Paper on Cuba after consultation with Secretary of State Rusk and the head of the Central Intelligence Agency, Allen Dulles. . . ."

The line of this piece of State Department propaganda is startlingly close to the line of Draper's pamphlet. Like Draper, the White House team assiduously avoids mentioning the role of American imperialism, both past, present, and projected, in relation to the Cuban revolution. The same key arguments as Draper's reach the same lulling conclusion; i.e., that the present warlike situation between Cuba and the United States is solely the fault of Fidel Castro. In fact, the two pamphlets coincide closely.

This is not just my impression. On April 5 Max Lerner of the *New York Post* hailed the State Department "analysis and manifesto" as "an important event in the technique of American foreign policy." It's "part of a new diplomacy of the intellectuals," a diplomacy aimed at the intellectuals in Cuba and the rest of Latin America.

And here's the word on Draper. "To complete the Schlesinger analysis," said the *Post* columnist, "I strongly urge you to read a long article by Theodore Draper—'Castro's Cuba: A Revolution Betrayed?' . . . makes mincemeat of the recent books on Cuba by C. Wright Mills, Paul Sweezy and Leo Huberman. . . . We still need a good book on Cuba, but until it comes the Draper and Schlesinger analyses are the best available."

Schlesinger and Draper omit the aggressive role of American imperialism because Allen Dulles's propaganda smokescreen requires it. Once this is left out of consideration, the defensive reaction of the Cuban Revolutionary Government loses its reason and appears pure madness. In such "analysis," everything is conveniently reduced to what *Bohemia Libre*, a counterrevolutionary magazine described by Draper as "the edition in exile of Cuba's most famous magazine," calls Castro's "paranoia"; or, as Draper phrases it for the audience he is shooting at, "my worst apprehensions have come true," Fidel Castro pushed "too hard, too fast, and too far" and "has given Cuba not a national revolution but an international civil war."

To omit the relation between American imperialism and the Cuban revolution has other conveniences, particularly in trying to make out that Castro "betrayed" the Cuban revolution—that is, turned away from the kind of democracy approved by the counterrevolution, the State Department, and Theodore Draper, and moved toward socialist-type institutions.

By dwelling on the limitations of democracy in Cuba, whether real, imagined, or imputed, these odd champions of democracy in the area between Haiti and Florida seek to divert attention from a crime against democratic rights that should make all Americans writhe over their country's role in world affairs. That is the crime of seeking to smash the Revolutionary Government, thereby denying the Cuban people the right to freely choose for themselves what form of government they want. By intervening in Cuba's internal affairs, by trying to strangle Cuba economically, by encouraging, financing, abetting, and arming the counterrevolution, American imperialism violates Cuba's national sovereignty, the main democratic right of any people.

Draper participates in this foul game of imperialist politics by maintaining that the real question at issue is *Cuban* democracy. That's after sixty years of American imperialist domination that imposed some of the cruelest dictatorships in Latin American history on the Cuban people. And with allies like dictator Chiang Kai-shek, Generalissimo Franco, the "towering" de Gaulle, and the indescribable little butcher Tshombe, who murdered Patrice Lumumba!

The Cubans are completely justified in dismissing the imperialist chatter about democracy in Cuba as nothing but war propaganda. They are right to demand of all Americans who raise the issue to please present their credentials in fighting McCarthyism—a test Kennedy, among others, cannot meet.

The Cubans score unanswerable points when they call attention to the way the most elementary democratic rights of Negroes and other minorities are denied and abused in the United States in contrast to the way they are respected in Cuba.

Every civil libertarian must wince when the Cubans note state election laws in "free" America that operate to bar minority parties from the ballot, and federal regulations that deny minority candidates equal free time on the air.

And so you can continue, making an inventory of the American Way of Life showing that a great erosion of democracy has occurred, that militarism is on the rise, and that there is now a vicious latent tendency toward totalitarianism, which makes itself known from time to time in the formation of such fascistlike groups as the John Birch Society. Too bad that a historian of Draper's caliber responds to the unworthy compulsion to leave rich, powerful America out of consideration when he thinks it politically advantageous to discuss democracy in poverty-stricken, beleaguered little Cuba!

Nevertheless, someone who has proved himself on all these

fronts, and perhaps believes in socialism as well, may say, "That's all very true. Still, just among ourselves, don't you think Draper made some telling points? For instance, what about Castro's failure to build a political party, and his letting the Rebel Army and the 26th of July Movement die on the vine? Isn't the Communist Party moving into power, and isn't Castro guilty of a one-man dictatorship? What about elections? How can the workers and peasants exercise democratic control over the government without elections?"

I will admit without the least hesitation that Cuba bears little resemblance to the democratic paradise to be found in Draper's head, if nowhere else on earth. Cuba is being badgered and bullied by the mightiest imperialist power on earth and threatened with a counterrevolutionary invasion in which the Pentagon and the Central Intelligence Agency are deeply involved. The CIA missionaries are out to shove "democracy" down the throats of the Cubans at the point of a machine gun, the way they shoved it down the throats of the Guatemalans in 1954, when Carlos Castillo Armas restored United Fruit to power.

The odds are greater against the Cuban people than they were against the Yugoslavs when they faced German imperialism, yet they have vowed to fight to the death for the freedom they won at such cost. They really believe in the democratic right to self-determination! They have taken up arms, much like our American revolutionary forefathers. Struggles like that, involving civil war, are notoriously hard on the forms of democratic civil life; the rules and laws of war come into operation.

This constitutes the true frame for discussing Cuban democracy. How then can Draper be honestly credited with a single telling point about Cuban democracy when he does not even start with the first requisite for a meeting of minds—the unconditional defense of Cuba against counterrevolutionary and imperialist attack? To blame Castro for departing from the norms of democracy in organizing the defense of Cuba's democratic right to national sovereignty is not only unjust, it is a way of evading the real issues and covering up and excusing the worst enemies of Cuban democracy—and of American democracy, for that matter.

Let us consider more closely several of the principal charges of the State Department propagandists.

"The history of the Castro revolution," say the Dulles-Rusk-Kennedy-Goodwin-Schlesinger harmony five, with a succinctness which soloist Draper might profitably study, has been the history of the calculated destruction of the free-spirited rebel army and its supersession as the main military instrumentality of the regime by the new state militia.

It has been the history of the calculated destruction of the 26th of July Movement and its supersession as the main political instrumentality of the regime by the Communist party (Partido Socialista Popular).

This is doctored history. Draper has assembled a few facts that will help us to show this.

First, let's get an idea of the size of the Rebel Army and the 26th of July Movement:

In the mountains at this time [April 1958, less than nine months before the revolutionary victory], Mills was told, the armed men under Castro numbered only about 300. Four months later, in August 1958, the two columns commanded by Majors Guevara and Camilo Cienfuegos, entrusted with the mission of cutting the island in two, the biggest single rebel operation of the entire struggle, amounted, according to Guevara, to 220 men. Sartre was informed that the total number of *barbudos* in all Cuba from beginning to end was only 3,000.

These forces suffered a high rate of casualties. "Sartre was told that Batista's Army and police killed 1,000 *barbudos* on the last clashes in the mountains. . . ."

Of course hundreds of thousands of Cubans actively sympathized with the *barbudos*; but, as the fighting cadres of the revolution staking their lives on the outcome, they constituted a very small force. This was not Castro's fault. To construct even this body of revolutionaries under the Batista dictatorship was a remarkable achievement.

What about their political quality? The young ones—that is, the great majority—were only at the beginning of their political education. This was true not only of the ranks but of the leaders as well. The following estimate, made by Draper last year in "The Runaway Revolution," an article in the May 12, 1960, *Reporter,* gives us an intimation:

Long after the rebellion in the Sierra Maestra had taken hold, Castro did not head a homogeneous movement, and the larger it grew, the less homogeneous it became. It included those who merely wished to go back to the democratic constitution of 1940 and those who demanded "a real social revolution." It included some who were friendly to the United States and some who hated it. It included anti-Communists and fellow travelers.

A variegated initial political formation of this kind would have undergone internal differentiation, with subsequent splits and possibly fusions with other forces, even in normal times. The revolutionary process accelerated this development, and the counterrevolutionary pressure of American imperialism gave it a breakneck pace. The main direction of the class struggle favored the wing that demanded "a real social revolution."

This evolution toward the left, a typical phenomenon of every revolution, was not a "betrayal" but the political reflection of a deep shift of class forces in Cuba. Of course the apologists and defenders of American imperialism are not concerned with analysis here; they are simply engaging in invidious epithet, an ancient custom among war propagandists.

What happened to the *barbudos* after the victory? A remarkable blindness afflicts the writers in the State Department stables. Draper mentions in "The Runaway Revolution" that 764 cooperatives had been formed when he visited Cuba and 500 more were in the planning stage in the cane lands. Describing "how the system works," he tells about a rice cooperative he visited near the town of Bayamo. After listing the various projects, he notes: "The 'administrator' was a former rebel fighter who had been an ordinary day laborer." The significance of this fact escapes him. To staff each of the cooperatives with a single *barbudo* like this one would require the majority of cadres who survived the struggle against Batista!

We, if not Draper, can appreciate Guevara's dry comment, after the big nationalizations of last fall, on the impracticality—aside from the political inadvisability—of the government taking over the 150,000 really small individual businesses in Cuba. "Just to get 500 interveners for the factories we had to break our heads, and every day we have to replace someone who doesn't work out!"[2]

A less resolute, less self-confident leadership would have felt defeated even before it started the gigantic task of staffing the government and the institutions that grew out of the revolution. The fact is that in the first months after the victory the *barbudos* worked around the clock, sometimes until they dropped and had to be carried out on stretchers. The dissemination of the cadres into the sea of tasks confronting the Revolutionary Government

---

2. *Obra Revolucionaria,* January 6, 1961, p. 29.

is termed by the State Department propagandists "calculated destruction." They make up for this, of course, by pinning "hero" badges on those that were really destroyed—the small number who turned traitor.

It is quite gratuitous to explain to the Cuban leaders the value of a party big enough and capable enough to undertake with smoothness the tremendous revolutionary tasks facing the country. They know from hard experience the value of such a party— how it would have facilitated the struggle for power, what an enormous difference it would make now in solving current problems. But that's not the kind of party the State Department advises for Cuba.

Draper, who knows all there is to know about building a revolutionary party except its practice, condemns Castro for allegedly blocking formation of a party that would properly measure up to the Cuban revolution. This is all the more ludicrous in view of the evident maturing of conditions in Cuba for the appearance of a mass revolutionary socialist party.

Two developments indicate the trend. The first is the formation of the militia.

We have seen how the State Department views the organization of the militia as part of the "calculated destruction of the free-spirited rebel army." Draper uses the epithets "amorphous," "impersonal," and "anonymous" to describe the armed people. This strange historian, in his babbling over the perilous state of democracy in Cuba, is capable of forgetting that America's revolutionary founders considered a militia such an important feature of democracy that they listed it as Article II in the Bill of Rights, next to freedom of religion, speech, the press, and right of petition. To save Draper researching it, here is what the Constitution declares: "A well-regulated militia being necessary to the security of a free State, the right of the people to keep and bear arms shall not be infringed."

If we judge by this criterion of democracy, Cuba under Castro is a free state; America, which has today adopted the Prussian military system, is not. Shouldn't Draper, as a firebrand of democracy, agitate for the militia system in the United States and, for instance, the free distribution of arms to Negroes in Mississippi?

The militia, as a democratic institution of the most fundamental kind, provides a great arena, involving hundreds of thousands of the most patriotic Cubans, for the development of a revolution-

ary socialist consciousness, the main requirement for the formation of the kind of party Cuba needs. Didn't Draper listen to the
political talks that accompanied the militia drills he witnessed
when he visited Cuba? Evidently not. In Draper's humble
opinion, even Castro "makes virtually the same speech every
time"; why listen to mere rank-and-file revolutionary cadres as
they explain the revolution to units of an armed population the
length and breadth of the island?

The other important development pointing the direction of
politics in Cuba was the firm stand taken by the Revolutionary
Government against any imitation of McCarthyism. This defense
of freedom of thought cost the defection of such anti-Communist
figures as Luis Conte Agüero, for whom Draper shed a few
sympathetic tears last year. But by refusing to join in the anti-
Communist crusade which has been such a blight in American
politics since 1948, the Revolutionary Government opened the
possibility for a new realignment of radical political tendencies in
Cuba. The principal grouping affected by this is, of course, the
Communist Party.

To the propagandists of American imperialism, this, naturally,
was nothing less than "betrayal" of the Cuban revolution, for
which, of all the revolutions on its calendar, Dulles's Central
Intelligence Agency has the most tender concern.

By refusing to deny the Communist Party its democratic rights
the way they are denied in "free" America, Castro failed to
conform to the loyalty standards of the House Un-American
Activities Committee. However, this was not equivalent to agreeing with the politics of the Communist Party, as the witch-
hunters would have us believe; it was a principled stand in
defense of democracy.

The Cuban Communist Party rallied to the revolution, while
the bourgeois parties, under guise of fighting the "inroads of
communism," began organizing the counterrevolution in conspiracy with a hostile foreign power, thereby placing themselves
outside any legitimate claim to democratic rights under the
Revolutionary Government.

The witch-hunters and their dupes picture the Cuban Communist Party as a totalitarian force rolling like a Soviet tank to
power, if it does not already "dominate the government," as the
State Department claims. The truth is quite different.

This party, like other Communist parties, is favorably affected
by the melting of the great iceberg of Stalinism, which began

with the Soviet triumph in World War II and continued with the Yugoslav revolt, the victory of the Chinese revolution, and the shattering of the cult of Stalin. The running ideological differences between Moscow, Peking, and Belgrade prevent the party from reverting to the deadly sterility of thought so characteristic of such parties in the thirties and forties. In addition—and this is decisive for the fate of the Cuban Communist Party—the members are under the influence of a great, successful revolution that broke over their heads and in which they must now prove themselves. They are subject to two sources of enormous revolutionary pressure: masses on the move and the radical Castro leadership, which demonstrated once and for all that you don't need a Stalinist background or Moscow advice or backing to topple a tyrant and set out on the road to a planned economy.

Viewed with cold objectivity, it is clear that the Cuban Communist Party is not a contestant for power but is instead one of the main components of a potential new political movement whose ultimate shape is yet to be determined. The chances are excellent that what will finally emerge in Cuba is a mass party with a revolutionary socialist program.

This will scarcely meet with the approval of the Central Intelligence Agency experts on party building in Cuba. What the cloak-and-dagger crew would like to see is a party in power committed to capitalist property relations and—in due time—"democratic elections." Since they are unable to get it any other way, they now propose to brush all democratic considerations aside, shoot their way in, and set up a puppet dictator like Castillo Armas of Guatemala.

The State Department slanders Castro in accusing him of totalitarianism. Castro's basic outlook is deeply democratic. He proved this in the most decisive way by taking an overturn in property relations as the key to extending democracy on the widest possible scale. This is one of the real reasons why Washington regards him with such hate. The imperialist rulers of America are afraid that if Cuba is left alone, if it is permitted to enjoy normal economic and diplomatic relations with the United States, the Revolutionary Government will soon set such an example of democracy in action that the American people would not be long in saying, "That's real democracy! We are entitled to some of that in America, too."

Against the efforts to smash the Castro regime, American supporters of democracy, in defending the democratic right of the

Cubans to self-determination, have every reason to put extra vehemence in the cry, "Hands off Cuba!"

The central thesis of the State Deparment's "White Paper" is that Castro "betrayed" the Cuban revolution. Section III is headed: "The Delivery of the Revolution to the Sino-Soviet Bloc." We are informed in this section that arms "have poured from beyond the Iron Curtain into Cuba" and that trade and financial agreements have "integrated the Cuban economy with that of the Communist world," 75 percent of Cuban trade now going in that direction.

"The artificiality of this development is suggested," the White House authors blandly assert, "by the fact that at the beginning of 1960 only 2 percent of Cuba's total foreign trade was with the Communist bloc."

The "White Paper" does not even mention that Washington cut off all sugar imports from Cuba in 1960 and then imposed a virtually total trade embargo on the island. What were the Cubans supposed to do in face of Washington's artificial political decision to stop all American businessmen from trading with them? Sit down in the shade of a royal palm and quietly starve to death while offering up thanks to Eisenhower and Kennedy for this American aid in speeding them on to a better world?

The Cuban government exercised its democratic right as a sovereign power to trade where it could on the world market. To have done otherwise would have been a real betrayal of the revolution.

The complaint about arms purchases is even more outrageous. Operating with seemingly unlimited funds from mysterious sources, the Cuban counterrevolutionaries, with the connivance of the Pentagon and the Central Intelligence Agency, opened up recruiting agencies for mercenaries throughout the United States, set up training camps in various areas, armed themselves to the teeth, and began invasion preparations by dropping incendiary mechanisms from Florida-based planes and by planting bombs in Cuba's big cities. What should the Cubans have done in the face of this "international civil war," as Draper calls it—bare their throats and say, "Please don't spoil my hair by cutting past my ears"?

In these circumstances does acceptance of aid wherever it can be obtained signify "Delivery of the Revolution to the Sino-Soviet Bloc"? According to that kind of reasoning, George Washington delivered the American revolution to imperial France because he accepted aid from Louis XVI and Marie Antoinette. We can see historian Draper, who at that time hung around the court of George III, beating his wig in anguish over such "treachery." The Americans were clearly "betraying" the anti-French and anti-Indian cause for which they had fought with the British in the French and Indian War not so long before.

But the practical, democratic-minded American revolutionaries took a different attitude toward French aid in their struggle for freedom from British tyranny. In fact, American gratitude was so lasting that almost a century and a half later, in World War I, the most popular slogan the propagandists could think up to cover the landing of American troops in France was "Lafayette, we are here!"

On the other hand, Americans who remained loyal to the crown, Benedict Arnolds who sold out their country's cause, and the Hessian mercenaries who were hired by the British to fight the rebellious colonials are held in deserved infamy to this day.

As another "proof" of its central thesis, the State Department claims that "so far as the expressed political aims of the revolution were concerned, the record of the Castro regime has been a record of the steady and consistent betrayal of Dr. Castro's pre-revolutionary promises. . . ." Draper declares that "Castro promised one kind of revolution and made another. The revolution Castro promised was unquestionably betrayed."

To substantiate his point, Draper has compiled "a brief inventory" of typical declarations made by Castro between 1953 and 1958. They indicate that Castro did not envision going beyond bourgeois democratic measures and that he specifically favored "free enterprise and invested capital" and rejected "wholesale nationalization." In taking over Cuban and American capitalist holdings, the Revolutionary Government clearly went far beyond bourgeois-democratic measures.

By disregarding the economic, social, and political pressures that forced this course, in particular those emanating from Wall Street and the State Department, Draper "unquestionably" has no difficulty in picturing Castro as having "betrayed" the revolution; that is, assuming leadership and responsibility for undertaking measures that went beyond and even conflicted with the original concepts of the revolutionary leaders.

As a professional historian, Draper, you might imagine, would realize that Castro is not the only revolutionary figure he is accusing of "betrayal" for permitting himself to be pushed forward by the revolutionary process. Here is a brief inventory for his consideration:

• In 1774 John Adams wrote that independence was "a Hobgoblin of so frightful mien, that it would throw a delicate Person into Fits to look it in the Face." Later he was a leader in the fight for adoption of the Declaration of Independence.

• In March 1775 Benjamin Franklin testified in London that he had never heard in America one word in favor of independence "from any person, drunk or sober."

• Even after the Battle of Lexington, George Washington told his Tory friend Jonathan Boucher that if ever he heard of Washington's joining in any such measures as the colonies separating from England, Boucher "had his leave to set him down for everything wicked."

• More than two months after the Battle of Bunker Hill, Thomas Jefferson, author of the Declaration of Independence, wrote in a private letter that he was "looking with great fondness toward a reconciliation with Great Britain."

• The delegates to the First Continental Congress, which met in the autumn of 1774, assured the King: "Your royal authority over us and our connection with Great Britain we shall always carefully and zealously endeavor to support and maintain."

• In 1775 the Second Continental Congress, while setting forth colonial grievances, explicitly assured "our friends and fellow subjects in any part of the Empire . . . that we mean not to dissolve that union which had so long and so happily subsisted between us, and which we sincerely wish to see restored." One year and two days later the same congress issued the Declaration of Independence.

Is this contrast between the convictions of one stage and the actions of the next to be accepted by the court as damning evidence of "revolutionary schizophrenia," as Draper labels comparable phenomena in the Cuban revolution? Tom Paine, one of the leading promoters of the American independence movement, saw it more clearly. In "The American Crisis" he wrote: "Independency was a doctrine scarce and rare, even towards the conclusion of the year 1775; all our politics had been founded on the expectation of making the matter up. . . ."[3]

---

3. The above quotations are taken from "The Movement for American Independence" by William F. Warde in *Fourth International,* July-August

Similar brief inventories could be drawn up for other revolutionary struggles. For instance, although he disliked slavery personally, Abraham Lincoln publicly pledged that the slaveholders need not fear a Republican administration. "We must not interfere with the institution of slavery in the states where it exists, because the Constitution forbids it and the general welfare does not require us to do so." As late as September 1861 he told a group of antislavery Republicans: "We didn't go into the war to put down slavery, but to put the flag back; and to act differently at this moment would, I have no doubt, not only weaken our cause, but smack of bad faith."

A year later, in view of the crisis in prosecution of the war, Lincoln overturned property relations in the South. He freed the slaves despite his public commitment to the contrary. We look forward with interest to Theodore Draper's history of the Civil War exposing Honest Abe, the Great Emancipator, as Bad Faith Abe, the Great Betrayer.

Historian Draper's forgetfulness of some major lessons of history is probably not due to any tendency to underrate the importance of facts; at least in his two volumes on the history of the American Communist Party he showed sufficient respect for them to let the record speak pretty much for itself. In the case of Cuba arbitrary preconceptions which he holds affect his selection and arrangement of facts. His "theory" dominates his analysis.

"How could a revolution basically middle-class in nature be turned against that class?" Draper asks. "How could a revolution made without the official Communists and for the most part despite them become so intimately linked with them? How, in short, could Fidel Castro promise one revolution and make another, and what consequences flowed from this revolutionary schizophrenia?"

The Cuban revolution, Draper answers, "belongs to a new type of system, neither capitalist nor socialist, that emerges where capitalism has not succeeded and socialism cannot succeed." According to this view, there is something inherent in the revolution itself that makes it go wrong and compels a leader like Castro to "betray." Naturally, if what is wrong is *inherent* in the revolution, the field of research is correspondingly narrowed, and

---

1950. This article offers an illuminating discussion of the lag between revolutionary consciousness and revolutionary events.

the relation of American imperialism is irrelevant. Even if the White House had remained friendly and the State Department had pumped aid into Cuba instead of attempting ruthlessly to bring down the economy and the new government, Castro would have "betrayed."

What is this inherent poison or congenital disease in the Cuban revolution? Where "capitalism has been successful," Draper tells us, no "impoverished, class-conscious proletariat exists." Therefore, in countries like the United States, which have the technological base for socialism, no socialist revolution can occur.

Where capitalism has not been successful, Draper continues, no "advanced industrial economy" exists that could support a socialist structure as conceived by Marx. However, in the latter areas, the middle class, faced with poverty and lack of opportunity, revolts and turns irresistibly toward the ideology of socialism. "They cannot be faithful to the fundamental ideas of the socialist tradition—that the proletariat should liberate itself, that there are prerequisites of socialism, especially an advanced industrial economy, and that socialism must fulfill and complement political democracy." But they "can find in Marxism an ideological sanction for the unrestricted and unlimited use of the state to change the social order, and they can find in Leninism a sanction for *their* unrestricted and unlimited power over the state."

The result of a revolution under these conditions, Draper contends, is something qualitatively different from either capitalism or socialism.

> The order of development cannot be inverted—first the revolution, then the prerequisites of socialism—without resulting in a totally different kind of social order, alien to the letter and, infinitely more, to the spirit of socialism. These inverted revolutions from above belong to what, for want of a better word, we must call the Communist family of revolutions, which, in practice, serve to industrialize the peasantry rather than to liberate the proletariat.

For about thirty years there was only the Russian variant, Draper continues. Then in 1948 came the "Titoist variant." In late 1949, the "Chinese variant." "Now a new branch of the family has begun to emerge." These are national-revolutionary movements that begin under figures like Nkrumah in Ghana, Sékou Touré in Guinea, or Fidel Castro in Cuba, but soon fall prey to Communism. Since local Communists are, in the beginning, no match for such leaders, they were "advised to bide their time." "First the national-revolutionary movement could win power, then the Communists could win power in the national-revolutionary movements." And that, in effect, is what has been happening in this world of ours.

Having read this, you have read about all of Theodore Draper on this subject. His articles on Cuba offer little more than the dust caught in the bag of this theoretical vacuum cleaner.

The sterile and reactionary character of the politics entailed by this theory is striking. I could find only two sentences in the entire pamphlet suggesting an alternative to nationalizing industry in Cuba and introducing economic planning: "After World War II, Cuban interests were strong enough to buy a substantial share of U.S.-owned sugar production which fell from 70-80 per cent of the total at its high point in the 1930s to about 35 per cent in 1958. Government encouragement of 'Cubanization' would easily have cut the figure in half again in a short time under a post-Batista democratic regime." In short, Draper's advice, for what it is worth, is that Castro should have encouraged "free enterprise" in Cuba.

Behind that program stand two postulates: (1) National capital in countries like Cuba is capable of successfully competing in the modern world with imperialist capitalism on the one hand and the system of planned economies on the other. (2) Imperialist capitalism is preferable to a "new type of system" that is presumably "neither capitalist nor socialist."

If these postulates are true, no rational explanation exists for the great wave of anticapitalist and anti-imperialist revolutions in the world today. Everything ends up in the "paranoia" of a demagogue. But why paranoia should prove so attractive and politically efficacious among hundreds of millions of poverty-stricken people remains a book sealed with seven seals.

Other oddities follow as logical consequences from Draper's preconceptions. He equates the anti-Semitic—and anti-Communist!—mass demonstrations engineered by Hitler and Mussolini with the anti-imperialist crowds that gather to hear Castro. He equates the cult of Trujillo, a puppet of American imperialism, with the popularity of Castro, who stands in the eyes of millions of Latin Americans like a David against Goliath; and he sees little difference between Trujillo's "neo-democracy" and the beginnings of proletarian democracy in Cuba. He equates Stalin's purge of the Old Bolsheviks, a phase of the degeneration of the Russian revolution, with Castro's moving beyond the initial program of the 26th of July Movement, a phase of the rise of the Cuban revolution. Draper, criticizing red-baiter Nathaniel Weyl, the author of *Red Star Over Cuba,* declares: "Communists, ex-Communists, non-Communists and opportunists are indiscriminately lumped together. Every bit of evidence that does not fit the book's thesis is ruthlessly suppressed or glossed over. All the hard problems of Castro's political developments are oversimplified and vulgarized." It's a fair, if not perfect, description of Draper's own analysis.

Under compulsion of the same logic, Draper is unable to see that the working class or peasantry played much of a role in the Cuban revolution. Batista fell, we are told, because the middle class deserted him. This was due, Draper argues, to Castro's "guerrilla tactics," which "aimed not so much at 'defeating' the enemy as at inducing him to lose his head, fight terror with counterterror on the largest possible scale, and make life intolerable for the ordinary citizen." (What class does that "ordinary citizen" belong to?) We are then given this priceless pearl: "The same terror that Castro used against Batista is now being used against Castro. And Castro has responded with counterterror, just as Batista did." Thus Castro = Batista. Q.E.D. History is reduced to terrorist bomb-throwing.

But worse than the old-time anarchists, who distinguished between the terror of reaction and the terror of the self-sacrificing idealist, Draper draws no distinction. A bomb is a bomb, and any bomb is equal to any other, if not sometimes more. Draper, who thus takes the democratic outlook to its ultimate absurdity, complains about C. Wright Mills's lack of sociological imagination. How carping can you get?

This happens to be the theory behind the counterrevolution's hopes for an easy victory over the Revolutionary Government. Since the inert and unthinking masses of workers and peasants play no part in Cuban politics, and since a section of the middle class has now deserted Castro, it follows that a few mad bombers prowling among the Sunday crowds can prove sufficient to induce the leaders of the revolution to lose their heads, "fight terror with counterterror" and thus open the way for the restoration of the landholders and capitalists to their properties. They probably found the theory in a book of useful household hints— "How to Cork a Volcano."

The counterrevolutionary mercenaries would be well advised to ponder the following observation, made by Theodore Draper last year in "The Runaway Revolution":

No matter what one may think of the theory behind Cuba's land-reform program and no matter how the program turns out in practice, there is no getting around the fact that for the poor, illiterate, landless outcast *guajiros,* the cooperatives represent a jump of centuries in living standards. They also represent a vast increase of constructive activity in the rural areas that were formerly the most backward and stagnant part of Cuba.

Will these *guajiros* prove inert to the plot to return them to the backwardness and stagnation of past centuries? I. F. Stone, who has a more vivid sociological imagination than Draper, said after a recent visit to Cuba: "Guerrillas who offer peasants aid against a hated landlord or village usurer are one thing. But can you see a U.S. guerrilla knocking on a peasant's door late at night, 'Give me water; hide me; I bring a message from United Fruit Company: we've come to take back your land.'?"

\*                    \*                    \*

The tendency for a bourgeois revolution to transcend its bourgeois-democratic limits, that is, proceed toward socialistic forms of property, was noted by Marx and Engels in the upsurge they participated in as young men. In fact, they began their revolutionary careers as bourgeois democrats and ended as the founders of scientific socialism. It was not until the appearance of Leon Trotsky, however, that this tendency received rounded theoretical development. As early as 1904, the youth who was to become coleader of the 1917 Russian revolution had reached that deep insight into the main course of the revolutions of our time which was to win him world recognition as one of the greatest of revolutionary theoreticians. He named his theoretical contribution "Permanent Revolution," taking the title from the following suggestive declarations made by Marx and Engels in an Address of the Central Committee to the Communist League, dated March 1850:

While the democratic petty bourgeois wish to bring the revolution to a conclusion as quickly as possible, and with the achievement, at most, of the above [reform] demands, it is our interest and our task to make the revolution permanent, until all more or less possessing classes have been forced out of their position of dominance, until the proletariat has conquered state power, and the association of proletarians, not only in one country but in all the dominant countries of the world, has advanced so far that competition among the proletarians of these countries has ceased and that at least the decisive productive forces are concentrated in the hands of the proletarians. For us the issue cannot be the alteration of private property but only its annihilation, not the smoothing over of class antagonisms but the abolition of classes, not the improvement of existing society but the foundation of a new one.

The battle cry of the workers must be, said the Address in conclusion: "The Revolution in Permanence."

The basis of Trotsky's theory was the uneven development of capitalism on a world scale. In the old capitalist centers, technology is so advanced that society is rotten ripe for socialist reorganization. In the underdeveloped areas of the world, however, precapitalist relations are still strong, and the main revolutionary tasks are thus bourgeois in character. But the pattern of change does not simply repeat the pattern of the early bourgeois revolutions, in which the working class was scarcely developed. The underdeveloped countries do not live in isolation from the rest of the world. In fact imperialist capitalism has penetrated them, bringing the most advanced technology. ("Brazil seems to have jumped from the ox cart to the age of the air," notes Charles Wagley, professor of anthropology at Columbia University; ". . . young Brazilians who have never driven an automobile have 'soloed' in the air.") And along with this, imperialism injects the most advanced class relations into the antiquated social structure. (Highly exploited sugar workers, for instance, in Cuba.) The working class, even though it may be numerically thin, consequently has far greater political weight than its prototypes at the dawn of capitalism. When it enters the political arena, it tends to draw on the most advanced political thought of the world's great metropolitan centers. Together with backwardness, even primitiveness, is combined the very latest in scientific thought and achievement.

It is possible, therefore, for the working class, in alliance with the peasantry—which is pressing for bourgeois reforms in property relations on the land—to win political power in a backward country even sooner than in an advanced country. In power it has no choice but to proceed with the economic and social tasks inherent to its class position: expropriation of capital, building of a planned economy, etc. These are socialist in principle no matter how limited or distorted they may be in fact. The victory of the workers in such countries cannot be maintained, however, without the aid of the workers of the advanced centers; that is, without the extension or continuation of the revolution on an international scale, above all into the old capitalist powers.

Through this theory, Trotsky was able to predict correctly the course of the 1917 revolution in Russia, some twelve years before it occurred.

Interestingly enough, Lenin did not agree with Trotsky's prognosis. In 1905 Lenin wrote: "We cannot jump out of the bourgeois-democratic framework of the Russian Revolution, but we can considerably broaden that framework." He repeated this in innumerable articles and speeches year after year until *after* the February 1917 revolution. Not until April of that year did he change his views. When he finally did change, it precipitated a crisis in the Bolshevik Party, which was convinced that the revolution had only a bourgeois-democratic character as Lenin had repeatedly insisted. But Lenin's prestige was such that he succeeded in getting the party to adopt the new position despite the cries of capitulation to "Trotskyism."

It was on the solid basis of this shift, plus his own recognition of Lenin's correctness on the need for a democratic-centralist party, that Trotsky, together with his following, joined the Bolsheviks and helped the second revolution to emerge from the first one.

Of course it can be argued, as it was at the time and has been perennially ever since, that the Bolsheviks did wrong in accepting power in an underdeveloped country like Russia. A book could be devoted to this topic alone. Aside from the "morality" of it all, the point is that Trotsky's theory of the permanent revolution enabled him to foresee with accuracy the actual main pattern of the Russian revolution and that this theory offers the only rational explanation for such revolutions as the one in Cuba.

No utterly novel "new type of system" has emerged, as Draper maintains. Cuba has simply gone beyond capitalism in some important respects and begun to build institutions that are basically socialist in principle. The country is in *transition* between capitalism and socialism. How long it remains in transition depends on international forces and events, primarily the ultimate fate of the old capitalist powers. When the United States goes socialist, Cuba will be among the first to benefit and will certainly complete the changeover in record time.

The question of the absence of direct proletarian leadership in the 1958-59 Cuban revolution offers a complication, it is true, but on the main question—the tendency of a bourgeois-democratic revolution in an underdeveloped country to go beyond its bourgeois-democratic limits—Cuba offers once again the most striking confirmation of Trotsky's famous theory. That the Cuban revolutionaries were unaware they were confirming something seemingly so abstract and remote makes it all the more impressive.

The fact that these same revolutionaries, without knowing Trotsky's theory, proved capable of transcending their own limited previous political positions speaks completely in their favor. It demonstrates that in caliber they belong to the great tradition of genuine revolutionary leaders, beginning with the leaders of our own American Revolution.

Cuba is at present a fortress under siege by American imperialism. To offer to judge what goes on inside that fortress without taking into account the siege represents the utter prostration and abasement of theory. That Draper's preconceptions required him to do this is sufficient to discount his views completely.

The Cuban revolution is another link in the chain of revolutions going back to the Paris Commune of 1871 and the revolutionary upheavals of 1848. As such, it has much in common with these revolutions, although like all revolutions it has its own peculiarities. It offers great new lessons, above all on the pattern to be expected in other coming revolutions in Latin America. All of these revolutions, it can be predicted with absolute surety, will proceed from the bourgeois-democratic to the proletarian stage with extraordinary speed. If for no other reason, they will do this because American imperialism offers them no choice but death or permanent revolution.

# Trotskyism and the Cuban Revolution—
## an Answer to Hoy
## (1962)

What has been the response of the other leaders of the Cuban Communist Party to the vigorous measures undertaken by Fidel Castro against Aníbal Escalante and the bureaucratic practices he fostered? All reports indicate that they were among the most enthusiastic in applauding the sudden downfall of their comrade. Never have they appeared so warm in their congratulations to Castro over a timely action in behalf of the welfare and advancement of the Cuban revolution.

Out of gratitude to Castro for such a felicitous measure against what could have developed into a bureaucratic cancer, one might expect a contribution from these other leaders of the Cuban Communist Party, a bit of self-examination and self-criticism that would help explain why Escalante felt that he could get away with it.

How did it happen, for instance, that none of them took the initiative in exposing Escalante's practices? How did it happen that none of them stood up in active opposition to this factional-minded bureaucrat who set out to build a personal machine? Were they afraid to speak up? If so, what made them afraid? Were they involved, too? Or were they just blind to the glaring faults of their fellow leaders? If so, how explain this blindness? Was it due to the long years of training in the school of Stalinism where bureaucratic practices and bureaucratic personalities were so much the norm that they could develop into a cult?

Honest answers by Escalante's associates to questions like these could provide instructive educational material for young revolutionists—and not only in Cuba. Some self-criticism did take place, at least enough to make the record. But considerations other than the educational needs of young revolutionists have evidently preoccupied Escalante's former intimate collaborators.

Fidel's moves against bureaucratism hold certain implications. If Fidel persists in this course, Escalante's comrades no doubt have reasoned, it will inevitably lend impetus to the antibureaucratic mood. Indeed, the ruin of Escalante signified in itself a considerable strengthening of the tendency to democratize the revolution along Leninist lines. But how can pressure be placed in the opposite direction without openly challenging Fidel? An indirect approach is needed. To influence Paul, attack Peter. This is especially shrewd if Peter happens to be gagged or the victim of much prejudice.

Such, we may surmise, were the calculations behind the campaign which *Hoy*, the daily newspaper of the Cuban Communist Party, recently opened against "Trotskyism."

Because of the imperialist embargo of Cuba and the consequent communication difficulties, we do not receive *Hoy* regularly. We are therefore unable to measure the campaign with precision. But we do have at hand six articles, some of them quite long and quite evidently placed on target with painstaking care. These are sufficient to indicate the real state of mind among at least some of the leaders of the Cuban Communist Party since the news was broken to them about Escalante being no longer at his desk. In no other sector of the world Communist movement is such alarm evident over "Trotskyism."

Before getting into an analysis of the articles published by *Hoy* it will prove useful to state the essence of Trotskyism:

1. It offers the most profound theoretical appreciation of the development of the Russian revolution and, by extension, all modern revolutions, especially in colonial and semicolonial areas. (This is the theory which Trotsky developed, in the light of Russian experience, from some observations Marx made about "permanent" revolution.)

2. It offers the only logically coherent explanation of how a bureaucratic caste could rise in the Soviet Union and the only program that, in the Leninist tradition, combines opposition to bureaucratism with unconditional Soviet defense.

3. It offers the most thorough-going program of opposition to fascism and all similar reactionary tendencies symptomatic of the decay of capitalist democracy.

4. It is the most consistent present-day proponent of the revolutionary socialist way out of the wars and other horrors of a world capitalist system in its death agony.

*Hoy* does not offer its readers these facts about Trotskyism. It offers a different picture. In the June 16 issue, for instance, the editors devote an entire article purporting to present the history of Trotskyism beginning with 1909. That year is chosen instead of the more appropriate one of 1905 because of a bitter factional dispute in the Russian Social Democratic Party which reached its culmination in 1912. At one point in this dispute Lenin angrily called Trotsky a "Judas." What the real issues were in that dispute of a half century ago remains obscure in *Hoy's* account. But it must be admitted that the epithet "Judas," which *Hoy* hauls out of the dusty archives, does help divert attention from the more troublesome word of current political interest—*Escalante*.

*Hoy's* presentation of Trotsky's role in the 1917 revolution adheres quite faithfully to the version concocted by Stalin for use in the infamous Moscow frame-up trials of the thirties. For instance, Trotsky "entered the Bolshevik Party with the aim of struggling within it against Leninism." After the triumph of the revolution "Trotsky continued opposing Lenin in a series of major questions. . . ." In 1921 Trotsky "began a factional struggle inside the Bolshevik party. . . ." With the death of Lenin in 1924, Trotsky "directed his principal attack against Stalin, who had been ratified as General Secretary of the Party."

In 1927 came "expulsion," these Cuban partisans of General Secretary Stalin inform us, and Trotsky "went abroad and organized a rabid campaign of calumnies against the Soviet power, while directing conspiratorial activities of his followers inside the Soviet Union itself."

And so on and so forth. All that is required to answer this falsified version of history is an asterisk and a footnote for the serious newcomer to the radical movement.*

What Escalante's former collaborators leave out of their lying account is more interesting than the concoctions they put in. Two items have special pertinence to the problems of the Cuban revolution.

---

* For better appreciation of typical Stalinist statements like these, consult the investigation and conclusions made in 1937 by the "Commission of Inquiry into the Charges Made Against Leon Trotsky in the Moscow Trials," which was headed by the well-known educator and philosopher John Dewey. In two volumes, available in most libraries, *The Case of Leon Trotsky* and *Not Guilty*, both published by Harper &

One is Trotsky's role, as the intimate colleague of Lenin, in organizing the political and military defense of the Soviet Union against the combined imperialist and counterrevolutionary assault undertaken first by Germany and then by the Allies. This period holds many lessons which partisans of the Cuban revolution could profitably study.

The other is Lenin's initiation in 1923 of the struggle against bureaucratism in the Soviet Union, which he began by seeking Trotsky's collaboration in a fight to depose Stalin. The Escalante case vividly demonstrates the relevance of this chapter in the history of the Soviet Union to the current problems of the Cuban revolution.

But it is precisely these historical lessons which Escalante's former friends and collaborators wish to keep the Cuban revolutionists from studying. The reason is simple. Anyone who objectively examines the facts of that heroic time cannot help concluding that Leninism and Trotskyism are identical. Still worse from the viewpoint of the Cuban Stalinist faction, all the lessons of those days speak against the basic policies represented by the Escalante tendency.

For people addicted for a quarter of a century to the dope of the Moscow frame-up trials, it is not possible to stay on such mild stuff as vague references to 1909, etc., in talking about "Trotskyism." The craving for something that foams better in the mouth is well-nigh irrepressible.

Unfortunately the de-Stalinization process in the Soviet Union cut off the habitual drug at its very source and it is not easy to find a substitute. However, Escalante's former comrades are not completely devoid of imagination; and they have come up with something that can give you quite a jag. *Hoy* devotes its June 17 article to presenting this synthetic drug.

On the one hand they minimize Cuban Trotskyism. "Trotskyism in Cuba," *Hoy* proclaims, "never represented anybody and never had any influence." On the other hand they saddle Cuban

---

Brothers. For the truth about Trotsky's life, his relations with Lenin, and his revolutionary views and activities, consult Trotsky's autobiography, *My Life*, or the standard three-volume biography by Isaac Deutscher. For easily available evidence of Trotsky's view of Lenin see the biographical article written by him in the thirteenth edition of the *Encyclopedia Britannica*, vol. 30, page 697.

Trotskyism with a figure who never belonged—the biggest labor czar under Batista.

Eusebio Mujal, deservedly one of the most hated bureaucrats in the history of the Cuban labor movement, began his career as a member of the Cuban Communist Party. As *Hoy* explains it, he was expelled in the thirties. According to these same historians, Mujal, after his expulsion from the ranks of the Communist Party, became "leader of Trotskyism in Cuba."

We are next informed that Mujal's role is "well known." Among other things, he "placed himself at the unconditional service of North American imperialism." Mujal's record as a witch-hunter, company-serving bureaucrat, and imperialist servant is then recounted as if this had some connection with "Trotskyism" rather than his original training ground, the Cuban Communist Party.

The absurdity of such an amalgam can perhaps be better appreciated if we put it in terms of the U.S. labor movement. Namely, that the Socialist Workers Party "never represented anybody and never had any influence." Moreover, its leader was George Meany, well-known bureaucrat of the AFL-CIO, who placed himself at the unconditional service of Wall Street and then followed reactionary policies in accordance with the character of "Trotskyism."

To indicate the true record of Cuban Trotskyism at the time in question a few paragraphs from a report published in the October 1935 *New International*, magazine of the American Trotskyists, should prove of interest:

The army of Cuba (a country without national frontiers) reaches the exorbitant figure of 18,000 soldiers, with a budget of $18,000,000, which means, consequently, per capita expenditures higher than in Europe or in America. To this must be added several thousands of men of the technical and secret police who devote themselves exclusively to the political persecution of every person and organization opposed to the government. In addition, there is the rural police, controlled by the municipal governments, which is only an appendix of the general staff of the army and which collaborates loyally in the persecution of all opponents. In general, the soldiers as well as the police are recruited from the most degenerated social strata, the slum proletariat of the cities and the famished peons of the country. They are very generously paid and enjoy all sorts of privileges which assure their unconditional submission to the government.

To supplement the oppressive apparatus, directed essentially against the working class, exceptional tribunals have been created which judge all affairs of a political nature. These tribunals have put into practice a series of laws of a Fascist nature, like the prohibition of strikes, of trade unions, the suppression of proletarian propaganda. They have likewise prohibited the right of free speech, free assembly, etc. This series of laws, put into effect by the regime of Mendieta and Batista, wipes out all democratic rights and puts the working class of Cuba in a position known only in the completely Fascist countries.

The exceptional tribunals have pronounced sentences of from six months to ten years against members of the Bolshevik-Leninist party [the Trotskyists] and have condemned our trade union militants for the sole crime of possessing a membership card. At the present time, thirty of our comrades, eminent political and trade union leaders for the most part, are in prison. With the rank-and-file members of our trade unions, a total of nine hundred workers have been imprisoned, including a minimum of sixty women. These figures refer exclusively to the city of Havana.

Outside of those mentioned above, hundreds of students and petty-bourgeois revolutionists have been imprisoned. The repressive conditions are at present undoubtedly much more violent than in the years of the Machado dictatorship. In addition to imprisonment, the number of workers assassinated rises every day.

The report tells in more detail about the terror:

Even in the day-time it was considered a criminal misdemeanor to walk the street by twos or more. The police and the military hordes invaded the streets and fired on the workers wherever they dared to assemble. The headquarters of every proletarian organization were raided, sacked and demolished. Our trade union center, the Havana Federation of Labor, was raided, all the furniture in it smashed, the documents taken, and all found there arrested and beaten. The government admits a total of thirty dead, although the figure is actually much higher. Among the dead was our comrade Cresencio Freire, the head of the bakers' union; the student leader Armando Feito and the leader of the Cuban Revolutionary Party, Enrique Fernandez, who was a member of the Grau San Martin cabinet. After the general strike, the military tribunal sentenced to death the young revolutionist Jaime Greenstein, who was executed at Santiago de Cuba, and condemned comrade Eduardo Galvez and others to perpetual incarceration. . . .

The persecution is becoming increasingly intense. Our comrades imprisoned in the penitentiary of the Isle of Pines are forced to work in the swamps and quarries that surround the prison.

Of special interest in the radical movement at the time was the rapprochement between Antonio Guiteras, head of Young Cuba, and the Trotskyists. The report refers to this:

Guiteras had a broader view than his successors. He had an international perspective for the Cuban revolution. To achieve this goal he had the intention of convening a continental congress in Mexico of all the parties of the Left and he insisted a good deal on inviting all the sections of the International Communist League [the Trotskyists] on the American continent, as he informed our party.

But early in May, Guiteras was taken by surprise by the army near the town of Matanzas, just at the moment of embarking for Mexico. Together with the Venezuelan Colonel Carlos Aponte, he was assassinated.

The death of Antonio Guiteras created a different situation on the Cuban political scene.

Today Antonio Guiteras, who might have developed into the Castro of the thirties, is revered as one of the martyrs of the Cuban revolution. Rightly so, for it was the independent current represented by him and the Trotskyists and similar revolutionists in the thirties and preceding decades that finally produced a leadership capable of toppling the Batista dictatorship and winning the first great victory of socialism in Cuba.

Where was the Communist Party in those days? It had its martyrs and its heroes, too, and they will always be remembered for their valiant and self-sacrificing struggles. But the policy makers of the Cuban Communist Party did not look towards the rank and file for inspiration and guidance. Their eyes, like those of Earl Browder in the United States, were on Moscow, and this was the time of the great purges, the frame-up trials, the savage witch-hunting of "Trotskyists"; the time of blood which was capped by sinking a pickax into Trotsky's brain; the time which *Hoy*, like its sister publications throughout the world, today euphemistically calls the time of "the errors of Stalin."

In 1934 Stalin initiated his "people's front" policy. In the U.S.A. this meant switching to support of Roosevelt, a policy which Browder carried to its ultimate logic of open support for Wall Street. In Cuba it meant switching to support of Roosevelt's and Wall Street's man, Batista. In June 1935, shortly after Batista murdered Guiteras, the *Communist International* commented approvingly on the change in tone in the Cuban Communist Party press as the new line went into effect:

This is a splendid beginning. The Party is ridding itself of the mistaken idea which restricted its initiative, the idea that the proletariat is opposed by one reactionary front composed of all parties from the A.B.C. to the Guiteras group. It is beginning to differentiate in its approach to these organizations. It is beginning to seek its allies—albeit even inconsistent and temporary allies—in the organization of a genuine national revolution. . . .

The supreme reward for this turn was posts in Batista's cabinet. In return the grateful leaders of the Cuban Communist Party hailed their "inconsistent and temporary" ally Batista as a "man of the people."

The Cuban people, however, paid a bitter price for this policy. Instead of winning their revolution in the thirties as might have occurred had Guiteras lived, had the Trotskyists survived Batista's terror, or had the Communist Party followed a revolutionary socialist policy such as was advocated by the Trotskyists, the Cuban people had to wait for a new generation of revolutionists intelligent and audacious enough to hew their way around the Escalantes.

It may seem odd that *Hoy* would venture to refer to the historic record in attacking Trotskyism. Great as the risk may appear, *Hoy*'s need is greater. To make the attack appear impressive, learned-sounding, if falsified, references to history are required. The "lessons of history" pitch is a convenient guise for pushing current interests. Besides, the risk is not too great. The Escalantes were instrumental in suppressing the Trotskyist newspaper in Cuba. The victim is thus hampered in meeting the slander and in pointing out the falsifications. Nor can he easily call attention to the real lessons of history in opposition to the aims of the slanderers.

The ax which *Hoy* is grinding is plain enough. The Trotskyists, *Hoy* affirms, work "to combat the Revolution by presenting themselves as more revolutionary than the Revolution itself." The Stalinist newspaper continues,

Their labor is to try to sow confusion, to divert people from serious revolutionary work in order to launch them into senseless discussions and discussions, to sow doubt in the future of the Revolution and to create whatever obstacles they can to its development.

In brief, *Hoy* stands against the right of revolutionists to discuss freely whatever they feel needs discussing, even if for the moment they may sound more revolutionary than the Revolution itself, and brands those who might wish to discuss or debate policies—whether with the aim of clarifying, modifying, or changing policies—as sowers of doubt and confusion and creators of obstacles.

From this it follows by a not-so-strange logic that *Hoy*, whose discussions, as we see, offer impeccable examples of lack of confusion and avoidance of diversionary topics, should have the right to block or to censor any thoroughgoing discussion of such sensitive subjects as the meaning of the obstacles to the revolution created by Escalante and his tendency.

While *Hoy*, in its campaign against "Trotskyism," does not go so far in its series of articles as to demand that discussion be put in a straitjacket, it nevertheless cites with strong approval the way Stalin ended the right of free speech in the Soviet Union after the death of Lenin under guise of putting a stop to "anti-Soviet activities."

*Hoy* puts it this way:

> The Trotskyists complain that in the Socialist States they have no freedom of action.
>
> In the Soviet Union they had it until 1927.
>
> What did they use it for?
>
> To attack the Party, to foment division, to distract militants from constructive revolutionary work with interminable discussions, to weaken confidence in the possibility of the Soviet Revolution triumphing in face of its enemies and constructing socialism among the peoples of old Russia, to conspire and sabotage.
>
> The Soviet people, because of this, had to end their freedom of action.

The inference of this repetition of old, long-ago exposed Stalinist slanders is that under the guise of fighting "Trotskyism" today Stalin's course should be emulated in Cuba.

But the Cuban revolutionaries are inclined neither to admire nor to emulate Stalin. This thoroughly healthy inclination has been strongly reinforced by the exposure of Stalin's crimes undertaken at the Twentieth and Twenty-second congresses of the Communist Party of the Soviet Union. Thus it is not so easy to put over a Stalinist line in Cuba today.

What Escalante's former comrades need to make up a plausible case is some current material. Where to find it? The mainstream of world Trotskyism does not appear very vulnerable. It is not only strongly for the Cuban revolution, it could with some justification even be called "Fidelista." Nevertheless, *Hoy* is not without resourcefulness. Scouting around for possibilities, *Hoy* ran into a singular piece of luck.

The world Trotskyist movement happens to be split into various tendencies. Among them is a minor one, the "Latin American Bureau" (BLA), which has adherents in Latin American countries. This current stands way out in ultraleft field.

It, for example, considers the Socialist Workers Party—which helped found the Fourth International in direct collaboration with Leon Trotsky—to be so opportunist that it "has had nothing to do with Trotskyism or with Marxism for a long time."

The Latin American Bureau is so "pro-Soviet," as *Hoy* might put it, and so little critical of Khrushchev that it hailed the resumption of nuclear testing by the Soviet government and even condemned those who expressed disapproval of the abrupt and arrogant way in which Moscow disregarded the feelings of the worldwide peace movement.

The Latin American Bureau is even further to the left on the crucial issue of war. Maintaining that U.S. imperialism will inevitably plunge humanity into atomic war no matter what the opposition may be, the BLA seriously proposes that it would be more to the advantage of the Soviet Union and the socialist cause if the Soviet government struck the first blow. Members of this group believe, something like the end-of-the-worlders, in a final Armageddon in which the international class struggle, taking geographic form, will be settled with nuclear weapons. They believe that humanity will survive this hell of modern science and construct a new civilization on the radioactive ruins left by the final war of capitalism.

The adherents of the Latin American Bureau are defenders of the Cuban revolution, and there is not the least reason to doubt their word that they would die for it. As might be expected, they are also critical of the leadership, especially Fidel Castro. (They seem to regard Che Guevara with a more comradely eye.) They work out in considerable detail numerous measures which they think ought to be put into effect in Cuba—at once.

A current like this can be found typically in all revolutions and broad revolutionary movements. The Russian revolution was no exception. The ultraleftists added to the complications facing the central leadership. Lenin, however, not only opposed the ultraleftists. He also recognized them as a legitimate current. The reason was thoroughly practical. While generally their proposals were bizarre or utopian or could lead to disaster if put into effect as policy, still their observations and criticisms might contain a grain of truth well worth noting. If they were wrong on a question they put forward it was better to argue the question openly so that everyone would understand why they were wrong. In any case, as people basically loyal to the revolution, they had a right to voice their opinions in accordance with proletarian democracy, to bring their views to the attention of other revolutionists, to be handled honestly and fairly, and to receive reasoned, if firm, answers.

That was Lenin's way. It is not *Hoy*'s way. *Hoy* saw the position of the Latin American Bureau as something that could be fitted—with the right tailoring—to its own peculiar needs. And so the artists went to work.

Instead of presenting the position of the Latin American Bureau in an honest way and debating it on its merits, *Hoy* set out to present it as serving American imperialism.

The technique, however revolting, is simple enough. A speech made last January in Brazil by J. Posadas, a leading figure of the Latin American Bureau, constitutes the raw material on which the operators bring their knives and scissors to bear. They do not name Posadas. They do not name the newspaper from which they took his speech. (The text is available in the March 7 *Voz Proletaria*, published in Buenos Aires.) They slice out phrases for quotation, glue them into new connections, trim them, "interpret" them in the light of the Moscow frame-up trials, and then assign them, not to Posadas, but to "the" Trotskyists.

An example or two will show how these Cuban practitioners of Stalin's methods operate.

Speaking of "the" Trotskyists, the June 23, 1962, *Hoy* says:

For them, "the policy of the Cuban leadership continues to be that of limiting the extension of the Latin American revolution."
Why?
Because "in all the speeches, in all the Cuban press, not a word appears indicating that the definitive victory of the Cuban revolution depends on the triumph of the world socialist revolution or of the triumph of the colonial revolution. Everything is placed exclusively upon the construction of socialism in Cuba.
"This is the conception of Socialism in one country."

*Hoy* then goes on to "interpret" this to mean that the Trotskyists hold that the Cuban revolution cannot triumph at all until the world socialist revolution first triumphs. From this it draws a series of ridiculous alternatives: the Cuban revolution must be renounced, or the struggle for socialism in Cuba must be given up, or revolutions must be made elsewhere before a revolution can be undertaken in Cuba. Against these absurdities, *Hoy* advances powerful arguments which, of course, are devastatingly sensible in comparison with the idiotic "Trotskyist" position which they "quoted."

But Posadas was not that absurd. Here is the first phrase used by *Hoy* above as it appears in context in the concluding paragraph of the speech made by Posadas:

> We can conclude, affirming that Cuba is part, but only part, of the permanent process of the world and Latin-American revolution. If the revolution does not advance and if Cuba does not intervene in order to make it advance, the dangers for the Cuban revolution will be immense every moment. It will be that much easier to defeat imperialism to the degree that its aggression occurs under conditions of extension of the Latin-American revolution. But to the degree that *the policy of the Cuban leadership continues to be that of limiting the extension of the Latin-American revolution*, the task of imperialism will be that much easier. [We have placed the phrase torn out of context by *Hoy* in italics for easier identification.]

The rest of the quotation cited by *Hoy* is taken from a much earlier part of Posadas's speech in which he is contending that "in Cuba" a "serious advance of the revolution and of socialism" cannot occur unless a similar advance occurs in other places.

In this completely different part of his speech, Posadas is simply wrong factually when he declares that "not a word" appears in the Cuban press or in speeches indicating that the "definitive victory" hinges on victories outside of Cuba. He is also wrong factually when he declares that "everything is placed exclusively upon the construction of socialism in Cuba." The truth is that the Cuban revolutionists are following an active international policy, especially in Latin America, where they correctly point to the revolutionary example which Cuba has set for all the other countries.

Here is another example of *Hoy*'s method of presenting the views of revolutionary opponents, this time dealing with Posadas's insistence on the importance of freedom of discussion:

With this propaganda they contribute directly to the campaign of imperialism on the lack of liberty in Cuba.

In consequence they demand:

"The masses of the continent must get the feeling that a revolutionary opposition exists in Cuba."

Neither the masses of the Continent nor the masses of Cuba need in the least way the existence of an opposition in Cuba which, whether with phrases of the left or with arguments of the right, would serve imperialism in its aims of promoting disturbances in our country and preparing favorable economic-social conditions for their criminal plans of new armed interventions against the Revolution.

Here is the original phrase, again italicized for easier identification, in the context from which *Hoy*'s artists extracted it:

The Trotskyists must be permitted to publish their newspaper and the masses must be permitted to organize freely. It is in this way that the North American masses can be influenced, since they will be able to compare this situation with the "democracy" of their own country, which does not permit the printing of a Communist daily. *The masses of the continent must get the feeling that a revolutionary opposition exists in Cuba* which, while fighting to the death in defense of the workers' state, holds an ideological position that seeks to carry the revolution forward. The Cuban revolution is on the rise, but it still does not meet the principal problems of this stage in which the Cuban revolution, the Cuban workers' state and the Latin American revolution are the same thing.

Despite the simplifications and the exaggerations, is there not a grain of truth in this? Would not fair consideration of this view help to enrich discussion among Cuban revolutionists? But *Hoy*, as representative of the Escalante tendency, has other purposes in mind than discussion of such questions. It passes by in silence the real points which Posadas makes and instead of taking them up—which would be easy enough for genuine Leninists—it doctors a single phrase so as to make it appear to be "proof" that "the" Trotskyists "contribute directly to the campaign of imperialism." Isn't this procedure a disservice to the Cuban revolution, if not worse?

Continuing in the same way, *Hoy* makes out that "the" Trotskyists are ignorant of some of the stages of the Cuban revolution. (Posadas makes some factual errors concerning the course of the agrarian reform.)

Taking up a different issue, *Hoy* makes out that "the" Trotskyists were against the victory at Playa Giron over the counterrevolutionary invasion mounted by Eisenhower and Kennedy. (Posadas makes the mistake of trying to weigh in a balance the relative importance of the victory at Playa Giron and the extension of proletarian democracy in Cuba.)

This is not all there is in *Hoy*'s roundup. With "quotations" the editors prove that "the" Trotskyists are against the huge mass mobilizations that have marked the Cuban revolution. (Posadas, not seeing too clearly through the ultraleft smoke in his glasses, misses the importance of these mobilizations and tends to brush them off as "plebiscites.")

Still another success in *Hoy*'s demonstration that "the" Trotskyists are against the Second Declaration of Havana. (The North American and European Trotskyists translated the Second Declaration and distributed it around the world; but Posadas believes that editorially he could improve on it and that politically it is a step backward.)

Finally—this is a real bombshell—*Hoy* established with nothing less than quotes from an original source that "the" Trotskyists are against Fidel Castro. (Posadas believes that Castro still has a long way to go before he can be trusted with the red charter qualifying him as a simon-pure Marxist-Leninist; and Posadas has the further quirk of believing that Castro is not an initiator and mobilizer but simply a reflector of pressure from below.)

In brief, *Hoy* takes an ultraleftist, who is a sincere defender of the Cuban revolution, deliberately misrepresents his views, grossly inflates his factual errors, calculatingly twists his remarks to make him look like an agent of imperialism, hides the fact that it is dealing with the opinion of one person, or at most a minor tendency, and then offers this literary frame-up to its readers as an analysis of the position of the world Trotskyist movement on the Cuban revolution.

This is the way *Hoy* seeks to put pressure on those who are concerned and worried about the Escalante tendency and its weakening effect on the Cuban revolution. With such means, learned in the school of Stalinism, it seeks to get them to back up. *Hoy* says to them in effect, "Watch out. You are playing into the hands of Trotskyists. And look where that can lead you!"

The April 16 *National Guardian* reported an exclusive interview with Blas Roca just before Aníbal Escalante was dismissed from his post. The final question asked Cuba's "top communist," as the *National Guardian* characterizes him, was: "Do you welcome to the ranks of Cuba's friends and partisans in the U.S. people of any orientation, for example Trotskyists? How can Cuba's U.S. friends best help Cuba?"

This was Blas Roca's written reply:

I am not well acquainted with those who call themselves Trotskyists in the U.S. We are separated from Trotskyists in general by fundamental points of view, and from some in particular by their actions as enemies. But I think that all in the U.S. who sincerely defend and support the Cuban revolution, and the right of self-determination of the Cuban and other Latin American peoples, do a worthy revolutionary job and we value them whatever their ideological concepts may be. North Americans who defend Cuba defend their own liberty and democracy. They make the most important contribution to the cause of peace, since any adventure by Kennedy and the Pentagon against Cuba creates a grave peril for world peace. And they take a step forward toward liberating themselves from their own imperialists, exploiters and oppressors.

Thus the defense of Cuba in the U.S. should be carried forward without any kind of sectarianism, with the greatest open-mindedness, with an objective spirit of judgment on the basis not of what people say but of what they do.

Blas Roca's disclaimer of knowledge about the role of the North American Trotskyists in defending the Cuban revolution is somewhat puzzling. But let us accept it at face value.

Now will someone please give Blas Roca the facts?

The only presidential candidate to defend the Cuban revolution in the 1960 campaign was the Trotskyist, Farrell Dobbs. In the homeland of Yankee imperialism, the Socialist Workers Party made defense of the Cuban revolution its major plank in that election and defended Cuba against both the Democrats and Republicans on countless local platforms and over radio and TV, including national hookups.

In the very insides of the imperialist monster, as they graphically put it in Cuba, members of the Socialist Workers Party have stood in the forefront of Cuban defense activities since the beginning—and without any sectarianism. At the time of the Playa Giron attack, the Socialist Workers Party mobilized its forces in conjunction with much wider layers from coast to coast for an all-out protest movement against the imperialist intervention.

It has circulated speeches of Fidel Castro and similar material on a nationwide scale and explained and defended the Cuban revolution against the strongest spokesmen of the State Department and before the most hostile audiences, in one of the most sustained and consistent campaigns in the history of the American Trotskyist movement. The effectiveness of this work was testified to by such an important independent figure as C. Wright Mills, author of *Listen, Yankee*.

These efforts were paralleled by the rest of the mainstream of world Trotskyism in Latin America, in Europe, and wherever Trotskyists have any influence.

When he has digested this information, we invite further comment from Blas Roca. We prefer that he say it to *Hoy*. It can be quite simple—a letter to the editor something like this: "I really meant what I said in that interview printed in the *National Guardian*. In basic approach I meant it not only for the United States but for Cuba. And what I said is especially applicable to Communists, who are duty bound to set an example. In accordance with those sentiments, *Hoy* ought to admit its slander and make up for it by printing the straight facts about the real position of world Trotskyism."

Escalante and his former friends, it is true, might not like a declaration of that kind; but, by countering *Hoy*'s divisive attack on partisans of the Cuban revolution, it would certainly help strengthen unity in the defense of the Cuban revolution.

And in the United States it would make it easier to call for fair play for Cuba if it could be reported far and wide that in Havana, critics who have the interests of the Cuban revolution at heart get fair play even in the pages of *Hoy*.

# "A New Field of Battle" for Che Guevara (1965)

At a public presentation of the new central committee of Cuba's Communist Party, Fidel Castro announced that Ernesto "Che" Guevara was no longer in the country. He had left earlier in the year for "a new field of battle in the struggle against imperialism."

Castro read a letter from Guevara which he said had been given him on April 1. The international press reported part of the letter, which was datelined Havana, as follows:

I feel I have completed the duty which the Cuban revolution gave me. I say farewell to you. I give up all my posts as minister in the party, as a major and as a Cuban citizen. . . .

My only fault has been that I did not understand more fully your great qualities. I am proud of having followed you. . . .

Other nations require my services and I must leave you. I leave behind my dearest memories and my most loved ones. I will take the spirit you inculcated in new fields of battle . . . in the fight against imperialism. . . .

I free Cuba of all responsibility. Should my end come elsewhere I will take with me your example. . . .

Castro did not say why he chose to make the announcement at this particular time. But it was clear enough he could no longer delay it. Only the day before, the news had been released that the top leadership of the Cuban revolution had been reorganized and Guevara's name was not on the list.

Among the significant changes was the name of the party. Formerly the United Party of the Socialist Revolution, it is now the Cuban Communist Party. That this is not a reedition of the old Communist Party of Stalinist days is clear from the further downgrading of former Stalinist officials, a process that has been going on for some three years. The Political Bureau is solidly Castroite, including Fidel Castro, Raúl Castro, Osvaldo Dorticós, Juan Almeida, Ramiro Valdés, Guillermo García, Sergio del Valle, and Armando Hart.

Leaders of the old Communist Party still occupy prominent positions, however. Blas Roca, for instance, is included in the party secretariat. A considerable concession in this direction was the appointment of Isidoro Malmierca as director of *Granma*, a new daily paper representing a merger of *Revolución* and *Hoy* (former Communist Party organ).

Malmierca was head of state security thoughout the Aníbal Escalante period. He was one of the most important figures to be removed from office at the time Escalante was ousted because of his systematic efforts to build a personal bureaucratic machine in the party and government. As head of the police, Malmierca joined with Escalante in this effort, and hundreds of illegal acts, including arbitrary arrests, were charged against him.

This appointment should serve to assure the Kremlin ideologists that tight control will be maintained over the critical propensities of Cuban journalists, particularly as they might concern Kosygin-Brezhnev.

The overall balance of the reorganization and renaming of the party, however, further emphasizes its independence from the old Stalinist machine, its identity with the activists who carried out the Cuban revolution, and its commitment to the ideology of revolutionary Marxism.

Where does Che Guevara fit in with all this? There is no really reliable information available. The Cuban government has maintained tight security on this secret.

The bourgeois press, of course, has indulged in considerable speculation about the whereabouts since last April of the man generally regarded up to now as being among the three top leaders of the Cuban revolution. In recent days it has reported Guevara twice arrested, once in Argentina and once in Peru, only as quickly to kill the rumors as unfounded.

Of the more serious papers, the Paris *Le Monde* offered the opinion in an October 5 editorial that it was a case of "revolutionary romanticism"; that Che Guevara "felt ill at ease in a regime that had accepted, more out of calculation than conviction, the principle of peaceful coexistence" and that he simply decided "to seek new fields of struggle."

The *New York Times* (October 9-10 international edition) was rather staggered, feeling that of the dozen men who survived the *Granma* landing and got up into the Sierra Maestra with Castro, "he is the first . . . to desert the leader of the revolution." Adds the *Times* editorial writer: "To those who knew him, he was the last to be expected to break away." The *Times* means a personal break with Castro in which Guevara "has now conjured himself away to some still mysterious ultima Thule of revolution somewhere in the world."

The *Times* continues:

> Possibly it is due simply to the fact that his extreme Marxist ideas of the Cuban economy had failed and had been abandoned or changed whenever possible. A further explanation could be that whereas Premier Castro's economic and military needs have forced him into close relations with Moscow, Guevara's leaning was to Peking.

As to that last guess, it is clear that the *Times* editorial writer has not been doing his homework on the voluminous material coming out of Peking. Guevara has been as conspicuously absent from Peking publicity as all the other top leaders of the Cuban revolution for a long time. The truth is that the Cuban revolutionists have done their utmost to indicate that within the general framework of revolutionary Marxism, their policy is an independent one, bowing to neither Moscow nor Peking.

In speculating on Guevara's departure for "a new field of battle," four outstanding facts call for consideration. They may offer a clue to the mystery.

The first one is the lengths to which Guevara went in dissociating himself from Cuba. He gave up his government posts, his army connection, his party standing, *even his Cuban citizenship*. As if this were not enough, he added: "I free Cuba of all responsibility."

It is evident that Guevara is projecting a political course that requires the Cuban government to be demonstrably and even ostentatiously free of all responsibility for his actions. Since it is agreed by all who know him, including his bitterest foes, that whatever he does it will be as a dedicated revolutionist who puts the cause even above his most intimate family ties, why should he have to publicly dissociate himself at all? Shouldn't the Cuban government be proud of being connected with the further revolutionary activities of Che Guevara, one of its principal founders?

The second fact is the line of the declarations made by Guevara during his tour in Africa last spring. These were all designed to advance the colonial revolution, to forge bonds of solidarity between the Latin American, African, and Asian revolutions; and he struck a few critical notes that evidently caused some fluttering in the dovecotes in Moscow. He spoke about the duty of "the socialist countries" to underwrite the revolution in the underdeveloped countries, not to profit in trade with these countries by taking advantage of their vulnerability on the world market, where they must compete with industrially advanced countries; and he advocated handing out arms freely to those who need them in revolutionary struggles.

The third fact is very simple. Upon returning to Cuba after gaining worldwide publicity for his declarations, Guevara did not make another public statement.

It would seem justifiable to surmise that the Kosygin-Brezhnev team lodged a stiff protest in Havana over Guevara's revolutionary declarations in Africa and certain criticisms that had come to their attention.

It would also seem justifiable to conclude that it was decided to make a concession to the Kosygin-Brezhnev team in this matter, for Cuba is extremely vulnerable under the enormous pressure of the North American imperialist colossus, only ninety miles away, and there is no other source of large-scale and effective material support except the Soviet Union. In relation to this, Castro has followed a most circumspect policy, evidently calculating that if there is to be an error it must be on the side of caution. The security of the Cuban fortress through maintenance of the best possible relations with the Soviet Union has, in fact, been the main axis of his foreign policy.

What happened between Castro and Guevara, we, of course, do not know. The top Cuban revolutionists, in their inner circle, have spoken frankly and often heatedly since they first constituted their team on every problem they faced. This occasion was most likely no exception.

But the incident may have brought out more clearly than ever before, the excruciating dilemma the Cuban revolutionists face. They have no choice but to do everything they can, including making painful concessions, to keep solid ties with the Soviet Union. On the other hand they are well aware that Moscow's policy of "peaceful coexistence" constitutes a grave and standing danger to their revolution. The Cuban revolution must receive fresh support from other revolutions, above all in the Western

Hemisphere, linking up with them within a certain time limit if it is not to suffer eventual defeat. This fundamental need has constituted the frame of reference of Cuban policy in relation to the rest of Latin America. Thus from the very beginning, Havana has appealed without letup to the peoples of Latin America to follow the Cuban example.

Guevara's name has been associated most intimately with the specific Cuban pattern—guerrilla warfare—not because his views on this are any different from those of the others, but because he took time to write a manual about it and to picture the Cuban example in detail as a practical way to achieve similar success in other countries where conditions might be propitious. His manual has been absorbed down to the last phrase in more than one guerrilla camp in the great *cordillera* running from Mexico down through the Andes.

And yet five years have gone by with no new victory. In fact a very grave defeat was suffered through the counterrevolutionary coup d'etat that brought General Castelo Branco to power in Brazil in April 1964.

Let us now fit in the fourth fact. This is Johnson's escalation of the war in Vietnam which began February 7, reaching a bloody crescendo precisely as Guevara returned to Cuba from his Afro-Asian tour. Havana's reaction to the escalation of the Vietnam War was quite different from either Moscow's or Peking's.

The Kosygin-Brezhnev team crawled under the bed. Its protests have not gone an inch beyond permitting students to stage a demonstration in front of the American embassy in Moscow, breaking a few windows. This, along with the hackneyed verbal protests that might be used in protesting the buzzing of a Soviet trawler, were discounted in advance by the Pentagon. In fact, the Kremlin bureaucrats have displayed such an ignominious attitude that the State Department has good grounds for presenting them as having a "common interest" in the escalation of the aggression.

Peking has done better, a least in displaying capacity to scream. Yet Peking, too, has failed to this day to undertake vigorous counteraction. And if it is correct for Mao to bear in mind the vulnerability of China to a nuclear attack in the absence of strong support from Moscow, he has still assiduously refrained from carrying out even the repeated promise to send volunteers—if needed.

Havana, in contrast, came out very quickly with a suggested

course of action calling for the firmest response as the only realistic way to stem the North American imperialist aggression and turn it back. These proposals were advanced by Castro himself in several public declarations; and the Cubans indicated their seriousness by earmarking material aid (shiploads of sugar) for the struggle.

The Cubans realize that not only is the defense of their country involved in Vietnam but that of the whole colonial revolution and all the workers' states. Moreover, they can see what is likewise clear to millions of people throughout the world—Johnson's escalation of the war threatens to end in a nuclear conflict. In brief, the White House has placed the fate of humanity at stake.

To Guevara, above all, it must therefore seem that extraordinary efforts must be made to overcome the setbacks, to reverse the effect of the defeat in Brazil, to move more energetically than ever before to achieve another victory, to bolster the defense of the Cuban revolution by advancing the world socialist revolution at any point where an opportunity might be found or created.

Is it so extraordinary to conceive a revolutionist like Guevara dedicating himself to personal responsibility in such a course? There is nothing of "revolutionary romanticism" in it at all. It is the same dedication to a great cause that made him a socialist in the first place and which gives meaning to existence for every revolutionary socialist in the world today. Besides, Guevara has taken some of the toughest assignments in the Cuban revolution, serving as a kind of "troubleshooter" from the start.

Such a decision on his part would automatically require his complete dissociation from the Cuban government, which must of course "coexist" with other governments, including those of completely opposite class character. In particular his activities could not be permitted to endanger relations with Moscow. If our surmise is correct, Guevara's "new field of battle in the struggle against imperialism" is something primarily on the level of revolutionary Marxist party politics, which is internationalist to the core and flatly in opposition to the dangerously subservient line of the Kremlin and the unimpressive performance of Peking.

It is pointless, in the absence of definite information, to discuss whether this was the best possible move for Guevara—whether whatever he can do in his new role is not more than offset by the harm of his dropping from public view.

In any case the central political problem facing the Cuban revolutionists, and Guevara's involvement in it, is clear enough.

As partisans of their revolution, we can only wish the Cubans well in their heroic efforts to safeguard its conquests and to strengthen their beleaguered fortress; and we hope that Guevara is able to do something effective to counter the passivity of Moscow and Peking, to help make up for the defeats and setbacks of the recent period, to break out of the encirclement and open up the possibility of reversing the headlong plunge taken by North American imperialism toward a nuclear catastrophe.

# Adolfo Gilly, Fidel Castro,
# and the Fourth International
# (1966)

One of the targets in Fidel Castro's January 15 speech attacking "Trotskyism" [see *World Outlook* February 11], was Adolfo Gilly, author of some informative and perceptive articles in the *Monthly Review* on the guerrilla movement in Guatemala and on developments in Cuba. These articles have been much admired among North and Latin American radicals.

In the April issue of the *Monthly Review*, Gilly replies to Castro, at the same time offering his own estimate of the Tricontinental Conference, which ended with Castro's controversial speech. In the same number of the magazine the editors of the *Monthly Review*, Leo Huberman and Paul M. Sweezy, weigh both Castro's appeal for united action against imperialism and his violation of that appeal in denouncing "Trotskyism." [See *World Outlook* April 8.] They also indicate certain differences with Gilly.

Actually, Gilly's reply to Castro takes the form of a sharp counterattack that raises broad new questions. His position is therefore well worth examining in determining the framework of the dispute and in coming to grips with the central issues.

First of all, at the risk of considerable oversimplification, let me state what appear to me to be the principal positions as they have been developed up to this point:

1. In his January 15 speech, Castro charged that "Trotskyites" of the "Fourth International" have been the "main spokesmen in the imperialist campaign of intrigue and slander against Cuba in regard to the case of comrade Guevara," going so far as to state that Guevara is dead—murdered by Castro; that "Trotskyite" agents have infiltrated the MR-13 [Movimiento Revolucionario 13 de Noviembre] guerrilla forces in Guatemala, thereby leading them into isolation from the masses; and that, in general, "if

Trotskyism represented at a certain stage an erroneous position, but a position within the field of political ideas, Trotskyism became in later years a vulgar instrument of imperialism and reaction."

2. The United Secretariat of the Fourth International in an "Open Letter" to Fidel Castro [see *World Outlook* February 18] replied that in every single "fact" cited by Castro to bolster his charges, the publications and personalities involved have nothing to do with the Fourth International. Included among these is Juan Posadas, quoted at some length by Castro; Posadas heads a small group that split from the Fourth International in 1962 but which makes the fraudulent claim that it constitutes the Fourth International.

The United Secretariat cited the consistent support given to the Cuban revolution by the world Trotskyist movement from the beginning and pointed to the responsible way in which it handled the announcement of Guevara's departure from the public scene in Cuba.

The "Open Letter" stressed the Stalinist origin of the slanders repeated by Castro, and asked him to make a rectification; or, if he preferred, five leaders of the Fourth International were prepared to argue the charges with him before a people's court in Cuba. Castro has not yet responded to the challenge.

3. On the other hand, Adolfo Gilly holds that Castro has become a virtual agent of the conservative-minded Kremlin bureaucracy; that as a result of this he eliminated Guevara from the leadership of the Cuban revolution, openly espoused the line of peaceful coexistence, cut his links with the Latin American revolution, and attacked the Guatemalan guerrilla movement, the socialist vanguard of Latin America, in a slanderous way.

The Tricontinental Conference, in Gilly's opinion, was a "failure." It "began with a disloyal and distorted attack on the Chinese, using rice as a pretext, and ended with the approval of a text with no political value, full of generalized declarations, and constituting a fraud on the responsible revolutionary movement."

4. The editors of the *Monthly Review* hold that the situation is much more complex and contradictory than Gilly pictures it. In their opinion the Tricontinental Conference was a "great historic achievement" insofar as it "laid to rest once and for all the illusion of peaceful coexistence between imperialism and its victims."

They consider Fidel Castro to still be a sincere revolutionist, although they think his attack on MR-13 was "ugly and perhaps ominous." They take issue with Castro's assertion that Trotskyism is an agency of imperialism, pointing out that this was the "accusation which provided the rationalization for the Soviet purge trials of the 1930's." The "malice" in this attack originated from some of Castro's advisers, they believe. In their opinion Castro acted in ignorance and they suggest that he take time out to study the history of the movement. Isaac Deutscher's biography of Trotsky, they indicate, would be a good work to begin with.

They agree with Gilly that the fate of Che Guevara—along with economic conditions in Cuba—will play an "important part" in determining the outcome of the present situation.

Both Gilly and the editors of the *Monthly Review* stress the importance of the Guevara affair. The statement by Huberman and Sweezy on this question carries all the greater weight because of its restraint. It is worth quoting in full:

In his final speech to the Conference, Castro said that "some day mankind will learn all the facts. That will be the day when the villains will see that comrade Guevara was not murdered; each of his steps will be fully known." Let us hope so, and let us hope that the day comes soon. For Fidel should be under no illusions that only imperialists and their agents are interested in Che's fate. More than anyone else, even more than Fidel himself, Che has come to symbolize all that is best, all that is pure, all that is beloved in the Cuban Revolution, a great historic event which belongs not only to seven million Cubans but to all the people of the Americas and indeed to all mankind. If, as some charge, anything untoward has happened or should happen to Che, those responsible (and that would necessarily include all who knew and kept silent) will be forever disgraced. A Cuban regime guilty of such a crime would lose its moral authority and either would be replaced or would degenerate into a police state. In the latter case, of course, the worst bureaucratic elements would rise to the top and do whatever was demanded of them by their more powerful counterparts abroad.

On the other hand, if the official Cuban story about Che turns out to be correct, if he reappears as a revolutionary fighter and theorist elsewhere, and if he retains his close ties to Fidel and his other former comrades in the Sierra Maestra, then the bonds linking the Cuban and world revolutions will be strengthened and the chances of a favorable evolution inside Cuba will be immeasurably improved. Is Fidel Castro aware of the real issues at stake in the Guevara affair? And does he realize that every day's delay in clearing up the mystery brings anxiety and doubt to honest revolutionaries everywhere and joy to their enemies?

Gilly repeats an argument first raised to my knowledge in an article I wrote in the *Militant* of January 31, 1966; i.e., the disproportion in Castro's attack on "Trotskyism." If the alleged agents of imperialism were utilizing Guevara's absence from the public scene in Cuba in order to damage the revolution and to disrupt unity in the struggle against imperialism, why didn't Castro answer in the easiest and most devastating way possible—by reading a letter or message from Guevara greeting the Tricontinental Conference, if he could not personally be present at this very important gathering?

Gilly goes much further than this suggestion, however. He asserts that "it is completely clear that one of the conditions of this alliance with the Soviet leadership and of this Conference was the disappearance of Guevara from the Cuban leadership."

As to the form of Guevara's disappearance, Gilly quotes with apparent approval the opinions of Juan Posadas, whom he characterizes as "a leader of the Fourth International." Posadas is "convinced" that "they" have "assassinated him, or that he is incapacitated or confined. . . ."

Perhaps Posadas has special sources of information. The rather broad selection of choices he leaves the reader, however, would indicate that he is engaging in mere speculation like many others. He excludes only that Castro might be telling the truth about Guevara.

Why does Gilly cite Posadas as an authority? We do not know. But he weakened his own authority in the field of Latin American radical politics by not taking the opposite course and helping to puncture the fraud that the Posadas group constitutes the Fourth International.

As Gilly sees it, Castro has gone over to the Brezhnev-Kosygin team and their line of "peaceful coexistence." This required sacrificing Guevara, who, in contrast to Castro, if we are to believe Gilly, held to the line of world revolution, the same line as the "Guatemalan guerrillas' program" and "the position of the Chinese." It would seem that Gilly is even tempted to imply that Guevara might have been moving toward the camp of Posadas. He includes a footnote quoting a conversation between Guevara and the followers of Posadas in Cuba on April 15, 1965, in which Guevara allegedly told them "that very soon all the works of the revolutionary, Leon Trotsky, would be published in Cuba." Guevara is also alleged to have said, "The Communists call me a Trotskyist and you Trotskyists call me an adventurer." Likewise:

"Very soon we will sweep out all these conservative bureaucrats."

It seems dubious that Guevara would discuss such matters in this way with the Cuban followers of Posadas. Guevara took the trouble to gain a rather accurate picture of the world Trotskyist movement as a whole, not hesitating to check with firsthand sources. He was well aware of the claims made by Posadas and discounted them.

Lest there be any doubt as to Guevara's own stand, up to the time of his last contact with real Trotskyists (in North Africa) he had not espoused Trotskyism, although he displayed a fraternal attitude to its representatives as he did to other sincere and dedicated revolutionists.

Gilly assumes—*assumes* is the right word—that differences of a most fundamental kind arose between Castro and Guevara. As to hard evidence of these differences, Gilly offers very little. No articles, no speeches, no declarations. This, of course, is easily explainable as due to the absence of established procedures in the Communist Party of Cuba for the expression of conflicting views.

The explanation, however, does not remove the difficulty. If differences arose between Castro and Guevara, what were they, exactly? We are left with little but deductions, and unfortunately—Gilly, I am afraid, is guilty of this, too—the deductions tend to fit preconceptions.[1]

If we check the fields where differences might have arisen, these are not nearly as great or profound as the fields of agreement between the two leaders. For instance, Guevara stressed the factor of morale, of revolutionary fervor, in the matter of economic incentives. His opponents pressed the virtues of material gain. A considerable public debate was conducted on this subject. Castro tended to side with Guevara's opponents but certainly did not reject Guevara's views.

---

1. A good example of this common-enough method of thought can be found in the opening page of Gilly's article. He asserts that Castro—despite being the leader of a socialist revolution and possessing revolutionary sentiments—"must" launch "an attack against and attempt to destroy the most politically influential guerrilla movement in Latin America: the leadership of the Guatemalan MR-13." Why? We are told by Gilly: ". . . in order to defend Soviet policy." Not a shred of evidence is offered for a single one of these assumptions, including the predominant influence of MR-13, although Gilly's subsequent deductions depend completely on them.

A sharper difference that was not made public may have arisen around some of Guevara's speeches in North Africa, particularly about certain "socialist countries" taking economic advantage of others through the mechanism of the world market, and about the duty of giving full and free material aid to the peoples struggling for liberation. If these remarks were interpreted by the Soviet bureaucrats as referring to Moscow, complaints may well have been sent to Havana to which Castro responded. This is a legitimate deduction inasmuch as Guevara did not again appear in public upon returning to Cuba. But there is no solid evidence to indicate that more than *tactical* differences might have arisen between Castro and Guevara.

As to the area of agreement between Castro and Guevara, it is only necessary to check their public utterances. They see eye to eye on a whole range of issues, not the least of them being insistence on the primacy of armed struggle in seeking to conquer power for the revolutionary forces. It was not without reason that Castro from the very beginning of his movement displayed the greatest personal confidence in Guevara by consistently asking him to take the most difficult and trying assignments. Guevara displayed equal consistency in accepting them. Until there is hard evidence to the contrary, Castro's assurances must be given due weight and not simply be brushed aside as unworthy of credence merely because it would fit in better with this or that preconception.

And what if it turns out that Guevara's disappearance is due to some kind of monstrous, as yet unexplained betrayal on the part of Castro? The editors of the *Monthly Review* have stated the consequences: "A Cuban regime guilty of such a crime would lose its moral authority and either would be replaced or would degenerate into a police state. In the latter case, of course, the worst bureaucratic elements would rise to the top and do whatever was demanded of them by their more powerful counterparts abroad." If this dire alternative envisioned by Huberman and Sweezy were to be realized, the Trotskyists would call such a structure a degenerated or deformed workers' state; and, regardless of the political character of the regime, would still defend it with all their energy and determination against imperialist attack.

For Trotskyist theory, this politically very unwelcome outcome would offer no difficulty. We have said from the beginning that the Cuban revolution must expand or it will go down in one way or another; revolutionary Cuba cannot remain isolated indefinitely. However, it still remains good advice not to cross bridges before you come to them.[2]

One of the decisive factors in a *qualitative* change in Cuba would be deep demoralization among the masses, particularly the *workers*. As Trotsky explained repeatedly, this was one of the most important elements in the rise of Stalin. To believe someone like Posadas, the masses are surging forward in Cuba—Castro is holding them in check. While not too clear on the subject, Gilly appears to lean in that direction. He claims, for instance, that Castro distorted Gilly's charge that Cuba failed to give "active support" to the Dominican revolution, by making this out to mean "the sending of soldiers and arms," whereas Gilly meant "mobilization of the masses." The purpose of the distortion, says Gilly, was "to contain the discontent of the Cuban masses who do not understand why Cuba did not act."

The Cuban people have provided history with the world's outstanding example to date of unremitting mobilization. It would be blind not to see the role Castro has played in this. Yet there are probably signs of weariness to be detected as year after year passes of unbroken imperialist blockade, continual threat of invasion, and international defeats like the one in Brazil. Accurate information on the mood of the Cuban people is needed to judge the state of health of the revolution there. Unfortunately, this is not easily obtained, one of the reasons being that Cuba is in the situation of a heavily besieged fortress.

Perhaps this is the place to mention another hypothesis advanced to explain Castro's attack on Trotskyism. Cliff Slaughter of the Socialist Labour League argues, in an article entitled with singular appropriateness, "How not to answer Fidel Castro," that "Without a shadow of a doubt, Castro's attack was part of a world-wide reaction by Stalinism to the growing influence of Trotskyism. . . ." (See the March 26 *Newsletter*.) Posadas antici-

---

2. The Socialist Labour League, a British ultraleft group, interprets Castro's attack on Trotskyism as crushing proof that Castro stands at the head of a capitalist state. The Posadas group, which for all its ultraleftism is able to see that Cuba is at least a "deformed workers' state," scores a telling point in criticizing the "brainless" SLL theoreticians for maintaining such a sectarian position. (See the March issue of *Red Flag*, the monthly newspaper devoted to publishing the declarations of Juan Posadas in English.)

pated the slower-witted British sectarian, declaring January 17: "Fidel Castro would not come out with such groundless statements if there did not exist within Cuba and within Guatemala a great development of Trotskyism." Gilly likewise sees a groundswell of opposition to Castro in Cuba which he identifies as *"guevarista* and pro-Chinese," indentified in turn with the line of extending the world revolution; i.e., Trotskyism.

Unfortunately, these statements correspond closer to wishes than to reality. The editors of the *Monthly Review* are more accurate in stating that "Trotskyism is certainly not a large or important political force in Latin America as a whole." My own impression is that Trotskyism has more prestige, standing, and influence than the editors of the *Monthly Review* realize, particularly in certain areas. This is especially true among the new generation of youth, who are not burdened with old prejudices and who are turning to the books with open minds, anxious only to learn something that can genuinely help them in the revolutionary struggles they are engaged in. But Trotskyism, it is true, has not suddenly begun advancing in a big way organizationally, and it remains a rather small minority current in Latin America as a whole. Castro's attack is thus not a reaction to a sudden phenomenal growth of Trotskyism, as the ultraleft sectarians hopefully assume.

What the sectarians leave out of account, either due to ignorance or to blindness, is that attacks such as Castro levelled against Trotskyism are not new in Cuba. The Stalinists, or those under Stalinist influence, have been campaigning consistently in this way against Trotskyism since the beginning of the revolution. In the July 30 and August 13, 1962, issues of the *Militant*, for instance, I had occasion to answer a series of articles in *Hoy* that attacked Trotskyism utilizing precisely the same frame-up and amalgam methods to be seen in the attack voiced by Castro. Even the same "leading Trotskyist" was utilized; namely, Juan Posadas. And he was not named. I had to name him and identify the source of the quotations ascribed to "Trotskyism."

Were these Stalinist-engineered attacks occasioned by the "growing influence of Trotskyism"? No. They were directed against the growing influence of Fidel Castro and his appeals to the rest of Latin America to follow the example of Cuba. From the Stalinist point of view, of course, Castroism does constitute a species of the genus "Trotskyism."

What is new in the current attack is that it is voiced by Fidel

Castro himself. This can be explained by a *weakening* of Castro's position in relation to Moscow. Which is not necessarily synonymous with the strengthening of Trotskyist influence.

Gilly pictures Fidel Castro as having become a completely servile agent of the Kosygin-Brezhnev "peaceful coexistence" team, so servile, in fact, as to willingly carry out orders to liquidate his co-leader Guevara. Likewise in accordance with his new role, Castro utilized the Tricontinental Conference, as Gilly sees it, to launch an utterly "disloyal and distorted attack on the Chinese, using rice as a pretext. . . ."[3]

And where does Gilly stand in the Sino-Soviet dispute? His article is filled with references to the Chinese. Not one of the references contains a word of criticism. Quite the contrary. "The same line," he tells us, "unites the Guatemalan guerrillas' program, the position of the Chinese, and that of Che's supporters in Cuba. It is the line of extension of the world revolution against the line of peaceful coexistence. . . ."

On this point it would seem that there is some substance to the boast made by Posadas (in the March issue of *Red Flag*) that Gilly is a "journalist influenced and orientated by the International"; that is, the group headed by Posadas.[4] For those who are not connoisseurs of the remarkable declarations of Posadas, it

---

3. The editors of the *Monthly Review* appear to agree with Gilly's view that Castro used rice as a pretext. They state that they do not wish to imply any criticism of the Chinese decision to cut shipments of rice to Cuba, the reasons given for this by the Chinese being "valid and justified." They add: "At the Tricontinental Conference Fidel talked a lot about the duty of all revolutionaries to help Vietnam and carry on the struggle against imperialism. Does he now presume to tell the Chinese, who are doing most of the helping and a large part of the struggling, that all that comes after the duty to supply Cuba with the amount of rice it asks for?" The irony is misplaced. From the viewpoint of defending revolutionary China against the escalating imperialist aggression in Southeast Asia, it would seem well worth while to make sure that no slashes occur in the rice ration of the fighters in the front lines ninety miles from Miami.

4. There is sometimes a curious coincidence between the views of Posadas and Gilly. For instance on the virtues of nuclear war, we learn in a declaration made by Posadas December 4, 1965, and published in the December issue of *Red Flag*: "The nuclear war is at the same time the

should be explained that among other oddities he believes that Mao has taken over a good deal of the Posadas line. In answering Castro, Posadas notes with satisfaction: "And the Chinese do not attack us; they have not said a word." Gilly could be charged with having been orientated to reciprocate.

Do the Chinese bear no responsibility for the strengthening of Stalinist tendencies in Cuba? Among the so-called pro-Chinese, two currents can be found. One consists of young revolutionists attracted by the guerrilla background of the Maoists, their firm declarations against imperialism, and even their ultraleftism. Castro and Guevara are outstanding examples. The other current is Stalinist to the bone. Examples can be found in many places besides Albania. Mao's rehabilitation of Stalin has encouraged and fortified this current. Posadas is simply dead wrong in his assumption that the strengthening of the "pro-Chinese" elements in Cuba equates automatically to the strengthening of Trotskyism. Depending on other factors, it can just as well have the

---

revolution." He predicts the annihilation of New York, London, and Moscow:

"When the masses of the world will see, will learn that 'New York is destroyed' all the faith in the capitalist system and in the bourgeoisie and in the strength of capitalism will vanish." The disappearance of Moscow will have an opposite effect. "On the other hand as we have said the bombardment of Moscow will be the rising of the world proletariat and will provoke the revenge of the world and European proletariat."

This is only the most recent formulation of a line advanced by Posadas since he split from the Fourth International. Earlier formulations are even more lurid, the suggestion being made that it would be wise of the Kremlin to launch a preventive nuclear war.

Now turn to Adolfo Gilly's introduction to the recently published *Studies in a Dying Colonialism* by Frantz Fanon: "And it is easy to imagine that if one day the transistor radio of a Bolivian miner, or a Colombian peasant, or an Algerian *fellah* tells them that Moscow and Peking have been destroyed by atomic bombs, they will rise up furiously and instantaneously to destroy in turn all that which represents their enemies. And if in the same moment they are also told that, on the other side, New York has disappeared from the map, their strength will be multiplied because they will see that their enemies no longer have any support, and they will feel that an immense weight has been lifted from their shoulders."

Gilly adds that "Perhaps this thesis is not very inspiring for a resident of New York." We can agree with him on that.

opposite effect of strengthening the elements bitterly opposed to the "de-Stalinization" process initiated at the famous Twentieth Congress of the Communist Party of the Soviet Union.

More importantly, Mao's policies are far from being Leninist. Often they are completely opportunistic, bearing the seeds of tragic defeats. An outstanding instance is the catastrophe in Indonesia.

The Indonesian Communist Party, under Aidit's leadership, espoused and followed the line of peaceful coexistence with Sukarno, the political leader of the Indonesian bourgeoisie. Class collaboration, practiced under the notorious theory of revolution "by stages," paved the way for the biggest debacle since the collapse of the German Communist Party under Stalin's genius-like guidance.

Peking, itself practicing "peaceful coexistence" with Sukarno, covered up Aidit's opportunism, if not directly fostering and encouraging it. Not before, during, or since the great mass slaughter of Communists in Indonesia, have the virtuosos in the thought of Mao provided the world revolutionary movement with a Marxist analysis of the disaster which the policy of peaceful coexistence led to in Indonesia.[5]

Coming still closer to home, we note Gilly's silence about Peking's open rejection of a united front policy in defending Vietnam against imperialist aggression. Mao publicly rejects a united front with revisionists and opportunists—as if Lenin's united front policy were designed for anything else except opening up the possibility for common action with revisionists and opportunists against a common enemy and thus proving in practice the superiority of Bolshevik policies and methods of struggle.

---

5. Last November 15 General Secretary Saturnino Paredes gave a report at the fifth national conference of the pro-Peking Peruvian Communist Party, the line of which did not differ in essentials from the line followed by Aidit, although it did stress the need for a long armed struggle. Paredes called for the formation of a "patriotic liberation front" that would include the "national bourgeoisie." The "strategic objective of the revolution is anti-imperialist and anti-feudal," said Paredes, and its objective is to "establish a new people's regime." Paredes warned that the prospective bourgeois ally "may" betray the revolution. Not a word about socialist revolution! (See the report in the March 9 bulletin issued by the Hsinhua News Agency.)

Mao's rejection of a united front policy has done immense harm to the international defense of Vietnam, making it much easier, for instance, for Brezhnev-Kosygin to reduce the flow of material aid to Hanoi to proportions far below what the situation calls for. One of the consequences was to block establishment of a common governmental front of all the workers' states that would have widened the opportunity for the Cuban government to play an independent role in relation to both Moscow and Peking.

The end result, given Cuba's geographical position and China's incapacity to substitute for the Soviet Union as a source of material aid, was to compel Havana to move closer to Moscow in the Sino-Soviet dispute than it may have wished to. It is absurd and ridiculous to equate Mao's error on this level with his position on the legal ins and outs of the protocol for exchanging rice and sugar. Behind the absurdity is the assumption that China with its 650 million people and Cuba with only 7 million (just off the coast of Florida) stand in equal relation to the threat of American imperialism.

In view of these facts is there not some justice to Castro's bitter accusations about Peking seeking to use economic blackmail in search of political concessions from Havana?

In this whole complex situation no greater error could be made than to lose sight of the correct stand taken by the Cubans in favor of an effective united front against the American imperialist aggression in Vietnam. Castro took an open public stand on this immediately after Johnson ordered the bombing of north Vietnam in February 1965. Castro called for vigorous defensive action and, as a token of what was meant, the Cuban government sent a shipment of sugar to Hanoi. Moreover the Cubans have repeatedly said they are willing to send volunteers to fight in Vietnam.

The Cubans made this one of the main themes at the Tricontinental Conference. Castro repeated it in a speech March 13, calling for sufficient "conventional" arms for the Democratic Republic of Vietnam to stop the American bombings. The Cuban delegation at the Twenty-third Congress of the Communist Party of the Soviet Union proposed that material aid be sent to the battlefront in such quantities as to convert North Vietnam into a cemetery for American planes.

How strange that Gilly, who has given considerable evidence of genuine perceptiveness, should see none of this! Preconceived notions indeed have power to blind one to real facts.

Finally let us note another remarkable oversight in Gilly's article. He does not make even passing reference to the Cuban-Yugoslav dispute. Yet this is so sharp that the Cubans exercised their influence to exclude the Yugoslav delegation from the Tricontinental Conference while voting to seat the Chinese!

The differences between Belgrade and Havana should be of concern to Gilly if he is really interested in substantiating his notion that Castro has committed himself to advancing the line of peaceful coexistence. This is precisely the key issue in dispute between the two sides. The Titoists condemn the Cubans for maintaining the position that the road to power lies through armed struggle; the Cubans score the Titoists for the opportunism and their friendly relations with bourgeois forces in Latin America, particularly the Betancourt and Leoni regimes in Venezuela.

Leaving aside the problem of bringing Belgrade into a united front against American imperialism (which is not easily solved in view of Tito's softness toward Washington and the failure of Moscow and Peking to set up an actual united front), the dispute between the Cubans and the Yugoslavs is of particular interest to revolutionary Marxists in gauging the limits of Castro's political concessions to the Kremlin. Since the dispute is a public one, it can easily be followed. Up to now the ultralefts have not commented on it, preferring to ignore it out of concern for maintaining their preconceived pattern.

The Tricontinental Conference should be judged against this background. Gilly labels it "a conference without glory and without program." In this judgment he comes close to the extreme sectarian view that the "main purpose" of the conference "was to provide a safety-valve for middle-class charlatans like Cheddi Jagan and upper-class demagogues like Allende to blow off steam against imperialism, neocolonialism and what-have-you." (Socialist Labour League theoretician Michael Banda in the February 5 *Newsletter*.) Posadas offers an intriguing variant: It was a "defeat" for Castro.

In a declaration dated January 21 (I do not have it in the original Spanish and must rely on the French version published in the February 25 issue of *Lutte Communiste*), Posadas maintains that the positions taken by the Tricontinental Conference were revolutionary "only in form" but not in substance since it did not issue calls mobilizing the masses against imperialism and did not come out with a revolutionary program. Nevertheless

Fidel Castro was "routed." ("C'est une déroute pour Fidel Castro.") The Tricontinental meeting at Havana, we are told, "demonstrated the enormous force of the revolution and the tendency, the objective necessity of unifying the Colonial Revolution." These forces were so strong that Fidel Castro "was compelled to make his first speech the very opposite of what he had been thinking of giving." Posadas, we must believe, has very good sources of information!

"Independently of the objectives it had, independently of the revolutionary resolutions, in form not more, independently of the interests and the objectives of the organizations present, it was the influence of the colonial revolution and that of the Workers State in its highest form—the Chinese Workers State—that triumphed," Posadas assures us. The triumph consisted of nine delegations opposed to peaceful coexistence who succeeded in influencing the other delegations. "It was a defeat for all the conciliatory perspectives sought by Fidel Castro."

Well and good. If there is any sense at all to this word salad, we are forced to conclude that Gilly is more sectarian than Posadas in his judgment of the Tricontinental Conference.

The editors of the *Monthly Review* perform a service for their readers, in my opinion, in taking a balanced view of the conference and its meaning, a view much closer to the contradictory reality. The conference did represent a positive achievement. It did strike a heavy blow against the illusions of "peaceful coexistence." And this was the line of the Cubans, both as hosts of the gathering and as participants in its deliberations.

Nevertheless the editors of the *Monthly Review* are fully justified in taking a reserved view as to how well the militant tone that characterized the proceedings is reflected in practice. They hold that the test will come in Cairo in 1968 when the second Tricontinental Conference is held. The object and goal for Cairo, in their opinion, must be "to take a giant step forward, to go beyond Havana, to proclaim socialism as the necessary and indispensable condition of real national liberation."

This would undoubtedly be a highly desirable step forward. I think, however, that we will be able to determine much sooner than that whether or not the Castro leadership has given up its policy of seeking to extend the Cuban revolution and sold out to the line of peaceful coexistence as practiced by the Kremlin. The continuation of the first Tricontinental Conference and the test of its real line will be observed in the development of the class struggle in the immediate future, above all in Latin America.

In agreeing that the first Tricontinental Conference did score positive achievements, I do not wish to imply that it did not suffer from serious limitations. The screening of the delegations was one of them.[6]

Gilly's completely negative reaction to the conference in its programmatic aspects is likewise not without an element of truth. If the conference was intended to found an International, it was certainly a prime example of "centrism." But then the sponsors of the conference, the Cubans in particular, made no claim to such an ambitious undertaking. It was a conference with limited aims. These included giving a boost to united action in behalf of the Vietnamese freedom fighters and to the concept that the road to power in countries where democracy has been suffocated lies through armed struggle.

Quite evidently the program of revolutionary Marxism encompasses much more than this. But it is evident that at this point the discussion can progress satisfactorily only if we turn to the broad problem of building mass revolutionary socialist parties.

When Gilly, for instance, refers to the Guatemalan guerrilla fighters as being "situated in the center of the political battle for the program of the world revolution," he exaggerates. The struggle being conducted by MR-13 is very important, but is there more to be learned from it either by way of program or example than from the struggle led by the Peruvian Trotskyist leader Hugo Blanco? Internationally, does the situation in Guatemala transcend in significance the situation in Indonesia? And what about Vietnam, which at the moment constitutes the key to the entire world situation?

It is very good that MR-13 opposes the line of peaceful coexistence with the Guatemalan representatives of Yankee imperialism and adheres to the program of socialist revolution. This program, however, can be discussed in relation to many situations besides the one in Guatemala where considerable factional heat has been generated. Thus without losing sight of

---

6. Posadas bears down heavily on this in his January 21 declaration. "Who elected the delegates to this Congress? Who designated them?" he asks cuttingly. The questions, pertinent as they are, do not lack in irony coming from the organizer of a rump congress that founded a counterfeit "Fourth International."

the specific situation there or the interests of the Guatemalan freedom fighters, it might prove profitable to take a more general view.

For example, the editors of the *Monthly Review* refrain from getting involved in the specific dispute as to whether or not there are "Trotskyites" in the MR-13 and whether or not it has a "Trotskyist program." Instead they pose the issue on a broader basis: "After visiting South America in 1963 we stated our opinion in these pages that there is no such thing as feudalism in Latin America and that it therefore makes no sense to talk about a bourgeois revolution." And again: "But if Fidel Castro and the Latin American Communist Parties duck the question of socialism, and still more if they attack as Trotskyites all those who openly struggle for a specifically socialist revolution, then the prospects for Latin American Trotskyism will be vastly improved. For the necessity, and indeed the inevitability, of socialist revolution, not in some vague future but as the next historical stage in Latin America is rooted in the underdeveloped, imperialist-enforced reality of that region."

Here we reach the root of the question. The specific contribution to revolutionary theory that has become labelled as "Trotskyism," is not merely unyielding recognition of the necessity for socialist revolution on a world scale—the ultraleft sectarians do this in all sincerity and they should be given credit for it.

What Trotskyism offers is a transitional political approach, the methodical search for points of contact with masses of workers and peasants who may have a backward outlook, who may be under the influence of conservative or demagogic leaders or opportunist parties. The approach consists of finding slogans, aims, or suggested measures that are acceptable to the masses at their given level of political development but which nevertheless correspond to objective necessities and which, once undertaken, tend to carry them toward socialist revolution and full political consciousness.

This transitional approach is applicable and required in the imperialist countries but has special meaning in the underdeveloped areas of the world where feudal conditions do exist, where the bourgeoisie has failed to carry out the tasks of the bourgeois democratic revolution, or where the struggle against imperialist domination leads to nationalist moods.

In tribute to Marx, who formulated the germinal idea, Trotsky named this theory, which permeates his writings and which guided all his political activities from 1905 on, the theory of "permanent revolution." The theory of permanent revolution is not at all something exotic. It was applied for the first time in the Russian revolution of 1917, where it provided the guidelines for taking the struggle against feudalistic tsarism into the socialistic phase that culminated in the establishment of the first workers' state in history.

It provides an incomparable key to understanding the inner logic of the revolutionary events of our time. It is very much involved in the problem under discussion—the question of extending the Cuban revolution. The Cubans, in fact, really owe it to themselves to become acquainted with the theory. They will be surprised to discover how well Trotsky foresaw the logic of the revolution they carried out by feeling their way through the more costly method of trial and error.

To return to the limitations of the Tricontinental Conference. If a question mark must be placed on its decisions being carried out in practice, the primary reason is the absence of mass revolutionary socialist parties in Latin America. They have yet to be organized. The Cuban revolution gave a great impulse in this direction, particularly by helping to end the authority of the fossilized Communist and Social Democratic formations. But the heavy and sometimes categorical emphasis on the efficacy of guerrilla warfare to the exclusion of other means, promoted by both Havana's and Peking's teachings, has tended to stand in the road of organizing parties built in the Leninist pattern. Perhaps this phase is coming to an end.

The contingents that will form the cadres of these parties are now separated in various formations, from independent revolutionaries to authentic Trotskyists, including the guerrilla movements and the youth sectors of some of the Communist parties that were represented at the Tricontinental Conference. If one of the effects of the conference is to bring them together in revolutionary actions, the party-building process will be hastened in Latin America. We hope that this proves to be the case.

In that event Castro's attack on Trotskyism will turn out to have been an episodic step backward and not the beginning of a major betrayal spelling doom for the bright hopes awakened by the Cuban revolution and its leaders.

# Stalinism or Trotskyism
## in the Cuban Revolution?
## (1966)

Why did Blas Roca feel impelled to take up the cudgel against Trotskyism? He says that Trotskyism, "in its politics and theory," is a "corpse." Wasn't Trotskyism reduced to that state by the late Stalin himself decades ago; not just once, but repeatedly, and not just polemically, but with frame-up trials, deportations, and executions? Didn't both Khrushchev and Mao in their polemics finish the dead dog once again? Finally, wasn't the cadaver disposed of so effectively by Fidel Castro in his speech of January 15 that any hope of its ever being resurrected was ended once and for all?

What an unexpected sight, then, only three months after Castro's speech against Trotskyism, to see the Earl Browder of Cuba rushing to the rescue of the prime minister, as if unexpected weaknesses had suddenly been exposed in the January 15 speech—or unexpected life in the overkilled corpse!

Karl Marx, and Hegel before him, taught that what men propose—even the most powerful and authoritative—often fails to be realized and indeed can end in just the opposite of their aims and intentions. This appears to have been the case with that section of Fidel Castro's January 15 speech which was directed against the "Trotskyites" and intended to consign them to oblivion.

By employing old Stalinist slanders, long ago exposed as frame-ups, by lumping opposites together—the method of amalgam typical of Stalinism—by eschewing reasoned political argument, Fidel Castro's attack led to an outcome utterly unexpected by the advisers who supplied the prime minister with the material he used in his speech. Three things happened:

1. The slanderous charge that "Trotskyism became . . . a vulgar instrument of imperialism and reaction" was not accepted.

The days of the Stalin cult are gone. The de-Stalinization process has destroyed forever the atmosphere when such vile accusations need only be asserted from on high to be believed. Castro's attack, on the contrary, provoked shock and dismay and led to widespread protests. The editors of the *Monthly Review* only voiced the general reaction in radical circles when they recalled that "the accusation has no foundation whatever, as anyone who has seriously studied the history of the communist movement since the October Revolution must know"; that it was "precisely this accusation which provided the rationalization for the Soviet purge trials of the 1930's"; that if "anything has been proved—and not least by the Soviet government itself—it is that the trials were a shameless frame-up"; and that Fidel Castro "should not deceive himself that he can sway any but cowards and syco-phants by mere denunciation."

2. Through the wide publicity it afforded and the sympathy it evoked for the slandered movement—undoubtedly the most maligned in all history—Castro's attack had the unanticipated effect of stimulating interest in the cause of Trotskyism and attracting further attention to its authentic ideas.

3. In the resulting discussion, the key issues involved in the attack began to emerge. They happen to be of vital concern to every revolutionary socialist and colonial freedom fighter: (a) What is the nature of the revolution now on the agenda in many countries, particularly Latin America? Must it first go through a bourgeois-democratic stage under bourgeois leadership? Or can a victory be projected under the leadership of a revolutionary socialist party that frankly espouses from the very beginning the need to pose socialist tasks? (b) What is the role of proletarian democratic norms in the revolutionary process, including free discussion and the exclusion of such abominations as slandering or muzzling oppositional views? Are these norms utopian, or are they really applicable and, in fact, a vital necessity?

These issues lie at the heart of the dispute and constitute its main interest. We will consider them in the process of analyzing Blas Roca's contribution in detail.

The basic content of Blas Roca's article in the May 1 [1966] issue of *Politica* merely re-echoes the central theme of Castro's attack: Trotskyism is "a vulgar instrument of imperialism and reaction"—which itself was an echo of the standard Stalinist slanders. He repeats the very phrase insistently, as if mere repetition a number of times by someone as authoritative as Blas

Roca would make up for Castro's unaccountable failure to make it stick.

There are, however, some instructive differences between the two attacks. While, in Castro's speech, the target was the Fourth International, you would never know that the references were to a fake "Fourth International" set up by one J. Posadas. Castro did not even mention the name of Posadas. The connection of members of this group with the MR-13 guerrilla movement in Guatemala was used to brand the movement as "infiltrated" by "Trotskyites" whom Castro dubbed "agents of imperialism" under the general slanderous charge levelled against Trotskyism as such. Then independent journals, or journals of organizations having no connection with Trotskyism, were *amalgamated* with the fake Posadas "Fourth International" either because they raised questions about Guevara's leaving the Cuban political scene or because they published articles by Adolfo Gilly, a revolutionary socialist journalist whose views on some points demonstrably coincide with those of Posadas. In brief, Castro's attacks read a great deal like similar attacks made by Blas Roca himself as far back as 1961. (See, for instance, Blas Roca's book *The Cuban Revolution* or the pamphlet I wrote in 1962, *Trotskyism and the Cuban Revolution—An Answer to Hoy*.)

In contrast to Castro's original presentation of "Trotskyism" as a single movement, the nature of which could be judged from statements judiciously selected from the writings of the unnamed Posadas, or the statements of a creature of the UPI like Felipe Albaguante, who was exposed in 1963 by the United Secretariat of the Fourth International, Blas Roca now presents "Trotskyism" as "a medley of such confusion, of groups and subgroups, that some Trotskyists deny that other Trotskyists are Trotskyists." As a result, for the first time to my knowledge, Blas Roca deigns to identify Posadas as the author of some of the quotations which he finds so useful. He refers to a genuinely Trotskyist newspaper, the *Militant,* for the first time, although in a very peculiar manner, as we shall see. And, ranging far and wide, he brings in the *Newsletter,* the newspaper of the Socialist Labour League in Britain.

The purpose of this procedure soon becomes obvious. Responding to the emergency, Blas Roca is picking up the pieces of Castro's January 15 attack on Trotskyism and trying to build a better structure by using more boards, stronger glue, sturdier mortar to plaster cracks, and a thick coat of demagogy to paint things and dazzle the eye.

This is a small-scale replica of the pattern Stalin followed in his notorious series of frame-up trials from 1936 to 1938. When glaring contradictions exposed the falsifications of his political police in a given frame-up, Stalin made up for it by staging a bigger and more imposing show trial. To use such methods in an effort to forestall Castro from rectifying a serious error—due, we may suppose, to bad advice—really injures the prestige and authority of the Cuban revolution; that is, if Blas Roca can get away with it.

Now that he admits it involves something broader than the tiny Posadas group, Blas Roca seeks to ridicule the Trotskyist movement by saying that in it such confusion reigns "that some Trotskyists deny that other Trotskyists are Trotskyists." The argument only makes its author look ridiculous. Ultrareactionaries likewise sneer at some Communists denying that other Communists are Communists; and they point to the polemics, which are not always models of comradeliness, between the Khrushchevists, Maoists, Titoists, and . . . Fidelistas.

What would an independent-minded revolutionist who knows the positions of the leaders of the Cuban revolution say if someone argued like Blas Roca and coolly told an audience that the Cuban leaders were "imperialist agents," the proof being the evident confusion and mutual recriminations because of different positions taken on crucial issues by the Communist capitals—such as Belgrade's friendly attitude toward the Betancourt-Leoni government in contrast to Havana's hostility, Moscow's class-collaborationist attitude toward U.S. imperialism in contrast to Peking's intransigence, and Peking's sectarian rejection of a united front in defense of the Vietnamese revolution in contrast to the appeals of all the others for a common front? The revolutionist would shout that this is utter nonsense and that the Cubans have their own positions—very good positions, as can be determined by reading their declarations and judging their actions. To which the orator would respond in the crushing style of Blas Roca: "What a joke! Everyone in this medley claims to be a Communist, whatever they call each other. I repeat what I said about the Cuban leaders no matter how much you squirm, and as proof I have scrupulously copied down the following stupidities from *Hsinhua* on the united front."

The truth is that Blas Roca belongs to the Stalinist school, which considers any critical opposition to the monolithic line handed down from the unchallengeable leader to be a reflection of imperialist pressure, if not a direct plot fomented by such agencies as the CIA. That the revolution should really be a "school of unfettered thought" is inconceivable to such ossified bureaucrats, for in a revolutionary party this involves the right to form tendencies and factions; and in a workers' state it means the right of the proletariat to form a multiple party system so long as the various parties remain basically loyal to the revolution and its conquests. Democratic centralism means *democracy* in reaching decisions as well as *centralism* in carrying them out.

To rise to the level of the great tasks it faces, a revolutionary party before and after coming to power requires the free play of thought, not only because this is the best way to develop and lift the intellectual level of its members and leaders, but because it is the most efficient way of exploring all possible political variants and of reaching solid decisions that truly reflect reality and thereby enable the revolutionary party to intervene in the national and international class struggle most effectively. This view is not peculiar to Trotskyism; it is as old as scientific socialism and constituted the essence of Lenin's method of party building.

That serious differences appeared in the world Communist movement after the decades of Stalinist monolithism was in itself a progressive development. Arising fundamentally from the victory of the Soviet Union over German imperialism, the postwar advance of the colonial revolution, and a balance of world forces favoring the socialist camp, these differences have helped pave the way for a resurgence of revolutionary Marxism. What is bad is the absence of provisions, customs, and institutions to carry the discussion of the differences forward to a democratic conclusion. And that lack reflects the continued existence of narrow, self-serving bureaucratic interests that deliberately block a normal resolution of the differences through the process of free discussion.

The Trotskyist movement did not remain unaffected by the advance of the colonial revolution, by the commencement of de-Stalinization, by the differences revolving around the Sino-Soviet conflict, and by other events. In fact the differential consequences of these developments can easily be found in the positions advocated by the various tendencies claiming adherence to Trotskyism.

A first-rate example of this was the impact of the Cuban revolution. The overwhelming majority of the Trotskyists throughout the world considered this to be the opening of the socialist revolution in the Western Hemisphere. The appearance of a new leadership, generated in the very process of a revolution, untainted by Stalinism and imbued with revolutionary determination, was hailed with immense enthusiasm. In the United States, the Socialist Workers Party took up the cause of the Cuban revolution as its own, and its candidates put defense of revolutionary Cuba as the first foreign policy plank in their national election platform in 1960 and 1964. The Fourth International as a whole responded in the same enthusiastic way. This common estimate provided one of the main grounds for the healing in 1963 of a major split in the world Trotskyist movement that had lasted almost ten years.

Two groupings, each of them representing small minorities, stood in opposition and came to consider their differences to be so great as to transcend their duty to adhere to the principles of democratic centralism. One of these engaged in a split (Posadas's Latin American Bureau) and the other rejected participation in the reunification of the world Trotskyist movement (Healy's Socialist Labour League).

Posadas, an energetic organizer, had been developing rather eccentric positions of his own inside the movement, and on splitting he cast aside all restraint. He advanced the idea that nuclear war and revolution are synonymous; i.e., a nuclear war will finish capitalism but not socialism, it is therefore to be welcomed, and in fact ought to be initiated in a preemptive strike by the Soviet Union. Among the various tendencies of the world Communist movement, Posadas expresses affinity with Mao's thought, which, as he indicates with satisfaction from time to time, often corresponds with his own "brilliant" analyses. Apparently he is convinced that Mao reads his speeches and reports. The Posadas group could be dismissed as a rather bizarre cult were it not for the fact that it has a few followers in Cuba, has contacts with the Guatemalan guerrilla movement, claims to be the Fourth International, and thus serves Blas Roca as a convenient club with which to beat the "corpse" of Trotskyism.

The Healy group, reflecting British insularity, took the position that the Cuban revolution has not reached the phase of a workers' state, that Cuba remains capitalist, and that Castro is just a demagogue if not worse.* In this respect, the quotations selected by Blas Roca were accurate enough reflections of Healy-ite views. It happens, however, that Healy's position, clearly a prime example of ultraleft sectarian thinking, was thoroughly debated by the world Trotskyist movement and overwhelmingly rejected as not in consonance with the reality.

In presenting Healy's nonsense about Cuba as the position of the Fourth International or the *Militant,* Blas Roca is deliberately dishonest. I say this not as an epithet, but as an easily proved statement of fact. *The very article in the February 5 Newsletter from which Blas Roca quoted ends up with an attack on the Socialist Workers Party for its position in relation to the Cuban revolution and Fidel Castro.*

Blas Roca could have brought in the conflicting position of still another group which claims to represent the Fourth International: a recent minor split-off headed by Michael Raptis (Pablo). Apparently this did not fit in with the immediate job at hand. Up to now this group has not developed views on Cuba differing distinctly from those of the Fourth International. Its differences are in other areas. It considers the de-Stalinization process to be irreversible and synonymous with democratization. In the Sino-Soviet conflict it favors Moscow over Peking and leans most strongly in the direction of Titoism. The sharpest differences with this group occurred over party-building methods, particularly the observance of democratic centralism.

Let us now consider Blas Roca's argumentation on how the Trotskyists allegedly serve as "very active auxiliary forces" in the effort of the Yankee imperialists "to destroy the prestige and authority" of the Cuban revolution. He seeks to prove this by

---

* The "theoreticians" of the Socialist Labour League consider that their abysmal ignorance of Latin American politics endows them with a special right to pontificate on the Cuban revolution. Naturally this offers sport to Blas Roca, who chortles over such boners as their informing the British public that the independent weekly *Marcha* of Montevideo is an "organ of the ultraleft Posadas group." For those hardy souls who try to keep up with the *Newsletter* this is but another sad instance of the notorious unreliability of this publication in handling such pedestrian things as facts. But what should we say then of the *Worker,* the voice of the American Communist Party, which, in its January 23, 1966, issue, printed a dispatch from its Havana correspondent listing *Marcha* as a "Spanish Trotskyite weekly?"

citing published statements by Posadas selected to coincide with the timing of various piratical forays fomented or engineered by the State Department or the CIA. Posadas coordinates his statements, if we are to believe Blas Roca, so that they appear in published form "as always" to "coincide with the intensification of the attacks of the imperialists. . . ."

Doesn't this sound like the red-baiting formulas of a comic book? Must we really submit this kind of argument to serious analysis?

1. What about the declarations made by Posadas between piratical forays? Did they fluctuate markedly in the direction of a friendly tone? If they did not, if Posadas maintained a uniformly critical position, then his declarations were not timed to coincide with the piratical forays—and Blas Roca's case falls to the ground.

2. If Posadas's purpose was to undermine the prestige and authority of the Cuban revolution, why did he make such self-destructive declarations? The very quotations carefully selected by Blas Roca are devastating—to Posadas. Read the sentences transcribed by Blas Roca from the article or report by Posadas on the discussions on architecture: "No congress of architecture can be posed without the war. It is insanity." And so forth and so on. Even Blas Roca is compelled to admit that the long text is "extremely confused and at times incomprehensible." He is completely correct. The utterances of Posadas damage only the prestige and authority of the author.

The alternatives are inescapable: Either Posadas appears bizarre to all who read such declarations, or the intellectual level of the Cuban cadres (and the cadres of the Latin American revolution as a whole) is so incredibly low that they can be swept off their feet by extremely confused and at times incomprehensible nonsense. Does Blas Roca hold to the latter alternative?

Personally, it pleased me to see Blas Roca quoting so extensively from Posadas while at the same time clearly indicating who the author was. One could only wish that Blas Roca would be more honest about indicating that this is a small sect and not the voice of the Fourth International.

Is Blas Roca more fortunate with his quotations from the *Newsletter*? He asserts that the nature of the *Newsletter* position "explains the coincidence between the most brazen attacks of Trotskyist propaganda with the piratical aggressions of the Yankee imperialists against Cuba"; but he does not even try to indicate any coincidence in dates as he does in the case of Posadas. Blas Roca relies on barefaced assertion and the impact of the outrageous theoretical and political positions voiced by the *Newsletter*.

We would like to know in greater detail from Blas Roca, however, exactly how the *Newsletter* proved to be a "very active auxiliary force" in the efforts of the Yankee imperialists. Can he name any group in all of Latin America that has been influenced by the *Newsletter*? We will go further. Can he name a single person in all of Latin America who considers himself a partisan of the *Newsletter*? The truth is that the position of the *Newsletter* on the Cuban revolution is in such utter contradiction to the reality that the Healy group stands in absolute isolation. Its position on Cuba doesn't play the dirty game of imperialism, as Blas Roca maintains; it only plays into the hands of Blas Roca. Even the half-dozen admirers of the Socialist Labour League to be found in the United States consider that Healy is completely wrong on this subject. They sedulously seek other reasons for praising him.

We thus come to a key question. Is this the best that Blas Roca can do in trying to bolster and shore up the contention that Trotskyism is a "vulgar instrument of imperialism and reaction"? The answer is yes. That's the best he can do.

Two omissions from Blas Roca's list are truly telling. The first is the Fourth International. He does not offer a single quotation from the genuine publications of the Fourth International. In all its declarations—and there are many of them—he could not find a single phrase that lent itself to his work! The reason is simple. The Fourth International espoused the cause of the Cuban revolution from the very beginning, has energetically participated in its defense, and has pointed again and again to the Cuban revolution as one more mighty verification of the validity of Trotsky's theory of the permanent revolution. That is why Blas Roca found nothing to say about the mainstream of the Trotskyist movement when he set out to do his smear job.

The other omission is the Socialist Workers Party. If Trotskyism became a "vulgar instrument of imperialism and reaction" and the Trotskyists are "very active auxiliary forces" in the efforts of the Yankee imperialists to destroy the prestige and authority of the Cuban revolution, the most crushing proof surely ought to be found in the imperialist U.S.A. itself. And this should be all the easier, one would imagine, because there is absolutely no question about who represents Trotskyism in the United States—it is the Socialist Workers Party.

Did Blas Roca fail to search here for evidence? We doubt it. He or his American cothinkers combed the pages of the *Militant* and the *International Socialist Review,* and the public declarations of the American Trotskyists, and their pamphlets and books, looking for something that could be used in the attack against Trotskyism.

The truth is that among the radical groupings in the United States the record of the Socialist Workers Party is unimpeachable and outstanding; so outstanding, in fact, that Blas Roca himself has been very cautious about attacking it even when pinned down on the subject. For instance, in June of 1962, Blas Roca did a smear job on Trotskyism in *Hoy,* utilizing quotations from Posadas (whom he did not name as the source) in the way now familiar to us. But only a few months before that, in its April 16, 1962, issue, the *National Guardian* printed an exclusive interview in which Blas Roca was asked if he welcomed to the ranks of Cuba's friends and partisans in the U.S. "people of any orientation, for example Trotskyists. . . ."

Blas Roca equivocated somewhat but obviously felt that he could not openly attack the American Trotskyists. "I am not well acquainted with those who call themselves Trotskyists in the U.S.," he said. "We are separated from Trotskyists in general by fundamental points of view, and from some in particular by their actions as enemies. But I think all in the U.S. who sincerely defend and support the Cuban revolution, and the right of the Cuban and other Latin American peoples, do a worthy revolutionary job and we value them whatever their ideological concepts may be. . . ."

The *Militant* has consistently printed the main declarations of Fidel Castro and Che Guevara despite the limited number of pages at its disposal, and is a well-known source of truthful information about the Cuban revolution. At the big turns like Playa Girón and the 1962 "Caribbean crisis," the *Militant* went all out in defense of the Cuban revolution and denunciation of American imperialism. It did this not from outside the country, but inside the imperialist monster itself. And its record of activity in defense of Cuba is superior to that of Blas Roca's sister organization, the American Communist Party.

The record of the *Militant* is so irreproachable in this respect that Blas Roca was apparently puzzled as to how to smear it. His

*Dynamics of the Cuban Revolution*

solution was the frame-up technique of the *amalgam.* He took the ultraleft sectarian position of the Socialist Labour League, which the Socialist Workers Party opposed so vigorously as to drive Healy to split from the Fourth International, and quoted it in close association with references to the *Militant.* To prove how deliberately this was done it is only necessary to take the January 31, 1966, issue of the *Militant,* in which we first responded to the attack in Castro's January 15 speech, compare it with the February 5 issue of the *Newsletter,* which deals with the same subject, including an attack on the Socialist Workers Party, and then check how Blas Roca pasted these opposites together in his article. It is an example for the textbooks on the polemical methods of the Stalinists.

There is still another remarkable omission. When Blas Roca wrote his article, he had before him a copy of the April issue of *Monthly Review,* which contains the stand taken by editors Leo Huberman and Paul M. Sweezy on Castro's January 15 speech. Yet he does not say a word about the *Monthly Review* or the very important issues raised by the two editors. He acts as if he had never heard about the deduction made by the *Monthly Review* concerning advisers who possibly supplied Fidel Castro with the material used in attacking "Trotskyism."

The proof that Blas Roca had this issue of the *Monthly Review* before him is, I think, compelling. In his article, he quotes the following sentence written by Adolfo Gilly, but without indicating its source: "The vertiginous political evolution of the Cuban leadership in recent months confirms the opinion that it is true that they have either assassinated Guevara or that they are restraining him by some means or other from expressing himself politically." The source of that quotation is page 29 of the April 1966 issue of the *Monthly Review.* This is the same issue that contained the editorial statement by Leo Huberman and Paul M. Sweezy. (We will return to the question of Guevara.)

Blas Roca failed to refer to the *Monthly Review* in order to facilitate evading the cardinal political issues. This is the same pattern followed by Gus Hall, the main spokesman of the American Communist Party, in his response to the stand taken by the *Monthly Review.* (See the *Worker* April 24, 1966, and my reply in the May 9 *Militant.*) Huberman and Sweezy challenged Fidel Castro on the "ugly and perhaps ominous" aspect of his speech in which he charged that Trotskyists are "agents of imperialism." "It was precisely this accusation which provided the rationalization for the Soviet purge trials of the 1930's," they said. Fidel Castro has not yet responded to the challenge issued by *Monthly Review*. Blas Roca chose to step forward instead. But he remained silent about the reference to the Moscow trials. Does he still support the "rationalization" used in purging Stalin's opponents or possible opponents? Does he think the Soviet government under Khrushchev was wrong in adding to the mountain of evidence proving that Stalin framed up his victims? He does not say.

However, we see that he proceeds as if Stalin had been vindicated. Thereby he provides a most illuminating insight into the nature of some of Fidel Castro's advisers, and offers confirmation of the reasoning of the editors of *Monthly Review* that to revive the accusation used in the Moscow trials is a "sure sign of either ignorance or malice" and that in this matter "the malice comes from advisers who never abandoned the attitudes and methods which underlay the trials."

Without naming the *Monthly Review,* Blas Roca does attempt an answer on Che Guevara's disappearance from the Cuban political scene. "Fidel," said the *Monthly Review* editors, "should be under no illusions that only imperialists and their agents are interested in Che's fate." They expressed the hope that Castro would soon clear up the mystery, but they asked: "Is Fidel Castro aware of the real issues at stake in the Guevara affair? And does he realize that every day's delay in clearing up the mystery brings anxiety and doubt to honest revolutionaries everywhere and joy to their enemies?"

Blas Roca simply repeats the accusations made in Castro's speech—the sole interest in the matter allegedly lies with the Yankee imperialists, whose "very active auxiliary forces" spread all the contradictory rumors about Che Guevara in order to undermine the prestige and authority of the Cuban revolution. The letter from Che read by Fidel last October was absolutely "definitive" for "genuine revolutionaries," says this prestigious authority. Blas Roca takes up only one new point, a point which I happened to advance in the article published in the January 31, 1966, *Militant*, from which Blas Roca quotes several times. On the assumption, which I accepted, that Castro told the truth about Guevara's taking a new assignment, I called attention to the *disproportion* in that part of Castro's speech. If it was true that imperialism was making a big and damaging campaign against the Cuban revolution by raising questions about Guevara's disappearance, then it was completely out of keeping to use this as a springboard for an implausible attack on "Trotskyism" which would only prove divisive in the revolutionary movement and would be rejected by the majority of today's revolutionary vanguard. On the other hand, it would have been devastating for Che Guevara to imitate Mark Twain and write a letter of greetings to the Tricontinental Conference indicating that the rumors about his death were grossly exaggerated.

Here is Blas Roca's response: "But in view of the facts, of what use would it have been? If before, with the last letter from *Che,* read by Fidel himself, the slanders and malicious speculations of these elements not only did not cease but multiplied, wouldn't they have responded in the same way to a new letter?" As if the content and style of such a letter would not be sufficient to establish its authenticity!

This is Blas Roca's answer not only to the *Militant* but to *Monthly Review,* both of which raised the question from the viewpoint of honest revolutionaries concerned about the welfare and prestige of the Cuban revolution. Does Blas Roca really think that the matter can be disposed of with the epithet "imperialist agents"? That kind of answer *is* alarming!

Since Blas Roca wants it that way, there is little choice but to raise some further questions:

1. Does Che Guevara know about the speculation over his disappearance from the public scene in Cuba? Yes or no?

2. If he does not know, how is this to be explained?

3. If he does know, why does he fail to respond to the concern of his comrades and friends? Why doesn't he indicate to the world that everything is all right with him? At the moment, what single act by him could conceivably be of greater assistance to the Cuban revolution?

Blas Roca becomes most effusive in praising the "stout and beloved comandante of our revolutionary war" Che Guevara and in defending him from the alleged slanderous attacks of the Trotskyists, who, we are told, seek to pit him against Fidel. But Che's opinion of the Trotskyists is quite different from the view contained in the slanders put into Castro's January 15 speech. I noted this in the article in the *Militant* which Blas Roca cited. Blas Roca ignored the paragraphs quoting the tribute paid by Che Guevara to the Peruvian Trotskyist peasant leader Hugo Blanco, who has been held in prison at Arequipa without trial for three years. Neither Guevara's tribute nor the picture of a

Trotskyist leader rotting in a Peruvian jail for the "crime" of leading a peasant struggle can easily be fitted into Blas Roca's slanderous picture of Trotskyism as a "vulgar instrument of imperialism and reaction."

While Blas Roca is answering the questions asked him above about Guevara, he might tell us also if he thought the stout and beloved comandante did wrong in paying tribute to Hugo Blanco. Speak up, Blas Roca, you have the floor.

Blas Roca singles out as one of his targets Adolfo Gilly and tries to make something out of the fact that "other Trotskyists" should both "defend" him and "denigrate him and his group." "It seems strange," says Blas Roca. ". . . But this is in perfect harmony with the fundamentally confusionist and provocative role of Trotskyism."

And in the very week that Blas Roca's article slandering Adolfo Gilly in the foulest way appeared in Mexico City in *Política*, Adolfo Gilly was arrested by the Mexican police and held without bail because the charges were so serious that he might receive more than a five-year sentence. And what are the charges? That he engaged in a "Communist conspiracy" to overthrow the Díaz Ordaz government; that he was involved in such "crimes" as seeking to organize protest demonstrations against the visit of President Johnson!

Where does Blas Roca stand in this? With the witch-hunters and red-baiters of the corrupt Mexican bourgeoisie? Or with the victim? We hope that Blas Roca will take a correct stand in this and express solidarity in the defense of Adolfo Gilly and the other victims despite his political differences with them.

Does a stand like that seem "strange"? It is perfectly comprehensible to every militant. And in the same way, the stand of *Monthly Review* in disagreeing with Adolfo Gilly's negative appreciation of the Tricontinental Conference and his estimate of Fidel Castro's course while agreeing with him on other issues is completely rational and understandable. The position of most Trotskyists toward Adolfo Gilly is not fundamentally different. They consider that he has made valuable journalistic contributions; at the same time, insofar as he is influenced by the views of Posadas on some issues, they would like to see him take a more independent course. No matter how mistaken they might think him to be in his views, they would unanimously reject with indignation the Stalinist slander that he is an "imperialist agent."

If Blas Roca chooses not to understand this, perhaps another case will sink home. I had barely begun this reply when the news came from Detroit that an ultrarightist, racist-minded gunman had entered the Eugene V. Debs Hall, the local headquarters of the Socialist Workers Party, to kill some "Communists." He ordered three young antiwar fighters there, one of whom belonged to the Young Socialist Alliance and two to the Socialist Workers Party, to line up against the wall. He then pumped nine bullets into them, killing Leo Bernard and critically wounding Jan Garrett and Walter Graham.

As Staughton Lynd said, "Leo Bernard is the first person in the peace movement to be murdered." I do not know whether this political assassination was reported in the Cuban press or what stand Blas Roca took on it. In the United States the entire antiwar movement has rallied in a spontaneous expression of solidarity in face of this murderous blow struck against the movement as a whole.

The Communist Party, U.S.A., made an official statement May 18 as follows:

The deliberate political murder in Detroit, Michigan on May 16 of Leo Bernard of the Socialist Workers Party and the shooting of Jan Edward Garrett and Walter Graham of the Young Socialist Alliance in an attempt to kill them is a shocking consequence of the anti-communist campaign of the ultra-Right. These three young men who were active in the struggle to end the war in Vietnam are also victims of the domestic hatred engendered by the warmongers.

For the past several months, the murderer had planned "to kill some communists." On March 3rd, the Detroit police were warned that this was the plan of this political hoodlum and did nothing about it. The Federal agencies were told about the murder plan before March 3rd by a consulate in New York and did nothing about it except to tell the Detroit police. The murderer lined up his victims and started shooting with a shout, "You are all Communists." This is cold-blooded political murder and all who have responsibility must be called to account.

This murder is related to the ultra-Right action organization of anti-Communist hoodlums in Detroit known as "Breakthrough" which tried to break up a meeting in Cobo Hall on May 6th at which Gus Hall was the main speaker. On that occasion, one who tried to break into the meeting carried a loaded 38 revolver with obvious intent to use it. That outfit gets its political direction from the Birchites.

This is also related to the bombings of the Communist Party headquarters building in New York, the bombing of bookstores in Detroit, Los Angeles and Chicago, the bombing of the DuBois headquarters in San

Francisco and the Vietnam Day headquarters in Berkeley, the acts of arson in Chicago and Indiana, the death threats through the mails and by telephone in various cities—all of which are known to city and Federal authorities who do nothing about them. The Detroit murder must serve to halt this brand of terror in our political life. All who advocate peace, democracy and political freedom have the responsibility to speak up and strengthen these struggles.

Dorothy Healy, the Southern California chairman of the Communist Party, voiced the following opinion:

The monstrous murder of Leo Bernard and the wounding of Jan Garrett and Walter Graham is a direct outgrowth of anti-Communist hysteria. This anti-Communism, which provides the justification for military aggression in Vietnam and domestic repression at home, has taken the life of Leo Bernard just as it has killed the Vietnamese fighting for independence. All Americans fighting to end the war in the Mekong Delta and those fighting for freedom in the Mississippi Delta should join in demanding an end to the hysteria which produced this attack on members of the Socialist Workers Party.

We leave it to Blas Roca to fit these statements into his slander about the Trotskyists being "very active auxiliary forces" of American imperialism when in reality they are recognized by friend and foe alike as "very active" in opposition to its "dirty wars" in Vietnam, Santo Domingo, and Cuba! No doubt Blas Roca will say nothing. Even silver-tongued orators sometimes find that silence is golden.

For a genuine revolutionary Marxist, it is not sufficient to determine that a position is "opportunist," or "ultraleft" or "sectarian." The reason why sincere and intelligent revolutionists can sometimes be found in any of the various blind alleys leading away from the road to socialism must be elucidated. Sociological reasons may be found, such as ties to the middle class or the pressure of a bureaucracy or caste.

Even if the analysis is carried far enough to reveal these underlying sources, a grain of truth may nevertheless be found lurking in their political positions. That is one reason why a figure of the stature of Lenin did not brush aside sincere revolutionists who argued for a position he disagreed with. His language could be very forceful, of course, but he nevertheless engaged in a reasoned discussion and he did not hesitate to appropriate something of value in an opponent's position. In the hands of Lenin, proletarian democracy was a genuine revolutionary tool.

It was injurious to the Cuban revolution to muzzle the Posadas group. Blas Roca quotes from the "mimeographed newspaper which was printed in Cuba by an organized Trotskyist group after the triumph of the Revolution with the assistance of Posadas and Adolfo Gilly." He does not mention that the newspaper was mimeographed because they were denied the use of a press. He does not add that even the mimeographed newspaper was put out of business through the arrest and imprisonment of those who produced and distributed it. Was the Cuban revolution so weak ideologically that it was incapable of answering the arguments of even a Posadas?

It may have seemed troublesome to pay attention to the "long, extremely confused and at times incomprehensible" articles or reports by J. Posadas which constitute the main grist of his small propaganda mill. No doubt there are youth in Cuba, however, who might have liked to argue it out with the followers of Posadas as a way of sharpening their own thought and advancing their revolutionary education. The overhead cost of suppressing the group was rather high, for it gave substance to the false charge that the Cuban revolution is going the way of the Russian revolution, i.e., is becoming *Stalinized*.

Particularly in the United States, where Stalinism has done untold damage to the revolutionary socialist cause, the suppression of the Posadas group did injury to Cuba. There were few campuses where the violation of the democratic rights of the Posadas group was not thrown at defenders of the Cuban revolution, particularly *Trotskyist* defenders of the Cuban revolution.

It is all the more brutally unfair of Blas Roca to tax the Posadas group with unwarranted criticisms of Fidel Castro in view of the unwarranted violation of their democratic rights. From their own experience they came to the conclusion that they had been given a raw deal and there are others who would agree on this despite the deepest repugnance for their political positions. The treatment of the Posadas group demonstrated that as yet the Cuban revolution has not evolved institutional forms providing for the free expression of dissident opinion within the framework of loyalty to the revolution. This is a grave weakness.

The mistake of the Socialist Labour League arises from the

incapacity of its insular-minded leadership to recognize a revolution when they see one. This is quite a condemnation of their theoretical and political capacities and signifies their doom as a viable movement. But there is one kind of revolution they would deign to recognize (we hope) if they saw it. That is a revolution that organized workers' power through soviets or councils and followed the norms of proletarian democracy laid down by Lenin in *State and Revolution*. Since the Cuban revolution has not yet achieved soviets, the SLL denies that a proletarian power exists in Cuba. From this they deduce that capitalism must still be in power no matter what measures have been undertaken and no matter what anybody says. They are, of course, mistaken. Their insistence on converting democratic norms into criteria marks them as sectarians; and their opposition to Cuba's revolutionary government despite its obviously tremendous achievements shows that they are ultralefts like Posadas. They are even less serious than Posadas, however. The entire colonial world remains a closed book to them. They are not really interested in it. They are quite content to vegetate in their placid little island where not even the cops carry guns. Periodically they announce grandiose plans about "reorganizing" the Fourth International and saving it from the "degeneration" brought about by such things as its support for the Cuban revolution and the Castro team.

Nevertheless there is a kernel of truth in their criticism which must be recognized. Cuba does not yet have a soviet form of government. And this, too, is a grave weakness.

The mainstream of the world Trotskyist movement has held since the beginning that the Cuban revolution is inherently the most democratic since the October 1917 revolution in Russia. Evidence for this abounded in the early years. The blockade and armed aggression mounted by imperialism cut across this tendency and prevented it from flowering. For instance, the humanist Cuban leaders abolished the death penalty but had to reinstate it in face of the murderous forays and bombings organized by Cuban counterrevolutionaries financed, armed, and instigated by the CIA. Under the tightening grip of the imperialist blockade Cuba necessarily took on some of the characteristics of a beleaguered fortress—which is not exactly a greenhouse for the development and observance of the norms of proletarian democracy. And still the Cuban revolution remained remarkably free of the bureaucratic sickness that wreaked such havoc in the Soviet Union. When the bureaucratic danger became acute in

1962, the famous move against Aníbal Escalante and his cohorts was undertaken.

The Cuban leaders have indicated their awareness of the weakness in the revolution on the side of political institutions and have expressed their intention many times of moving ahead in this field. They have made tentative experiments and have registered real progress in the construction of the Communist Party of Cuba. But they still have a considerable distance to travel before it need no longer be said that every important policy hinges on the decisions and the life of a single leader. The slowness of the process of setting up democratic institutions of proletarian rule in Cuba is of concern to many supporters of the Cuban revolution besides the world Trotskyist movement.

We come finally to what is really at the bottom of the attack against "Trotskyism." Blas Roca intimates it in his sneering references to the "superrevolutionary language" of the Trotskyists. You would think we were still back in the thirties, when the Blas Rocas were defending the Stalinist (not Leninist) "thesis of the possibility of the triumph of socialism in one country" as against the Trotskyist position that the very defense of the socialist achievements of the October revolution required the extension of the revolution and its culmination in an international revolution that would finally establish socialism in the industrially advanced capitalist countries. The correctness of the Trotskyist position has been confirmed by reality—in the extension of the revolution into Eastern Europe, in the toppling of capitalism and landlordism in China, and last, but by no means least, by the revolution in Cuba itself, only ninety miles from the world's major capitalist power.

A single additional socialist revolution in Latin America today could end the isolation of Cuba from the American continent at one blow and assure the rapid spread of revolutions throughout the Americas. Never has the Trotskyist program had such reality as today! This is precisely what the Blas Rocas, representing the miserable remnants of Stalinism in the Western Hemisphere, fear and are seeking to block.

Consider the following paragraphs from Blas Roca's article, in which he really tries to come to grips with Trotskyism:

With ultraleft slogans and calls for the immediate realization of the socialist revolution, they isolate this movement from the masses, they cut their road of development. With no little frequency they point to socialist

Cuba; but in 1958 the Rebel Army did not proclaim the socialist revolution, but united the people in the practical struggle to overthrow Batista's tyranny and to destroy his mercenary army which served to support him and which was the instrument of neocolonialism and all the reactionary social forces.

Whatever quotations Blas Roca may find in the articles and reports of J. Posadas, the Trotskyists do not call for the "immediate realization of the socialist revolution." This is a caricature, like the Stalinist caricature of former decades which claimed that Trotsky's theory of permanent revolution meant "simultaneous revolutions" everywhere.

Roca continues:

The Trotskyists like to say that the measures of socialist transformation were taken in Cuba under the pressure of the masses; what they are not even capable of understanding is that the *revolutionary leadership* under the guidance of Compañero Fidel Castro prepared each step and took it in consonance with the same state of consciousness which they had created in the masses. In 1959 the proclamation of socialism would have divided the country; in April 1961 the masses unanimously supported the declaration of Compañero Fidel Castro on the socialist character of our revolution and carried it to victory, with their blood, on the beaches of Playa Girón.

According to Blas Roca, "The Trotskyists like to say. . . ." Again, it is Posadas who likes to say. The decisive element in the victory of the Cuban revolution was unquestionably the leadership provided by Fidel Castro, who succeeded in overcoming the long default in leadership due to Stalinists like Blas Roca, bypassing them from the left. Naturally the masses responded. So did the Trotskyists and many other genuine revolutionists on an international scale. But Blas Roca's reference to Posadas here is only part of the smokescreen under which he advances a line in opposition to the line followed by Fidel Castro up to now of revolutionary struggle and declared socialist aims.

Blas Roca's line, as indicated in these paragraphs, is the same one advanced by the U.S. Communist spokesman Gus Hall in his criticism of *Monthly Review*. It is the concept that the revolutionary process in industrially underdeveloped countries must go through two separate stages, a bourgeois-democratic stage led by the progressive-minded bourgeoisie and a later stage in which the revolutionary leadership of the proletariat can come forward. The concept is the one advanced and defended by the Mensheviks in opposition to both Lenin and Trotsky. Something more is involved, however, than just a long-outmoded concept.

I do not deny that in 1959 a "proclamation of socialism" in Cuba would have been widely misunderstood. The reason had nothing to do with the class character of the developing revolution. It was due to the enormous discredit brought on the very name of socialism or communism by the record of Stalinism in the Soviet Union and in Cuba, where the Communist Party supported Batista. A "proclamation of socialism" would have been misunderstood as a proclamation of Stalinism.

It was correct of Castro to avoid that misunderstanding; to which we should add that Castro himself had been repelled by the record of the Communist Party and did not yet consider himself a Marxist. Instead of developing around a proclaimed program of socialism, the revolution moved forward under a slogan of action; namely, armed struggle against Batista. And even on this level, the Communist Party under Blas Roca's leadership failed miserably, attacking Castro's movement as adventuristic and putschist.

The truth is that Blas Roca's line, of avoiding the "superrevolutionary language" of socialism, of advancing the concept of two stages, had already been tried out in Cuba and had been found wanting, to say the least.

On December 4, 1939, the Cuban Communist Party nominated its candidate for the office of president. His name? Colonel Fulgencio Batista, the Chief of Staff of the Cuban armed forces. Blas Roca and his fellow Stalinist leaders backed Batista because they considered him to be a "man of the people," a good bourgeois democrat, a leader of the "first stage" of the revolution. And Batista rewarded his Communist Party supporters by giving them posts in his cabinet.

Without this coalition, Batista could never have gotten into a position to establish his bloody dictatorship. There were two stages all right. Two stages of a counterrevolution. In the first stage, the revolutionary forces were hoodwinked and duped into supporting a bourgeois democrat—a figure like Sukarno or Chiang Kai-shek, who was also touted by Stalin in the "first stage." In the second stage, the revolutionary forces were decimated as the counterrevolution consolidated its dictatorship. This tragic process was duplicated in Brazil two years ago when

Goulart was pictured as the good bourgeois democrat on whom all reliance should be placed in stage No. 1.

The Castelo Branco coup d'etat in April 1964 demonstrated in the most emphatic way that the line of a "two stage" revolution is still quite capable of paving the way for a "two stage" counter-revolution. This lesson has been freshened since October 1965 with the blood of hundreds of thousands of Communists in Indonesia. If Blas Roca's line is applied elsewhere in Latin America, it will most certainly guarantee another defeat as it did in Cuba in Batista's day, in China in 1925-27, Brazil in 1964, Indonesia in 1965, and many other countries where it has been tested.

The question then comes up: Can a successful revolution be organized around a mere slogan of action as happened in Cuba under Castro? To answer yes implies two things: (1) The indigenous bourgeoisie and their imperialist backers have learned nothing from the Cuban experience. (2) The masses in Latin America have learned nothing from the Cuban example of going forward to the socialist stage—in other words, "socialism" still has not recovered in their outlook from the terrible discredit brought on it by Stalin and his handpicked lieutenants like Blas Roca.

Both conclusions are wrong, in my opinion. American imperialism and its stooges are far readier to act in the most violent way at the first sign of a revolutionary upheaval no matter what attempts are made to disguise it. Johnson's occupation of Santo Domingo and the repressive measures taken against the Peruvian guerrilla fighters in the past year are proof enough without adding the lesson of Johnson's escalation of the war in Vietnam.

On the other hand, the Cuban revolution has had an immense effect on popular consciousness throughout Latin America, and this effect will grow as the contrast between Cuba's gains and the stagnation in the rest of Latin America becomes more glaring. In record time Cuba achieved such things as the liquidation of illiteracy. Unemployment was ended, social security guaranteed, an education assured to every child. Despite all the difficulties of the imperialist blockade and a number of serious errors, the planned economy is developing and offers a bright perspective for the future. And what an impressive fact—little Cuba, only ninety miles from the imperialist U.S., has been able to hold out against the world's mightiest power for seven years now! "Socialism," Cuban style, is bound to appear more and more attractive—as the socialist revolution was to the masses of the world in the first years after the October revolution. The Latin American masses will become increasingly impatient to achieve what the Cubans did—a socialist revolution. And why shouldn't they have it?

This rehabilitation of the word *socialism* and the program of socialism will likewise be listed in history to the credit of the Cuban revolution, and it will be achieved despite everything that the Blas Rocas, with their treacherous advice, can do to stop it.

In their editorial on Castro's January 15 attack against Troskyism, Huberman and Sweezy made the following point:

> Whatever its role in Guatemala, Trotskyism is certainly not a large or important political force in Latin America as a whole. But if Fidel Castro and the Latin American Communist parties duck the question of socialism, and still more if they attack as Trotskyites all those who openly struggle for a specifically socialist revolution, then the prospects for Latin American Trotskyism will be vastly improved.

Whatever it is called—consistent class struggle, revolutionary Marxism, revolutionary socialism, or Trotskyism—the prospects for socialist revolution in Latin America are already vastly improved. The prospects for class collaboration, peaceful coexistence, popular frontism, coalitionism, or Stalinism are on the decline. The great dividing line was drawn by the successful Cuban revolution. The popular appeal of the socialist goal, noted by Yon Sosa, the Guatemalan guerrilla leader, is but one indication of the deep processes at work in this direction.

The defeats and setbacks of the past few years will prove to be but temporary. Latin America's 200 million people are gathering their forces for another giant step forward. Nothing will be able to stop them—not all the dollars and guns of imperialism, and still less the pitiful labors of the Stalinist defilers of socialism.

# Fidel Castro and the
# Events in Czechoslovakia
# (1968)

What has happened to Fidel Castro's speech of August 23, in which he supported the invasion and occupation of Czechoslovakia by the Warsaw Pact countries?

Is it being hailed by Moscow? Has the Soviet command tried to put a copy in the hands of every citizen of Czechoslovakia, the better to explain why foreign troops have been stationed in their country? Have the Czechoslovak communications media opened a public discussion of the questions it raises?

If the speech is not being widely circulated, has it at least been placed on the agenda for discussion at a governmental level, or among the leaders of the Communist parties of the "socialist camp"?

The truth is that even the Communist Party U.S.A., one of the few pro-Moscow parties in the West to support the invasion wholeheartedly, has displayed an ambiguous attitude toward Castro's speech. While utilizing the fact that Castro approved the action of the Warsaw Pact countries, the top CPUSA leaders have refrained from disseminating or discussing Castro's speech as a whole.

The silence over what Castro said—one might justifiably call it a conspiracy of silence—is all the stranger in view of the fact that the Cuban leader remains the only one of all those who backed the action of the Warsaw Pact governments whose position can be characterized as internally consistent, if you accept the basic premise advanced by the Kremlin to justify sending troops into Czechoslovakia.

What led the Warsaw Pact allies to decide to block Castro's contribution from being discussed on a broad basis? Why did they decide that it was politically discreet to ignore it? To answer these questions, it is necessary to examine Castro's arguments closely.

The Cuban leader states his basic premise as follows:

We . . . were convinced—and this is very important—that the Czecho-slovak regime was dangerously inclined toward a substantial change in the system. In short, we were convinced that the Czechoslovak regime was heading toward capitalism and was inexorably heading toward imperialism. Of that we did not have the slightest doubt.

Castro, of course, is referring to the regime of Alexander Dubcek although he does not refer once to Dubcek by name.

The reasons advanced by Castro for coming to this conclusion include the interest displayed by imperialism in the ferment in Czechoslovakia, a certain responsiveness by some circles in the country to this interest, the slogans that were advanced concerning democratization of the political structure, the pressure for establishment of freedom of the press, "a process of seizure of the principal information media by the reactionary elements" which began "to develop," "a whole series of slogans of open rapprochement toward capitalist concepts and theses and of rapprochement towards the West."

He agrees that not everything was bad about the situation. Some of the slogans were "unquestionably correct." He also agrees that responsibility for precipitating a situation so allegedly favorable to the restoration of capitalism must be ascribed to the previous (Novotny) regime, to "incorrect methods of government, bureaucratic policy, separation from the masses. . . ."

Various "tendencies were developing simultaneously, some of which justified the change and others of which turned that change toward an openly reactionary policy."

It should be noted that Castro does not contend that the counterrevolution had reached the point of launching an armed struggle for power. It was the Dubcek regime itself that was in question, that was "dangerously inclined toward a substantial change in the system." Castro says at another point:

Provisionally, we reached this conclusion: we had no doubt that the political situation in Czechoslovakia was deteriorating and going down-hill on its way back to capitalism and that it was inexorably going to fall into the arms of imperialism.

I do not propose to argue here whether Czechoslovakia was going downhill and on its way back to capitalism. The accumulating evidence more and more confirms the opposite view—that a political revolution was maturing in Czechoslovakia which, if Moscow had not intervened, would have succeeded in bringing a revolutionary socialist regime to power.

On the basis of his premise, that "Czechoslovakia was moving toward a counterrevolutionary situation, toward capitalism and into the arms of imperialism" (which, of course, coincides with the justification advanced by the Kremlin for intervening with troops), Fidel Castro considers one of the main bits of propaganda used by the Warsaw Pact allies at the time to explain what they had done. They said they had received an appeal from prominent Communists in Czechoslovakia asking them to intervene. Out of international solidarity, they had responded to this request.

Castro notes that the names of the signers of the appeal had not been made public up to the time he spoke. However, he does not make much of that; he goes to the heart of the question.

The intervention, in his opinion, "unquestionably entailed a violation of legal principles and international norms." It "cannot be denied," he contends, "that the sovereignty of the Czechoslovak State was violated." To say otherwise would be "a fiction, an untruth. And the violation was, in fact, of a flagrant nature."

"From a legal point of view, this cannot be justified. . . . Not the slightest trace of legality exists. Frankly, none whatever."

Castro argues that the sole justification for the invasion was political necessity. "In our opinion, the decision made concerning Czechoslovakia can only be explained from a political point of view, not from a legal point of view."

As he sees it, the political situation had become so alarming "that it was absolutely necessary, at all costs, in one way or another, to prevent this eventuality [the restoration of capitalism] from taking place."

The essential point to be accepted, or not accepted, is whether or not the socialist camp could allow a political situation to develop which would lead to the breaking away of a socialist country, to its falling into the arms of imperialism. And our point of view is that it is not permissible and that the socialist camp has a right to prevent this in one way or another. I would like to begin by making it clear that we look upon this fact as an essential one.

Castro puts up a strong case for dismissing the appeal of the unnamed "group of personalities" as immaterial. Is a certain embarrassment detectable in his stress on this point?

Only last January Aníbal Escalante was put on trial for suggesting that the Kremlin intervene in Cuban affairs and utilize economic pressure to compel Fidel Castro to change his orientation. This was held to be a grave crime against Cuba's sovereignty, and Escalante was sentenced to fifteen years in prison. Others in his group were sentenced to terms ranging from two to twelve years.

It would have been somewhat inconsistent of Castro to have considered the appeal of the Czechoslovak personalities to be legal while maintaining that the appeal of the Cuban personalities had been correctly condemned as illegal.

He could have argued that the Czechoslovak personalities were within their rights in making their appeal, for it was directed against the allegedly procapitalist Dubcek regime, whereas in the case of Cuba the appeal of the Escalante group was directed against the revolutionary regime of Fidel Castro. But this is a political argument, hinging on the political aims of the two groups—the appeal of the faceless Czechoslovaks being revolutionary, Escalante's appeal being counterrevolutionary.

This line of argument would have run into complications when it came to explaining why the appeals of such disparate groups were in each instance directed to the same address—the Kremlin. Why would both the criminal Escalante group and the heroic Czechoslovak group each count on a favorable response from the Kremlin unless all three had something in common?

Castro avoided these quicksands by subordinating the issue of sovereignty to political necessity and frankly admitting that the action of the Warsaw Pact allies did not have the "slightest trace of legality."

Perhaps the Kremlin regretted that it had not been as outspoken as Castro on this point. The famous appeal of the discreet personalities turned into the opposite of what its originators had intended. It served to expose the fraudulent nature of their arguments.

To this day (November 17), the Warsaw Pact allies have felt it inadvisable to reveal the names of the signers. The ones to whom suspicion pointed denied any association. Thus, as no personalities, prominent or otherwise, stepped forward to claim the honor of having asked for foreign troops to be sent in, it became more and more evident that the population and the Communist Party were solidly opposed to the intervention. Even the few in the regime willing to serve as puppets were afraid to identify themselves! Consequently, within a few days the Kremlin dropped all references to the appeal.

But instead of acknowledging what a fraud had been perpetrated, the spokesmen of the Warsaw Pact sought to brazen it out.

Some quarters, secure in the knowledge that the reimposed censorship prevents the Czechoslovak Communists from replying, are even arguing that the invasion was intended to safeguard the sovereignty of Czechoslovakia.

Thus Gus Hall, the general secretary of the CPUSA, asks rhetorically in his pamphlet *Czechoslovakia at the Crossroads*: "Does anyone really believe that the five powers were really violating national sovereignty?" They were, he contends, only protecting their own sovereignty. "The intervention," he adds, "is a temporary one." He caps this reasoning with the following assurance: "It will leave Czechoslovakia's sovereignty intact and able to defend itself."

This is reminiscent of the famous defense put up by the rapist when he was hauled into the frontier court. "First of all, judge, does anyone really believe I am capable of really raping a defenseless woman? Secondly, I was only protecting my own virginity. Thirdly, it was only a temporary situation. And, last but not least, afterwards she still had her virginity intact and able to defend itself."

The fact is that Moscow prefers Gus Hall's reasoning to Fidel Castro's frankness. The Cuban leader's open recognition of the illegal nature of the Soviet intervention in Czechoslovakia was highly embarrassing to those in charge of justifying the operation. That was one reason why they sought to dispose of the speech as quickly and as quietly as possible.

It would be interesting to know what the real thinking of the Cubans is now on this point. How could the Moscow leaders have come in the first place to use such a clumsy and fraudulent device as the appeal from anonymous persons? And why have they said nothing about arguments like those thought up by Gus Hall, maintaining that Czechoslovakia's sovereignty was preserved by the intervention?

More needs to be said about this issue, but let us first follow Castro's reasoning after he assumes as his basic premise the contention of the Warsaw Pact governments that Czechoslovakia had to be saved from going capitalist.

It is not enough, he says, to simply accept as a fact that

"Czechoslovakia was headed toward a counterrevolutionary situation and that it was necessary to prevent it." Something more is required.

"We must analyze the causes," he continues, "and ask what factors made this possible and created the necessity for such a dramatic, drastic and painful measure." We must "analyze the causes, the factors and the circumstances" that brought about a situation leading a group of personalities "to appeal to other countries of the socialist camp to send their armies to prevent the triumph of the counterrevolution in Czechoslovakia and the triumph of the intrigues and conspiracies of the imperialist countries interested in tearing Czechoslovakia away from the community of socialist nations."

The question is of immense importance to Fidel Castro.

Gentlemen, is it conceivable that a situation could occur, under any circumstances, after 20 years of communism in our country, of communist revolution, of socialist revolution, in which a group of honest revolutionaries, in this country, horrified by the prospect of an advance—or rather a retrogression—to counterrevolutionary positions and toward imperialism, could find themselves obliged to request the aid of friendly armies to prevent such a retrogression from occurring? What would have happened to the communist conscience [consciousness] of this people? What would have happened to the revolutionary awareness of this people? To the dignity of this people? To the revolutionary morale of this people? If such a situation could arise some day, what would have happened to all those things which, for us, are the essentials of the Revolution?

What Castro is saying here, with complete consistency, is that if you adopt the position that Czechoslovakia was about to fall like a ripe plum to capitalism, then you must draw certain conclusions about the attractive power of communism. How is it to be explained that capitalism has such an ideological grip on the people of Czechoslovakia? And not only after twenty years of living under a workers' state in Czechoslovakia, but fifty-one years after the Russian October and ten years after the Cuban victory.

That's capitalism in its death agony, too. A capitalism that has given the world two global conflicts, a major depression, and any number of minor ones. It is a capitalism that has given the world fascism and, in the case of Czechoslovakia, the Nazi occupation. A capitalism, moreover, that has already wiped out two cities with nuclear bombs and that threatens to destroy all mankind in a nuclear holocaust. A capitalism that has won universal hatred and contempt because of such aggressions as the current one in Vietnam. A capitalism that has aroused a mood of deep rebellion among the youth living under it. A capitalism which in the United States has touched off repeated explosions in the ghettos.

In the face of all this, the Kremlin is compelled to say—in deeds if not in words—that capitalism is more attractive to the people of Czechoslovakia than communism!

It is hard for Fidel Castro to accept that. It is hard for any revolutionist to accept it. Yet the conclusion is unavoidable if you admit the premise that the counterrevolutionary danger in Czechoslovakia was so great that foreign troops had to be sent in to crush it.

A completely opposite conclusion follows if the truth of the matter was that a political revolution was maturing in Czechoslovakia. For this signifies that instead of wanting to go back to capitalism, what the people of Czechoslovakia wanted was to go forward to socialist democracy. If that is the case, capitalism cannot possibly be restored in Czechoslovakia. The battle is with bureaucratism—the pattern of Stalinist bureaucratism imposed on the country from the outside.

But let us follow Castro's reasoning further. He insists that "it behooves the communist movement as an unavoidable duty to undertake a profound study of the causes" that gave rise to the situation in Czechoslovakia.

The suggestion, again, is completely consistent. If such a glaring weakness has been uncovered, it would seem high time—fifty-one years after the victory of the Bolsheviks—to find out what went wrong and what might be done to remedy it. If the main strength of communism no longer lies in the power of its ideas and its example, but simply in the number and quality of its bayonets, then it is in a very dangerous position. Suppose that the men wielding the bayonets are likewise attracted by capitalism and begin welcoming it instead of battling it?

Every revolutionary socialist, one can be sure, will back Fidel Castro in pressing for a thorough analysis of the causes of the situation in Czechoslovakia. One can be just as sure that the Soviet bureaucracy will not prove responsive. The last thing Stalin's heirs want is a profound study of the causes of the situation in Czechoslovakia.

Another reason can be written down for the cool reception they gave Castro's speech.

Castro states that "this is not the time to make or pretend to make that profound analysis, but we can cite some facts and ideas." He lists these as "bureaucratic methods in the leadership of the country, lack of contact with the masses . . . neglect of communist ideals."

He deals in particular with the neglect of communist ideals, beginning with internationalism. "The communist ideal cannot, for a single moment, exist without internationalism," he says.

Communists who are in power must not forget the rest of the world. "They can never forget the suffering, underdevelopment, poverty, ignorance and exploitation that exist in a part of the world or how much poverty and destitution have accumulated there."

A truly internationalist outlook cannot be instilled in the people if they are allowed to forget these realities and the danger represented by imperialism. It is wrong to attempt to move the masses "through material incentives and the promises of more consumer goods alone." Castro continues:

> We can say—and today it is necessary to speak clearly and frankly—that we have seen to what extent those ideals and those internationalist sentiments, that state of alertness and that awareness of the world's problems have disappeared or are very weakly expressed in certain socialist countries of Europe.

What Castro has in mind, evidently, is the help which the better-off "socialist" countries should give to the poorer ones and to revolutionary movements still struggling to achieve power. Later he reveals some scandalous examples of Cuba's experiences in this field.

"On many occasions they sold us very outdated factories." They were eager to "sell any old junk. . . ." The Novotny regime sold weapons to Cuba that were the "spoils of war seized from the Nazis, weapons for which we have been paying and still today are paying for. . . ." The Tito regime even refused to sell arms to revolutionary Cuba, although it offered them to Batista.

This is a very telling point. The leaders of the Warsaw Pact must have squirmed a bit over the public exposure. Perhaps that was when they decided to throw the document in the wastebasket.

Castro could have said much more, however, under the heading of "internationalism." Even in its economic aspects he confines himself largely to the question of international solidarity in meeting the imperialist enemy and in dealing with underdeveloped countries. He leaves out completely how the parasitic economic interests of the bureaucracy affect international cooperation and interfere with correctly solving such problems as achieving the optimum ratios in the production of the various kinds of goods.

Castro's reticence on the political aspects of internationalism is even more striking. Where is internationalism best exemplified if not in trying to reach joint solutions to the common political problems facing the workers' movement, particularly in confronting imperialism?

But what international body, set up in accordance with the rules of democratic centralism, took up the problem of the drift in Czechoslovakia toward an alleged counterrevolutionary situation? What international body, composed of representatives of all the socialist countries, decided that no other solution was possible save a surprise invasion consisting in the main of Soviet troops?

Was Castro, for instance, asked for his views or for suggestions as to possible alternatives? Was he even notified in advance? Or was he merely told about the action after it had occurred?

All the evidence indicates that the decision was reached secretly by top bureaucrats in Moscow who preferred to remain anonymous. To this day, it is not known if some of those participating behind closed doors in these secret councils were opposed or if the decision was unanimous. Everyone else in the "socialist camp" was required to step forward after the event and be counted publicly for or against, a position hardly in accord with the dignity of communist man. And criticisms were not given much of a hearing, as we can see from the way Castro's speech was received.

Another practice of "certain socialist countries of Europe" which Castro condemns is "the preaching of peace." He, of course—as he patiently explains—is not advocating war. "We are not the enemies of peace; we are not in favor of wars; we do not advocate universal holocaust." But he thinks it is wrong to keep crying peace, peace, when there is no peace. "And those realities cannot be changed by simply preaching, in one's own house, an excessive desire for peace."

If peace must be preached let it be done in the enemy's camp and not in one's own camp.

What Castro is attacking here, without nailing it down, is the concept of "peaceful coexistence" peddled by the Kremlin, which plays into the hands of imperialism and which has led to disaster after disaster for the working class internationally.

A free discussion on this policy and its consequences would be highly useful, particularly "in certain socialist countries in Europe," above all the Soviet Union. But free discussions in those countries on such topics is taboo. That is why Castro's speech seems not to have been cleared by the "socialist" censors.

Some of Castro's sharpest criticisms refer directly to the Soviet Union. He says, for instance: "We are against all those bourgeois liberal reforms within Czechoslovakia. But we are also against the liberal economic reforms . . . that have been taking place in other countries of the socialist camp, as well." Quoting from an article in *Pravda* assailing an alleged tendency to introduce "mercantile relations" and "granting a broad field of action to private capital," Castro asks:

> Does this, by chance, mean that the Soviet Union is also going to curb certain currents in the field of economy that are in favor of putting increasingly greater emphasis on mercantile relations and on the effects of spontaneity in those relations, and those which have even been defending the desirability of the market and the beneficial effect of prices based on that market? Does it mean that the Soviet Union is becoming aware of the need to halt those currents? More than one article in the imperialist press has referred jubilantly to those currents that also exist within the Soviet Union.

This is not the place to debate whether the "economic reforms" in either Czechoslovakia or the Soviet Union point in the direction of a capitalist restoration. I think it can be shown that they do not transcend the limits of bureaucratic planning, whatever dangers that kind of planning may hold in general for the Soviet economy. What is to be noted here is Castro's consistency.

If the "liberal" economic reforms paved the way in Czechoslovakia for a counterrevolutionary situation, then the same holds true for the Soviet Union. And if the leaders of the Soviet Union are concerned about what happened in Czechoslovakia, they should be all the more concerned about what is happening under their noses in the Soviet Union.

Implicit in Castro's argumentation is the question: If the analysis of the trend in Czechoslovakia was accurate, then must it not be concluded that a counterrevolutionary situation is being fostered in the Soviet Union?

An even more cutting criticism concerns Moscow's relations with Washington. He says:

It disturbs us that, so far, there has been no direct imputation against Yankee imperialism in any of the statements made by the countries that sent their divisions to Czechoslovakia, or in the explanation of the events. We have been informed exhaustively concerning all the preceding events, all the facts, all the deviations, all about that rightist group, all about that liberal group; we have been informed of their activities.

The activities of the imperialists and the intrigues of the imperialists are known, and we are disturbed to see that neither the Communist Party nor the Government of the Soviet Union, nor the governments of the other countries that sent their troops to Czechoslovakia, have made any direct accusation against Yankee imperialism for its responsibility in the events in Czechoslovakia.

Castro emphasizes this important point:

Certain vague references to world imperialism, to world imperialist circles, and some more concrete statements concerning the imperialist circles of West Germany have been made. But who doesn't know that West Germany is simply a pawn of Yankee imperialism in Europe, the most aggressive, the most obvious pawn—that it is a pawn of the CIA, a pawn of the Pentagon and a pawn of the imperialist Government of the United States? And, certainly, we wish to express our concern over the fact that in none of the statements is a direct imputation made against Yankee imperialism, which is the principal culprit in the world plot and conspiracy against the socialist camp. And it is necessary that we express this preoccupation.

Castro made his speech just two days after the invasion. Almost three months have passed; yet this telling criticism has not been met.

In fact, the Soviet leaders have followed the opposite course. They have gone out of their way to display their friendliness to Washington. State Department officials, invited to talk with the Soviet diplomats, have leaked to the press that the Brezhnev-Kosygin team were anxious to assure the Johnson administration that there was no reason for the events in Czechoslovakia to alter the present détente in relations, since the invasion was intended only to normalize a family matter in the Soviet sphere of influence. The State Department and the White House, no doubt having in mind the need to normalize some family problems in the Western Hemisphere, indicated how well they understood Moscow's position.

In light of the record, it would seem difficult to avoid reaching the following conclusions:

1. There was no counterrevolutionary situation in Czechoslovakia engineered by the U.S., no matter what irons the CIA may have tried to heat in the fire.

2. Due to domestic ferment, the country was heading toward a political revolution and the establishment of socialist democracy.

3. Washington understood this and also understood the fear in Moscow, which it was not beyond sharing to some extent, over this perspective.

4. Washington indicated in advance that it would not react in a genuinely hostile way to any action undertaken by Moscow to normalize the situation, whatever propaganda value the imperialist communications media might try to squeeze out of it or whatever declarations officials of the Johnson administration might have to make for the record.

5. Castro's allusions to this subject irritated Moscow since they put in question its policy of maintaining "peaceful coexistence"; i.e., collaborating with U.S. imperialism to maintain the status quo. Hence the decision to give Castro's criticisms the silent treatment.

At the conference of the Organization of Latin American Solidarity in Havana last year, Castro criticized the Soviet policy of dealing with the tyrannical governments of the oligarchies in Latin America in face of their participation in the U.S. blockade of revolutionary Cuba. He raises the question again in his speech on the events in Czechoslovakia.

It is understandable that the countries of the Warsaw Pact sent their armies to destroy the imperialist conspiracy and the progress of the counterrevolution in Czechoslovakia. However, we have disagreed with, been displeased at, and protested against the fact that these same countries have been drawing closer economically, culturally and politically to the oligarchic governments of Latin America, which are not merely reactionary governments and exploiters of their peoples, but also shameless accomplices in the imperialist aggressions against Cuba and shameless accomplices in the economic blockade of Cuba. And these countries have been encouraged and emboldened by the fact that our friends, our natural allies, have ignored the vile and treacherous role enacted by those governments against a socialist country.

And at the same time that we understand the need for the spirit of internationalism, and the need to go to the aid—even with troops—of a fraternal country to confront the schemes of the imperialists, we ask ourselves if that policy of economic, political and cultural rapprochement toward those oligarchic governments that are accomplices in the imperialist blockade against Cuba will come to an end.

To drive his point home, Castro quotes dispatches from various cities in Latin America indicating that all these reactionary governments and their press were extracting everything possible out of the events in Czechoslovakia and shaking their fists at the Soviet Union. In the case of Venezuela, what a contrast between the attitude of the reactionaries in the government when the U.S. invaded the Dominican Republic and their attitude in the case of Czechoslovakia. In the former instance,

No relations were broken, no business was shelved, no economic relations were disturbed—nothing at all like this happened. And now they permit themselves the luxury of throwing in the face of the countries of the socialist camp this type of relations which the latter have actually been begging them for, this type of relations which they have been begging that government, which is one of the most reactionary and dyed-in-the-wool of the accomplices of Yankee imperialism. And now they throw it in the faces of the socialist countries.

These are the results of such a policy when the chips are down, at the moment of truth.

One wonders what Castro's basic thinking is about the Soviet bureaucracy. Does he believe that it will really listen to reason, that it can be reformed by pointing out some of the disastrous consequences of its reactionary policies? In any case, he is consistent in maintaining that if they have turned over a new leaf in Czechoslovakia, then they ought to do likewise in a number of other areas, including their attempts to woo the Latin American oligarchies.

In passing, Castro lashes the Communist parties of Europe, caught up in "indecision" at the moment.

And we wonder whether possibly in the future the relations with Communist Parties will be based on principled positions or whether they will continue to maintain a spineless attitude, to be satellites, lackeys—a situation in which only those that maintain a spineless attitude, say "yes" to everything and never assume an independent position on anything, would be considered friendly.

He contrasts the principled attitude of the Cuban Communist Party, which backed the Venezuelan, Bolivian, and Guatemalan guerrillas when they were abandoned by a "rightist and treacherous leadership."

Yet we were accused of being adventurers, of interfering in the affairs of other countries, of interfering in the affairs of other Parties.

I ask myself, in the light of the facts and in the light of the bitter reality that persuaded the nations of the Warsaw Pact to send their forces to crush the counterrevolution in Czechoslovakia, and—according to their statement—to back a minority in the face of a majority with rightist positions, if they will also cease to support these rightist, reformist, sold-out, submissive leaderships in Latin America that are enemies of the armed revolutionary struggle, that oppose the peoples' liberation struggle.

And, with the example of this bitter experience before them, I wonder whether or not the Parties of those countries, in line with the decision made in Czechoslovakia, will cease to support those rightist groups that betray the revolutionary movement in Latin America.

It can be seen how logical Castro is. All kinds of accusations were leveled at the Cubans bacause they backed minority groups of revolutionary guerrillas against Communist Party leaders who betrayed. The Cubans were even accused—crime of crimes!—of intervening in the internal affairs of other countries and other parties.

Yet, lo and behold, the Warsaw Pact allies sent more than 600,000 troops to intervene in the internal affairs of another country and another Communist party, the reason being that a minority there had appealed for help. Isn't an apology due the Cubans? And if the apology is skipped, shouldn't the Warsaw Pact governments, in all consistency, change their line by about 180 degrees in Latin America?

A broad discussion in Czechoslovakia on this point would have helped a great deal to bring clarity into the situation there. But clarity is not exactly what Moscow wants in Czechoslovakia.

All this is preliminary to one of the sharpest juxtapositions yet to be made by Castro between the revolutionary principles on which the Cubans stand and the line of "peaceful coexistence" with imperialism followed by the Kremlin.

Certainly we do not believe in the possibility of an improvement in relations between the socialist camp and imperialism under the present conditions, or under any conditions as long as that imperialism exists. We do not and cannot believe in the possibility of an improvement in relations between the socialist camp and the U.S. imperialist Government as long as that country performs the role of international gendarme, aggressor against the peoples and enemy and systematic opponent of revolutions everywhere in the world. Much less can we believe in any such improvement in the midst of an aggression as criminal and cowardly as that being waged against Vietnam.

Our position on this is very clear: one is consistent with world realities and is truly internationalist and genuinely and decidedly supports the revolutionary movement throughout the world, in which case relations with the imperialist Government of the United States cannot be improved, or relations with the imperialist U.S. Government will improve, but only at the cost of withholding consistent support from the worldwide revolutionary movement.

Castro's target is absolutely clear. However, he does not leavs it at this abstract level. He gets down to cases.

He cites a dispatch from Washington dated August 22 reporting a declaration by Secretary of State Dean Rusk that the Soviet intervention in Czechoslovakia compromises any improvement in relations between East and West and that the situation could block ratification of the Non-Proliferation Treaty by the U.S. Senate. Castro declares:

This can hardly fail to delight us. Our people know the position of the Cuban delegation regarding this famous Non-Proliferation Treaty, which virtually gives a permanent concession to the large powers for the monopoly of nuclear weapons and the monopoly of technology in a field of energy that is going to be indispensable to the future of mankind. We were concerned, above all, by the fact that many countries of the world, including our own, would be obliged to accept the U.S. imperialist Government's monopoly on those weapons, which could be used at any moment against any people, particularly in view of the fact that the proposed treaty was also accompanied by an astonishing declaration concerning the defense of the signatory nations that might be threatened with nuclear weapons. Such countries as Vietnam, countries such as Cuba, that did not choose to accept that type of treaty, and much less sign it in a situation in which the aggression against Vietnam is being constantly intensified, are left outside the realm of any protection, and thus fall into the category in which the imperialists would theoretically have the right to attack us with nuclear arms. And, of course, everyone knows our position.

The final reference here, no doubt, is to the famous 1962 Caribbean crisis, in which the Cubans accepted the placement of defensive nuclear weapons in order to deter Washington from attempting another Bay of Pigs invasion. Khrushchev's withdrawal of the weapons without consultation was bitterly resented by the Cuban government.

Since the Non-Proliferation Treaty was directed primarily against China, Castro's remarks on this point were undoubtedly read with interest in Peking. In fact, the following paragraph in Castro's speech coincides quite closely with Peking's position:

> In view of the facts, in the face of an imperialism that is always plotting, always conspiring against the socialist camp, we ask ourselves whether or not the idyllic hopes of an improvement in relations with the imperialist Government of the United States will continue to be maintained. We ask ourselves if, consistent with events in Czechoslovakia, a position may be adopted that will imply a renunciation of such idyllic hopes in relation to Yankee imperialism. And the dispatch states that an improvement in relations will be compromised and that there is the danger of nonratification of the treaty. In our opinion, that would be the best thing that could happen.

This is a stinging slap at Moscow's policy of trying to placate U.S. imperialism at the expense of the overall interests of the "socialist camp." However, it should not be concluded from this that Castro is preparing to join the cult of Mao. He is voicing independent, revolutionary opposition to the joint efforts of Moscow and Washington to maintain the status quo.

Castro scores even more directly and tellingly on the question of supporting the Vietnamese revolution against the U.S. aggression:

> The TASS statement explaining the decision of the Warsaw Pact governments states in its concluding paragraph: "The fraternal countries firmly and resolutely offer their unbreakable solidarity against any outside threat. They will never permit anyone to tear away even one link of the community of socialist States." And we ask ourselves: "Does that declaration include Vietnam? Does that statement include Korea? Does that statement include Cuba? Do they or do they not consider Vietnam, Korea and Cuba links of the socialist camp to be safeguarded against the imperialists?"
>
> In accordance with that declaration, Warsaw Pact divisions were sent into Czechoslovakia. And we ask ourselves: "Will Warsaw Pact divisions also be sent to Vietnam if the Yankee imperialists step up their aggression against that country and the people of Vietnam request that aid?! Will they send the divisions of the Warsaw Pact to the Democratic People's Republic of Korea if the Yankee imperialists attack that coun-

try? Will they send the divisions of the Warsaw Pact to Cuba if the Yankee imperialists attack our country, or even in the case of the threat of a Yankee imperialist attack on our country, if our country requests it?

When Johnson first escalated the war in Vietnam, Castro, it will be recalled, appealed at once for a massive response to the imperialist aggression. His appeal was not heeded by either Moscow or Peking.

The Cubans themselves redoubled their efforts to help Vietnam by opening up new revolutionary fronts in Latin America. This was one of Che Guevara's declared aims in starting a guerrilla struggle in Bolivia. Through the right-wing Communist Party leaders under its control, the Kremlin blocked these attempts.

But in Czechoslovakia, seeming to become alert all at once to a counterrevolutionary danger, the Kremlin, with extraordinary haste, mobilized and sent into immediate action 600,000 or more troops. Castro declares:

> We acknowledge the bitter necessity that called for the sending of those forces into Czechoslovakia; we do not condemn the socialist countries that made that decision. But we, as revolutionaries, and proceeding from positions of principle, do have the right to demand that they adopt a consistent position with regard to all the other questions that affect the world revolutionary movement.

Castro sounds almost ironic. The irony, however, is probably unintentional. He is convinced that basically the Kremlin is motivated by revolutionary aims. He hopes that it will respond to the power of reason and undertake to reform itself.

However, this hope is not realistic. It is a mistake to think that the basic flaw in the Kremlin's policies is inconsistency. Something more difficult to rectify sets the Kremlin's course. This something is the material interests of the Soviet bureaucracy as a parasitic caste. The needs of the bureaucracy do not happen to be the same as the needs of the world revolution. In fact, most often they are antagonistic to those needs.

That Castro seeks to subordinate all other political considerations to the needs of the world revolution is shown by the fashion in which he weighs the relative importance of Czechoslovakia's national sovereignty.

For Cubans, the question is especially important, he says. They have had to face the problem of intervention throughout their history. Thus "it is logical that many would react emotionally in the face of the fact that armies from outside the nation's borders had to come in to prevent a catastrophe." Castro is referring here to the widespread sympathy in Cuba for the Czechoslovaks. He continues:

And since, logically, for various reasons, our conscience [consciousness] has been shaped by the concept of repudiating such deeds, only the development of the political awareness of our people will make it possible for them to determine when such an action becomes necessary and when it is necessary to accept it even in spite of the fact that it violates rights such as the right of sovereignty which—in this case, in our opinion—must give way before the most important interests of the world revolutionary movement and the struggle of the peoples against the imperialists, which, as we see it, is the basic question. And, undoubtedly, the breaking away of Czechoslovakia and its falling into the arms of imperialism would have been a rude blow, an even harder blow to the interests of the worldwide revolutionary movement.

He concludes this point with the general assertion: "We must learn to analyze these truths and to determine when one interest must give way before other interests in order not to fall into romantic or idealistic positions that are out of touch with reality."

This is the source of Castro's consistency—he subordinates all other interests to the interest of the world revolution. Paradoxically this also happens to point directly to the weakest point in Castro's position. Where does the question of socialist democracy stand in relation to the interests of the world revolution?

Castro deals hardly at all with democracy in his speech. As for *socialist* democracy, the blunt fact is that he does not even mention it.

If anything, he indicates a bias against democracy. Thus he states that in Czechoslovakia a "real liberal fury was unleashed; a whole series of political slogans in favor of the formation of opposition parties began to develop, in favor of openly anti-Marxist and anti-Leninist theses. . . ." He states again: "A series of slogans began to be put forward, and in fact certain measures were taken such as the establishment of a bourgeois form of 'freedom' of the press. This means that the counterrevolution and the exploiters, the very enemies of socialism, were granted the right to speak and write freely against socialism."

What was really developing in Czechoslovakia, all the weight of the evidence shows, was a powerful proletarian current demanding the right to speak out against a stifling bureaucratic regime, the right to form independent *communist* political group-ings as in Lenin's time, and the right to institute socialist democracy in Czechoslovakia. This is not the same as a "bour-geois form" of democracy.

One wonders if it was not on this question that Castro was led into misjudging what was happening in Czechoslovakia. In the opening of his speech, he says:

A process of what was termed democratization began. The imperialist press invented another word, the word "liberalization," and began to differentiate between progressives and conservatives—calling progressive those who supported a whole series of political reforms, and conservatives the supporters of the former leadership. It was evident—and we must give our opinion about both: the conservatives and the liberals. . . . It rather reminds us of the past history of Cuba, that division between conserva-tives and liberals, a situation which, of course, was not to be expected in the political processes of socialist revolutions.

If we have understood Castro correctly, he believes that the aim of the democratizers in Czechoslovakia was to introduce dirty machine politics and petty "politicking" such as Cuba knew before the revolution. And, if we are not mistaken, he considers shallow, miserable politics of this type to be the "bourgeois form" of democracy.

Now there is absolutely no doubt about the mean, trivial, and fraudulent nature of bourgeois democracy in the political arena in prerevolutionary Cuba, and, for that matter, throughout the rest of the capitalist world today. But the question of "bourgeois forms" of democracy is not exhausted by this fact.

The question is much broader. In reality it involves some of the profoundest theoretical and political problems of the world revolution today and the connection of these problems with the heritage of previous revolutions.

Marxism does not reject the conquests of previous revolutions, such as the winning of democracy by the bourgeois revolution against feudalism. Marxism defends these conquests, seeks to deepen and develop them, to supersede, not do away with them.

Thus the Marxist appreciation of bourgeois democracy is that it represented an enormous gain for humanity, one of the great achievements of the revolutions of the past. The Marxist criticism of bourgeois democracy is that it remained limited; it did not go far enough.

One of the main charges leveled by the revolutionary Marxist movement against the capitalist system today concerns its tendency, as it exhausts all the progressive features of its earlier stages, to narrow down, pinch off, and reduce democracy in the political arena as well as elsewhere to an empty shell.

The culmination of this tendency is fascism; that is, a reversion to utter barbarism. As against fascism, revolutionists are duty bound—independently and with their own methods—to defend bourgeois democracy with all their strength. Not to do so is suicidal.

Even more than this is involved. Taking bourgeois democracy as a conquest of previous revolutions, the program of Marxism calls for expanding it into proletarian democracy, spreading democracy from its limited area of application under the bourgeoisie in their best days to the entire economic and social system, right down to the factory level. This is the key thought developed by Lenin in *State and Revolution,* where he also considers the problem of how this is to be accomplished.

As we can see from his speech, Castro is well aware of the significance and importance of national sovereignty. What is national sovereignty but one of the forms of bourgeois democracy? As soon as we view national sovereignty from this angle, we at once see the limitations of the bourgeoisie of today as either a revolutionary or progressive force. In the underdeveloped regions, the bourgeoisie are no longer capable of achieving national sovereignty in a genuine sense. They came on the scene too late. In the advanced sectors, the bourgeoisie, having reached the imperialist stage, systematically violate it. The dialectic of history has thus conferred on the proletariat the achievement or defense of national sovereignty. The situation in Vietnam today offers an almost perfect example.

Lenin was the first to grasp the political importance of this and to inscribe the right of self-determination in the program of the Bolsheviks.

The victory of the Bolshevik revolution did not settle the question even for the workers' state established under Lenin. The right of self-determination includes the right to secede from a federation like the Soviet Union. For a socialist state to stand outside this federation does not necessarily signify a catastrophe. This is shown in the cases of China, Korea, Vietnam, and . . . Cuba. In principle, why shouldn't any of the East European countries feel free to stand as independently of the Soviet Union as, say, Cuba? Why shouldn't this likewise hold for any of the republics of the USSR?

The truth is that exercising this democratic right would greatly strengthen the socialist camp. The experience with Cuba is living proof of this.

However, the question was not posed on this level in Czechoslovakia. There is no evidence that the workers, or the ranks of the Communist Party, or the bulk of Novotny's Communist opponents in the government wanted to sever relations with the Soviet Union, or the Warsaw Pact, or even to stand as independently as Cuba. What they wanted, concretely, was socialist democracy inside the country.

We come to the decisive question: Was it not in the interests of the world revolution to establish socialist democracy in Czechoslovakia?

Castro speaks depreciatively of people who are preoccupied over intellectual and artistic freedom and similar issues, although he grants that they have a point and that there have been abuses. But such interests are not of great concern to the masses of humanity living under imperialist oppression and neocolonialism.

And for the thousands of millions of human beings who, for all intents and purposes, are living without hope under conditions of starvation and extreme want, there are questions in which they are more interested than the problem of whether or not to let their hair grow. This might be a very controversial issue, but these are not the things that are worrying people who are faced with the problem of whether or not they will have the possibility or hope of eating.

This is very true. People faced with starvation are not inclined to be concerned about abstract democratic rights. This, however, hardly disposes of the problem. These same people may become highly interested in national independence, in a radical agrarian reform, in social equality, free education, and similar issues that belong historically to the bourgeois revolution and its democratic tasks.

It is true, moreover, that in seeking a way out of the abyss of misery and hunger to which they have been sentenced, they have accepted the models provided by the Soviet Union, China, and now Cuba. They know they do not need to follow the slow path of development charted by the highly developed capitalist countries.

Instead of centuries, industrialization can be achieved in decades under a planned economy. If this requires foregoing democracy, they are prepared to pay the price, a decision reached all the easier in view of its virtual nonexistence anyway in their part of the world.

However, things are altogether different in the imperialist sector—which is also involved in the world revolution. The imperialist sector, if we may state an elementary truth, is of crucial importance in the development of the world revolution. Great as the victories have been elsewhere up to now, the final, and, we may believe, the biggest and most bitterly contested battles will be fought there. Consequently, in weighing the interests of the world revolution, it is absolutely essential to take into account the problems faced by the revolutionary Marxists in the heartlands of the capitalist system. The ultimate victory hinges on this.

In the imperialist sector, the issue of democratic rights is of key significance. Having won these rights in immense and often bloody battles in the past, the masses are not inclined to give them up readily. They are inclined instead to defend them. They can easily understand the virtue of deepening and extending them or trying to win them where they have not already been gained. The current student struggles in various imperialist countries and the black freedom struggle in the United States are cases in point.

The problem for revolutionary Marxists in these countries is to find ways and means of converting these struggles into struggles for socialism. This cannot possibly be done if the masses believe that socialism signifies taking away what they have already achieved.

The greatest single obstacle to a socialist victory in Western Europe and the United States for decades has been the treacherous role played by leaderships committed to Stalinism; and, in particular, the totalitarian image conferred on socialism and communism by the practices of Stalin and his heirs.

The purges, the frame-up trials, the forced confessions, the deportations, the labor camps, the liquidation of all political opposition, the suppression of all free thought in politics, the schools, art, and even some of the sciences—horrors such as these, which became common knowledge in the West despite Stalin's censorship and the dithyrambs of his retainers, dupes, and sycophants, made the task of building a revolutionary socialist movement in the advanced capitalist sectors almost insuperable up to recent years.

The reversion of the Soviet Union to a *precapitalist* level so far as democratic rights were concerned was pictured by the bourgeois spokesmen as synonymous with socialism. And this propaganda—ably assisted by the cult of Stalin and the dictator's claim to be the incarnation of socialist wisdom—gained widespread acceptance among the masses.

If there is one thing needed to counteract this lie of socialism and Stalinism being one and the same thing, it is an example of socialist democracy in practice.

The Twentieth Congress of the Communist Party of the Soviet Union aroused hopes among some circles that this marked the beginning of a process that would soon lead to the reestablishment of socialist democracy in the Soviet Union itself. The hope proved illusory because the bureaucratic caste which Stalin represented still remained in power. The "de-Stalinization" consisted of concessions designed to relieve social tensions the better to maintain the rule of the parasitic bureaucracy. The bureaucrats have not hesitated to tighten the screws again when they deemed this advisable.

The proletarian upsurge in Poland in 1956 gave hopes of the appearance of socialist democracy there. The upsurge was contained and its energy drained away and the hopes died.

The proletarian uprising in Hungary in 1956 was even more promising. It was crushed with tanks.

One of the reasons for the great response to the Cuban revolution, particularly among the youth in the United States, was precisely the impression that it favored the development of socialist democracy. The way Havana became a crossroads for all kinds of revolutionary tendencies, the free rein given to artists, the welcome extended to intellectuals of many hues, the rebuff given the bureaucratic tendency headed by Escalante—all this gave an immensely favorable impression not only of revolutionary Cuba but of socialism in general.

It must be said, however, that the development of this tendency in the political and governmental arena has not flowered, and this has prevented Cuba from serving as a model of socialist democracy.

Could Czechoslovakia have moved into this position? There is every reason to believe that this would have been possible if the Kremlin had kept its hands off. That, of course, was precisely why the Kremlin ordered the invasion. The example of a working socialist democracy in Czechoslovakia would have been altogether too contagious for the workers of the East European countries and the Soviet Union. The fate of the bureaucratic ruling caste was at stake.

But from the viewpoint of the interests of the world revolution, the establishment of socialist democracy in Czechoslovakia would most likely have marked a point of qualitative change for the advance of the socialist revolution in the imperialist sectors.

That is why, so far as the world revolution is concerned, the invasion of Czechoslovakia was one of the worst crimes ever committed by the Stalinist bureaucracy.

It is to be regretted that Castro does not see this. Perhaps he will come to this view as more facts accumulate and it becomes increasingly difficult for the Kremlin to cover up the real reasons for the invasion and occupation.

At the same time, Fidel Castro's criticisms of the policies of the Kremlin deserve the closest attention. Every revolutionist will surely do everything possible to help circulate them where they will do the most good.

# Glossary

**Abd El Krim** (1882?-1963)—Moroccan guerrilla leader defeated by Spanish and French in 1926. Escaped from internment in 1947 and became a leader of the North African independence movement.

**APRA** (Alianza Popular Revolucionaria Americana—American Popular Revolutionary Alliance), also called the Partido **Aprista**—founded in 1924 by Haya de la Torre, a Peruvian. At its peak, APRA movements existed in Cuba, Mexico, Peru, Chile, Costa Rica, Haiti, and Argentina. Aprismo was first movement to urge economic and political unification of Latin America against imperialist domination. A populist movement, it later degenerated into a liberal, anti-Communist, procapitalist reform party.

**Auténtico Party**—radical bourgeois party led by Grau San Martín against Batista. When Grau became president in 1944, Auténtico ministers continued traditional graft and corruption. A new opposition party was formed in 1947—the Ortodoxo Party.

**Batista y Zaldívar, Fulgencio** (1901-1973)—president of Cuba 1940-44, 1954-58. After he seized power by a coup in 1952, the brutality and corruption of his regime provoked rebellion culminating in the victory of the July 26 Movement, January 1, 1959. Batista fled to Dominican Republic, later died in Spain.

**Béjar, Héctor**—Peruvian guerrilla leader in the sixties. After defeat and imprisonment, he criticized his former guerrilla strategy for underestimating mass work. After 1970 general amnesty for political prisoners, he capitulated to Velasco regime and got a job in the government.

**Blanco, Hugo** (1935-    )—led movement of Quechua peasants of Peru for land reform; their unions seized land and defended it against army and police. Captured in 1963 and sentenced to death, Blanco was saved from execution by international solidarity campaign. He was amnestied in 1970, and except for brief intervals lived in exile in Mexico, Argentina, Chile, and Sweden.

**Bravo, Douglas**—Venezuelan guerrilla leader; developed criticisms of guerrillaism for its overestimation of the importance of "shooting," its underestimation of the problems of organizing the workers and peasants, and its dismissal of the role of the revolutionary party.

**Browder, Earl Russell** (1891-1973)—secretary-general of American CP, 1930-44; president of Communist Political Association, 1944-45. Led CP through zigzags in policy from ultraleft "third period" to support of Roosevelt, to opposition to U.S. war preparations during Stalin-Hitler pact, to collaboration with Roosevelt against the American workers during World War II. Expelled from CP in 1946, blamed by the rest of CP leadership for previous policies they had all supported.

**Cannon, James Patrick** (1890-1974)—a founder of American CP; expelled in 1928 for supporting Trotsky against Stalin. Became one of the founders of the American and international Trotskyist movements.

**Castillo Armas, Carlos**—colonel in Guatemalan army, placed in power by CIA-backed coup in 1954, assassinated in 1957.

**Castro Ruz, Fidel** (1925-    )—Cuban revolutionary leader, premier of Cuba from February 16, 1959, until December 3, 1976, when he was elected president by the National Assembly of People's Power.

**Céspedes, Carlos Manuel de** (1871-1939)—son of a leader of revolution of 1868, participant in revolution of 1895 and Spanish-American War. Provisional president of Cuba August-September 1933.

**Communist International**—organized in 1919 under Lenin's leadership as revolutionary successor to the Second International, which had supported bourgeois governments in World War I and crushed 1919 revolution in Germany. After Lenin's death and with the Stalinization of the Soviet Union, the Communist International was converted into an instrument of Soviet foreign policy of class collaboration and "peaceful coexistence," and was finally dissolved in 1943 as a gesture to Stalin's imperialist allies in World War II.

**Conte Agüero, Luis**—classmate and friend of Castro, recipient of his letters from prison after Moncada trial. Broke with the revolution in March 1960, used his position as TV-radio commentator to appeal to Castro to "save" Cuba from Communism, sought asylum in Argentine embassy when faced with demonstrations and public denunciation by Castro.

**La Coubré**—French ship carrying ammunition from Belgium for the Cuban armed forces, exploded in Havana harbor March 4, 1960, killing 100. Cause of explosion was never established.

**entrism sui generis** (entrism of a unique kind)—tactic used by Trotskyists in the fifties and sixties. Unlike the entry of Trotskyists into Social Democratic parties in 1930s, with the right to express their own views as a faction, publish their own newspaper, and thus influence a growing left wing, entrism sui generis meant reducing the size of public Trotskyist organizations and intensifying work inside the Social Democratic and Communist parties. The tactic was abandoned in the late sixties.

**Escalante Dellundé, Aníbal**—a leader of old Cuban CP (People's Socialist Party) censured in 1962 for forming bureaucratic clique in unified revolutionary organization; went to Czechoslovakia; returned in 1964 and headed an experimental poultry farm. CP Central Committee again censured him for factionalism in January 1968; his pro-Moscow "microfaction" opposed Cuba's critical stance toward Soviet policies in Latin America and Vietnam, the armed-struggle line for revolution in Latin America, and reliance on political motivation ("moral incentives") in organizing production in Cuba. Escalante was sentenced to fifteen years in prison by a people's tribunal.

**Fourth International** (World Party of Socialist Revolution)—the political movement founded in 1938 as revolutionary successor to Second and Third Internationals. Led by Trotsky until his death in 1940. Split in 1953 (*see* International Committee *and* International Secretariat); reunified in 1963 on a principled basis.

**Gómez, José Miguel** (1858-1921)—president of Cuba, 1909-13. Participated in Ten Years War and revolution of 1895; led uprising after losing election in 1905 and won subsequent election under U.S. occupation.

**Gómez y Arias, Miguel Mariano**—president of Cuba 1936, impeached after he dismissed 3,000 pro-Batista government workers.

**Good Neighbor Policy**—proclaimed by Roosevelt in 1933; said U.S. would no longer resort to armed interventions in Latin America and the Caribbean, but would function like a good neighbor.

**Grau San Martín, Ramón** (1887-      )—president of Cuba, September 1933–January 1934, 1944-48. Remained in Cuba after revolution.

**Guatemalan revolution**—period of reforms from 1944, culminating in labor and agrarian reforms under Jacobo Arbenz Guzman (president, 1950-54), including expropriation of United Fruit and other foreign plantation owners. Arbenz government did not mobilize the masses to defend these moves or extend them to combat the national bourgeoisie; it was overthrown by CIA-backed coup in 1954.

**Guevara, Ernesto "Che"** (1928-1967)—Argentine physician and student radical, took part in 1952 protests against Perón dictatorship. Went to Guatemala. When Arbenz regime was toppled, he moved to Mexico where he met Castro and joined Cuban guerrilla struggle. After victory of revolution, headed Cuban national bank and served as minister of industry. Travelled to Africa in June 1959 and January-March 1965 for discussions with leaders of nationalist movements there. Dropped from public view at end of March 1965; led guerrilla movement in Congo and then Bolivia; was captured and executed October 9, 1967, by Bolivian army.

**Healy, Gerry** (1915-      )—a former leader of British Trotskyist movement and International Committee of the Fourth International. Took position that Cuba had not become a workers' state because there was no revolutionary socialist party there. Remained outside reunified

Fourth International as head of sectarian Socialist Labour League (since 1973 called Workers Revolutionary Party).

**International Committee**—public faction of the Fourth International formed in 1953 by opponents of some of the political views and organizational practices of Michel Pablo, then secretary of the organization. The IC was supported by the majority of Trotskyists in Argentina, Chile, Peru, Canada, the United States, Britain, France, and Switzerland, and the Chinese Trotskyists in exile. The formation of the IC was used by Pablo as grounds to formally split the International in 1954.

**International Secretariat**—until 1953 the top body of the Fourth International between world congresses. Under Pablo's leadership the IS pursued the policy of entrism sui generis in the Communist and Social Democratic parties, and functioned as a factional center for the majority of Trotskyists in continental Europe, some parts of Latin America (headed by Posadas), and Ceylon (although Ceylon remained politically neutral between the two factions).

**Laredo Brú, Federico** (1875-1946)—fought in war of independence 1898-99; led movement against President Zayas 1920-24; president of Cuba 1936-40 under influence of Batista.

**Lumumba, Patrice Emergy** (1925-1961)—a leader of the All-African Peoples Conference and president of the Congolese National Movement. First premier and minister of defense of the Republic of the Congo (now Zaïre). When Belgian troops invaded to "protect European lives" Lumumba appealed for United Nations aid; but the government was overthrown by Mobutu Sese Seko in an army coup, and Lumumba was arrested by the army and killed in Katanga (now Shaba) Province.

**Machado, Gerardo** (1871-1939)—president of Cuba 1925-33. His police terror led to a general strike, loss of army support, and U.S. intervention. Machado fled Cuba, later died in Miami.

**Marcy, Sam**—a leader of the Socialist Workers Party in Buffalo in the early fifties. His support to the crushing of the Hungarian revolution in 1956 and his other deep differences with the SWP majority led Marcy to split in 1959, forming the Workers World Party and Youth Against War and Fascism.

**Martí, José Julian** (1853-1895)—Cuban essayist, poet, revolutionary leader. Arrested and exiled at age 16; lawyer, journalist; founded Cuban Revolutionary Party in 1892; led rebel troops and was killed in war of independence.

**Mendieta, Carlos** (1873-1960)—participated in revolt against Spain, 1896-98; led attacks against Menocal and Machado administrations; was arrested and exiled in 1931; after fall of Machado, led opposition to Grau; provisional president of Cuba, 1934-35.

**Menocal, Mario Garcia** (1866-1946)—conservative president of Cuba 1913-21.

**Miró Cardona, José**—civilian resistance leader against Batista; prime minister of Cuba, January 2–February 13, 1959; then ambassador to Spain until he requested political asylum in U.S. in 1960. President of Council of Cuban Refugees in Miami, 1961-63; resigned when Washington failed to launch new invasion.

**Muñoz Marin, Luis** (1898-    )—governor of Puerto Rico, 1949-65.

**Nasser, Gamal Abdal** (1918-1970)—Egyptian army officer and political leader. Led coup that deposed King Farouk, 1952. President of Egypt 1956-70; nationalized Suez Canal and other resources, but maintained capitalist ownership of the land despite "Arab Socialist" rhetoric.

**Oehler, Hugo**—a member of National Committee of Workers Party, a predecessor of Socialist Workers Party, in 1930s. Opposed entry into Socialist Party as unprincipled. Was expelled in 1935 with his followers for issuing a public periodical without party permission. Founded Revolutionary Workers League, a sect which survived into the 1950s.

**Ortodoxo Party**—formed in 1947 to combat government corruption; attracted young, idealistic supporters, including Castro, but failed to organize an effective struggle for democratic rights and land reform.

**Pablo, Michel** (Michel Raptis)—former secretary of the Fourth International. Early in the fifties came to the conclusion that World War III was imminent and that under war conditions revolutionary wings would develop that could be won to Trotskyism. He therefore called on the Trotskyist parties to enter the mass Communist and Social Democratic parties. Within the Fourth International, his practices led to a prolonged split. After the 1963 reunification, Pablo developed political disagreements and left the Fourth International in 1965. He continues to lead a small movement in several European countries. Pablo served as a technician in the agrarian reform in Algeria under the Ben Bella government in 1962-64.

**Platt, Orville Hitchcock** (1827-1905)—U.S. senator from Connecticut, author of **Platt Amendment**. This rider attached to Army Appropriations Bill of 1901 stipulated conditions for American intervention in Cuban affairs and permitted the United States to lease land for naval base at Guantánamo. The amendment was forced into the Cuban constitution. After interventions in 1906, 1912, 1917, and 1920, the treaty was abrogated in 1934, but the United States retained Guantánamo.

**Posadas, Juan** (Homero Cristali)—Argentine leader of International Secretariat's Latin American Bureau. He split from Fourth International in 1962. Posadas believed that a nuclear war would inevitably end in victory for world socialism; therefore he advocated that the Soviet Union launch such a war. His Cuban followers were imprisoned from 1963 to 1965. Members of his group joined MR-13 guerrillas led by Marco Antonio Yon Sosa in Guatemala in 1966; it was these "Trotskyists" that Castro attacked at the Tricontinental Conference. The Posadistas were expelled by MR-13 for embezzling movement funds.

**Robertson, James**—an early leader of Young Socialist Alliance; broke with SWP over reunification of Fourth International. Attempted to align his group with Healy's rump "International Committee of the Fourth International" but failed in 1967. Heads Spartacist League, a small sectarian group.

**Roca, Blas**—central leader of Cuban CP from 1934; initially called for popular front with bourgeois ABC Party against "fascist" Batista. In 1938, declared Cuba had "semi-democratic conditions," Batista could be influenced. In 1939, after CP was legalized, Roca appeared with Batista in presidential palace, urged people to "support his progressive endeavors."

**Shachtman, Max** (1903-72)—expelled from American CP along with James P. Cannon and Martin Abern in 1928 for Trotskyism; a central leader of the Trotskyist movement until 1940, when he and others split from SWP over such questions as the class nature of the Soviet state and democratic centralism; formed the Workers Party, which was dissolved into the Socialist Party in 1958.

**Socialist Labour League** (later Workers Revolutionary Party)—British ultraleft sect led by Gerry Healy.

**Sukarno** (1901-1970)—leader of radical nationalist movement of Indonesia, founded in 1927; was jailed and exiled by the Dutch; cooperated with Japanese occupation in World War II. First president of Indonesian republic; assumed dictatorial powers in 1962 and proclaimed himself president for life in 1963. Deposed by military coup in 1965; was stripped of titles in 1966 and kept under house arrest until his death.

**Touré, Sékou** (1922-    )—president of Guinea since 1958; was a union leader and delegate to French national assembly before independence. A "Marxist" who has maintained capitalism in Guinea.

**Transitional Program** ("The Death Agony of Capitalism and the Tasks of the Fourth International")—founding document of Fourth International, written by Trotsky, outlining a method for mobilizing the masses despite their misleaders, raising their consciousness in the course of the struggle, and leading to the conquest of power by the working class and its allies.

**Tshombe, Moise Kapenda** (1919-1969)—led attempted breakaway of Katanga (now Shaba) Province from Republic of the Congo when it gained independence from Belgium in 1960. Was charged by UN with complicity in murder of Lumumba in 1961. When attempt to secede failed, he was forced into exile (1963), but was made premier of a government of national reconciliation in 1964. Dismissed in 1965, accused of treason in 1966, went into exile in Spain, and was sentenced to death in absentia. In June 1967 a plane in which he was flying was hijacked to Algeria, where he was jailed and then kept incommunicado until his death.

**Wohlforth, Tim**—an early leader of Young Socialist Alliance, broke with Socialist Workers Party over reunification of Fourth International. Leader of Workers League until 1974. Broke with Healy during witch-hunt for "CIA agents" in WL. Began to criticize WL abstention from antiracist struggle. Rejoined SWP in 1976.

**Yon Sosa, Marco Antonio**—leader of Guatemalan guerrilla movement MR-13. Unlike other guerrilla leaders, he called for socialist revolution, not just democratic reforms and anti-imperialism. His movement was defeated and dispersed in 1966.

# Index